PHOENIX
AND THE BIRDS OF PREY

PHOENIX

AND THE BIRDS OF PREY

The CIA's Secret Campaign
to Destroy the Viet Cong

MARK MOYAR

NAVAL INSTITUTE PRESS
Annapolis, Maryland

Library of Congress Cataloging-in-Publication Data

Moyar, Mark, 1971–
    Phoenix and the birds of prey : the CIA's secret campaign to destroy the Viet Cong / Mark Moyar.
        p.   cm.
    Includes bibliographical references and index.
    ISBN 1-55750-593-4 (cloth : alk. paper)
    1. Vietnamese Conflict, 1961–1975—Underground movements. 2. Counter insurgency—Vietnam.   3. United States.   Central Intelligence Agency.   4. Mât trân dân tôc giải phóng mi`ên nam Việt Nam.   I. Title.
DS558.92.M69   1997
959.704'3—dc21   96-53438

Printed in the United States of America on acid-free paper ∞
04 03 02 01 00 99 98 97   9 8 7 6 5 4 3 2
First printing

To those Americans who served their country well in Vietnam, and to those of their Vietnamese allies who resisted the enemy as best they could

In memory of William T. Moyar (1909–1996)

Contents

PART FIVE Damage Inflicted on the Shadow Government

PART SIX Villager Attitudes

PART SEVEN Postlude

Foreword

Over two decades since the fall of Saigon and after literally tens of thousands of books and articles on the Vietnam War, that conflict remains almost completely misinterpreted and misunderstood. One reason is that the passions of the time were so intense that many became prisoners of those passions and forever resistant to any evidence to the contrary.

The result was a distorting lack of context. To antiwar protestors it was axiomatic that the war in Vietnam was the most awful, most barbaric, most terrible war in the history of mankind. What such beliefs really reflected was an almost complete ignorance of history. If one wanted a base line for the horrors of war, one need search no farther than the family Bible, especially Numbers 31:7–18:

> And they warred against the Midianites, as the Lord commanded Moses; and they slew all the males. And they slew the kings of Midian [and] took *all* the women of Midian captives, and their little ones. . . . And they burnt all their cities wherein they dwelt, and all their goodly castles, with fire. . . .
>
> And Moses was wroth [and] said unto them. . . . kill every male among the little ones, and kill every woman that hath known man by lying with him. But all the women children, that have not known a man by lying with him, keep alive for yourselves.

By that standard, the Vietnam War was an exercise in gentility. Even by comparison with the Korean War that preceded it, military operations against the civilian population were restrained. An infantry veteran of both the Korean and Vietnam Wars, nothing in my Vietnam experience came even close to the horrors of the "scorched earth" policy during our retreat from North Korea in the winter of 1950. On the explicit orders of the Eighth U.S. Army commander, all houses were burnt, all livestock killed, and all food supplies destroyed to prevent the Chinese from living off the land. Millions of civilians, mostly old men, women and children, were forced to flee their homes in sub-zero weather, and the sight of those poor souls dying in the snow during that terrible trek south still haunts me.

Much has been made by the protestors of the "carpet bombing" of Hanoi, a propaganda campaign so pervasive that I was shocked on my first visit there in 1974 to discover a city relatively untouched by war. By comparison, Pyongyang, the capital of North Korea, was flattened by aerial bombardment, including a 1,403-plane raid in August 1952, far larger, and far less concerned with "collateral damage," than the Hanoi raids.

As Moyar relates, humanitarian concerns were a major constraint against U.S. bombing of the Red River dams and dikes, concerns that did not manifest themselves in Korea. There the dams and irrigation systems were fair game. The last bombing campaign of that war in May 1953 was against North Korean irrigation dams in order to disrupt their food supplies and force them back to the negotiating table. Civilian casualties in the three-year Korean War are estimated at 2.5 million, compared to an estimated 365,000 in the ten-year Vietnam War.

Even worse than the lack of context, the failure to see the Vietnam War in its entirety severely distorts an understanding of that conflict. Almost all the literature on the war concentrates on the period of intense U.S. military involvement during the 1960s, with most works ending with the Tet Offensive of 1968. As the late William Colby noted, this is like ending a study of World War II with the battle of Stalingrad, the North African invasion, or the capture of Guadalcanal in the Pacific.

Not only does this ignore the fact that the war continued for another seven years, it gives inordinate weight to the Viet Cong and the guerrilla war, ignoring the fact that after 1968 the guerrilla movement withered away to the point where in the North Vietnamese Army's 1975 final offensive they had almost no part to play. That twenty-two-division cross-border blitzkrieg had more to do with the fall of France in 1940 than to any notions of guerrilla war. It was a Soviet-supplied T-54 main battle tank, not a black-pajama-clad guerrilla, that broke down the gates of the Presidential Palace in Saigon on April 30, 1975.

"The ultimate irony," said Colby, "was that the people's war launched in 1959 had been defeated, but the soldier's war, which the United States had insisted on fighting during the 1960s with massive military forces, was finally won by the enemy." An even greater irony, however, is that that irony is still not widely appreciated. In 1996, for example, a BBC interviewer asked how the Viet Cong had won the war.

It had to be explained to her that in fact the Viet Cong were the war's ultimate losers. They lost to the Americans, they lost to the South Vietnamese and, most conclusively of all, they lost to the North Vietnamese. As such critics of the war as Stanley Karnow and Morley Safer discovered on their return to Vietnam, the founders of the National Liberation Front are among the most bitter veterans of the war.

Sadly, that misperception is shared by those whose business it is to know better. The 1996 Bernath Book Prize of the Society for Historians of American Foreign Relations, for example, was awarded to a work that once again truncates the war and perpetuates the myth of a guerrilla victory, a victory that even Hanoi's Military History Institute would now deny.

That's why Mark Moyar's *Phoenix and the Birds of Prey: The CIA's Secret Campaign to Destroy the Viet Cong* is so important. Not only does Moyar place the Vietnam War in context, he also details one of the main reasons why the Viet Cong guerrillas, after some impressive initial successes, faded into irrelevance by the end of the war.

Beginning with a new interpretation of the rise of the Viet Cong and the crucial role of their shadow government, or Viet Cong Infrastructure (VCI), he then provides a balanced, detailed account of the efforts to destroy that shadow government. Arguing against the conventional wisdom, he finds that it was the South Vietnamese themselves, particularly their much maligned Provincial Reconnaissance Units and their local militia that "devastated the Viet Cong shadow government, as well as the Viet Cong guerrilla forces."

When it came to the "people's war," the people won. Moyar discovered "that the majority of villagers actually favored the Saigon government over the Viet Cong during the latter years of the war." The people, however, were not the center of gravity of the war, as we had erroneously believed. The center of gravity was the North Vietnamese Army. As former Phoenix adviser Stuart Herrington remarked, "Like us, Hanoi failed to win the 'hearts and minds' of the South Vietnamese peasantry. Unlike us, Hanoi's leaders were able to compensate for this failure by playing their trump card—they overwhelmed South Vietnam with a twenty-two division force."

Today, as the United States draws on the "lessons" of Vietnam to undergird "operations-other-than-war," its new euphemism for dealing with revolutionary war, it is critical that those "lessons" reflect reality. In words that gently chide much of the Vietnam War "scholarship," Moyar concludes that "For a history of a revolutionary war or for a theoretical work on revolutionary warfare," scholars should try harder "to examine as much of the available evidence as possible and to interpret it before coming to any conclusions about the validity of particular theories." And in this work, he has done just that.

Col. Harry G. Summers, Jr., USA (Ret.)

Preface

M y research on this subject began in 1991, when, as a sopho-more at Harvard University, I took an introductory course on the Vietnam War. The campus climate was no longer what it had been during the Vietnam War, not even when the Gulf War erupted that year. The students did not target university property, protest in great numbers, or lavish praise on the Iraqis. The mainly conservative minority that disagreed with the antiwar students was considerably larger, more vocal, and better organized. Had the war been longer or had the United States instituted a draft, however, perhaps the campus would have turned into something more closely resembling its state during the late 1960s, for the majority of students did not differ greatly from their Vietnam-era predecessors in their political beliefs.

Many student radicals of the Vietnam era have become professors at Harvard or other prestigious universities across the land. They are now using the "system," which they once despised, to their own ends. One of the professors teaching the Vietnam course that I attended fit this description, and his lectures made clear that his views about the war have not changed significantly over the years. Most of the students taking the course and the teaching assistants embraced the tenets of the antiwar movement, and, without reservation, they devoured lectures and course readings that supported those views. Many of these people prided themselves on their ability to question and renounce the beliefs offered to them by previous generations or other established authorities. They reminded me of Rakitin, the divinity student in *The Brothers Karamazov*. They seemed much less willing, however, to question their own beliefs. Most of them found it easy to believe that almost every aspect of the Vietnam War validated their political and philosophical beliefs. Although they generally advocated affirmative action, campus programs for minorities, and greater acceptance of minorities in order to promote "diversity," they had little respect for the idea of intellectual diversity. They did not welcome or, in some cases, even tolerate those who challenged their views, as might have been expected, but ignored or ridiculed them or attacked their motives. Despite their condemnation of the

American elites of the 1950s and early 1960s for alleged right-wing dogmatism and intolerance, this new elite of the left was dogmatic and intolerant of those who disagreed with it. Not all members of this group acted in this way, but enough of them did to obstruct a great deal of worthwhile discussion.

I was more skeptical about the information I received in the course than most of my peers. At that time, I knew little about the war known to Americans as the Vietnam War, but I had learned enough about human nature to distrust people who believed that one side rarely did anything wrong and the other side rarely did anything right in a conflict as complicated as this war. Having been something of a zealous liberal at an earlier stage in life, moreover, I knew firsthand that many of my liberal colleagues had not scrutinized their own opinions as thoroughly as they should have.

When it was time to do research for my term paper, these doubts made me eager to seek other sources in the stacks of Widener Library, and I embarked on a period of reading that continued long after the course ended. I began by reading standard texts on the war, most of which suggested that all aspects of the Vietnam War were rather easy to understand. I noticed that most of these books focused on the period up to 1968, even though Saigon did not fall until 1975. They gave the years after 1968 either cursory treatment or none at all and often left the impression that the military and political situation in South Vietnam did not change much during the last seven years of the war. I also found, as I became interested in the counterinsurgency initiative known as the "Phoenix program," that most books described this highly controversial subject with a few broad and thinly substantiated generalities. Later, as I began to find documents and to talk to people who had participated in the war, I realized that a great deal of the war's history had escaped the innumerable books written about it. I decided to write my senior thesis—and then this book—out of the conviction that too many facets of the war have been ignored or misunderstood.

Limited evidence and the resultant scarcity of detail do not inherently discount a historical interpretation, particularly when a subject is small or simple. But the war against the Viet Cong shadow government, the war in which the Phoenix program tried to play a central role, was such a large and complex undertaking and publicly available information about it so limited that only a thorough investigation could hope to discover its true nature. The war against the shadow government, unknown to many historians, involved a vast array of programs and people who functioned in many diverse areas over a long period of time. To avoid using an unrepresentative sample, I employ evidence of all types covering every Allied program, every province, and every year from 1967 to 1972. As I sifted through the details of my research, I found that the war against the Viet Cong shadow government did follow certain patterns in many different times and places but, in many cases, not the patterns that most commentators thought.

Proper selection and usage of sources are crucial for any type of history, but they are especially important for histories of the Vietnam War. A large percentage of interviews, documents, and other types of sources on the war contain false or misleading information, and the reliable sources are frequently used to support arguments that they do not actually support. The vigilant researcher, however, can discern the useful from the useless if he or she knows what sorts of biases to expect and if enough sources are available. Before using any source for this book, I looked at the contemporary situation in the place or places in question, the ways in which the source's vantage point might have limited its perspective of events, the motives that the source might have had for giving accurate or inaccurate information, and the truthfulness of other information that the source had given. Because a large number of my sources came from more or less the same type of environment, I also was able to gauge their reliability by checking them against each other. I do not discuss the validity of individual sources in this book, however, except in a few cases where the issue is particularly noteworthy. In most instances, because of space constraints, I give only one or two illustrative examples when I make a general statement, but, in virtually every case, I have many other sources that confirm the statement.

I focus on the period 1967–72 because the Allies made their most comprehensive attack on the Viet Cong shadow government during this period. The Americans also monitored the various programs more closely than in preceding and subsequent years, so more relevant information is available. I organized this book thematically rather than chronologically, because thematic organization allows more thorough analyses of most topics. Important changes over time, of course, are mentioned where appropriate.

In this book, I normally refer to the Communist organization in South Vietnam as the Viet Cong or the Party, rather than the National Liberation Front as some historians do, because the Communist Party, not the NLF, actually controlled the South Vietnamese Communists. In addition, the term *Viet Cong* is more familiar to most readers. When I use the term *Communists* without mention of Northerners or Southerners, I refer to the North and South Vietnamese who served in any of the organizations controlled by Hanoi, whether political or military. Many members of these organizations did not embrace Communist political ideology, but seldom do all who serve a dictatorial regime share the political beliefs of the leaders.

Part I presents a new interpretation of the rise of the Viet Cong and of the crucial role that the Viet Cong shadow government played in that ascent. It also describes and explains the environment in which the Viet Cong played out this success and the Allied attempts to stop them. Parts II through IV describe in detail the efforts of the Allies, principally the United States and the Republic of Vietnam, to destroy the shadow government. Because many critics have accused Phoenix and related programs, such as the Provincial Reconnaissance Units, of targeting non-Communists and assassinating people, I pay particular attention to such charges. In the course of my investigation, I found that these allegations were accurate in some ways. South Vietnamese government personnel, with varying amounts of support from their American backers, arrested, tortured, and killed certain South Vietnamese civilians who were not Viet Cong. On the other hand, the Allies sometimes went out of their way to keep such abuses from occurring. By looking at only one of these two types of behavior, as many historians unfortunately do, one can paint a picture of the Allies as either wicked oppressors or upstanding saviors. Choosing to avoid such black-and-white interpretations, I attempt to describe the various shades of gray that existed. I argue, nevertheless, that the gray of the Allies tended to be lighter rather than darker.

Part of the book's purpose is to uncover and explain the grayness of the war, the mixture of good and bad that resulted when ideals ran into reality. Those individuals who do not recognize the harsh realities that limit their ability to put their ideals into practice succeed only in committing foolish actions that can make the world worse. When they fail to temper idealism with realism, they can even become desperate and destructive. The more radical members of the opposition to the Vietnam War suffered this fate, as they turned from ideals of love and peace to hatred of American soldiers and the dangerous delusion that the motives of their ideological adversaries were necessarily base.

Part V argues that certain components of the war against the shadow government, most notably the Phoenix program, were ineffective. Other Allied programs, such as the Provincial Reconnaissance Units, which most people mistakenly identify as Phoenix, and the territorial forces, succeeded in hurting the enemy to varying extents. Together they devastated the Viet Cong shadow government, as well as the Viet Cong guerrilla forces.

Part VI looks at the effects of the war against the shadow government on the South Vietnamese villagers. Many commentators argue that it alienated the hamlet populations and thereby reduced their desire to resist the Communists. Most also claim that the Viet Cong always enjoyed greater overall popularity with the villagers than did the South Vietnamese government in Saigon. On this issue, the shortage of scholarship is most surprising, given the casual manner in which people often generalize about it. I discovered that the majority of villagers actually favored the Saigon government over the Viet Cong during the latter years of the war, and that the attack on the shadow government did not estrange many villagers.

This book provides information that should prove useful in future wars of a similar nature. Whether or not one believes that the U.S. Central Intelligence Agency and military forces should help other countries fight insurgencies, we need to understand how these organizations can intervene most effectively because they will continue to do so. Even President William J. Clinton, who avoided service in what he called an immoral war in Vietnam, has deemed it necessary to involve the Central Intelligence Agency and the military in the morally ambiguous internal conflicts of such foreign lands as Somalia, Haiti, and Bosnia. The extent to which future wars will resemble the Vietnam War, of course, is not clear, especially because relations among the world's strongest powers have changed tremendously during the past decade. An insurgent war of some type, nevertheless, is raging somewhere on the globe at almost all times.

Unfortunately, certain categories of history are segregated in America today. Too few historians study the interaction between social, political, economic, and cultural history, on the one hand, and military and intelligence history on the other. My intent is to synthesize social and political history with military and intelligence history and, in the process, to illuminate a subject that occupies an important place in the American consciousness.

Acknowledgments

his book could not have been written without the help of a great many individuals. I am deeply indebted to several people whom I was fortunate enough to know at Harvard University. Professor Ernest May served as adviser for my undergraduate thesis. He offered much valuable advice and helped me in many other ways. The indefatigable Robert Johnson instructed and advised me for much of my four years, and he critiqued my writing more often than I reasonably could have expected of anyone. Professor Christopher Andrew of Cambridge University, while visiting for a semester, enlightened me on the study of intelligence during memorable afternoon conversations as part of an independent study. Professor Akira Iriye supported and advised me when I needed it. Mark Bradley, John Connelly, Timothy Naftali, Jeffrey Richter, Professor Stephen Peter Rosen, and Professor Stephan Thernstrom also provided helpful criticisms and suggestions during my university years. I owe thanks, in addition, to the Charles Warren Center at Harvard for a grant that made possible some of my research.

The war's participants who told me of their experiences are especially deserving of my thanks. They taught me a great deal about the Vietnam War and war in general, and much of this book relies heavily on their testimony. Candidly and patiently, they not only discussed events and programs but also told me their private thoughts that, in many cases, they had not talked about with anyone since leaving Vietnam. Their names appear in the introduction to the Notes section. Some also introduced me to other veterans. I owe a few of these people special recognition. Peter Scott sparked my interest in this subject and encouraged me along the way. Bob Boyke went out of his way to help organize my trip to Vietnam. Comdr. Frank C. Brown, Col. Walter B. Clark, Robert Komer, Col. Chester B. McCoid, and Richard Welcome were my proponents during the book's early days. Colonel Clark and his wife, Ellen, were as hospitable as any people I know. The late William Colby read through my thesis carefully and offered valuable suggestions for improving it. Any inaccuracies of interpretation or fact, of course, are my responsibility.

Dale Andradé, Zalin Grant, William Laurie, Gary Linderer, Harry

Maurer, Lt. Gen. Harold G. Moore, Al Santoli, Lt. Col. Kalev Sepp, Lewis Sorley, and Douglas Valentine put me in touch with people who participated in the war against the shadow government. Stanley Karnow and Col. Harry G. Summers, Jr., gave me support and encouragement. Gen. John Vessey, Lt. Gen. Harold G. Moore, and Dr. Lewis Stern helped me to find people for interviews in Hanoi. Luu Lan Phuong of Vietnam's Foreign Press Center dutifully organized my interviews with Communist leaders in Hanoi and, along with Nguyen Bao Mai, interpreted for me. Nguyen Tan Loc served as interpreter in the United States. B. G. Burkett and Steve Sherman helped me to investigate some individuals who had made false statements about service in Vietnam. J. C. Fischer, who has compiled long lists of American advisers in Vietnam, verified the identity and time and place of service of individuals whom I interviewed. Phoebe Spinrad provided information on misperceptions of Vietnam veterans. The Deutscher Akademischer Austauschdienst gave me a scholarship for a year of study in Germany between the writing of the thesis and the writing of the book. Randy DeGeer, Sean McBride, and Mike Popiel of Marakon Associates allowed me to take time off from work during the book's final stages. At the Naval Institute Press, Mark Gatlin stood behind me the whole way.

Archivists at the U.S. Army Center of Military History, the U.S. Military History Institute, the National Archives Suitland Branch, and the Lyndon B. Johnson Library located documents for me. Of particular note, Dale Andradé and Richard Hunt at the Center of Military History went out of their way to provide me with numerous documents. Both have authored books on Vietnam and shared their insights with me.

Friends who have helped during my travels and during other times include Stephen Anderson, Scott Braming, Evan Clark, Omar Darr, Paul Dean, George Downing, Ari Epstein, Chandler Fulton, Joseph Grossman, Gregory Harper, Peter Kuechle, John Lardas, David McIntosh, Andrew Narten, Mark ("Chip") Poncy, Jr. and family, James Reddinger, Piotr Sobieszczyk, Rüdiger von Stosch, Susanne von Stosch, Juan Zarate and family, and Robert Zirovich and family. Others who helped me at various times include Robert Shurtz, Todd Heath, Douglas Smith, Robert Hanson, John Klaymen, and Thomas Everett.

A few of the people who contributed to this book cannot be mentioned by name because they prefer to avoid publicity.

Finally, I wish to express my deepest gratitude to my family: Mom, Dad, Dean, David, Grandmother Moyar, Grandmother Capous, the Papases, and my future wife, Kelli Meilander. Their love and support made this book possible.

Part One: Origins

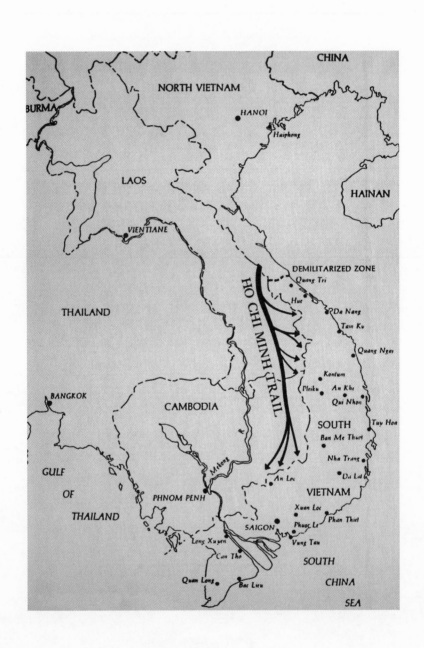

1

Vietnam at War: Before Phoenix

egend has it that Phoenix tore through the South Vietnamese countryside like a hell-driven hurricane. Phoenix, it is said, radically redirected the war in the villages and exposed the village populations to indiscriminate torture and assassination on an unprecedented scale. In truth, Phoenix's nature and its relationship to the preceding time period were far different. The onset of the Phoenix era did not represent the addition of a new dimension to the conflict. Instead, it signified changes in the power of dynamic forces that had already been operating in one of the war's dimensions. Only in the context of the war's preceding phases, therefore, can the Phoenix program and related efforts be understood.

The Vietnamese Communist movement first took root in southern Vietnam during World War II. Founded in northern Vietnam under the leadership of Ho Chi Minh, the Communist Party attracted modest numbers of members farther south before 1945. The Viet Minh—the front of the Communist Party at that time—initiated uprisings in August 1945 and took control of Vietnam's major cities. For a short time, it seemed that the future of all Vietnam would lie with the Communists. The French colonialists, however, soon took the cities back. During the next decade, the Communists fought the French colonialists in an effort to drive them out and simultaneously eliminated many of their Vietnamese political rivals. After the Communist triumph at Dien Bien Phu in 1954, the French decided to give up the fight.

The ensuing Geneva Accords divided Vietnam into the Democratic Republic of Vietnam in the North, which the Communists governed, and a non-Communist Republic of Vietnam in the South, led by Ngo Dinh Diem and supported by the United States. Each of these entities received half of Annam, the central third of Vietnam, which differed economically and culturally from the northern and southern thirds. Several hundred thousand anti-Communist North Vietnamese, the majority Roman Catholic, moved to the South at this time. Although prejudice against Northerners was strong in much of South Vietnam, some of these northern refugees eventually would assimilate into the southern culture and lead strong opposition to the Communists. After the Geneva settlement, the Communist leadership in Hanoi decided to keep between ten thousand and fifteen thousand of its supporters in the South as secret organizers. The Communists moved between fifty thousand and ninety thousand more Southerners to North Vietnam for training. Years later, the Communists would send these people back to their native land to lead an insurgency against the South Vietnamese government, known as the Government of Vietnam (GVN). They would become, for a time, the Communists' greatest asset in South Vietnam.

Shortly after Ho Chi Minh's reign began in Hanoi, he launched a campaign to crush the wealthiest classes of North Vietnamese citizens, along with other alleged enemies of the state. Thousands perished, and many others endured torture and internment in prisons and labor camps. While Ho solidified his control over the North Vietnamese people, he considered taking South Vietnam as well. Ho initially hoped to conquer South Vietnam through political agitation. Prepared for the worst, however, he ordered his supporters in the South to start building up clandestine military forces as they simultaneously pursued the political route. Ho devised a plan for full-scale "revolutionary warfare" in the South, based on the Chinese Communist model, should the GVN stifle his political initiatives. The plan called for three phases: (1) the organization of opposition movements in the rural areas, (2) the mobilization of the rural population into guerrilla units to wear down the enemy forces, and (3) the buildup of conventional army (main force) units that ultimately would attack the towns and cities in conjunction with urban uprisings. At times, Ho knew, the Communists might operate in more than one of these phases simultaneously.

President Diem proved that Ho's caution was warranted; Diem decided to eradicate his political opponents, much as Ho had done in North Vietnam. During the middle and late 1950s, Diem's police imprisoned or killed thousands of Communists and their sympathizers, former Communist soldiers and supporters, non-Communist political opponents, and others whom the police disliked. As in North Vietnam, no one knows how many suffered imprisonment or death in the South. Diem hoped to destroy his enemies in the countryside, as well as in the towns and cities, through this program, and he largely succeeded. He also strengthened the GVN presence in the most populous rural areas. The bulk of the nation's rural inhabitants lived in the many provinces of the Mekong Delta, in the provinces surrounding

Saigon, and near the coast in the provinces north of the capital city. As Diem's actions ate away at the Communist strength in South Vietnam, the North Vietnamese concluded that only with force could they achieve a Communist takeover. In 1957, the Communists initiated the first of many terrorist campaigns against GVN employees and supporters and sent more military advisers to the South. Ho did not call for open warfare against the GVN until 1959, however, and fighting did not begin in most places until at least 1960. By this time, Diem's tactics had crippled the Southern Communists.

During the early 1960s, the Communists who had moved north in 1954 returned to lead the Southern Communist movement into the second phase of revolutionary warfare. The insurgent war blazed through the Vietnamese countryside. The Viet Cong (another term for the Southern Communists) took control of many South Vietnamese villages, and their armed forces expanded rapidly. GVN forces who tried to quench the Communist fire suffered many humiliating setbacks, and their losses mounted. Many of the GVN personnel who had served full time in the rural areas retreated into the towns and cities where they could enjoy better protection from the danger in the countryside, but the enemy was growing and surrounding the GVN's enclaves.

These developments set off alarms in Washington, D.C. President John F. Kennedy, deeply concerned about Communist encroachment in Southeast Asia, decided to establish a military command center in Saigon and expand the U.S. advisory effort in South Vietnam. Despite their many weaknesses, Diem's military and police forces, with American help, still seemed capable of preserving the southern regime in the near future. Whether Diem could have held out for many more years, however, shall never be known. During 1963, Kennedy became extremely dissatisfied with Diem's harsh treatment of political dissidents and his conduct of the war. He encouraged a group of South Vietnamese generals to overthrow Diem but not to kill him. The generals ousted Diem at the beginning of November 1963 and killed both Diem and his influential brother Ngo Dinh Nhu. Kennedy's decision, which displayed the administration's considerable ignorance about South Vietnamese politics and potential successors to Diem, severely damaged the GVN war effort. For two years after Diem's death, several men held the top GVN office. None of them proved capable of strengthening the Army of the Republic of Vietnam (ARVN) and staving off the Communists while also maintaining the favor of the United States and key South Vietnamese political groups. The turbulence in Saigon and the poor quality of Diem's replacements greatly undermined the stability and effectiveness of GVN counterinsurgency programs. Communist control over rural South Vietnam grew by the day, and the Viet Cong (VC) main force units were approaching the strength necessary to implement the final phase of revolutionary warfare. In late 1964, Hanoi decided to hasten the main force buildup by infiltrating North Vietnamese Army (NVA) units into the South. The North Vietnamese assumed that the United States would not respond to this escalation with ground forces, one of the biggest errors in judgment of the Vietnam War. They apparently had taken President Lyndon B. Johnson at his word when he made his infamous promise during the 1964 presidential campaign that he was not about to send American boys halfway around the globe to do what Asian boys ought to be doing for themselves.

In early 1965, Johnson initiated "Rolling Thunder," a campaign of bombing both North Vietnam and the infiltration trails in Laos to keep the Communists from destroying the GVN. Rolling Thunder was not designed to produce decisive military results. It spared many important targets, both to minimize civilian casualties and to leave the United States the option of threatening escalation later on. The bombs were intended to weaken North Vietnam's will to fight, damage the morale of the Communists in the South, and bolster GVN morale, but Rolling Thunder attained none of these objectives during its 3½-year life span. The American civilian leaders who designed the bombing plan showed that they, like Ho, did not understand their enemy, for the Communists could tolerate the damage inflicted by limited American air strikes. These same Americans also overestimated the positive impact of the bombing on the morale of their South Vietnamese ally.

Rolling Thunder soon drew U.S. troops into Vietnam to protect the air bases, troops that the world's leading democratic power would find difficult to withdraw without losing face. In July 1965, afraid that backing down would damage America's prestige and credibility both at home and abroad, and that the South Vietnamese Army could not withstand the Viet Cong and North Vietnamese onslaught much longer, Johnson inserted one hundred thousand U.S. troops. Many more would follow during the next few years. The ineffective South Vietnamese Army, relieved of most of the responsibility for fighting the Communist main forces, turned its attention to wresting control of the villages and their people from the VC, a task known as "pacification."

The well-prepared U.S. troops blunted the Communist offensive in short order. Communist forces continued to seek some main force battles with U.S. units but only when they greatly outnumbered the Americans. In virtually all of these lopsided main force engagements, the U.S. troops, thanks to their superior combat capabilities, repulsed the larger Communist forces and killed many of them. Such battles persisted during the first two years of the American intervention, despite complaints from some factions in Hanoi that the Communists take a less aggressive course. The Communist forces also relied on guerrilla tactics to harass the Americans. They hit the Americans at times and places of their own choosing and then tried to withdraw before the Americans could hit back. The guerrilla approach succeeded more often and incurred fewer Communist casualties than the main force battles, but it took a smaller toll on American manpower.

Gen. William C. Westmoreland, who commanded the U.S. forces through the Military Assistance Command, Vietnam (MACV), hoped to defeat the Communists by locating and destroying their troops and bases until Hanoi lacked the will and manpower to continue the fight. In the lingo of the day, Westmoreland was pursuing an "attrition" strategy and employing "search-and-destroy" tactics. The Americans also tried to shut off the flow of men from the North to the South. To complement the bombing of North Vietnam and Laos, the U.S. Navy prevented transportation by sea between North and South Vietnam, and the Air Force and the CIA-supported Hmong forces tried to reduce the infiltration of young North Vietnamese men through Laos. A strategy of attrition is often the most effective way to fight a war, but it proved problematic for the Americans in Vietnam because they could not find and destroy enough of Hanoi's manpower to halt its offensive in the South. The North Vietnamese soldiers who slipped through Laos and the Southerners whom the VC shadow government continued to conscript compensated for the horrendous Communist losses. The Communist Party leadership in Hanoi never considered giving up, no matter how many thousands of men were sacrificed. After the infusion of U.S. troops in 1965, however, the fortunes of the Communists began to decline steadily. Suffering heavy losses, they yielded control of many areas and lines of communication. The Allies had the upper hand.

During this same time, the Allied pacification program functioned poorly. The Allies did not eliminate the Communist presence in many villages, nor did they strengthen their own permanent presence in the villages appreciably. ARVN units either did nothing or conducted largely ineffective operations against the VC. Their leaders believed that their nation was safe as long as the Americans kept fighting, so they did not see any need to prosecute the village war more forcefully. Other GVN organizations made modest attempts to bolster the Allied pacification effort in areas where the VC did not have firm control over the villages. The Communists repeatedly attacked them when they showed much determination and usually prevented them from making substantial progress.

2　The Shadow Government and the Viet Cong

he astonishing success of the Viet Cong has mystified Westerners ever since the initial VC uprisings attracted their attention in the early 1960s. In most underdeveloped countries of the world, governments no stronger than the GVN have crushed such revolutionary movements with little outside help. Yet, the South Vietnamese peasant revolutionaries brought the GVN to its knees and forced the world's strongest army to come to its rescue, and even then they bowed only slowly. Despite the tremendous attention that Americans and other Westerners have paid to the Vietnam War, few have investigated in detail the reasons behind the Viet Cong's triumphs. The involvement of the shadow government has remained particularly obscure. In truth, of all the factors at work in the village war, the actions of the shadow government's cadres played by far the largest role in propelling the Viet Cong to victory.

Although the war during the early 1960s varied from province to province, and indeed from village to village, it followed certain general patterns. Each side had a set of organizations that it used in most parts of the country, and each of the organizations operated according to fairly uniform general procedures. On the Viet Cong side, three basic types of units engaged in armed activity: main forces, local forces, and guerrillas. VC main-force units possessed better soldiers and heavier armaments than the others. They attacked the large Allied military units, as did the North Vietnamese Army units once they started arriving. Because of the personnel and equipment needed for main-force units, the VC main forces developed slowly at first but became a formidable entity by 1964. The local forces screened and maintained bases for the main forces, attacked the enemy territorial and main forces at times, and protected the guerrillas. Unlike the men in the main forces, local-force members were native to the district in which they operated, although the units usually hid in unpopulated areas.

The VC guerrillas fell into two categories. Some guerrillas divided their time between farming their land in their native villages and serving the VC. Others worked full time for the VC in their villages and surrounding areas and, in many cases, were not allowed to live with their families. The guerrilla units lacked the competence of the main and local forces, who had already taken the best young men from the villages, either directly or after they had distinguished themselves as guerrillas. Guerrillas harassed the Allied troops by sniping and setting mines and booby traps, and they attacked small GVN security forces. They also collected intelligence for the main- and local-force units and provided them with guides, porters, and other assistants when needed. Within the hamlets, they investigated the arrival of strangers, served as sentries at night, and assisted the shadow government. At times, the guerrillas also persuaded or forced other villagers to help them.

All three types of VC forces usually had good leaders and excellent discipline. They regularly received accurate intelligence about enemy forces, which allowed them to avoid or attack the enemy as they chose. Distinctions among the main forces, local forces, and guerrillas became confusing at times because the main and local forces often operated in small groups and fought in guerrilla fashion. Although the Communists knew that eventually they would have to defeat their enemy in large conventional battles, they knew they often lacked the capability to win such battles and thus relied on slow erosion of the enemy's main forces via guerrilla warfare. All of the units, nevertheless, remained separate bodies.

The GVN tried to use militia forces, or "territorial forces" as they were called more often, to hold the village areas, but VC assaults usually destroyed them or drove them into the towns and cities. Their departure left the ARVN regular units as the GVN's only effective armed forces. The ARVN had air support and heavy artillery, which the VC did not, but its shortcomings far outweighed these advantages. It lacked intelligence capabilities equivalent to those of the Communists, and it seldom operated effectively at night against an enemy that did most of its work at night. The ARVN's use of large units severely limited the area that its forces could cover, inhibited their ability to move quickly, and gave VC spies in the villages and within the GVN a good chance to detect their movements. Because of their size, supply needs, and use of motor vehicles, ARVN units regularly traveled on major roads where the Viet Cong soldiers and guerrillas could ambush them. Static defense of important locations made ARVN units vulnerable to attack by concentrated VC forces. For these reasons, the VC inflicted increasingly heavy losses on the ARVN until the Americans arrived in 1965. The impressive firepower and mobility of the Americans, their fighting spirit, and their night warfare capabilities and surveillance devices reduced the Communists' effectiveness. Even against the Americans, though, the Communists fought, more often than not, at the time and place of their choosing.

To understand the VC's ascent and their persistent strength, however, one must look further, to the Viet Cong shadow government, or the Viet Cong infrastructure (VCI), as the Americans often called it. The Viet Cong were not a ragtag collection of South Vietnamese villagers, driven by discontent with the GVN, who met informally to discuss a few general plans. The drive and guidance of the VC, rather, came from a highly dedicated, competent, and well-organized shadow government. Under the direction of Hanoi, the members of this shadow government, known as "cadres" or simply as "VCI," formed the political and military leadership of the Viet Cong. The shadow government consisted of the Communist Party structure in South Vietnam that organized and directed the VC, as well as the leadership and administration of the National Liberation Front (NLF), an entity that the Communist Party had created to carry out its policies. The VCI did not include regular soldiers, rank-and-file guerrillas and members of NLF organizations, and other people who assisted the Communists in some way. Estimates of the shadow government's size in the mid-1960s varied considerably. U.S. agencies responsible for estimating enemy strength regularly quarrelled over how to measure it, as well as how to define membership in the VCI. The shadow government, it is certain, expanded greatly from 1960 to 1965, then shrank somewhat from 1965 to 1967. The most reasonable estimate of political cadre strength in 1967 probably came from the Central Intelligence Agency (CIA), which concluded that it lay somewhere between 80,000 and 150,000.[1]

The Southern Communist Party—first called the Southern Arm of the Workers' Party and later rechristened the People's Revolutionary Party—operated through committees at five administrative levels: nation, region, province, district, and village. During the early 1960s, Vietnamese from the southern half of Vietnam comprised the bulk of Communist Party members in the VC. During the half decade following the Geneva Accords of 1954, Communist cadres who stayed in South Vietnam had tried to conduct political activities in secret. They inserted agents into GVN organizations, assassinated GVN officials and informants, and spread propaganda among the populace. Most of the cadres, however, were jailed or killed during this five-year period, thus leaving the burden of leadership to the Southern cadres who had gone to North Vietnam for training in 1954 and returned to the South in the early 1960s. As the Communist ranks quickly expanded during the early 1960s, many villagers also became leaders.

True Northerners, though few in number in the South at that time, occupied important positions in the hierarchy. The Central Office for South Vietnam, the title assigned to the national-level Communist Party leadership, took its orders from the Communist leaders in Hanoi. North Vietnam, through this mechanism, maintained firm control over the VC throughout its lifetime. A number of Southerners did hold very high Party positions in Hanoi. Some of them, especially those from central Vietnam, endeared themselves to the Hanoi regime by casting aside their regional loyalties, but many others retained their Southern identity and, at times, influenced Hanoi's policy choices in the South's favor. When certain Northern Communists proposed reducing the fighting in the South to facilitate building up the North, for instance, these Southerners helped to convince the Party leadership to reject the proposal and to continue pressing for victory in the South. The North Vietnamese, nevertheless, made the final decisions. Many ardent critics of the American war effort at the time denied that Hanoi pulled the strings of the South Vietnamese Communists, but no one now disputes this fact.

The Communist Party's Central Office for South Vietnam (COSVN) sent directives down through the hierarchy of Party committees. The region and province committees had considerable freedom to adapt the directives to local conditions before they passed them down to the district and village committees, whose independence varied from place to place. The committee members at each echelon debated issues freely, but a small number of senior Party members made the important decisions, and the Party secretary played a prominent role within this group. The committee contained sections for handling specific activities and policies, such as military affairs, finance and economy, communications-liaison, and security. The political cadres of the military affairs sections commanded the armed forces.

Joining the Party required proof of one's dedication and skill over an extended period of time. Candidates for Party membership gradually received greater responsibility, while the Party simultaneously increased the limitations on their personal freedom. This process ensured that the VC's elite leadership, upon which the success of the Viet Cong depended, included only capable and dedicated people. The village-level Party structure carried out all of the functions necessary for controlling the general population. At the village level, only the most important political cadres belonged to the Party. The VC hamlet-level political infrastructure, a subdivision of the village-level infrastructure, had even fewer Party members. When the VC firmly controlled an area, the hamlet and village VCI often lived in the hamlets or villages for which they were responsible. The Vietnamese village is not a single cluster of homes, as Americans might think of it; such a cluster is called a hamlet in Vietnam. Rather, a village is a group of several of these clusters, sometimes with a larger cluster in the middle. Cadres above the village echelon guided the village-level apparatus but did not execute policies in the field. Most members of the shadow government above village level—the middle- and upper-level leaders—were Party members. They normally had armed protection and stayed either in hamlets that were free of GVN presence or in the wilderness. Many Party members also served as cadres or soldiers with VC military units, but they were not considered to be VCI.

The National Liberation Front committees at any given level did not take orders from higher echelons or give orders to lower echelons, as the Communist Party committees did. The Party committee at each level controlled the corresponding NLF committee by choosing and controlling its leaders. Hanoi used the NLF to mask its involvement in the South so as to convince Westerners that the Communists in Hanoi did not control the Viet Cong.

During the early 1960s, the political and military cadres together orchestrated the seizure of hamlets from the GVN across the country. Their basic objective was to replace the GVN governing apparatus with a Communist government. The greatest obstacles to the revolution were the GVN officials, policemen, territorial security forces, informants, and teachers who lived or worked in the hamlets, for they could identify and attack the VC and get the villagers to assist them in this task. Armed VC drove these people out of the hamlets by killing, kidnapping, or threatening them. The shadow government frequently chose to abduct and indoctrinate the targeted individuals or force them to flee, rather than kill them. In some cases, too, the Viet Cong cadres allowed GVN officials and soldiers to remain in the village areas, as long as they did not carry out any duties that could harm the VC cause. The VC feared that killing them would turn the victims' families against the Communists. When the VC did decide to kill someone, they typically staged a sham trial before the public. The cadres read a list of charges against the "traitor," received approval from pro-VC elements in the crowd, and then killed the person, often by beheading or disembowelment. Because the VC cadres had excellent intelligence and their superiors insisted that they target only people whose involvement with the GVN could be proved, they seldom accused and executed the wrong people. Only in areas where they had relatively little influence did the VC resort to less discriminate terrorist attacks, such as executing bus passengers or throwing grenades into restaurants.

Usually, a few threats, abductions, or killings caused the rest of the GVN's apparatus, except for certain spies, to flee to the safety of towns, cities, or military outposts. The bulk of the GVN's leaders, from Saigon down to the hamlets, lacked commitment to their cause, so they failed to motivate themselves, their subordinates, or villagers to resist the VC in the face of stiff opposition. Some GVN personnel continued to visit the hamlets during the day, but they did not function as effectively as before. The VC often closed the roads leading to hamlets by digging ditches, blowing up bridges, and setting up regular ambushes, thereby decreasing the ability of GVN personnel in the district and provincial capitals to participate in the war for the hamlets; the GVN still held all of the district and provincial capitals, which were either cities or towns, although some of the towns scarcely exceeded villages in size. Once the GVN infrastructure abandoned a hamlet, the population gave up any hopes of overthrowing the Communists, and VC envelopment became complete. Thereafter, the shadow government executed only a small number of people, primarily those who passed information to the GVN or who refused to join the VC or pay taxes.

As the GVN lost its ability to govern, the VC's ability to make use of village resources grew. One of the VCI's first tasks in gaining control over a population was the recruitment of villagers into mass political organizations, such as the Liberation Farmer Association, Liberation Youth Association, or People's Liberation Committee, or into the guerrillas. The Liberation Farmer Association was the most important association, for the Party distributed land through it once the GVN lost its power in the village. Most of this land came from wealthy landowners, especially absentee landowners; less often, the GVN or French citizens owned the land. The Liberation Farmer Association also tended land whose owners had left the village, and it organized village labor to increase agricultural production. Although these organizations held allegedly democratic elections to enhance the members' sense of participation, Party members appointed from above actually controlled them.

Initially, the shadow government obtained most of the VC's personnel through the mass organizations, although it would later resort to forced conscription as well. Party members within the organizations assigned various tasks to the villagers, and the cadres promoted those who performed well. They tried to get most of the young males to join the local guerrilla forces, which could be a stepping stone to the main and local forces and perhaps even cadre status. Women joined the guerrilla ranks as well but in small numbers. More often and more effectively, they performed political tasks, such as wooing young men away from the GVN and organizing public protests against GVN policies. The VCI employed women, children, and the elderly to carry out menial tasks as needed, such as transporting rice at harvest time, digging tunnels, and distributing propaganda leaflets.

During the early years of the war, the shadow government enjoyed great success in expanding the ranks of full-time VC. According to American estimates that probably were close to the truth, the VCI recruited roughly three thousand villagers in South Vietnam per month from 1961 through 1964. During this time, the VC depended almost exclusively on recruits from the South Vietnamese rural population to build itself into a force capable of dominating the hamlets. Only at the end of 1964 did the North Vietnamese Army begin to enter South Vietnam in force. As both sides stepped up their war efforts in 1965 and the VC changed its methods, VC monthly recruits rose to an estimated ten thousand.[2] Recruits per month then declined to seven thousand in 1966 and, as the war began to turn in the Allies' favor, fell to somewhere between three thousand and five thousand in early 1967, which was not enough to replace VC losses.[3]

Taxation of the rural population constituted another crucial shadow government activity, for it gave the VC much of its income and most of its food. Sometimes the cadres took cash, but most often they expropriated rice and other agricultural products. In keeping with the VC's empathy for the poorer villagers, the shadow government's tax rates rose sharply in proportion to the volume of agricultural production—the more a farmer produced, the higher the percentage of taxes. The cadres used the agricultural taxes to feed the full-time soldiers, guerrillas, and cadres. Cash taxes, revenue from the sale of surplus food, and large sums gained by extorting money from capitalist enterprises allowed the Communists to buy medicine and other supplies in GVN-controlled areas, pay informants, and acquire other necessary commodities.

The shadow government also ran an extensive logistics network. It carried food from agriculturally rich areas, particularly the Mekong Delta, to Communists who had to tread less fertile ground. It also transported arms and ammunition to the fighters. Initially, the VC relied principally on American rifles and ammunition captured or extorted from the GVN but, by 1963, they began to receive sizable shipments of light and heavy weapons and ammunition from North Vietnam via Laos and Cambodia. After North Vietnamese and American troops entered the war en masse, the shipments became much larger. Wounded soldiers were transported, as well as lighter items, such as medical supplies and money. The VCI often forced civilians to carry most of the payloads in order to use VC personnel for other endeavors.

Intelligence collection was another invaluable but little-understood shadow government function. VC cadres organized the guerrillas and other villagers to conduct surveillance in and around the villages in order to determine where GVN forces operated. Relatives of VC cadres proved to be especially good sources of information in the hamlets. Through surveillance, the Viet Cong also received advance warning of GVN forces approaching the village. Observers used drums and other signals or raced back to the village on foot or by bicycle or boat to inform the VC so they could hide or flee. The VCI recruited and utilized many informants and agents in the GVN armed forces, police, and civil service who told them of imminent GVN attacks. Many VC had relatives serving in the GVN, and they were invariably the most willing and most reliable spies. The nature of the VC's armed successes made the intelligence tasks easier, for it often forced GVN forces to operate in large units. Once the VC developed some military strength in an area, which did not take long in places where they fomented uprisings successfully, the GVN usually tried to track down the VC only with its large forces during daylight hours. Its leaders feared that the VC main and local forces would destroy units smaller than company or battalion size. Usually, Communist observers near the hamlets detected the large GVN units easily, and the planning and support required for their operations involved many people who, potentially, could pass information to the VC.

The VCI skillfully organized activities designed to frustrate GVN intelligence collection. The cadres devoted great energy to locating and eliminating GVN informants and agents. They often convinced certain families in a hamlet to report any suspicious undertakings by members of other families. The families with members who worked for the GVN or who frequently traveled to GVN areas and families with large landholdings received extra attention, but even the families of Communist cadres and soldiers did not escape this surveillance. In some hamlets, the shadow government had cadres whose primary duty was spying on other villagers. They did nothing in public that would reveal their VC affiliation and thus hid their identity from the villagers. These covert cadres received the title "legal" cadres because they had legal South Vietnamese citizenship and the documents to prove it, whereas the overt cadres were "illegal"; the GVN knew most of the illegals and arrested them when they had the chance. Some legals tried to infiltrate GVN organizations, and, occasionally, killed GVN officials or civilians, but the need for secrecy normally limited the activities of these cadres. The security affairs cadres even had informants in the hamlets who reported other VC cadres when they collaborated with the enemy or performed poorly. The Party secretaries themselves did not know the identities of these informants.

Villagers had to report any strangers in their villages to the VC cadres, who then questioned the newcomers to determine if they might be GVN spies. In many areas, the cadres forbade villagers from visiting district or provincial capitals or put other restrictions on their movements to prevent them from passing information to the GVN. Informants living near GVN bases provided the VC with information about visitors to the bases, some of whom might have been GVN spies arriving to give reports. Some VC informants who worked within the GVN also identified GVN informants and agents.

The shadow government navigated cadres and military forces, particularly the alien North Vietnamese, through dangerous territory. When Communist forces passed through an area, the local cadres arranged for villagers to quarter the troops and often established primitive hospitals for them and gave them clothing and personal items. The carrying of countless messages, which enabled the VC to issue orders and report from the field, depended on VCI guidance and coordination. Along with other cadres and members of the NLF organizations, VC "agit-prop" cadres inundated the villagers with Communist rhetoric. They used "agitation," whereby one communicated a few general ideas to many people, and "propaganda," whereby one person communicated many ideas to a single listener.

3   The Shadow Government
and the People

A complete explanation of the shadow government and the Viet Cong requires an investigation into the reasons why so many South Vietnamese villagers supported the Communists and why some entered their ranks and carried out the multitude of military and political functions described in chapter 2. During the Communists' war against the French, the revolutionary movement convinced large numbers of educated urbanites and rural elites to join the Communist cause. The Communists attracted the heirs of the Mandarinate by promising to rid Vietnam of the French colonialists as previous generations had driven out other imperialistic foreigners and, less often, by promising to create a socialist society. These elites, many of whom went to the North in 1954 for training, played prominent roles in leading the revolutionary warfare of the 1960s. The shadow government was not able to engineer takeovers in the towns and cities as it did so effectively in the hamlets and villages in the 1960s. Ho Chi Minh, realizing that the shadow government could not mobilize the masses of the towns and cities against the GVN, argued that the rural peasants, not the proletariat, would have to lead the revolution in the South. He had borrowed this idea, like many of his ideas on revolutionary warfare, from the Chinese Communist leader Mao Tse-tung.

Many GVN employees and their relatives lived in the towns and cities, as did others eager to earn rewards for naming VC agitators. The urban population, therefore, was likely to report suspicious people to the local GVN authorities. Because the VC could not know everyone or restrict everyone's movement, they could not identify many of the GVN's spies. GVN police and military forces stationed in the towns and cities moved quickly to hunt down any reported VC before they escaped. Most town and city residents did not farm for a living, so the shadow government could not develop a group of supporters by offering the same prizes that attracted the peasants. In the urban centers, the VC could conduct only covert activities, such as terrorist attacks, incitement of anti-GVN demonstrations and riots, infiltration of GVN organizations, and recruitment of a few people into the VC ranks. Most shadow government activity occurred in the countryside, so the enemies of the shadow government had to focus most of their efforts there.

In order to present a serious threat to the GVN, the Viet Cong had to attract large numbers of people in the rural areas of South Vietnam to their movement. In the early 1960s, roughly 85 percent of South Vietnam's population lived in the villages, so the pool of potential converts was large.[1] Explaining how the shadow government attained this objective is not easy. The world of the South Vietnamese villager during the 1960s scarcely resembled anything that most Americans have ever encountered. The hamlets of South Vietnam varied by culture, religion, and race, as well as by income distribution and economic structure. Nevertheless, a thorough examination of VC documents, interviews with VC prisoners and defectors, and other sources reveals that the shadow government gained the villagers' cooperation for the same basic reasons in most areas.

Before the Viet Cong infrastructure came, villagers were loyal to their native villages. Most Vietnamese villages enjoyed a tradition of autonomy and self-sufficiency, and their residents seldom ventured far from home. This insularity prevented villagers from forming attachments to entities outside their village boundaries. Interdependence among neighbors, which further promoted local unity, tended to be stronger in the central coastal areas than in the southern third of Vietnam. Relations between wealthy and poor villagers were fairly harmonious, although modernization in the twentieth century eliminated some of the interdependence between these groups and increased disparities in wealth. Rulers from distant places could and did come to collect taxes or demand men for their armies, often in return for something that benefited the peasants, but otherwise they left the villagers alone. Both the rulers and the villagers believed strongly that political power should operate according to such principles. This arrangement inspired the famous Vietnamese maxim, "The emperor's authority ends at the village gate." The Vietnamese, like most people, were not particularly inclined to adopt new relationships between the rulers and the ruled overnight.

Of considerably greater importance than the village was the family. Villagers saw loyalty to family members as a sacrosanct duty that superseded any other allegiances. Because of Confucianism and other cultural traditions, as well as an economy that, in many cases, did not require great cooperation among families, individuals put their families and themselves before anything else. For Vietnamese peasants, the good life meant having a close and loving family, farming the land as they saw fit, and acquiring and enjoying as much wealth as was possible within socially acceptable bounds. Because of religion, custom, and human nature, farmers wanted to tend the land where their ancestors had lived. They hoped that their offspring would live there as well and venerate their spirits once their bodies no longer walked the earth. External forces on their lives interested the villagers only in terms of how the forces facilitated or hindered attainment of these objectives.

Many Americans, then and since, have failed to understand or recognize this mind-set. Some opposed their country's patronage of the GVN and believed that the Vietnamese peasants were noble idealists fighting to free themselves from GVN oppression or American neo-imperialism. They considered themselves idealists who, free of ethnocentric prejudices, understood foreigners better than did most Americans. They assumed that the Vietnamese outlook on life did not differ fundamentally from their own. These Americans expected that some sort of political ideology, akin to the ideologies that inspired Americans during their war for independence and their Civil War, motivated the Vietnamese masses. Some also were duped by Communist propaganda claiming that the South Vietnamese farmers fought for the same reasons as the Communist Party's elite Southern and Northern leadership.

Americans have most often cited nationalism as the key to the VC's widespread appeal. The villagers who comprised the vast majority of VC recruits during the 1960s were not actually nationalistic. They cared little about anyone or anything outside of their families and villages. "The VC promise to give a good future to the people by advocating the liberation of the country," a high-ranking Communist defector explained to a South Vietnamese interviewer, "but the people only believe in immediate facts, in something they can enjoy right now. If you give the people what they want right now, that is, tranquillity and wealth, you will win in the countryside and, consequently, win the war."[2]

The VC's Marxist principles did not attract the peasantry. Ordinary villagers did not understand basic Communist ideology. Except for a few senior Party members, most of the South Vietnamese Communists themselves did not understand the teachings of Marx, Lenin, or Mao. Communist doctrine was difficult for the people to understand, and it would not have appealed to them. The Communist desire to abolish private property, the struggle of farmers and workers against international capitalism, and even the oppression of other Vietnamese peasants did not excite the passions of people who were indifferent to those outside the family and merely wanted land and bountiful harvests. Another high-level cadre who defected to the GVN explained:

> The peasants in the rural areas have a very limited outlook. Some have never in their lives left their village to visit Saigon or even their own provincial capital. They live close to the land and are concerned with nothing else. While the country is in the middle of a war, while there is industrial progress and some are even using tractors, mechanical pumps, etc., they do not have enough water buffalo to plow the land, and they still use a simple plow. Thus they do not have the time or the concern for large matters like the future of communism—such matters are of no concern to them. . . . Their concern is to see that their immediate interests are protected, and that they are treated reasonably and fairly . . . if the Party were to say: in the future you will be a laborer, your land will be collectivized, you will no longer own any farm animals or buildings, but will become a tenant farmer for the Party or the socialist state—if the Party were to say that, the peasants would not heed them. Thus the peasants never think of the distant future of communism. Indeed, Party cadres are instructed never to mention these things, because, according to the teaching of Lenin, the peasant is the greatest bourgeois of all: he thinks only of himself. Say one word about collectivism, and he already is against you. This is a truth the Party has studied and learned to exploit. [3]

American supporters of U.S. involvement in the war who thought that the peasants decided to follow the VC in great numbers because the shadow government intimidated them were also mistaken. Communist intimidation alone could not win over enough of the rural populace to carry on the revolutionary cause. The Communists had to offer the villagers something they liked. The shadow government adopted the capitalist tactic of exploiting the individual's self-interest for the benefit of the group, rather than exploiting the individual's supposed sense of class solidarity and desire for economic equality, as Karl Marx would have liked. The cadres identified the unsatisfied desires of the individual villager and then offered to satisfy them.

The most common desire, and thus the most important, that the VC could try to satisfy was ownership of land. A high percentage of villagers did not own the land they farmed or their agricultural tools and farm animals, especially in the southern areas of the country. Rather, they paid rents to landlords or village officials to use these commodities and frequently had to borrow money to pay the rents. In much of the country, rents and interest rates were fairly high, which kept the incomes of farmers low and made them dependent on others, two conditions that grated harshly against the temperament of the individualistic peasants. Diem had created a land reform program in an effort to help the poorer peasants, but it effected only marginal changes by 1960. To persuade villagers to join the VC, or more often to convince family heads to make some family members join the VC, the shadow government offered them possession of the precious land. Where the VC cadres thought that they lacked the strength needed to enforce land redistribution, they promised lower rents and interest rates and protection against crop failure. Viet Cong taxes usually exceeded those of the GVN, especially after the American intervention in 1965 prompted a massive VC tax hike. Nevertheless, for poor peasants who no longer had to pay rent or who paid the lower rent and interest rate that the VC imposed on landowners and creditors, the reduction in rent and interest payments more than compensated for any tax increases.

Most of the material rewards that the VC offered served the interests of the have-nots, villagers who worked as tenant farmers or worked for other farmers. When asked which people cooperated most often with the VC, Communist prisoners and defectors invariably gave responses similar to this one: "Most of them belonged to the very poor class or to the lower middle class," whereas those who cooperated the least belonged to the "middle-middle class and upward."[4] This political reality explains why the VC generally enjoyed more support where more people were poor, such as in the provinces on the coast from Phu Yen to Quang Nam. The commitment from the poor secured by the agricultural policy was so strong and reliable that the VC chose to fill most of their important positions with the dispossessed. By contrast, they drove the wealthier people out of the villages and gave important positions to villagers who did not have much money. A Viet Cong document from a village in Kien Phong province indicates how much the VC depended on its agricultural policies for mobilizing the people: "The Party knew well how to make use of the farmers' interest in land. On it we built a mass movement. And for that reason the revolutionary movement made great progress and resulted in a great success."[5]

Many villagers also wanted to stop the excessively corrupt or oppressive activities of particular landlords and GVN personnel. Common abuses included extortion, misuse of GVN funds, arrest and torture of people with marginal ties to the Communists, looting, monopolization of commodities that villagers needed, and impressment of the villagers for GVN construction projects. Some GVN officials also carried out GVN policies that many villagers disliked intensely, most notably the forced relocation of people to hamlets that the GVN deemed more defensible. In their minds, many villagers lumped abusive landlords and GVN personnel together. In most villages not yet transformed by the Communists, the rural elites influenced or directly controlled the hamlet and village administrations and used them to serve their interests. Some of the GVN's village administrative positions went to officials and soldiers from other villages or from towns or cities, particularly in areas where the VC had driven away the original village councils, policemen, and territorial forces. As outsiders, they were less likely to have sympathy for the villagers, particularly the lower classes, and more likely to arouse the resentment of villagers accustomed to local rule.

Outsiders controlled the GVN administrative organs and armed forces above the village level as well. The ARVN soldiers who came to the hamlets when the VC became too strong for local militias rarely operated in their native hamlets. They treated villagers worse than anyone else and displayed little concern for civilian lives when fighting the VC. The arrival of American ground troops in 1965 brought something else to Vietnam that hurt the villagers physically and financially—a much more destructive war. This phenomenon, however, had quite different effects than other damaging Allied activities; it is examined in chapter 25.

The GVN's district-level leadership, in conjunction with the rural elites, appointed hamlet and village officials during the Diem era. After Diem's fall, the general population sometimes had a voice in choosing hamlet and village council members, but GVN leaders above the village level and the village elites often influenced the selection process. The masses' dissatisfaction with hamlet and village officials, however, did not stem from an absence of democracy. For centuries, villages had chosen their own leaders, but the village elites usually had made the selections and chosen people from their own class. The rest of the people had accepted those choices. Therefore, the poorer peasants of the 1960s did not believe that they had to choose their leaders in order to respect them. The shadow government showed that a political power could gain the approval of numerous villagers without holding elections for leadership positions.

Many landlords and members of the GVN infrastructure did not mistreat the peasants to any great extent. Enough of them went beyond tolerable bounds, nevertheless, that the VC could gain supporters by promising to eliminate these groups. A Communist Party member who served in the VC local forces told a story similar to thousands of others across South

Vietnam. He recalled that ARVN forces "didn't oppress people," and "[t]he Village Council behaved correctly and didn't do anything wrong. Only the SDC [Self-Defense Corps, the GVN village militia] made people dissatisfied. . . . The Self-Defense soldiers beat people and did not let them explain. They stole poultry from the villagers. . . . The VC took advantage of that and proselytized people. They convinced me, and I followed them."[6]

Initially, most villagers were not concerned with bringing down the wealthiest villagers and bestowing the greatest share of money and power on the poorer peasants or even on themselves. As in most authoritarian societies of the world, the poorer people in rural South Vietnam had long accepted their low status as an immutable reality of life. Until the Communists arrived, most of the masses had never questioned the legitimacy of the village elites. They desired only the limited, but important, social status that resulted from ownership of small pieces of land, along with the accompanying economic independence and material benefits. Few of the people who joined the Viet Cong longed for positions of considerable authority. A villager who joined the VC could not obtain power easily. As in any hierarchy, only a small number of individuals held positions of significant authority, and these individuals received the jobs only after a lengthy period of service in subservient positions. Further, as discussed later in this chapter, the VC spent a great deal of energy in their attempts to destroy the self-interested ambitions of the members, such as the desire for power, and they rewarded the most selfless among them.

Although the shadow government's offers of benefits played a major role in the VC's rise to power, these offers, by themselves, were not enough to bring many villagers into the VC. The Communist Party's ability to win villager approval depended heavily on the successes of the VC in defeating the GVN militarily and politically. The Confucian tradition, which the Chinese had brought to Vietnam, had instilled the belief that the masses must obey the emperor and other authorities who possessed the "mandate of heaven," a divinely sanctioned legitimacy. They heeded this famous Confucian proverb: "The ruler is like the wind and the commoners like grass blades. When the wind blows, the grass blades have to bend under it." If rival groups were trying to rule, the villagers had to decide which group had the mandate. Their decision, however, was a response to circumstances, not an exercise of free will. The villagers watched to see which group best satisfied the conditions that, according to the will of heaven, a ruler had to satisfy to possess the mandate. They then followed that group.

Strength stood at the top of the list of conditions. When either the VC

or the GVN inflicted heavy military defeats on the other or when one conducted governmental functions better than the other, many of the villagers cooperated more willingly with the successful group. Numerous villagers said that they and others followed the Communists, in part or in full,
because they were stronger than the South Vietnamese government. Hai
Chua, a former Communist party secretary at the village level, said that
virtually all the people in his village supported the VC by 1965, and that
the support "was given willingly because the people were nearly certain
that the future lay with the Communists."[7]

In a close contest between the rivals, many villagers remained as neutral as possible until one power clearly demonstrated that it had the mandate. If and when one power gained a decided advantage in strength, these
villagers obeyed the will of heaven and joined forces with the dominant
power. This opportunistic mode of behavior put the villagers on the side
that most likely would attain complete control, thereby ensuring that they
would enjoy the favor of the future rulers. It accelerated the victory of that
side, which would bring strife to an end. Fighting for a winning cause also
meant a greater chance of survival during the war; soldiers on the side of
the victors were less likely to die on the battlefield or endure torture or
execution at the hands of vindictive captors.

Strong leadership also played a crucial role in bringing the peasants into
the VC, a role that few Westerners, other than the advisers to Vietnamese
units, understood. Defeating the GVN and wooing the people required able
and determined leaders. The force of charisma itself prompted many villagers to support or join the VC. The Vietnamese masses, because of their
traditions of obedience, were inclined to follow and serve anyone who was
dedicated, competent, articulate, and strong enough to have a chance of
winning. As an official Communist Party newspaper put it, "Although fighters are skillful, the armed forces cannot develop their revolutionary nature
and combativity if cadres are not good organizers and commanders. . . .
Party leadership is the cause of, and the decisive factor in, the birth, growth,
and victories of our Army."[8]

The shadow government's leaders relied heavily on propaganda to persuade villagers to side with the VC. They had to convince the villagers that
the Viet Cong would help them get what they wanted. Before the Communists came, most villagers had accepted unfavorable land distribution,
high rents and interest rates, and abusive authorities as facts of life that
they could change no more than they could change the seasons of the year.
A former cadre from Dinh Tuong province, who said that almost all GVN

village officials in his area "took advantage of their power to oppress the people," described the prevalent attitude of the villagers before the VC revolts: "Since they did not see any way out of this oppression, they had to resign themselves to it. Therefore, whenever they spoke of GVN officials, they liked to say: 'If a good official is assigned to our village, then tell your-selves you have been lucky. If a bad one comes over to rule us, well, it's only bad luck! We have to accept any fate which befalls us.'"[9]

The villagers considered resisting the GVN only after the cadres came and ceaselessly explained how the Viet Cong, with their help, would destroy the GVN and bestow upon them greater wealth and independence. In some places where the VC succeeded in distributing land and driving out the GVN infrastructure, the villagers still avoided active involvement in the VC until they heard enough propaganda to persuade them to do otherwise. In many cases, the Communists kidnapped uncooperative people and convinced them to join their cause. Even when reality did not correspond closely to what the cadres said, eloquence sometimes proved more compelling than the truth. For example, one young man, who had served in the VC for a time, recalled that the VC cadres "made a lot of propaganda in the village. People had a lot of sympathy for them. They talked very well, even to the point that people who worked for the GVN followed them and accepted their ideas."[10]

The shadow government had many excellent propagandists who did much to advance the VC cause. Secret Party documents consistently empha-sized the importance of propaganda. The following is a good example:

> Daily the masses are oppressed and exploited by the imperialists and feu-dalists and therefore are disposed to hate them and their crimes. But their hatred is not focused: it is diffuse. . . . They swallow their hatred and resent-ment or resign themselves to enduring oppression and terror, or, if they do struggle, they do so in a weak and sporadic manner. For all these reasons agit-prop work is necessary to stir up the masses, to make them hate the enemy to a high degree, to make them understand their rights and the pur-pose and method of the Revolution, and to develop confidence in our capa-bility. It is necessary to change the attitude of the masses from a passive one to a desire to struggle strongly, to take part more and more violently to win their rights for survival. Good or bad results in our Revolution depend on whether agit-prop action to educate and change the thinking of the masses is good or bad.[11]

Assertions of power and authority were the peasants' best gauge of the mandate of heaven, but leaders also had to abide by certain rules of moral conduct and attend to their subjects' needs in order to fulfill the mandate's requirements to the greatest possible extent. The VC usually governed the people fairly, at least those toward the lower end of the income scale. Their fairness contrasted sharply with the GVN's tendency toward arbitrariness and oppressiveness. Most cadres were less concerned than GVN officials were about using their positions to help themselves or their families, and they reprimanded fellow cadres who tried to do so. A peasant of middle income expressed the most common view of the VC in many villages: "To me, frankly, the NLF cadre are much better than the GVN. They keep strict discipline and never take anything away from the people. When they come to your house, they go to the kitchen and help your wife or go to the garden to help you do whatever you do. After that they talk and go away without taking advantage of their position of authority in the village."[12] When the cadres chose to conscript, collect taxes, kill someone, or perform other unpopular tasks, they explained articulately why they had to take these measures, which most GVN officials did not do.

During the early 1960s, the VC, by defeating the enemy in battle and by leading and recruiting the villagers, showed the people that they had the authority conferred by the will of heaven. Their initial victories caused the masses to flock to the VC, and the South Vietnamese Communists experienced explosive growth. The GVN tried to keep its grip on the mandate in the same way, but it performed less effectively and could not reverse the VC's momentum. In the villages where the VC wore the mantle of divine authority, most families gave them enough men to run the insurgency. These families also provided the VC with taxes, intelligence, shelter, and other necessities, and tried to avoid giving these things to the GVN. Only in a relatively small number of cases during this time did the shadow government rely on coercion or trickery to obtain villager cooperation. In 1965, as both the Communists and the Allies stepped up their war efforts, the VC needed many more soldiers and laborers. The shadow government, in response, began conscription on a large scale. Those who resisted faced abduction and "reeducation," or even execution.

In some rural areas, the Viet Cong failed to win significant support. Many of these areas contained members of non-Vietnamese racial groups who disliked the ethnic Vietnamese and hence both the GVN and the VC. The two largest of these groups were the Cambodians, who were a mixture of Chams and Khmers, and the Montagnards, tribes of various mixed races that had once lived in the fertile lowlands but had been driven into the sparsely populated highlands by the Vietnamese. About 20 percent of South Vietnam's population was not Vietnamese by race, although the percentage in the country's most important rural areas was lower because of the remoteness of the Montagnards and the almost exclusively urban presence of a large Chinese minority. Other places where the VC found little support included villages occupied by members of certain religions that opposed the Communists, particularly the Buddhist sects known as the Hoa Hao and Cao Dai and the Roman Catholics, or by members of anti-Communist political factions, primarily the Viet Nam Quoc Dan Dang (VNQDD) and the Dai Viet movements. Often, especially after Diem's fall, the GVN granted these groups a large degree of autonomy so that local elites governed instead of outsiders, and the Americans often assisted them in a variety of ways. Ethnocentrism, religious beliefs, political loyalties, or faith in a group's leaders convinced villagers that they preferred their present situation to anything that the Communists could offer.

Getting people to enlist in the VC was not the same as motivating them to perform well once they joined. All of the reasons cited above, especially leadership, contributed in some way to the motivation of cadres and soldiers. The Party, though, used additional devices to make people operate the complex machinery of the shadow government and fight in the military units when the job became very dangerous or when a normal farmer's life seemed far more pleasurable than cowering in a foxhole during an American air strike. Many commentators on the Vietnam War ignore the crucial difference between the reasons for joining the VC and the reasons for performing well in the VC. They tend to attribute the VC's strength simply to factors, such as the positive appeals of nationalism and land reform, that they believed caused the peasants to support the VC. Other commentators believe that intimidation alone caused the Viet Cong machine to function as well as it did. Like most soldiers, VC soldiers persisted in the struggle for reasons different from the reasons that caused them to join. The political cadres remained committed for most of the same reasons as the soldiers, an exceptionally impressive achievement because leaders normally lack the tools to motivate political officials with as much success as they can motivate soldiers.

The VC wanted both their soldiers and cadres to give the movement their undivided allegiance. For this reason, the Party sought to destroy the villagers' traditional concerns and allegiances, with two exceptions: village loyalty and racial ties. The Party largely kept village loyalty in order to promote the cohesion of VC villages. It did not try to break racial ties because they were too strong; instead, it tried to recruit cadres from each racial group and use them to build the insurgent movement within their own group. Preoccupation with the self and family, which the Communists exploited in luring villagers with land redistribution, was the strongest traditional attachment and hence the one that the cadres tried the hardest to eradicate once it had brought people into the VC ranks. A Communist Party instructional document attacking "individualism," which the document defined as concern with the interests of both the self and the family, states:

> We must try to overcome the disease of individualism, because it weakens the Party.... People affected with individualism, when the revolution encounters difficulties, when it meets the increasingly terroristic enemy, when the movement in the villages temporarily withdraws, are very agitated, no longer have confidence, bring up questions of food, are only concerned with their own life, do not think of the people or the Party or the movement. They will abandon the work, even the Party cells; they will abandon the revolution.[13]

The peculiar conditions of the Viet Cong presence in the hamlets made possible the destruction of the sacred Vietnamese loyalty to the family. An examination of the differences between the GVN and the VC makes this point clear. Because GVN employees were paid regardless of how they treated the villagers, they could afford to mistreat and extort money from the villagers and take the money home to their families. They could retreat to the towns and cities at night if they needed to avoid angry peasants. GVN leaders also had many opportunities to embezzle from direct and indirect American aid programs. The Americans did not keep close watch over this aid money, in part because they thought this laissez-faire approach would encourage the growth of South Vietnamese autonomy. In addition, GVN leaders devised various schemes to swindle money from town and city residents, who owed much of their wealth to the American presence. People in the GVN even took from others who occupied places below them within the GVN hierarchy by making them pay to hold their jobs or by skimming off part of their salaries. Some officials became so corrupt that they lost interest in any aspects of their positions that did not enhance their family's bank accounts. Wealthy villagers who served in their local hamlet or village governments thought that they could maintain their power because of their private wealth and the support of the territorial forces, an assumption that would prove to be incorrect in most cases, and thus did not see a need to curry the favor of the rural masses.

The VC, by contrast, lived among the rural population and depended on its good will to survive. If they did not treat most of the villagers kindly, they might not be able to win over enough peasants to obtain the personnel and food needed to overpower the GVN. Absolute necessity forced the VC to behave benevolently. The absence of temptation also affected their conduct. VC personnel did not have access to the wealth of American aid programs or of the towns and cities, as GVN officials did, so they could not choose a life of greed aimed at building a family fortune. After the war, when the Communists had uncontested control of all of South Vietnam, they no longer needed to win over the support of the rural masses or organize opposition to the Allies by behaving well, and they had access to urban wealth. As a result, greed and corruption became as rampant within the new order as it had been within the old.

Favorable circumstances alone, however, did not sever the people's traditional loyalties. One of the most important techniques that the shadow government used to tear them down was isolation from family and other external influences. The Party sent many VC, especially cadres and main force soldiers, to serve in areas distant from their birthplaces for long durations. One political cadre who went to North Vietnam for training described the effects of isolation: "Sometimes we were very lonely and wanted to go home to see our families and friends. But we learned after a while not to be lonely, and learned to find strength in our revolutionary struggle. We learned not to think much about our families any more. We learned not to miss our families any more—like Ho Chi Minh."[14] The VC who served in or near their native villages were prohibited from living with their families and interacting with religious groups and independent political factions. The Party cadres rigidly regimented the daily schedules of the VC in order to deny them free time to spend with relatives or fellow worshipers, but some VC managed to visit their families on occasion.

The VC also eliminated traditional family loyalties by acting as a surrogate family. A former Party member commented: "Regarding family ties, [the cadres] just ignore or forget them; their new family is their comrades at work."[15] The shadow government primarily recruited males in their teens and early twenties, in part because they were more impressionable and less committed to family than were older men. These traits made them more likely to find a new "family" in the Viet Cong. The VC "family unit" was the cell. Regular military units contained three-man cells, and guerrilla units, the Party, and the NLF and its associations used cells with up to seven members. Every cell, for obvious reasons, had a Party member as its leader. The cell leaders monitored the other members to make sure that they performed effectively, behaved properly, and maintained allegiance to the revolution.

Frequent "self-criticism" and "criticism" sessions, during which members discussed their shortcomings and those of others, helped to destroy privacy and individuality. As in any effective military organization, mutual participation in difficult or dangerous tasks and the great amount of time spent together built bonds of loyalty among members. One Party proclamation states that cell members had to "build their cell into a three-member collective, glue-welded on the basis of comradeship and mutual life and assistance, stemming from a thorough revolutionary spirit, a noble class spirit, and good revolutionary virtues. To this end each cell member must tell his colleagues facts about his private life. . . . They must consider their [cell] as their home and their [cell members] as brothers."[16] This sense of commitment to other Communists inspired the VC, especially the leaders, to great acts of bravery and sacrifice.

The VC, like most Communist movements, also tried to subvert religious organizations. As it did with its political opponents, the Party attempted to ally itself with an organization at the local level or to infiltrate Party members into its local leadership. Then, it used such ties to monitor and influence the organization and, if possible, to dominate it eventually. In areas where the Communists could not get the religious groups to help them, they sometimes shut down pagodas and churches and prevented the organizations from meeting. The Party also fought religion with propaganda. A VC schoolteacher recounted that the shadow government did not forbid villagers to worship in his village, but he added that "we stand for the eradication of religious worship through the gradual education of the people so that they become conscious of the dangers of religious indoctrination to the present struggle of the people. We know that when people follow a religion, and believe in religious tenets, they do not have much mind left to understand and heart left to believe in the Party."[17] The most popular religions in Vietnam were Mahayana and Hinayana Buddhism, both of which usually included elements of Confucianism, Taoism, and ancient Vietnamese beliefs in ancestor worship and animism. The members of these Buddhist sects did not organize resistance against the Viet Cong particularly well and often fell under the influence of the shadow government. The Hoa Hao and Cao Dai Buddhist sects, both with large followings, and the Catholics usually resisted the Communists fervently, so the VC did not often manipulate them.

The shadow government succeeded in shifting the primary loyalty of many people from family, religion, or race to the Communists and their cause. For some VC, particularly those of low rank, this transformation never happened. For many others, it occurred only partially as they struggled to maintain their traditional commitments while serving the VC as faithfully as possible. Most of the VC's key leaders, nevertheless, were more committed to the VC than to anyone or anything else. This commitment accounted for some of the key differences between the performances of VC and GVN leaders. The concern of the latter for furthering personal and family interests made them much more likely to abuse their authority and less likely to take the aggressive but risky actions that could have weakened the VC. One villager illustrated the importance of this factor while describing the behavior of local VC cadres: "I think that the majority of the local officials are worthy cadres. Only a few of them are bad since they are still strongly attached to their family relationships. Consequently they have sometimes neglected their duties."[18] The actions of the GVN personnel were no worse than those of government leaders and servants in most Third World countries. The Vietnamese Communists were one of the few groups in the Third World that were able to achieve the subversion of individual and family loyalty that is needed to build a more effective and fair government.

Ideology, although unimportant in bringing the peasants into the movement, helped to motivate villagers to a moderate extent once they became a part of the VC hierarchy. The shadow government's indoctrination convinced most soldiers and cadres to believe a few simple, and simplistic, ideas. In their lectures to new Communists, the cadres aroused hatred of the "imperialist" Americans, their GVN "puppets," and the "oppressive" landlords. Col. Huong Van Ba, an artillery officer who went to the North for training in 1954, described the effects of the propaganda: "We had been thoroughly exposed to anti-Saigon and anti-American propaganda in the North. We had seen pictures of the South Vietnamese people being beaten, arrested, and tortured. We had seen documentary movies of Ngo Dinh Diem's cruel suppression of the Buddhists, of people being shocked with electricity and women being raped. These pictures had built up our rage and our determination to liberate the South."[19]

Above all, the Viet Cong's entire motivational system depended on strong leadership. The shadow government's village-level cadres turned the masses into revolutionaries by severing them from their families and their self-interests with strict methods. They developed the discipline and effectiveness of their subordinates by indoctrinating them, keeping them busy with tough jobs, monitoring them, and rewarding or punishing them for good or poor performance. The leaders had to set good examples by renouncing their own individual interests and earn the confidence of their followers by demonstrating competence and exposing themselves to danger. They persisted even in the face of violent opposition from the GVN and later from the Americans. Although good leadership traits are important in any organization, they proved particularly crucial in South Vietnam because its people could be quite obedient. Without strong leadership, all of the Viet Cong's other advantages would have brought them nothing.

Leadership was most important at the highest levels of the Communist Party, not just because the top leaders formulated strategy but also because they selected, trained, and tried to motivate their subordinates, who in turn selected, trained, and tried to motivate the people below them. The rank and file had some opportunities to make suggestions about particular decisions, but the quality of decision making rested mainly on the leaders. The strength of the Viet Cong, therefore, hinged on the ascetic dedication and superb leadership abilities of Ho Chi Minh, other top North Vietnamese Communists, and the highest Communist leaders who had grown up in the South. Ultimately, the allegiance of the South Vietnamese masses and the fate of their country would depend on whether the top Communist leaders or the top GVN leaders could lead more effectively in the face of danger. During the early 1960s, the Communists clearly performed better.

The Viet Cong shadow government, then, successfully ran an insurgency in South Vietnam during the first half of the 1960s under Hanoi's general guidance. To summarize, the shadow government organized the obliteration of the GVN political apparatus and the construction of a VC apparatus. It built mass organizations in the villages by persuading and prodding villagers to join and used them to mobilize the manpower of the villages. Cadres collected taxes and ran a sophisticated logistics network for transporting food and other commodities. Intelligence and counterintelligence, vital in this type of war, depended on the cadres' diligent work. Through their startling successes and eloquent speeches, they convinced the villagers that they possessed the mandate of heaven. Extremely well disciplined, the shadow government also treated the villagers less abusively than did the GVN. The VCI ensured the loyalty of the VC to the revolution through the demolition of their normal attachments and through the power of leadership.

Perhaps nothing better illustrates the importance of the shadow government to the Communist Party than statements from the Communist leaders themselves. Ho Chi Minh once said, "The success or failure of everything depends on whether cadres are good or bad," and "with good cadres, everything can be done."[20] A Party document concerning the village-level

Party organization (chi bo) asserts that the mass movement could not exist without this policy-executing echelon of the shadow government:

> The development of the *chi bo* is extremely important and in fact is the fore-most principle in the development of the Party. . . . The *chi bo* is the bridge between the Party and the masses, the eyes and ears of the Party among the masses, the brain of the masses, the source of Party plans and policies for the masses, and the leadership organization in the struggle of the masses. Without the *chi bo*, Party plans and policies could not be transformed into the strength of the mass struggle. Thus the revolution could not possibly succeed, and the interests of the masses could not possibly be protected.[21]

4

The War against the Shadow Government: Before Phoenix

government facing an enemy that possesses both guerrilla and main force capabilities can choose from a great variety of political and military countermeasures. Between 1960 and 1967, the GVN and its allies used virtually every type possible, with the exception of chemical and nuclear warfare and the bombing of population centers. Numerous critics of the Allied war effort attribute the Allied failures during this period to an inability to recognize and focus on the countermeasures that worked best. In reality, the Allies generally attempted to use suitable political and military programs against the enemy. Their failure resulted from the lack of competence and will among the South Vietnamese charged with implementing these programs.

During the late 1950s, President Diem had demonstrated that he knew how to fight the nascent VC shadow government. His secret police, the Cong An, understood the purpose and methods of the shadow government and used informants and agents to identify its members. A direct descendent of the colonial-era secret police, the Cong An eliminated most of the Communist infrastructure that had stayed in place after the 1954 cease-fire. The Communist Party nearly ceased to exist in South Vietnam at this time; subsequent Communist histories would refer to this period as the Party's "darkest hour." The effectiveness of the Cong An declined sharply during the early 1960s because VC armed forces usually denied the police access to the villages after they had driven away the territorial forces, and the shadow government had eliminated many of the Cong An's informants. In 1962, Diem put the Cong An, by then called the Special Police, with the marginally effective paramilitary Combat Police and other police organizations under an umbrella organization called the National Police. The GVN's police suffered another major setback in the aftermath of Diem's assassination. The new GVN leaders imprisoned many of the police officers, either for having abused their authority or for having been loyal to Diem, and many others fled to avoid reprisals. Throughout the war, the CIA advised and supported the Special Police, and employees of the U.S. Agency for International Development (USAID) advised other elements of the police.

The territorial forces constituted Diem's second means for fighting the insurgents. With advice from the CIA, Diem had built up the territorial forces during the late 1950s. The troops often lived in outposts near the hamlets and tried to keep the Communist intruders away from the hamlets. Many units suffered from poor leadership. A large number of the province and district chiefs who commanded them had been chosen by Diem and his successors because of political reliability or personal connections, rather than military competence, and many were inept. As a consequence, the territorials usually failed to offer serious resistance to the VC shadow government when it began mobilizing the peasants. The fixture of the territorial forces in static positions also allowed the Viet Cong to confront them with large forces and annihilate them or force them to flee.

In early 1963, at the suggestion of the CIA, Diem created the Chieu Hoi program, which offered amnesty to members of the Viet Cong who wished to leave the Communists. Chieu Hoi personnel questioned the "ralliers" (the term often used for the people who defected through this program) about VC methods of operation, the identities of specific cadres, and other important topics. They indoctrinated the ralliers and then tried to get them to work for the GVN or resettled them in GVN areas.

Diem tried to isolate the population from the shadow government through forced relocation, an old and often effective means of fighting against revolutionary warriors. In 1959, Saigon began moving villagers into "agrovilles," new rural villages that featured better schools, sanitation facilities, and other amenities. Modeled after similar British constructions in Malaya, the agrovilles allowed government security personnel to watch over the population and keep intruders out more easily than they could in the old hamlets. The agroville program did not work well, and the GVN decided to abandon it in early 1961. In 1962, however, U.S. military advisers and the British counterinsurgency veteran Robert Thompson convinced Diem to resuscitate it. The "strategic hamlets," as the new settlements were called, received greater support from Saigon than did the agrovilles. The GVN gave security a higher priority and built fortifications at the hamlet level, whereas the agrovilles' fortifications were at the larger and less controllable village level. The program expanded too rapidly, however, and spread GVN resources too thinly. Strategic hamlet security forces sometimes kept the guerrillas and cadres out, and, at first, the strategic hamlets allowed the GVN to increase its control over the population. The program's good fortune was short-lived in most places, however, because the VC's superior leadership and motivation, as well as their ability to concentrate large forces against a single hamlet, allowed them to overcome the small fortifications with relative ease.

More modest programs, aimed at fortifying hamlets in certain areas of religious, racial, or independent political fervor, often succeeded in keeping the Communists out during the early and mid-1960s. The largest of these, the Civilian Irregular Defense Groups (CIDGs) in the highlands, encompassed several hundred villages of Montagnards. The CIA funded the CIDGs and similar programs and gave the hamlet inhabitants medical help, sanitation equipment, and other benefits to win their support. The CIA staffed the programs with U.S. Special Forces soldiers, who organized and armed local militia units, indoctrinated the villagers, built fortifications, and developed intelligence and counterintelligence systems. In 1963, the U.S. Army took over operational control of the CIDG hamlets and moved the CIDG soldiers and their families into separate camps in order to deploy them against the Communists' main forces, rather than against the Communists' small forces and cadres in the villages.

During the chaotic years following Diem's downfall, the CIA took an even more prominent role in developing unconventional programs for countering the Communists. With Diem gone and the American and South Vietnamese armies focusing on the burgeoning Communist military forces, the CIA had to assume chief responsibility for the pacification programs. The CIA had considerable experience with counterinsurgency warfare, and it was more flexible than either the American or South Vietnamese military. It could create and staff programs appropriate to new and unusual situations better than most U.S. government organizations. One CIA innovation was the Static Census Grievance program, which sent people into the villages to survey one member of each family in order to identify the villagers' grievances against the government and to gather intelligence. The Armed Propaganda Team program used armed men to approach the Viet Cong and their family members and encourage defection via the Chieu Hoi program. For interrogating important civilian prisoners, the CIA established a Province Interrogation Center in each province. The Special Police staffed the centers under the supervision of CIA advisers.

The most highly touted and ambitious of the CIA initiatives was the Revolutionary Development (RD) Cadre program, which imitated the Viet Cong's cadre system. At first, the CIA controlled the program tightly, but some energetic South Vietnamese officers soon took control and, after many disputes, convinced the CIA to give them most of the managerial responsibility. On the Vung Tau peninsula, the RD Cadre program leaders trained young South Vietnamese men and women to live in the villages and use the methods of the shadow government, such as helping the villagers with their work, propagandizing the villagers frequently, building public facilities, recruiting people into militia units and mass associations, and eliminating the enemy's local infrastructure, but the RD Cadres did not accomplish much. When confronted by the VC, they usually withdrew to safer environs rather than fight.

Counter-Terror Teams, which the CIA controlled completely, also copied Viet Cong methods. These small, elite groups of North and South Vietnamese men collected intelligence on the VCI and other VC and then captured or killed them, usually at night. Because they had good leaders, they could operate with sufficient stealth to hit targets in areas where the VC possessed sizable military forces. In late 1966, the CIA gave the teams the more gentle name of Provincial Reconnaissance Units (PRUs), put more emphasis on capturing rather than killing, and required that the teams have more concrete evidence before operating against a suspected cadre. Although the Americans created, funded, and advised most of the GVN's pacification programs, the PRU program was the only one over which the Americans had direct command authority.

Another program, known as the Kit Carson Scouts and run largely by the U.S. military, organized VC defectors into small, elite units. Most often, these units performed reconnaissance missions or guided U.S. military units rather than targeting members of the VC in the villages. Another South Vietnamese paramilitary organization, the National Police Field Forces (NPFF), consisted of combat police under the sponsorship of USAID. The Americans intended to have the NPFF provide additional reaction forces for attacking the VCI directly, but they did not perform well and often wallowed in inactivity. Regular police forces also captured some members of the VCI, usually in the urban areas or at checkpoints where they searched all passersby for clues of Communist involvement. Other military organizations participated to a small extent in the attack on the VCI during this time. American intelligence and counterintelligence units and the Military Security Service, which was the internal security branch of the South Vietnamese Army, made the most significant contributions. Main force units affected the VCI indirectly when they operated in the village areas.

Some Americans hailed the end of the Diem regime as the best thing that could happen to South Vietnam. Soon, however, Diem's successors showed that they could not fight the insurgents as well as he had. As premiers came and went from the end of 1963 through the first half of 1965, they replaced most of their predecessors' province chiefs and many other key officers with their own cronies. The discontinuity of leadership gravely weakened all of the GVN's war efforts. Eventually, the June 1965 coup of generals Nguyen Cao Ky and Nguyen Van Thieu returned a measure of political stability, although the regime became considerably more stable after Thieu pushed Ky aside two years later and emerged as the sole leader. Throughout the period 1963–67, none of Diem's replacements led or allocated power as well as he had.

Once the GVN's pacification programs fell apart, the ARVN became the sole means by which the Republic of Vietnam could stave off defeat. The use of large ARVN units in daytime "search-and-destroy" operations has been the subject of much criticism by dissident U.S. military men, certain CIA officers, academic historians, and political scientists. Most of the critics argue that the ARVN and the American advisers who played a large role in determining ARVN activities could have combated VC guerrilla warfare much more effectively with less conventional means. The U.S. military, they contend, had spent most of its time preparing for a conventional war in Europe and was unable to construct military organizations and train men to fight a different style of war. Therefore, the argument continues, the ARVN maintained command structures designed for conventional large-unit battles that were inappropriate for the insurgency environment. ARVN main forces wasted too much time in vain searches for enemy military units away from the villages. They could not keep the Communists out of the villages, and their efforts to find the Communists in the villages usually bore little fruit. When they did find the Communists in the villages, they attacked them with too much heavy firepower, thereby damaging the villages and alienating the citizenry. Instead, critics say, the ARVN should have deployed its troops primarily in small, lightly armed units in and around the villages to isolate members of the shadow government and other VC from the population. These ARVN units could have received information from the villagers and pounced on the enemy forces more frequently because the VC had to visit the hamlets to obtain the resources of the local population.

This argument appears attractive on the surface, but it is flawed. Organizing the South Vietnamese army along conventional lines was hardly foolish. Diem had built up the ARVN with much help from his American military advisers. He envisioned this army not as the primary weapon for suppressing the Communist activities in the villages—the Cong An and the territorial forces were supposed to handle that task—but rather as protection against the possibility of a North Vietnamese invasion or a Viet Cong main force buildup, both of which occurred in 1964. When the shadow government drove the Cong An and the territorial forces out of the hamlets, however, the South Vietnamese generals and the Americans agreed to use the ARVN against the VC guerrillas as a last resort.

In the areas to which the ARVN sent troops, most ARVN commanders conducted operations only in large units, an approach that turned out to be quite ineffective. When smaller ARVN units tried to operate in areas dominated by the VC, which allowed them to cover more territory, the larger Communist main force units found and destroyed them. Poor leadership, together with the VC's excellent intelligence and operations capabilities, deterred the ARVN from conducting effective small-unit and night operations. The ARVN's leadership suffered greatly from the same subordination of performance to political considerations that put so many weak men into district and province chief positions. Diem and his successors promoted the officers whom they deemed most loyal to them and least likely to mount a coup. They also encouraged ARVN commanders to avoid heavy casualties by not engaging in sustained and bloody battles; they wanted to preserve the strength and morale of ARVN units so that they would side with the president and protect him should any other ARVN generals attempt a coup. The mere allocation of ARVN troops to division-sized units did not necessitate that the ARVN attack the VC guerrillas with large sweep operations. Such units can be broken down easily into small forces suitable for fighting guerrilla warfare, as both Communist and Allied commanders did at times. Thus, in determining the ARVN's tactics, doctrinal inflexibility was much less important than the limitations of the situation.

Numerous critics of Allied policy also fault the GVN and the Americans for not devoting enough resources to developing militias, police forces, or guerrilla-type units for use in combating the VC cadres and guerrillas in the villages, even after the Communists acquired significant main force strength in the 1960s. Some also believe that the GVN needed to institute political reforms to counter those of the VC. In both ways, they reason, the GVN could have defeated the VC with the same methods that the VC had used to overpower the GVN during the early 1960s. Jeffrey Race, arguing the first position in his highly influential book *War Comes to Long An:*

Revolutionary Conflict in a Vietnamese Province, criticizes an American general for advocating the destruction of large Communist military units first, then the local forces, the guerrillas, and the cadres in that sequence. "The reason why [this strategy] was not successful in Long An," writes Race, "can be seen by noting that this strategy is exactly the reverse of the strategy successfully employed by the Party, despite the fact that by 1965 the government in Long An was in a position roughly comparable to that occupied by the Party in 1959."[1] Frances FitzGerald, in the Pulitzer Prize-winning *Fire in the Lake: The Vietnamese and the Americans in Vietnam*, claims that the GVN could have improved its position in the countryside only by changing its rural political system so that it benefited the villagers more than that of the Viet Cong. As it was, she continues, the way in which the Allies used force alienated the villagers and drove them into the arms of the VC:

> For the NLF, military victories were not only less important than political victories, but strictly meaningless considered in isolation from them. Those few American officials who studied the NLF saw the political focus, but did not understand its significance. Had they understood it, they might have warned that it would be better to send the Saigon regime's army to fight without weapons than to send it to fight without a political strategy, as was the case.[2]

These theories have attained considerable popularity and have not received the scrutiny they deserve. The GVN's position in 1965 differed greatly from the VC's position in 1959 and prevented the GVN from imitating the Viet Cong program. The VC had made their village-domination program work from 1959 to 1965 with good leadership against an enemy beset by poor leadership. Poor leaders, even if they possessed large advantages in material resources, could not make the same program work against a well-led and strong enemy, as Race suggests that the GVN leaders should have done in 1965. As chapter 3 indicates, the GVN lacked effective leadership in 1965 and the preceding years, and the nature of the South Vietnamese political system—barring a colonial-style takeover by the Americans—prevented the GVN from narrowing the leadership gap.

Without leadership and the concomitant discipline and stealth, no GVN militiamen or other village security forces could hope to imitate the VC in conducting small-unit or night operations effectively, any more than could ARVN main force units. Weak leadership, as well as the absence of support from the villagers, prevented village security forces—or "pacification forces" as they are sometimes called—from sneaking around in the wilderness for long periods of time without visiting base camps for rest and resupply. Of all the GVN forces that functioned between 1959 and 1965, indeed, only the well-led Counter-Terror Teams used guerrilla tactics effectively on a regular basis. Because of popular support and excellent leadership, the VC obtained much better intelligence on the location and size of enemy forces than did the GVN pacification forces. As a result, the VC often could attack and overwhelm the GVN forces when they dispersed into small groups, and could avoid them when they formed into large main force units. The VC's stealth and the absence of any need to defend towns, cities, fixed bases, and roads also contributed to their ability to avoid battle when they needed to do so; the GVN did not possess such advantages in 1965.

The GVN's only chance to hurt the Communists in the village areas during the mid-1960s, and it was not a very good chance, was to attack the Communist main forces with large ARVN units. Even Robert Komer, an adviser to President Johnson who initiated and managed a major expansion of the Allied pacification program, believed that the Allies could not achieve any progress in pacification until they destroyed the biggest Communist main force units with their own conventional units. By 1964, Komer says, "thwarting the VC/NVA 'main forces' had become indispensable to creating a climate in which pacification could get started again. After 1964 it was essential to fight both main-force and village wars. . . . Only after U.S. military intervention staved off GVN collapse and regained the initiative in the big-unit war, and a measure of political stability returned, did greater attention begin to be paid to reviving some form of pacification to complement the big-unit war." [3] Komer also states: "The local security requirement had grown far beyond the capability of the police or paramilitary forces to meet." [4] ARVN soldiers often treated the villagers poorly in areas under VC dominance. Had they not gone into those areas, however, the VC simply would have had an easier time of dominating the populace and would have suffered fewer casualties.

Another enormously important difference between the VC in 1959 and the GVN in 1965 that proponents of Race's theory overlook was that the GVN had to hold the towns and cities at all times, whereas the Viet Cong never did. The cities and towns provided the GVN with great quantities of resources, both of people and of wealth, especially after huge numbers of villagers began fleeing to the urban areas in 1965. They also served as command and control centers, as safe areas for troop bases, and as symbols of

GVN power and prestige. Given the GVN's weakness in the countryside, it had to rely on the towns and cities for sustaining its war effort. The Communists, too, recognized the importance of these areas and repeatedly proclaimed, in accordance with Mao Tse-tung's theories, that they would have to capture them with their main forces to win the war. Considering the substantial military power at the VC's disposal by 1964, the GVN had no choice but to employ many main force units to defend its holdings against Communist conventional forces, the only ones capable of seizing the urban areas. The ARVN had to find and engage the enemy as frequently as possible in order to hold the initiative and inhibit the massing of Communist main forces. It also had to allocate large numbers of troops to guard the towns and cities, as well as the lines of communication connecting them. These deployments severely restricted the number of GVN armed forces available for fighting a counterguerrilla war in the villages.

The GVN stood no chance of mobilizing the rural masses through political action. Its employees did not and could not treat the villagers as kindly as did the Viet Cong for a reason not especially amenable to change, namely, an environment that encouraged selfishness and inferior high-level leadership. The VC's agricultural policies had touched most key rural areas already, so the GVN could not win over the peasants by offering to distribute land or by lowering rents and interest rates. The GVN could have scored a modest propaganda victory by allowing the peasants under its control to keep the redistributed land or to continue paying the lower rents and interest rates, but some people with considerable influence over the GVN leadership opposed such reforms. The United States could not force the GVN leadership to enact these policies or other political reforms unless it was willing to exert more authority over the Vietnamese.

Even had the GVN leaders tried to institute new programs to obtain the villagers' cooperation, they could not have done so in many hamlets where the VC already had some power. As in the case of the pacification forces, GVN political officials tended to avoid areas under VC influence as much as possible because of the GVN's poor leadership and the enemy's strength. Without the regular presence of capable officials, the GVN could not redistribute land, implement civic action projects, encourage village self-development, or institute other political actions to gain the cooperation of the villagers. More important, the GVN could not propagandize and lead the masses on a regular basis, as the VC did with such effect. When the VC had access to the hamlets, they could steal or destroy medicine, bridges, schools, roads, new farming technology, and most other gifts to the populace. Because of the VC's success in mobilizing rural man-power and driving pro-GVN elements from the villages, the GVN had a far smaller pool of potential recruits in most villages in 1965 than the VC had possessed in 1959.

When the American forces arrived, they fought far better than the ARVN and promptly eliminated any chance of a quick Communist victory. They were not able to find enemy forces and engage them on favorable terms often enough, however, despite their high-tech intelligence equipment. As in the ARVN's case, many observers blame this on the U.S. military's emphasis on large, conventional search-and-destroy operations. General Westmore-land, they contend, erred in focusing on conventional warfare and leaving pacification, which he called the "other war," to the South Vietnamese. The critics argue that the Allies could have defeated the Communists by focus-ing on the "other war" instead of on the Communist regular forces. The Americans, they say, should have assigned most U.S. troops to small-unit territorial security roles, preferably in combination with knowledgeable Vietnamese. They particularly admire the Combined Action Program (CAP) that the U.S. Marines implemented in a small number of villages in the northern provinces. Each CAP platoon consisted of a squad of Marines and a platoon of Vietnamese militiamen who guarded and patrolled a par-ticular village.[5]

CAP platoons inhibited guerrilla and shadow government activity in the hamlets rather effectively, and they improved the fighting capabilities of the territorial forces. They allowed the Allies to engage the enemy more often than did most American units involved in search-and-destroy oper-ations. Westmoreland, nonetheless, never had enough troops to use this type of technique on a large scale. He needed too many of the troops that Washington had allotted him to prevent the Communist main forces from concentrating into large units to seize the urban areas and overrun Allied pacification forces. Although increased control over the villages could have undermined the entire Communist war effort in the long run, a stronger pacification effort could not have undermined it quickly enough to stop many large-unit VC attacks on small pacification forces. Even with the great amount of protection that the Marine main force units actually did offer to the small number of CAP platoons, large VC forces often overran the static CAP outposts.[6] The frequently heard claim that the Communists overran only one of them during the entire war is patently false. Had the U.S. military used the CAP concept more extensively during the mid-1960s, it most likely would have suffered higher casualties because of VC attacks on the platoons, thereby undermining support for the war in the United States, and would have jeopardized large bases and population centers.

By directing the pacification war for the South Vietnamese with the CAP platoons, the Americans would have allowed the GVN to avoid taking responsibility for pacification and for the war to an even greater extent than they actually did. Communist activities in the villages did not threaten to topple the GVN immediately, so the United States did not need to sacrifice additional lives to prop up the GVN pacification effort temporarily. Brig. Gen. Robert Montague, one of the most influential of the U.S. Army officers who favored greater emphasis on pacification and less on conventional operations, agreed on this point. A top graduate of the West Point class of 1947, Montague spent most of his time from 1963 to 1969 working as a special assistant for pacification to General Westmoreland, Robert Komer, and others, so he had a very good view of this issue. Montague said:

> I was not a big fan of U.S. units in pacification. The Marine Combined Action Platoons were the wrong way to go. The program didn't have a permanent effect, and it wasted resources. The Vietnamese weren't making them work—the U.S. Marines were, and everyone knew the Marines weren't going to be there very long. Other U.S. units got involved in pacification, and they weren't very successful, either. It was better to put U.S. forces into search-and-destroy missions than into pacification. If we were going to win the war, the Vietnamese would have to do it. We could help them, but ultimately they had to win it.[7]

Later in the war, the use of U.S. troops in pacification on a large scale became feasible because the Communists did not have substantial main force strength in most of the country. From 1969 to 1971, many U.S. units did break into small groups, a fact that most advocates of CAP platoon expansion ignore. Some of the CAP platoons began to operate without static bases during this period, which frequently reduced their casualties. Yet, these efforts did little to propel the GVN toward victory.

A more accurate criticism of the U.S effort, heard less from Westmoreland's harsh critics than from Americans who served in Vietnam, is that the U.S. forces became too heavily involved in the war in the South. Those who advance this argument agree that U.S. forces had to step in during 1965 to prevent South Vietnam's defeat, but they believe that the U.S. forces should not have stayed as long as they did, unless they had been employed exclusively to fight NVA infiltrators in Laos, Cambodia, or the South Vietnamese hinterlands. The use of American forces in the South, according to this school of thought, caused the ARVN to sit back and do nothing rather than to develop its fighting capabilities. Some advocates of this hypothesis underestimate the strength of the VC and undervalue pacification, but the basic points of their argument are accurate. Had the United States withdrawn its forces earlier and left only its advisers and air support in the country, necessity would have forced the South Vietnamese to attempt to improve their performance sooner. The ARVN, in all probability, would have taken up the slack earlier on and the Americans would have suffered fewer casualties, thus reducing the U.S. public's aversion to aiding the GVN. As the Easter offensive of 1972 would show, the ARVN could protect the nation from the NVA when endowed with U.S. advisers and sufficient firepower.

From the uprisings of the early 1960s until 1967, the many components of the Allied war effort combined to damage the Viet Cong shadow government significantly. The pacification forces, most notably the Counter-Terror Teams/PRUs and the Special Police, eliminated some of the VCI and the VC guerrillas in the village areas. Allied main forces, in the course of conventional military operations, captured or killed an unknown number of Viet Cong political cadres. Although Allied forces failed to keep the shadow government out of many hamlets throughout this period, their intensified military activities from 1965 onward and the consequent flight of villagers to urban areas did disrupt the VCI's operations seriously in some places. A large number of Communist cadres, most of them low in rank, rallied to the GVN through the Chieu Hoi program. The need for more Communist military units, meanwhile, caused the transfer of some political cadres to the military. By 1967, the shadow government lacked enough cadres to fill all VCI positions in many areas and it was forced to replenish its ranks with less capable cadres.

A CIA national intelligence estimate from 1967 states, "The overall availability and quality of VC political cadres at the lower levels have declined in many areas where losses have been heavy and replacements generally inferior."[8] Despite losses of lower-level cadres, however, the shadow government retained a great deal of power in many villages. As another CIA report from 1967 puts it, "Although shaky in some areas, the infrastructure remains largely intact at middle and higher echelons, and poses a formidable obstacle to the pacification program."[9]

5   The New Attack on the Shadow Government

n 1967, the Allies knew they would have to fight a long and difficult battle to reassert lasting GVN control over the rural population. During that year, they took a number of steps to improve the arsenal that they would use in this battle. Although most of the work would ultimately fall to the South Vietnamese, the initiative came from the Americans. During the first six months of the American ground force intervention, President Johnson and key administration figures had kept their attention on the main force engagements, which the U.S. forces had to win to avert the GVN's obliteration. By the beginning of 1966, however, their inability to defeat the Viet Cong decisively in the war's opening months and the rising influence of the CIA and other critical voices outside the military command had given the Johnson administration cause to wonder whether pacification deserved greater support. In February 1966, Johnson hastily called a conference in Honolulu for all of the top U.S. and GVN leaders to discuss ways to improve the pacification effort. The conference did not yield any concrete gains for pacification despite its lofty calls for new programs, but it did indicate that the Americans had become more interested in dealing with the "other war."

In March 1966, Johnson chose one of his administration's heavyweight thinkers, Robert Komer, as his chief adviser on pacification. During his trips to Vietnam, Komer became acquainted with the bright, slightly rebellious group of Americans—men like John Paul Vann, Richard Holbrooke, and Daniel Ellsberg—who believed that the United States was expending too many of its resources on the main force war and not giving pacification the attention it needed. He also came to know William E. Colby, then chief of the CIA's Far East Division, who had spent many years in Southeast Asia. In contrast to the younger men, the brilliant Colby was an insider who enjoyed considerable respect among some of the top American policymakers. Yet, he too complained fruitlessly that the United States was not devoting enough resources to pacification. These men soon convinced

Komer, and he started formulating plans for revamping the pacification effort. Moving among the highest circles in Washington, he repeatedly told President Johnson and his closest advisers that the United States had to do something about the "other war."

Komer decided that the United States desperately needed to improve coordination among its organizations involved in pacification: the CIA, the military, the U.S. Agency for International Development, the State Department, the U.S. Information Agency, and the Joint U.S. Public Affairs Office. Each controlled or advised pacification programs that ranged from aggressive paramilitary teams to agricultural development teams. Perhaps the greatest shortcoming of this fragmentation was the failure to coordinate civilian pacification programs with those of the military. The agencies responsible for political and economic development needed the armed forces to protect them from the predatory Viet Cong in the hamlets where they were trying to work, but the military forces often operated elsewhere in areas of their own choosing. Colby described the problem as it stood in the mid-1960s: "You'd find the U.S. civilians resettling villagers in one place, while the military was putting a defense force in a different place where there weren't villagers. It didn't make any sense. You needed to have the defense force, the self-defense force, the elections, the tin and cement to build houses, and the propaganda support as one program for a village."[1]

After the Honolulu conference, the United States attempted to put all of the civilian pacification organizations under a single command. That endeavor failed. In November 1966, President Johnson decided to make a more serious effort to create a "single manager" system for the civilian organizations. He gave ostensible authority over the civilian agencies to a central body called the Office of Civil Operations. This creation improved bureaucratic interaction somewhat, but the civilian bureaucracies generally managed to avoid obeying its commands or surrendering their autonomy. Johnson and Secretary of Defense Robert McNamara did not care much whether the Office of Civil Operations succeeded; they saw it primarily as a way to prepare the civilian agencies for their placement under military command. The military, for its part, set up an agency known as Revolutionary Development Support to coordinate its pacification undertakings more effectively.

Johnson, on the advice of McNamara and Komer, decided to unify the civilian and military pacification activities in May 1967 under the command of a single, strong organization, called Civil Operations and Rural Development Support (CORDS), to be headed by Komer. CORDS became a part of Westmoreland's Military Assistance Command, with Komer serving as a deputy to Westmoreland in Saigon. Komer explained why he favored putting CORDS under Westmoreland's command despite objections from many of the pacification organizations: "The military could handle the logistics. If I needed men, AID and State and CIA could provide me with men very slowly. Maybe a dozen a month. The military could give me twenty thousand men. If I had to have trucks to move stuff around the country, who had all the trucks? The military."[2]

Westmoreland seldom exerted his authority over CORDS, which left control to Komer. This arrangement satisfied both Westmoreland, who wanted to concentrate on the main force war, and Komer, who wanted uninhibited authority over the U.S. portion of the pacification effort. Lt. Gen. Phillip B. Davidson, who served as Westmoreland's chief intelligence officer in Vietnam, recalled: "Westmoreland's interest always lay in the big-unit war; pacification bored him. He welcomed Komer's two-war ploy in that it freed him from anything more than a titular responsibility for pacification and allowed him to concentrate himself and his MACV staff on the shooting war."[3]

CORDS assumed control of the military's pacification advisory staffs and the civilian organizations' staffs at all administrative echelons. During 1967, roughly 4,000 military and 800 civilian personnel served in CORDS. The organization reached its peak size at the end of 1969 with 6,400 military personnel and 1,000 civilians, then gradually shrank until it disappeared at the end of 1972.[4] Most of the people who found themselves in CORDS were advisers to GVN organizations and had counterparts in positions of authority within the organizations they advised. The adviser's functions usually included monitoring performance, providing funds and supplies, and offering advice. At every echelon down to the district level, CORDS designated a military officer or civilian as senior adviser with authority over all of the other pacification advisers at that level except for the CIA's advisers. The deputy senior adviser was a civilian if the senior adviser was a military officer and vice versa, which eased civilian fears of military domination. No military command in American history had ever encompassed so many civilians or had counted an ambassador—Komer held that rank—among its subordinates. CORDS greatly improved the coordination of civilian and military programs and allowed the United States to keep a better account of GVN personnel involved in pacification.

The CIA's province officers in charge and region officers in charge maintained independent control of CIA pacification advisers at the provincial and regional levels, respectively. The CIA had convinced Komer that its officers would perform best if they remained independent of the other pacification organizations. Komer did share control over the CIA's pacification division—known as the RD Cadre division—with John Hart, the CIA station chief in Saigon, and he gave instructions to the division's head, Lewis ("Lew") Lapham, more often than did Hart. For the most part, however, Komer and Hart let Lapham run the division as he saw fit.

Once the Americans had established CORDS, they began helping the Vietnamese improve their pacification efforts. The GVN system of district chiefs and province chiefs already provided unified command of most Vietnamese pacification programs, but ARVN division commanders often prevented these programs from working as well as they could have. A national pacification organization analogous to CORDS that could have dealt with this problem did not exist on the Vietnamese side; Komer and his successor, Colby, convinced President Nguyen Van Thieu to build one during 1968 and 1969. Much more significant, however, was the assistance that CORDS gave the GVN in replacing ineffective district and province chiefs and in expanding and improving the pacification forces. Aided by the advent of general conscription in June 1968, the territorial forces grew from approximately 418,000 to 680,000 men between 1967 and 1972, and the National Police from 66,000 to 121,000.[5] CORDS assigned many more American advisers to work with the territorial forces and accompany them on operations. In its early years, CORDS provided the initiative, planning, and funding for most GVN pacification programs, but it began leaving more to the GVN during the early 1970s as CORDS approached its end.

During 1967, Komer also came up with a program for unifying efforts against the Viet Cong shadow government. At that time, the sharing of intelligence on the VCI among the relevant organizations varied from one area to the next, but many organizations shared little with the others. No central mechanism existed to induce sharing, so whatever cooperation did take place occurred because of informal arrangements among the various agencies or because one person controlled several agencies and made them work together. To make matters worse, the Special Police, who were supposed to play a key role in locating the VC cadres, were not doing the job very well.

For a number of reasons, Komer chose the CIA to create a program for improving coordination of the attack on the VCI. The CIA had been trying to attack the VC in the village areas for years and had enjoyed some success in the field. It already had great influence over many of the organizations best designed for attacking the VCI. By contrast, MACV's military intelligence staff, which announced that it wanted to coordinate the attack on the VCI once the issue came into prominence in Saigon, had been ignoring the matter for the most part. In addition, Komer had served in the CIA for thirteen years, so he had the knowledge of the organization and the personal contacts within it that made close cooperation relatively easy.

In 1966, the CIA had begun experimenting with programs to pool information from all of the intelligence agencies through a central mechanism. If effective, such a system would yield a highly detailed picture of the VCI, instead of several pictures with fewer details, and would permit more efficient use of operational units because each unit would have more information on which to act. It also would reduce duplication of effort because each agency would know what intelligence the others had already collected and what they were trying to collect currently. The CIA tested a pilot coordination program known as CT-4 in November 1966. Intelligence personnel from the CIA, the U.S. military, and the South Vietnamese National Police in Gia Dinh province and in the Saigon metropolitan area participated. This program performed poorly, and the CIA eventually phased it out.

CIA officer Robert ("Bob") Wall created a second pilot program, called the District Operational Intelligence Coordination Centers, in I Corps during early 1967. Wall said that he took as his model the coordination centers developed by Claude Fenner, deputy chief of the Malayan Special Branch during the Malayan insurgency of the 1950s. "I was the chief of station at Kuala Lumpur for nearly four years," Wall explained. "I worked very closely with Fenner, who developed the basic concept of district intelligence and operations coordination that I used in Vietnam."[6] Representatives from the CIA, the U.S. military, and GVN organizations provided intelligence inputs from their respective agencies to Wall's centers, which then circulated these reports to the other representatives. The representatives, in turn, added any relevant information that they had to the reports. The participating South Vietnamese and American organizations strongly supported the effort, which facilitated the sharing of much intelligence. Initially, the centers actually concentrated on tactical military intelligence because the U.S. Marines were the only operational forces who used the intelligence product regularly.

Nelson Brickham was one of the CIA officers in Saigon studying the attack on the VCI at that time. Brickham envisioned a plan for a national organization that would supervise the intelligence and operations coordination of the American and, later, the South Vietnamese organizations. After a visit to Wall's centers, Brickham decided that the centers could simplify the task of coordination significantly. Brickham said, "I talked to the Vietnamese police officers and the U.S. military, i.e., the Marines. They went over the records of what they'd done and how they'd done it. That convinced me that these centers were a very effective tool."[7]

CIA officer Evan J. Parker, Jr., who had just arrived in Vietnam, had final responsibility for creating the new program. He compiled suggestions from Brickham and other CIA officers and passed a final proposal to Komer. On 14 June 1967, Komer took it to the MACV staff, which turned it down. Not someone with patience for obstructionism, Komer brought the proposal directly to Westmoreland and Ambassador Ellsworth Bunker two days later, and they quickly approved it. Komer gave Parker and the CIA responsibility for setting up the new program within CORDS, under the title Intelligence Coordination and Exploitation (ICEX).

ICEX started establishing District Intelligence and Operations Coordination Centers (DIOCCs) in the most suitable districts. As in Wall's centers, representatives from the various agencies were supposed to provide intelligence to their local centers, although they did not always circulate their reports to each other for review as before. Separate sections of the DIOCCs handled tactical military intelligence and VCI intelligence. The ICEX staff hoped to achieve the greatest improvements in intelligence and operations coordination at the district level; better coordination already existed at the provincial level. The province ICEX coordinator, who was normally the senior CIA officer in the province, and the province senior adviser supervised the establishment and functioning of the DIOCCs. At the provincial level, the province ICEX coordinator coordinated the CIA and CIA-sponsored agencies and, through the Province Intelligence Coordination Committees, attempted to gain the cooperation of GVN agencies not tied to the CIA. ICEX committees and staffs functioned at the corps and national levels as well, and the CIA controlled them with subordinate assistance from MACV. These upper echelons provided general guidance to the lower levels but did not play a part in the day-to-day functioning of ICEX. The ICEX structure spread fairly quickly throughout the district and provincial capitals of South Vietnam. By the end of 1967, thirty-nine provinces had ICEX committees, and twenty-nine had permanent Province Intelligence Coordination Centers, where full-time staffers processed information. One hundred three districts had District Intelligence and Operations Coordination Centers.[8] At the beginning of 1968, the CIA rechristened the program as "Phoenix." CIA veterans gave me a variety of explanations for the name change; none of these explanations can be clearly documented.

American advisers to the district Phoenix centers began arriving in early 1968. Initially, Komer had tried to get the CIA to staff the district-level Phoenix centers, but the CIA refused on the grounds of personnel shortages. He then asked the military for the necessary 250 lieutenants and eventually received them. In most places, therefore, the Americans had not fully built up the Phoenix program before the Communists struck with their massive Tet offensive of 1968. This unexpected onslaught stalled Phoenix for a short time because the intelligence and operations organizations had to concentrate their energies on stopping the Communist attacks. DIOCC formation resumed after the Tet offensive died down; by the end of 1968, most of South Vietnam's 239 districts had Phoenix centers. During 1968 and 1969, Phoenix merged all of the Province Phoenix Committees into the Province Intelligence Coordination Centers to form Province Intelligence and Operations Coordination Centers (PIOCCs). All provinces had PIOCCs by the end of 1969.

ICEX tried to get the intelligence agencies to obtain information that would facilitate the targeting of specific VC cadres at specific times and locations. It wanted less reliance on the "cordon-and-search" method, by which operational forces sealed off an entire hamlet and searched it for suspicious characters. "The operational concept at the cutting edge is analogous to a 'rifle shot' rather than a 'shotgun' approach," Komer wrote at the time. "Instead of cordon and search operations, it will stress quick reaction operations aimed at individual cadre or, at most, small groups. Cutting off the heads of the infrastructure at local levels will tend to degrade the whole structure."[9] Primary responsibility for mounting operations against the cadres went to the PRUs and the National Police Field Forces. Other operational forces, however, helped to attack the shadow government, especially at the beginning when the National Police Field Forces had not yet deployed many units to the countryside.

Komer slowly persuaded the GVN to participate in the new attack on the Viet Cong shadow government. The nature of South Vietnamese participation became a matter of dispute within the secret chambers of the GVN high command. The Americans never knew for sure what issues most concerned the South Vietnamese, but they suspected that some elements of the GVN leadership thought that the program gave too much power to the Americans or that it would favor certain GVN political factions over others. One of the most important GVN leaders who did not like ICEX was Gen. Nguyen Ngoc Loan, chief of the National Police, who became known to all the world during the Tet offensive when he shot a VC prisoner in front of a cameraman. "I don't think Loan was really ready to go along with ICEX," Parker told me. "Ultimately, he realized that it was going to happen because the ambassadors and Westmoreland were behind it. He had to accept it."[10]

On 20 December 1967, GVN Prime Minister Tran Thien Khiem announced the birth of a South Vietnamese organization parallel to Phoenix and called it Phung Hoang, the name of an all-seeing bird from Vietnamese legend, similar to the Occidental phoenix. President Thieu, however, did not commit the GVN to the program until July 1968, when he issued a supportive decree and a standard operating procedure for Phung Hoang with much help from the Americans. By the beginning of 1969, the South Vietnamese had begun taking over some of the responsibility for the program from the American advisers.

At the outset, ICEX had no personnel other than its director, Evan Parker, Jr., and several assistants assigned to him. Parker assigned tasks to CIA officers and a few other civilians and military officers in addition to their other duties. ICEX and Phoenix always relied on preexisting intelligence and operational organizations that functioned independently of the coordination program. Contrary to popular belief, ICEX and Phoenix did not create or control any intelligence agencies or operational forces. Later, when large numbers of Americans became Phoenix advisers, they still did not control substantial intelligence or operational assets in most cases. This state of affairs accounts for the differentiation in this study's title between "Phoenix"—a coordination program—and "the birds of prey"—the armed operational forces that actually sought out and went after VCI. Phoenix and Phung Hoang, however, did influence the activities of the birds of prey. Komer delegated some of his authority over the CIA's pacification division to Parker, who used it to focus the Special Police and other CIA-sponsored pacification resources on the anti-VCI attack. "The Vietnamese had considerable respect for Ev Parker, as I did," Komer said. "He would deal with the Chief of the Special Police. He had a great deal of influence over the Vietnamese, and he did exert it."[11] The CIA station in Saigon ordered its province and region officers in charge to follow Parker's directives. Parker and subsequent directors also tried to influence other GVN organizations, with modest success. The South Vietnamese Phung Hoang directors, on the other hand, had little influence over anyone.

After their complete establishment in mid-1968, the Phoenix and Phung Hoang programs underwent several major transformations between then and 1972. At the end of 1968, the CIA began reducing its direct involvement in Phoenix while MACV increasingly took control and expanded its personnel commitment. On 1 July 1969, the CIA relinquished its management and support responsibilities to the staff of CORDS and made only minor contributions to the program thereafter, although a CIA officer continued to hold the position of Phoenix director. In this same year, the South Vietnamese created Village Intelligence and Operations Coordination Centers as the National Police moved down to the village level. Between the end of 1971 and the middle of 1972, the South Vietnamese gave the police complete control over Phung Hoang by gradually merging Phung Hoang into the National Police. Some U.S. Phung Hoang advisers remained after this merger, along with American advisers to various other South Vietnamese pacification organizations. The Phung Hoang advisers all departed at the end of 1972, but a few of the other advisers, most of them with the CIA, stayed behind and advised the Vietnamese during the final years of the Republic of Vietnam. Phoenix, Phung Hoang, and the other components of the attack on the shadow government changed in other ways, as well, during the period 1967–72. These developments are covered in subsequent chapters.

The attack on the shadow government, like many other GVN and Communist enterprises, continued after the Paris Peace Accords in violation of the so-called cease-fire.[12] This book focuses primarily on American and South Vietnamese activities during the period 1967–72, when the Allies made their most concerted attack on the instigators of the South Vietnamese insurgency, the Viet Cong shadow government. This period was a time of tremendous change for the war as a whole, for the war against the VCI, and for the people of South Vietnam. The remainder of this book explores the dynamics of the war against the VCI during these years and this war's overall effects.

PART TWO: Intelligence

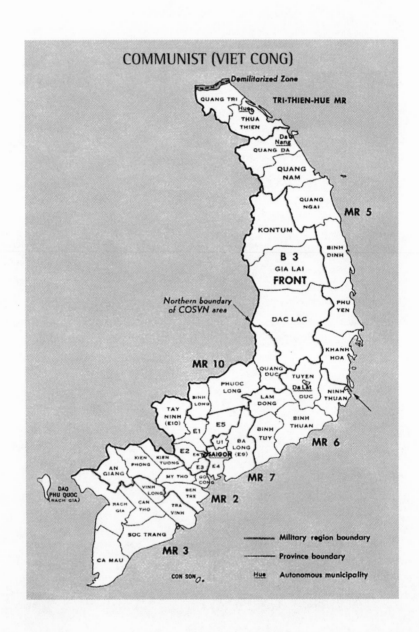

COMMUNIST (VIET CONG)

Demilitarized Zone

TRI-THIEN-HUE MR

QUANG TRI

Hue

THUA
THIEN

Da
Nang

QUANG DA

QUANG
NAM

QUANG
NGAI

MR 5

KONTUM

BINH
DINH

B 3
GIA LAI
FRONT

Northern boundary
of COSVN area

DAC LAC

PHU
YEN

KHANH
HOA

MR 10

QUANG
DUC

TUYEN
DUC

Da Lat

NINH
THUAN

PHUOC
LONG

BINH
LONG

LAM
DONG

TAY
NINH
(E10)

E5

E1

U1

BINH
TUY

BINH
THUAN

E2

SAIGON

BA
LONG
(E9)

MR 6

KIEN
PHONG

KIEN
TUONG

E3

E4

AN
GIANG

MY THO

GO
CONG

MR 7

DAO
PHU QUOC
(RACH GIA)

VINH
LONG

BEN
TRE

MR 2

RACH
GIA

CAN
THO

TRA
VINH

SOC TRANG

MR 3

CA MAU

CON SON

Military region boundary

Province boundary

Hue   Autonomous municipality

6   Targets

he war against the shadow government in the villages often involved the sorts of violence that characterize most wars. People shot at other people, bullets ripped through flesh, and those who died or surrendered were deemed the losers. Yet, the forces of human will, courage, and steel did not play as great a role in the village war as they did in more conventional wars because another factor assumed a more prominent position. In this war, as in most insurgent wars, the participants depended on intelligence for their success to a much greater degree than in most conventional contests. Because the Communist armed forces and illegal cadres did not defend any fixed positions or areas except for relatively small secret bases, the Allies had to scour the countryside to find them. Sound intelligence made this task far easier. In the case of the legal VC cadres who operated secretly amid the populace, the Allies could stop them only with intelligence.

One important type of intelligence identified someone as a Communist political cadre. Most often, the Allies determined that specific individuals belonged to the shadow government by learning their names and other personal information from various sources or by obtaining their photographs in locations or situations that suggested they served the Communists. The Allies drew wiring diagrams (charts resembling family trees) of the local hierarchy and tried to identify by name the person who held each position on the chart. If they identified particular civilians as legal cadres, they could find and arrest them easily because these cadres lived as normal citizens. When the Allies obtained information on the identity of illegal cadres, they improved their chances for specific identification of those individuals if they happened to capture them during an operation. They also could use the information to find friends or relatives of cadres who might convince the cadres to defect or spy for the Allies.

The other major type of intelligence gave the location of political cadres, which was crucial for neutralizing illegal cadres. It could locate them in the villages where they lived or visited, in secret bases, at meetings away from the population, or in areas where they traveled. Ideally, it pinpointed cadres at specific places and times, but, in many cases, it could identify only trails or areas that the cadres frequently traversed, where the Allied forces stood a good chance of capturing or killing them. On occasion, intelligence provided other, more subtle facts. It could, for instance, indicate which cadres bore grudges against other VC, information that the Allies could use to recruit them as informants or agents or induce them to defect.

When trying to identify a VCI, the Americans and South Vietnamese often found it difficult to determine whether the individual was a VCI, a VC supporter, or a VC soldier. Sometimes, villagers to whom the Communists did not assign specific posts in the shadow government hierarchy—and who thus could be classified only as VC supporters—performed more or less the same tasks as the cadres. The structure was not always highly formal and rigid. Many Americans and South Vietnamese, moreover, did not always understand which people on the VC organizational charts were VCI and which were VC supporters.

By the late 1960s, many political cadres served in some type of military unit because of personnel shortages, which made them difficult to differentiate from the VC soldiers. In some places where the VC were strong, especially in the Mekong Delta during 1967–68, overt political cadres remained in the hamlets and relied on the counterintelligence methods that had protected them so well in the early 1960s or on the protective screen afforded by large Communist military units. The day-to-day activities of most village-level illegal cadres across the country, however, had undergone a major transformation by the late 1960s, a fact that fundamentally altered the war against the VCI and the war as a whole, yet one that eluded most outside observers. These cadres no longer lived in or near the hamlets under their jurisdiction because Allied pacification pressure made it too risky. They lived with military units or, on occasion, in villages other than those in which they worked, as the upper-level VCI had done all along. Most illegal cadres at all echelons visited their operational areas only periodically, if at all, to carry out the essential functions of the shadow government, such as conscription and recruitment, tax collection, and intelligence gathering. The comments of Le Van Thai, a deputy PRU chief at the provincial level during the late 1960s and early 1970s, apply to the illegal cadres in most parts of the country from 1968 on: "The Viet Cong cadres did not live in the hamlets because it was too dangerous for them. They lived in camps. They put mines and grenades around the camps, and only they knew how to get in and get out. Many soldiers protected them. We could get them in the camps only by bombing them. Sometimes the camps were near villages, which made them difficult to bomb."[1] As the war moved into its later years, Communist main force units themselves assumed many of the shadow government's functions. These units had their own cadres who propagandized and intimidated the village populations and obtained recruits, taxes, and intelligence from them, for the local VCI did not have enough people to perform these tasks.

Because of these circumstances, a clear distinction between the shadow government's overt political cadres and the VC soldiers and guerrillas operating in small units near the villages seldom existed. In most cases, the Allies did not try to distinguish between the two groups because it usually proved too difficult. Most often, they attacked any enemy force they could and assumed that they would get some VCI in the process, rather than spend much time in trying to pinpoint specific cadres or cadres within groups of VC. "We tried to go after any VC we could find," said John Mullins, a CIA adviser to the PRUs in Thua Thien and Quang Tri provinces during 1969 and 1970. "We didn't make much of a distinction between political and military VC."[2] The attack on the shadow government, therefore, was almost always intertwined with the attack on all the Communists who operated in the villages.

Most of the legal cadres stayed in the villages. Starting in 1969, the VC decided they would try to increase the number of legal VCI. Allied operations had been making life so difficult for the illegal VCI and the VC armed forces that the VC no longer stood a realistic chance of mobilizing the village populations as they had before. Hanoi's strategists, by this time relying primarily on main force units from the North rather than on armed forces developed in the South, decided that they could best use Southern Communists as legal VCI who collected intelligence through observation and infiltration of the GVN to help the North Vietnamese forces. A typical report from the American Embassy during 1971 states, "The enemy continues to place great stress on the political struggle and on the need for implanting large numbers of legal cadre."[3] The Communists, however, failed to recruit large numbers of legal cadres in most places during 1969 and the 1970s.

The legal cadres and other VCI employed several tactics to keep the Allies from discovering their identities. Most cadres had aliases. The VCI took the most common names as aliases, which provided a particularly effective cover because certain names belong to a great many people in Vietnam. Sometimes, the only information that the Allies had about someone was a name, so aliases often frustrated efforts to learn much about a particular cadre. The VC's use of aliases, along with the tendency for one person to hold multiple jobs, quite frequently led the Allies to open several different dossiers on one VCI. In 1970, Komer reported: "Until we find better means of identification (photos and fingerprints), we may have as many as 10–12 dossiers on the same man (he may have several AKAs, operate in several districts and provinces, have several different VCI jobs)."[4] With the help of other sources of information, however, particularly those originating within the VC, the Allies succeeded in overcoming the alias problem in many cases.

The VC cadres, especially those who did not live in the villages, sometimes tried to confuse the GVN intelligence organizations by changing their areas of operation. Because relocation placed cadres in unfamiliar environments, they usually moved only when they thought the Allies knew enough about them to put their lives in serious danger. When a VCI moved to a new place, the Allied intelligence agencies in that area and their sources usually knew little about him or her, especially if the migrant went to a different province. Allied attempts to build national databases to identify transient VC cadres failed. Sometimes cadres lived in new villages where they operated undetected and with relative ease as they mixed with the local people. Newcomers abounded in many places. Workers came in to help plant or harvest, refugees arrived from the hot war zones, and GVN deserters and draft dodgers wandered from place to place.

"People were moving in and out of an area all the time, especially if it was a contested area," said Peter Scott, a U.S. Army officer assigned as a Phoenix adviser in Chau Doc and Chuong Thien provinces during 1968 and 1969. "They were carrying messages. They were trading. They came in at the time of planting or harvesting. A lot of young men were avoiding the draft, and they would change identities, buy different IDs, and move to different villages. The more shadowy you could be in that society, especially as a male, the better chances you had of staying alive."[5] Some cadres also took refuge in the urban areas without being detected. A male between the ages of sixteen and fifty, however, was never completely safe from suspicion anywhere unless he had an excellent cover story backed by impeccable documentation. The GVN knew that any man who was not working for it was most likely a VC or a draft dodger.

Chapters 7 through 9 discuss the methods that the Allies used to obtain intelligence concerning the shadow government. Although many of the VCI spent most of their time with military units and locating them was essentially an exercise in tactical military intelligence, I do not examine all of the Allied military intelligence efforts. They were too numerous, and many had no direct connection to the village war. Rather, I focus on the intelligence work of the organizations involved in pacification because they assumed the main responsibility for trying to stop the shadow government and its guerrilla warriors in the hamlets.

7   Informants and Agents

n many hamlets of South Vietnam, suspicions dominated relations among the villagers. Many villagers had to help relatives in the GVN or the VC who worked in the area. All tried to keep the enemy and its eyes and ears in the countryside from knowing about this assistance. If the enemy discovered them, they would die. Secret information moved between individuals in whispers or on scraps of paper—information that determined the fate of the protagonists in the village war.

The population of rural Vietnam knew all sorts of information about the VC cadres and other VC who operated in the village areas which the Allies could use to defeat them. When the illegal political cadres conducted most of their important business, such as recruitment and conscription, tax collection, dissemination of propaganda, and public execution of their enemies, they came into face-to-face contact with village residents. By the late 1960s, the villagers had watched the Viet Cong shadow government at work for so many years that they knew all of the illegal cadres who operated in their own village. Some observant villagers also knew who some of the legal cadres were, if careless VC had contacted the cadres where these villagers could see them.

The villagers, of course, also knew the location of illegal cadres who lived in the hamlets, but by the late 1960s virtually all of the illegal cadres lived elsewhere and made short visits to the hamlets. The villagers knew when, where, and in what strength the illegal cadres and their cohorts most often operated in the hamlets. When these overt members of the shadow government visited a hamlet, of course, the villagers knew where they were at that moment. Such information helped Allied forces if they happened to arrive while the cadres were still there. If the cadres tried to hide upon arrival of the Allies, the villagers knew where they were. When no Allied forces came to the hamlet during a VCI visit, however, the cadres usually did not stay long enough for a villager to sneak away and fetch the Allies. Allied informants in the hamlets also feared leaving their hamlets while the VC were there lest the VC catch them and suspect them of spying. Some villagers, primarily those who had close ties to the VC, had access to information pinpointing specific illegal cadres and other VC at particular times and places. Other useful facts known to the villagers included the identities of the VC cadres' relatives and the location of VC mines and booby traps.

During the Tet offensive of 1968, many legal cadres surfaced in the hamlets and thus revealed their identities to the villagers. All types of political cadres from the countryside and legal cadres living in the towns and cities took to the streets in many district and provincial capitals during the offensive. They tried to lead attacks on Allied forces and installations and exhorted the people to rise up in rebellion. Their calls to action, however, failed to rouse the urban masses. Always unsympathetic toward the VC, the town and city populations repeatedly reported the identities of the Communists to the GVN forces. Dean Almy, the CIA's top man in II Corps from 1967 to 1969, recalled, "During Tet, two North Vietnamese units came into Nha Trang to attack the Korean headquarters and ARVN headquarters. The local VCI came out and led these troops to their objectives. The populace saw these VCI and reported them to the Special Police and ARVN, who picked them up."[1] A North Vietnamese soldier who rallied in Binh Dinh province during the offensive said that the VC "thought the city people would support them, but it turned out that they didn't. . . . I think the people in the cities hate the Viet Cong very much. I know this hatred because while staying in the [GVN] Sector office, I saw people coming in to the Sector to report the information they had about the Viet Cong in their areas."[2]

In the countryside, the village informants communicated with Allied intelligence gatherers in a variety of ways. In some cases, they voluntarily approached a GVN employee or agency and told what they knew. Many ordinary villagers who provided information on the shadow government, however, did so only when Allied personnel or their agents asked them for it because they desired payment or wanted to pass information only to select people. Every police, paramilitary, and military organization on the Allied side sought out informants among the general populace. So did the South Vietnamese chiefs at every echelon, from hamlet chief up, as well as certain American advisers. Many informant efforts did not focus primarily on the Viet Cong shadow government or the village war, but some of them did yield information on the cadres. When villagers and members of the shadow government became informants, they typically provided information only on an irregular and informal basis.

A few villagers became Allied agents. Agents differed from informants in that they generally had better access to information. Among villagers, relatives of people in the VC, the wealthy or influential who cooperated with the VC, and leaders of racial or religious groups generally had the best access. In some cases, a single person served as a principal agent, an agent who recruited other informants or agents—often relatives—to tell him or her what they knew. Some of these subsources in turn had other people who reported to them, whether or not the latter knew where the information ultimately went, so one principal agent could draw on a large number of people. The Allies went to great trouble to recruit agents. They tried to identify people who could get the information they wanted and who had reasons to dislike the Communists, then looked for ways of contacting them. Agents communicated with their contacts regularly, and they received more money than informants. Because effective agents were much harder to find than effective informants, the Allies had far fewer agents than informants among the hamlet populations.

People within the Communist ranks, not surprisingly, also knew a great deal about the shadow government. The VC's leadership tried to keep its members from knowing anything they did not have to know in order to minimize information leaks, but most Communists nonetheless had good access to information about the cadres and other members of the VC. The illegal cadres usually had to live and work together with many other VC, thus making their identity, location, and activities known to them. Communist leaders and others in administrative positions knew large numbers of illegal cadres and, in some cases, legal cadres. Certain individuals within the VC ranks knew ahead of time when and where particular cadres or other VC would be operating or meeting with other cadres. Most Communists, in addition, knew the locations of secret bunkers, supply depots, bases, and other places where cadres might be hiding, as well as the locations of mines, booby traps, escape routes, and other information needed for mounting operations. They could tell the Allies which VC were disgruntled and how they could be contacted for defection or employment as informants or agents. Most agents who lived with Communist military units, however, could not communicate with the Allies or transmit urgent information in a timely manner, for they could not leave their units easily. The legal cadres who spied for the Allies, because they lived in GVN or contested areas, contacted Allied intelligence personnel with no more difficulty than other villagers.

Many organizations had informants who worked for the Communists. The Special Police, the South Vietnamese military, a GVN national-level strategic intelligence organization called the Central Intelligence Organization, and the CIA recruited agents within Communist organizations as well. These agents occasionally provided outstanding reports on the shadow government. The best CIA agent in the VC, known most commonly as "Hackle," operated in Tay Ninh province and obtained some of the Communists' most sensitive information from senior Communist officials at the district and provincial levels. The CIA officers who worked with Hackle now suspect that he might have been a double agent, for he chose not to leave Vietnam at the end of the war. They know for certain, however, that he provided a great deal of information during the war that subsequent events proved to have been accurate. A small portion of this information aided the attack on the shadow government. One of the officers who worked with Hackle was Frank Snepp, an analyst in the CIA's Saigon station from 1969 to 1975 who later ran afoul of the CIA for writing an unauthorized and highly critical account of America's evacuation of South Vietnam in 1975. Because of Hackle, said Snepp, "we knew who all the VCI in Tay Ninh province were. He provided us with a wiring chart of many, many of his comrades."[3] The Allies, however, usually did not ask their better agents for information that would help in attacking the VCI or other VC in the villages. The information they provided on other matters had a higher priority than information concerning the VCI and the village war, and exploitation of the lower-priority information would have increased the Communists' chances for discovering their identity.

CIA case officers also recruited agents within the GVN who gave them information about the VC in the villages and about GVN activities and intentions. Many of these agents had good contacts with others in the GVN or in the villages and thus served as principal agents. Thomas ("Tom") Polgar, CIA station chief in Saigon from 1972 to the end of the war, remarked, "We had some very good sources in the Government. Those could be handled directly by Americans, and some were very effective."[4]

A large number of the CIA's agents in the GVN worked for the Special Police. CIA advisers recruited single members of the Special Police, instructed them in detail on what information they wanted, and discussed with them their means of obtaining it. Working with the police as a group, rather than with an individual, involved too many security risks. Lew Lapham, who replaced John Hart as CIA station chief in Saigon at the beginning of 1968 and held that position for almost a year, explained the situation:

> Recruiting agents unilaterally was almost impossible. You needed cutouts.
> If the Vietnamese police helped you, you could not control who had access
> to that information, and we knew that many of the police elements were

penetrated by the VC. It was almost essential, therefore, that you work with an individual in the police the Americans had been working with. He had to have been vetted adequately, and he had to be loyal, to the point that he didn't even keep records of the work within his own service. We were basically using them as agents to get other agents. In a liaison relationship, you're normally totally dependent on what the host government wants to give you. In Vietnam, our expectations were higher than that, simply because we were in a war, and we were making a much greater investment of U.S. money and lives than the U.S. normally makes with respect to a host government. If the Vietnamese did not cooperate, our province officer would get together with his region officer in charge and see what they might do to get the Special Police officer replaced or to get some influence brought on him to be more cooperative.[5]

In some cases, a CIA adviser took an operation that he had discovered through the Special Police and started running it without the Special Police, but in most cases this method did not produce much intelligence. Donald ("Don") Gregg, who went to Vietnam to become the III Corps region officer in charge in 1970 and held that position until 1972, told me, "We were constantly trying to get the Special Police to share more of their leads with us. They did not give us a ton of viable leads. If you had a good and cooperative police chief, everything was much better. So much depended on the individual, and his character, and how he felt about what the Americans were trying to do."[6]

Informants and agents seldom were willing to disclose all of their knowledge about the shadow government to the Allies, for most knew some cadres in their areas whom they would not betray. Where loyalty to village, religion, or race was strong, they would not divulge information about cadres in those groups, and no one would betray a relative. Bruce Lawlor, a CIA case officer who spoke Vietnamese fluently, observed this phenomenon while he was in I Corps during the early 1970s:

> There was always loyalty to the family and to the village. Let's say you have an informant who's getting information from a cousin in the VC, and then a VC cadre who's not from the village comes into that village. The informant probably has no loyalty to that cadre, so he will tell you the cadre is coming. If the cousin comes into the village, however, or a group of VC with the cousin comes into the village, you'll never hear about it. Many informants were also wary of providing information that would affect people in their village's structure. As a result, the cadres we'd get information on most often were guys from outside of the village coming into the village.[7]

Allied military operations damaged informant and agent operations. The Allies inevitably killed some informants and agents, just as they killed innocent civilians and VC. The intelligence agencies usually did not tell other organizations who or where their informants and agents were because of possible security leaks. Thus, a GVN territorial forces patrol would not know that one person out of an eight-man group of VC moving across a rice paddy at night was a valuable CIA informant, and the GVN troops would kill all eight men if they could. Daniel ("Dan") Mudrinich, the CIA's IV Corps region officer in charge from 1969 to 1971, said, "You couldn't tell the PRUs, 'Don't touch that guy over there because he belongs to us.' The PRUs might let it slip that the guy was working for you, and then he would be finished. The PRUs or the military forces might kill your source, but the source understood that. That could happen to him whether he was working for you or not."[8] When one organization arrested another organization's source, the contact organization usually went to the prison and secured the person's release. The arrest of a VC or a villager, however, often made the Communists distrustful of that person thereafter and thus more likely to keep secret information from the individual.

The attack on the VCI, by its very nature, also made penetrating the VC more difficult. The South Vietnamese and Americans with authority over action forces made some attempts to recruit VCI as agents or get them to defect, but more pressing priorities usually discouraged them from pursuing such delicate matters. In some cases, their superiors pressured them to neutralize large numbers of the VCI right away, and many were themselves inclined by nature to focus on immediate results. Allied forces could achieve quicker results by capturing or killing VCI than by appealing to cadres to spy or defect. Unsuccessful appeals, moreover, especially to legal cadres, were liable to cause people to go into hiding or operate more carefully, thus eliminating the possibility of recruitment, arrest, or killing. As a result, the Allies apprehended or killed some cadres who might have been developed into GVN agents over a long period of time. The emphasis on quick results diminished somewhat for CIA officers during 1969 and afterward as the CIA put more emphasis on penetrating the VC, but it remained a major concern for the South Vietnamese.

According to Daren Flitcroft, a highly regarded CIA officer who held the top CIA post in III Corps from 1968 to 1970, "The Special Police were far less interested in penetrations and authenticated operations than the Agency was. They were fighting a war. As soon as they knew someone was working for the other side, they'd go get him." Flitcroft recognized that the Special Police and other organizations had worthwhile missions that inevitably conflicted with penetrating the VC. He added, "It was pretty hard to encourage people to go out and destroy the infrastructure and at the same time to preserve certain elements of it to get intelligence information out of it. That problem was always there."[9]

Informants and agents provided information for a large variety of reasons. Money and other material amenities, such as American medical treatment, naturally motivated some South Vietnamese to become informants or agents. CIA case officers usually could spend as much as they wanted for information. CORDS and the U.S. military had more limited funds. The GVN had fewer funds still, although the South Vietnamese often asked for and received money from the Americans. Phoenix offered fairly small rewards for information leading to neutralization of VCI; the Americans could have funded higher rewards, but they feared that doing so would make the program more vulnerable to misuse by GVN officials, who often found ways of slipping American money into their own pockets. The Americans also suspected, justifiably, that high rewards would encourage many South Vietnamese to give false information to GVN officials and then split the reward with those officials. Most observers thought that money elicited some very useful information. Col. Chester B. McCoid, who served in Vietnam for eight years, including one as deputy Phung Hoang director, said that "the Vietnamese would do almost anything, if the take were big enough."[10] Vo Van Dinh, an officer in the South Vietnamese Rangers who spent some time working on Phung Hoang at the provincial level, asserted, "With money, you could get all the information you wanted."[11]

Many former intelligence personnel, however, believed that people motivated by money alone did not make reliable or loyal sources. Rex Wilson, who served a tour in Vietnam with the U.S. Army during the late 1960s and then returned as a CIA adviser to the Special Police in An Xuyen and Bac Lieu provinces from 1970 to 1972, subscribed to this view. Of the agents run by the Special Police and the CIA, Wilson said, "There were plenty of cases where we recruited people just with money, but those agent relationships were dangerously thin, and they were a great problem to run."[12]

The most dependable informants and agents had reasons more important than money for helping the Allies. Some excellent sources gave information because they hated the Communists. Many villagers and even some of the VC resented the heavy-handed methods and broken promises of the Communists or the dominant role of the Northerners in the Party leadership. Col. Viet Lang, the III Corps PRU director from 1970 to 1972, commented, "When the people were treated poorly by the Communists, they gave us information sometimes."[13] Other informants and agents disliked particular individuals and informed only on them; within the VC, informing provided a convenient way of eliminating rivals and other adversaries. Some VC cadres, especially those in higher positions, decided to help the GVN because they became disillusioned with the Communist political ideology. They had come to believe—presciently—that Communist rule inevitably meant less freedom and prosperity for the people than did GVN rule.

Allied success and improved GVN leadership caused many villagers to provide information to the Allies, just as VC success and leadership had. After the Americans arrived in 1965, the GVN started to fare much better in the little wars for individual hamlets and in the war in general, and most villagers thought it might win in the end. Hoping to get on the GVN's good side, many became more cooperative, although some also continued to assist the Communists because at times they still seemed to have a good chance of winning as well. Francis J. West, Jr., served with the U.S. Marines in Vietnam and observed how the CAP platoons obtained intelligence by fighting well: "Most CAPs have to go through a testing period of several months' duration subsequent to establishment during which both the PFs [territorial forces] and the villagers watch carefully for signs of timidity or quick abandonment. With confidence in the CAPs' capability and staying power comes information, first from the PFs, later from the villagers through the GVN agents who have relatives or friends in the hamlets."[14] GVN leadership also improved considerably from 1968 through 1972, which boosted the villagers' respect for the GVN. Confidence in the GVN leadership generally provided a more reliable incentive for cooperation than did opportunistic support for the stronger side.

Sometimes, the Allies gained valuable information from children in the villages. When asked what he or she knew about certain relatives or neighbors who belonged to the VC or where the VC had placed mines, a child usually did not have the same fears of telling the truth that an adult had. The key was to get to the children before the parents could do anything to hush them up. "If we questioned the older people, sometimes they were scared," said Nguyen An Tien, who served in the Special Police in Chuong Thien province. "They knew the truth, but wouldn't say it. The children, however, would tell the truth."[15]

In certain cases, the Allies coerced hamlet dwellers into talking, although they used this tactic less often as time went on and the villagers became more cooperative. Bruce Lawlor saw the Quang Nam PRUs, with whom he worked extensively, employ coercion: "Often a PRU guy would recruit a villager that he knew was a VC sympathizer with a very crude method—'You either tell me, or you're gone. You can either cooperate with us, or when we find out, we'll come get you.'"[16]

The Allies obtained information most frequently and most effectively through relatives of GVN personnel. Most people in GVN organizations had family members in the villages, many of whom were involved with the VC in some way. These relatives often told all they knew. Through their assistance alone, the GVN could identify all of the VCI in many villages, which accounts, in part, for the decision by most illegal cadres to live away from their villages. "The PRUs got most information in the villages from their relatives or their friends," recalled Pham Huu Chinh, who worked at the national level of the PRU program in the early 1970s. "The information from the relatives was the best."[17] Even some of those serving in the VC ranks, where people were supposed to lose their family loyalty, put family first and informed on their VC comrades. In some instances, family members who worked on opposing sides exchanged valuable information about their own side, information that guaranteed the deaths of others, so that each could please his superiors. GVN intelligence personnel also obtained information about the VC with relative ease from their friends and, in some cases, neighbors or members of the same religious or racial group. Mudrinich said, "Many Vietnamese were inclined to rely on old friendships somewhere or other. 'I know the mother of this guy so he'll talk with me and I'll talk with him,' that sort of thing."[18] The GVN took advantage of family and other personal relationships more and more often after 1967, as the number of villagers employed in their native areas rose.

When villagers or VC pondered the decision to inform on the shadow government, their most important worry by far was whether the VC would find out what they had done. By the late 1960s, the VCI did not control the villagers' movements as often or surveil them as effectively as it had before, but it still had effective ways of identifying enemy informants and agents. If the Allies were not careful, the villagers knew, VC informants might see Allied informants talking to GVN intelligence personnel. When someone visited a GVN base area, the Viet Cong agents and informants who worked or lived near that base might very well spot that person and report this suspicious activity to the shadow government. Other people feared that the VC might guess who had provided particular information when only certain people could have known it. Brig. Gen. Tran Van Nhut, a South Vietnamese officer who held the position of province chief in Binh Long from 1970 to 1972, said that the Communists discovered some informants this way and killed them. "If we bought some information, and the information told us a guy was a Communist and we caught him, the VC would wonder how we knew. Maybe there was only one person who knew, so the Communists could figure out who he was."[19]

In some cases, villagers and VC were reluctant to cooperate because they suspected that GVN intelligence collectors and their coworkers lacked the motivation to act on the information or, much worse, that they secretly worked for the VC and would divulge their identities. One of the main reasons why villagers cooperated so readily with relatives was that they knew their relatives would not betray their identities to the VC. Many people chose to work with the Americans, rather than strangers from the GVN, because they believed that the Americans did not have Communist spies in their ranks, with the possible exception of their interpreters, whereas they knew that the GVN did. Rex Wilson observed that some VC would cooperate with him, "but they wouldn't work with the Special Police because they knew the Special Police had been penetrated by the VC." Wilson added, "Getting most information depended on whether someone trusted the person he was passing the information to."[20] Successful operations against the VC also helped to build the villagers' faith. The villager in Marine CAP hamlets, according to one study, "is hesitant at first . . . but when he sees his tip acted upon successfully, and sometimes immediately, his confidence increases and the flow of information follows suit."[21] Agencies that, over a period of time, had shielded their informants and agents well had better success in recruiting others.

VC personnel and the villagers knew that if the VC cadres identified them as informants or agents, Communist security squads likely would kidnap or kill them. Most members of the VC normally lived and operated with other Communists, so the shadow government could easily arrest and punish those whom it suspected of espionage. Most villagers and legal cadres were seemingly less vulnerable to Communist retribution because, by this time, the Communists did not live in most hamlets or visit them often and their counterintelligence capabilities had deteriorated dramatically. The Party still had the ability, however, to sneak into most hamlets at night and kidnap or kill someone. The odds of meeting resistance from Allied forces were considerably higher since the Allies had increased activities in the village areas at night, but, even when the Communists failed, they often tried again. "You could not physically protect every hamlet and every house in the district," Lt. Col. John L. Cook, a district-level Phoenix adviser in Bien Hoa province from 1968 to 1970, told me. "It was just a physical impossibility. No matter how hard you tried, the Viet Cong could kill a few people in a hamlet when they wanted to."[22] The numbers of civilians kidnapped or killed by the VC fluctuated from 1967 to 1972, but they did not display a marked downward trend.[23] They decreased substantially only in less important areas where the VC had become almost completely inactive.

The danger of reprisal discouraged some villagers and people within the VC from supplying information, yet many others decided to cooperate because they thought that the Allies would keep their identities hidden from the Communists. The Allied intelligence collectors employed a number of schemes to prevent the VC intelligence system from observing their contacts with particular spies. In many cases, they arranged secret meetings with their sources in out-of-the-way places. Sometimes, they sent letters back and forth to secret drop-off locations. Most agents and a few informants communicated with Allied agencies through "cutouts," inconspicuous intermediaries who passed along the correspondence wittingly or unwittingly. Typical examples included slipping information inside a shipment of food; delivering information through a VC's relative who was visiting a secret VC base, ostensibly on family business; concealing a letter on the body of a child; and sending messages in invisible ink.

Most Americans did not communicate directly with informants and agents, in part, to protect the sources from suspicion. A tall white American attracted much more attention in a Vietnamese hamlet than a Vietnamese rice trader, a dealer in black-market goods, or even a local militiaman; an African American could be even more conspicuous. Meeting an agent in a remote area to converse through an interpreter required more time than many Americans had. Most Americans also recognized that the South Vietnamese intelligence collectors normally had much greater knowledge than they did and thus had better ideas of whom to question and what to ask.

The Allies hid the identity of numerous informants and agents by meeting, one at a time, with large numbers of villagers so that the VC would not know which ones actually supplied intelligence. The Census Grievance Program employed this tactic on a systematic basis nationwide. Census Grievance cadres visited hamlets and interviewed someone from every family to find out what the peasants wanted the GVN to do differently. They kept tabs on each family's members and tracked the flow of people into and out of an area. In the course of their duties, these cadres developed intelligence on potential informants and on the VCI for their CIA sponsors. Most American advisers, both with the CIA and the military, thought that the program worked quite well, although frequently they could not verify or disprove everything in the cadres' reports. "The Census Grievance Program worked very well in some places," said James R. ("Jim") Ward, the CIA's region officer in charge in the Mekong Delta during 1967 and 1968. "It produced a heck of a lot of good intelligence. It identified many VCI, as well as grievances."[24]

Census Grievance information proved particularly valuable to armed forces not familiar with the hamlets in which they operated. U.S. Marine Col. William Corson, who headed the CAP and was not known to give compliments freely, notes, "The Census Grievance cadres do their work well. They prepare detailed maps of each hamlet indicating who is a VC sympathizer, who has a family member in the VC, who will inform, who provides material assistance to the VC, and so forth." Corson obtained a map from a Census Grievance cadre. "In subsequent weeks we staked out a house which the map indicated as that of a VC sympathizer, and intercepted, captured, or killed sixty active VC attempting to use the house for resupply, rest, or medical treatment."[25]

RD cadres also talked to all families in any given hamlet on a regular basis. Some of the cadres were intelligence specialists who reported to CIA officers and other people. From 1969 on, they interviewed the people more often as they took over many of the functions of the Census Grievance program, which the CIA dissolved in that year. Col. Carl Bernard, who served as province senior adviser in Hau Nghia, Vinh Binh, and several other provinces during the late 1960s, said of the RD cadres, "When you had that many guys working in a hamlet, they learned a lot. They were a considerable source of information. The police chief also had people in RD cadre uniforms working for him."[26]

Members of other intelligence agencies simply met with large groups of villagers on their arrival in an area. In addition, they often arrested substantial numbers of villagers and brought them in for questioning. Not only did the arrests provide them an opportunity to speak with informants, but they also caused the VC to suspect that everyone arrested might be a GVN informant, thus increasing the VC's counterintelligence burden. In some cases, intelligence collectors used other pacification operations as a screen behind which they met with much of the population. Comdr. Frank C. Brown, then a medic in Chau Doc province, regularly visited different hamlets as part of a program to provide free medical services to the villagers. Some

Kit Carson Scouts went along to talk to the many people who milled around the medical team. Brown said, "We always took three or four Scouts and they would mingle with the crowd. In some cases they had informants that were in that area and they would check in with them. Later when we got back to the team house, there would be a briefing about what the Scouts found."[27]

Some informants and agents had jobs, or claimed to have jobs, that allowed them to make contacts with various people and perhaps to dole out money without arousing too much suspicion. Jobs such as teacher, black-marketeer, merchant, pimp, drug dealer, and doctor worked well, for people in such positions had to meet privately with the village population as well as with GVN or American personnel, and some normally carried large amounts of money. Other people, such as woodcutters and smugglers, had good excuses to go into unpopulated areas and look around. Sometimes, intelligence gatherers who worked for the GVN in various capacities disguised themselves as ordinary villagers or VC in order to reach their meeting places without arousing suspicion. Lt. Col. Dao Quan Hien, the National Police chief of III Corps from 1968 to 1971, recalled: "In the villages, some people from the Special Police had to dress as VC to infiltrate the jungle, the forest, the village to get intelligence or make contact with their secret agents."[28]

The VC acknowledged that the Allies enjoyed considerable success in concealing their informants and agents when using these guises. A 1971 captured document, for instance, states, "The enemy has applied the 'fine tooth comb' tactic throughout [South Vietnam] and planted his spies among the merchants who travel between [GVN] controlled areas and our liberated areas to collect information. Disguised Special Forces troops have mingled with the people in our liberated areas to discover our transportation corridors and messing and billeting areas."[29]

In certain places, the GVN accepted anonymous tips, thus allowing voluntary village informants to conceal their identities. In Dinh Tuong province, for example, villagers put notes addressed to the police into mailboxes, and these notes apparently provided a considerable amount of useful information.[30] This type of system offered villagers complete safety, except in the very unlikely event that a VC source in the police recognized an individual's handwriting. The big shortcoming, though, was that the Allies did not know the reliability of the source unless the person chose to give a pseudonym each time he or she wrote and established credibility through a series of good reports.

Intelligence bureaucracies tried to limit the amount of money given to informants and agents. A sudden increase in someone's wealth would suggest to the VC that he or she was receiving money from the Allies. Almost no informants received large sums of money. "Informants didn't receive enough money to attract attention," said Gary Mattocks, a region-level PRU adviser in IV Corps and II Corps during the early 1970s. "It really wasn't that much money."[31] With some penetration agents, the amount of money was high enough that an agency had to be careful how much it paid out at a time. Mudrinich told me, "You wouldn't give him money to take back to his village in amounts that would attract attention. You wouldn't give the person a fistful of money and say, 'Okay, we'll see you again next month, and if you produce again, we'll give you another fistful of money.' He was usually only given what he could reasonably account for with his friends. Sometimes you'd give him other things, like medical care for family members."[32] Some agents received payments in escrow accounts, which they could obtain when they stopped reporting or, if they were in the VC, when they defected.

On occasion, Allied intelligence gatherers or their informants or agents thought that exploitation of a source's information might alert the VC to the source's identity. The information would go unused unless it was so important that it warranted risking exposure of the source. If the Allies thought that they should act on it, the collector or the source had to decide whether the source should try to remain in place and hope to avoid detection or flee to an area held by the GVN. "There were some instances where sources disappeared after we used their information in an operation," recalled Warren Milberg, the CIA's province officer in charge in Quang Tri and then a member of the CIA I Corps staff in the late 1960s. "We always attempted to balance the need to use information against the potential harm to the provider. Sometimes we succeeded, sometimes we did not."[33] The intelligence agency in question, if its officials were particularly uncaring, also could exploit the intelligence without telling the source of the dangers that he or she faced. This fate befell a small number of informants and agents.

The Allies also tried hard to prevent VC spies within Allied organizations from discovering Allied informants and agents. Many commentators have exaggerated the presence of VC sources in GVN organizations from the late 1960s onward. Most of them used as their main piece of evidence a 1970 CIA report that estimated the Communists had thirty thousand agents in the GVN.[34] Just how many full-time agents the VC actually had shall never be known, but thirty thousand is far too high. Secret Communist documents from this period express considerable disappointment with the number of Communist agents in the GVN, a development detailed in chapter 23.

CIA officer Rudolph ("Rudy") Enders, who served in Vietnam during most of the period 1966–72, investigated this matter and found out why the estimate was so high. When Enders returned to the United States for a short time in 1969, he examined the calculations of Sam Adams, the controversial CIA analyst who had come up with the figure of thirty thousand, and discovered a flaw that rendered the estimate meaningless. Enders explained to me, "Sam got his information from reading the captured documents, but those documents were worthless. The Communists lied to their superiors so that they wouldn't look bad, just as a lot of people on our side did. As an example of the VC's penetrations, Sam used the military proselyting section of Sub-Region 23, which was under the command of Tu Thang. Sam said, 'Tu Thang has five hundred penetrations in Hau Nghia province.' I told him, 'That's ridiculous. There aren't even five hundred people in ARVN and the police for the VC to penetrate in Hau Nghia.'" Later, after Enders returned to Vietnam, a rallier helped him and other CIA advisers to capture a large number of cadres in Hau Nghia. After interrogating all of the prisoners, talking to ralliers, and cross-checking the testimony, the CIA advisers concluded that the VC proselyting section had only two penetrations, not five hundred, in Hau Nghia. "One was the valet of the province chief," Enders told me, "which was a very good penetration because the guy had access to a lot of information. The other was a policeman."[35]

The VC, indeed, regularly inflated all types of success. A Party document from August 1968, for example, claims: "Recently, the U.S. troops also suffered great losses. The casualty rate was very high: one hundred and forty thousand casualties in seven months."[36] The United States actually suffered approximately sixty-one thousand casualties during the entire year of 1968.[37] The comments of a former district-level VCI are typical of those of many ex-VC leaders:

> I don't think the higher cadres were well informed about what was going on in my area. . . . The reports [to higher cadres] were only about fifty percent correct, because we based them on the reports from village and hamlet cadres, which were mostly not well-founded. And we didn't have enough time or means to check them. Many low cadres only thought of falsifying favorable reports to set a commendable record.[38]

When estimating the number of VC agents, one also has to be careful about definitions. The VC might have received bits and pieces of information at one time or another from twenty or thirty thousand people within the GVN. Far fewer, however, possessed the full-time commitment to the VC to qualify as agents. The value of informants and agents also varied greatly. Considering the poor internal security in GVN organizations of minimal importance, such as the People's Self-Defense Forces, the VC easily could have acquired large numbers of informants or agents in such organizations. During the late 1960s, in fact, when the shadow government became much less effective in conducting its overt activities, it stepped up efforts to infiltrate such programs. A whole host of these low-level informants or agents would have been far less useful than one spy on the staff of a province chief.

Most of the Communist informants and agents in the GVN could not inform the Communists of all, or even most, of the operations to which they had access. They needed to let some of these operations succeed in order to avoid arousing suspicion in their colleagues. Col. Douglas ("Doug") Dillard, deputy Phoenix coordinator in IV Corps during 1968 and 1969, recalled, "The VC sacrificed some of their men so as not to compromise their penetration in our system."[39] Many of the spies, in fact, performed well in their GVN jobs to fool others into believing that they detested the Communists. Gary E. Masters, who spent most of the war's last years in Vietnam with the U.S. Army First Military Intelligence Detachment and then with the CIA in Phu Yen and Bien Hoa provinces, explained, "GVN employees were probably the VC's best source of information, but often they had to do good work for the GVN to keep their jobs. So who benefited most?"[40]

Allied organizations, of course, sought to avoid hiring people tied to the VC and to remove any who were already embedded in their ranks. The South Vietnamese Military Security Service identified and neutralized some of the applicants and Allied personnel who spied for the VC, as did other organizations. The organizations with the best leadership generally succeeded most often at finding the guilty, although, in many cases, the information resulted from luck—such as the appearance of a captured document or a cooperative rallier—more than anything else. In some of their documents, the Communists reported that the Allies had identified their spies within the GVN and put them out of action. A 1970 report from the VC's Ba Ria–Long Khanh Province Party Committee stated that the enemy "intensified

Phuong Hoang activities, destroyed our espionage installations by collecting information (on our) intelligence activities, discovered our agents and attacked them, kept the people from making contact with us, and classified and organized the people into groups."[41] Most of the South Vietnamese whom I interviewed said that GVN counterintelligence discovered some Communist spies in their ranks but left a considerable number of others untouched because they were too hard to find. "The Military Security Service helped us find PRUs who worked for the VC," Col. Viet Lang told me. "They had good information and gave it to us. When we found out someone was a traitor, we shot him and reported, 'We went on an operation and the guy was killed during the operation.' A few PRU leaders were caught spying, but we had a trial for them and put them in jail. Still, the Communists had other spies we did not find."[42]

Americans tried to make sure that their interpreters, principal agents in the GVN, and cutouts did not work for the Communists. The CIA regularly gave these individuals polygraph tests and checked their loyalty through other intelligence sources; it succeeded in weeding out many who were suspicious. Other American organizations, however, did not enjoy much success in vetting their South Vietnamese assistants because they lacked polygraph machines and good intelligence assets of their own.

The Allies took additional precautions that often prevented information from leaking to Communist spies. In cases where the Allies had identified possible VC collaborators but had not removed them, they kept sensitive information away from them. Most people in GVN organizations feared spies throughout their own ranks anyway, regardless of whether they knew who they were, and limited the distribution of information to the greatest extent possible. Leaders of intelligence agencies had their subordinates employ trusted family members and friends to collect information as much as possible. They knew that intelligence collectors would guard the identities of their relatives and friends very carefully from possible VC penetrations into the organization.

Counterintelligence tasks called for skilled and vigilant leadership, which the Americans possessed more often than the South Vietnamese. Of all the pacification organizations staffed by the Vietnamese, the PRUs possessed good leadership most consistently and, therefore, they suffered least often from information leaks. Gary Mattocks said of the PRUs, "The loss of informants to Communist countermeasures never was a problem on a large scale."[43] On the whole, Allied intelligence-gathering organizations generally had leadership of sufficient quality to prevent the Communists from identifying most of their informants and agents. At times, the VC conceded their inability to identify and neutralize most Allied informants and agents. A Sub-Region 2 document of February 1970 declares, "We have not yet been determined to . . . eradicate enemy spies"; it adds, "Neither have we succeeded in detecting the enemy's underground elements and personnel."[44]

In the first phase of the Phoenix era, CIA case officers obtained a great deal of useful information on the VC and VCI in the villages from their own informants and agents. Some CORDS advisers and U.S. military intelligence personnel also tried to get the same sort of information from informants and agents. They had fewer funds and poorer interpreters than CIA officers, however, and their training, experience, and innate skills usually did not match those of CIA personnel. Few generated much useful information on the shadow government and its cohorts in the village war.

During the initial years of Phoenix, the informants and agents of the Special Police generated a considerable amount of information on the VCI in some areas and at some echelons. Inadequate intelligence personnel impaired the informant and agent operations of the Special Police and most other GVN organizations at the district level and, to a lesser extent, at the provincial level. Many members of the Special Police lacked the experience or skills necessary for cultivating informants during these years. In March 1968, legendary pacification adviser John Paul Vann wrote, "The majority of the Special Branch Police do not presently possess sufficient qualifications or training to enable them to do the job, and . . . there is a very limited number of them present in the districts."[45] The armed forces had the highest personnel priority. They also offered better chances for promotion and, until 1971, much better pay than did the police. As a result, the military generally took the cream of South Vietnamese youth and left the less capable to the nonmilitary organizations, with the exception of the PRUs, at all levels. The police did attract some people with raw talent but not necessarily with the desire to use it. As Masters observed, "Many people in these jobs were the children of rich families and had the positions bought for them. They knew them to be safe places from which to watch the war."[46]

More important than the abilities of the rank and file, however, was the quality of leadership. As a general rule, the Special Police performed well where they had good leaders and performed poorly otherwise. Good leaders trained the rank and file and stimulated them to seek intelligence sources aggressively and persistently. "When you are commander," Lt. Col. Dao Quan Hien said, "the way you command determines whether the men under you perform well or poorly. If you are a good leader, your men are effective. If you do nothing except try to make money, your men don't do anything."[47] Robert ("Rob") Simmons served in Vietnam for a year and a half during the 1960s as a U.S. Army intelligence officer and returned in 1970, after learning the Vietnamese language, for two years as a CIA adviser to the Phu Yen province Special Police. Simmons observed, "If you had a police chief or Special Police chief who was not dynamic, not a lot would get done."[48] The military provided the police's leadership and, during most of the Phoenix era, did not assign many of its better people to the police; the police generally had good officers only at the provincial level in the more important provinces. Komer and Parker persuaded and pressured the district and province chiefs, who controlled the Special Police in part, and the Phung Hoang section of the Special Police in Saigon to get the Special Police to generate more intelligence on the shadow government. Their efforts caused some improvement, but the South Vietnamese did not cooperate as much as they wanted.

The role of the Special Police in the attack on the VCI shifted somewhat at the end of 1968 when Ted Shackley replaced Lew Lapham as CIA station chief in Saigon. Shortly after his arrival, Shackley began withdrawing a large chunk of the CIA's resources from pacification programs and reallocating most of them to strategic intelligence collection. Shackley took the CIA advisers out of the RD Cadre and Census Grievance programs, which CORDS had controlled since mid-1968. CORDS advisers began staffing the RD Cadre program. Shackley dissolved Census Grievance and assigned its functions to the RD Cadre program and other organizations. He also phased out the CIA's management role in the Phoenix program by mid-1969 and let CORDS personnel take over. Shackley did not remove the CIA from its relationships with the PRUs and the Special Police, but he did reduce the number of CIA Special Police advisers charged with attacking the shadow government and assigned many more CIA case officers to Special Police and unilateral operations aimed at penetrating the Viet Cong and the GVN.

Shackley pressured his officers to recruit more upper-level VC as agents and to use informants and agents less often for tactical intelligence on low-level VC and VCI and more often for strategic intelligence. Until that time, the CIA had recruited few agents in the VC above the village level and had emphasized low-level tactical intelligence over strategic intelligence. Neither Shackley nor then–CIA Director Richard Helms, who had to approve the policy, agreed to speak to me about the reasons for this major change. Shackley, however, discussed the decision with others in Vietnam, among them William Colby, Evan Parker, Jr., and Col. Doug Dillard. Helms, and perhaps Shackley as well, wanted to get the CIA out of pacification as much as possible because of negative publicity about Phoenix and the PRUs that was beginning to emerge. Apparently, Helms or Shackley, or both, also had concluded that strategic intelligence collection deserved more of the CIA's resources and pacification deserved fewer of them. Perhaps the decline of the VC and the growing importance of the North Vietnamese Army in the South convinced them that strategic intelligence was more important at that time.[49]

With the added emphasis on penetrations, the CIA and its agents in the Special Police made limited headway in penetrating the VC at the district level and above. Most of the targets lived in remote, protected areas, where only family members or other VC, if anyone, could contact them. Usually, the Special Police or CIA officers had to convince the family members to cooperate and to urge their VC relatives to cooperate; this was difficult because high-level VC were the most loyal VC. Other cutouts and agents were generally too unreliable for this type of work. The Special Police and CIA case officers chased many possible leads and some claimed to have penetrated the enemy. In only a few cases, most of which involved a good deal of luck, did the CIA or its helpers actually penetrate the VC structure at the district level or above. Gregg said, "The good officers were very frustrated. The guys who sort of went along to go along were less frustrated. They basically accepted what was given out."[50]

The South Vietnamese hid their valuable penetrations of the VC from the Americans. "Most of the Special Police chiefs weren't of any use to us Americans," Flitcroft said, "but we had so little information about what they were doing. I'm sure the Special Police had all kinds of stuff going on that they didn't tell us about. Why should they have told us? In the first place, we'd immediately have told them how to do it."[51] Several senior GVN officers told me that the GVN had penetrations at the highest levels of the Communist hierarchy. Others who had spent time in reeducation camps after the war said they met prisoners there who had been high-ranking VC cadres and had been imprisoned by the Communists for spying. American advisers told me that people in the GVN had informed them, during the war and since, that they had high-level penetrations of the VC. In most cases, the high-ranking VC passed information to relatives in the GVN. Captured VC documents noted, on occasion, that the Allies had spies in positions of considerable importance who caused VC personnel losses. A circular from VC Military Region 5 concerning activities during 1970, for example, affirms, "Some enemy spies did work in our district Party Committees and provided guidance for the enemy to kill 55 friendly personnel."[52] The distinction between CIA and Special Police intelligence operations escaped the Americans who claim that the Allies enjoyed almost no success in penetrating the VC.

The reorientation of the CIA's Special Police advisory effort did not substantially reduce the Special Police's output of low-level VCI intelligence because a gradual improvement in the quality and quantity of Special Police personnel offset this change. The increased GVN emphasis on the "other war" after the Tet offensive improved the personnel situation within the Special Police and other pacification organizations. During 1971, however, the Special Police still had considerable room for improvement. John S. Tilton, Phoenix director from mid-1971 to late 1972 and subsequently the CIA's deputy station chief for a year, wrote in August 1971: "The problem of lack of trained and experienced people . . . remains, both with the National Police and Police Special Branch."[53] American advisers noticed that the Special Police leadership and performance improved greatly from 1971 to 1973 as the GVN put substantial effort into strengthening the organization. CIA case officers, although continuing to recruit many informants and agents, were less likely than before to use their assets to root out the shadow government.

In most provinces and at most times, the PRUs enjoyed more success than other South Vietnamese organizations in collecting information for operational use in the village war from the populace and the VC. The PRUs relied only on informants, not agents, and few of their informants occupied high positions in the shadow government. Through their informants, nevertheless, the PRUs amassed a high volume of tactical intelligence on the lower-ranking members of the shadow government. "We had good coverage," Bruce Lawlor told me. "We had informants almost everywhere."[54] Col. Viet Lang said, "The PRUs had informants in almost every hamlet. Most were relatives or acquaintances of the PRUs who lived in the villages the PRUs came from."[55]

Most of the credit for this success belongs to the PRU leadership, which was usually first-rate, and the presence of relatives of PRU members in the villages. Other organizations over which the Americans exerted considerable control, such as CAP platoons and, until 1969, RD Cadres and Census Grievance, developed good informants in some cases for most of the same reasons. Usually, they were not as successful as the PRUs—their achievements were closer to those of the Special Police—because their leadership quality was usually a step below that of the PRUs and they did not have as many indigenous personnel. The territorial forces, when favored with able leaders, as they often were, obtained a large amount of information through their local contacts. The rest of the GVN organizations generally performed less well. They acquired many useful informants only when they had good leadership, which they often lacked.

Communist sources confirmed that Allied informant and agent activities caused serious problems for Communist personnel in and around the hamlets, although most of their statements about the attack on the VCI have focused on its overall effects, rather than on the effects of specific portions. They spoke increasingly often of these troubles after the Tet offensive. COSVN Resolution 9 of July 1969, perhaps the most famous and momentous Communist document of the war, states:

> The American imperialists are very obstinate and cunning; although forced to gradually de-escalate the war, they strengthen and expand their espionage war in order to serve their "hold and sweep" strategy and their pacification scheme. . . . [Our] movement to guard against espionage and protect secrets has prevented, in part, the enemy's attempts to sabotage us, but it has not become an extensive and strong people's security network which is highly effective in guarding against and fighting the enemy. . . . The Party's organization principles and activities, and the systems and internal regulations regarding anti-espionage and secrecy preservation work, have not been strictly enforced. The enemy has taken advantage of those deficiencies to attack and cause damage to us.[56]

8 Prisoners: Interrogation, Torture, and Execution

n the war against the shadow government, success followed upon success. Sometimes. Communists and Communist supporters who were captured during fruitful operations, like the Allies' informants and agents within the VC, knew a great deal about the shadow government. The only differences between the Communist prisoners and the Allied informants and agents as sources of information were that prisoners no longer had continuous access to information and that, once the Communists learned of their capture, they could take steps to reduce their own vulnerability should the prisoners cooperate with the GVN. Many prisoners, of course, were reluctant to give information to the Allies. In this type of war, the process of extracting information from these prisoners was bound to involve many mistakes and considerable brutality.

A great variety of organizations interrogated prisoners, and multiple organizations often interrogated a single prisoner if he or she seemed important. Which organization would have an opportunity to interrogate a person became quite controversial at times. When an operational unit captured someone, it frequently had one day to interrogate that person. During this time, it might pass along the prisoner to interrogators from other units in the area as well. The unit then turned its catch over to higher authorities at the district or provincial level. Soldiers captured by pacification forces might be sent to ARVN or U.S. military interrogators or, along with prisoners classified as civilian detainees, be sent through nonmilitary channels for further interrogation.

The responsibility for handling nonmilitary prisoners ostensibly belonged to the National Police. Senior Americans and South Vietnamese with other organizations in a district or provincial compound, however, were supposed to send notice of any potentially important prisoners to their superiors at the echelon above them—province, corps, or Saigon—who might want to take custody of the prisoners themselves. The people at the higher tiers picked up prisoners from local compounds when they thought that these prisoners could supply strategic intelligence. In addition, some officers at the upper echelons wanted to interrogate prisoners, even if their importance was dubious, because they satisfied their own bosses and gained promotions by extracting as much information from prisoners as possible.

Often, a helicopter from higher headquarters snatched away a prisoner so quickly that the local interrogators did not have a chance to obtain much tactical information. Sometimes, the higher level sent a report of the interrogation or, in a few instances, the actual prisoner to people in the district or province where the prisoner had been captured. Unless the organizations involved were particularly sophisticated or well organized, this feedback usually arrived weeks or months later when much of the information was useless. The higher-level interrogators, moreover, usually did not put as much effort into asking about local details of the village war as those at the lower level did and, typically, did not know enough about this subject to interrogate most effectively. These problems exasperated many people at the lower levels who needed intelligence about the local VCI. Warren Milberg frequently witnessed the movement of prisoners to higher levels. "Interrogation reports resulting from such situations," Milberg laments, "did not filter back to the province where the prisoner originated until months later. Far too much time elapsed for the interrogation report to be useful in identifying other VCI and mounting operations to neutralize them."[1]

Sometimes, the people at a lower level were so certain that they deserved priority in interrogating a prisoner that they hid the prisoner from higher levels. Lloyd Pomeroy, a CORDS Phoenix adviser in An Xuyen and Kien Hoa provinces in 1969–70, recalled, "Because of lack of feedback when headquarters took prisoners, it was not unknown for the Vietnamese in Kien Hoa to withhold from higher headquarters knowledge that prisoners had been captured. This withholding was temporary, a matter of a few hours, perhaps, or a couple of days on the outside, until they could evaluate what or who they had. It took some courage."[2]

In many cases, the actions of the higher echelons were justified. Interrogators at higher administrative levels tended to be more capable and experienced and had a better view of strategic issues. If they were Americans, they more likely spoke Vietnamese or had better interpreters. As a result, they frequently obtained strategic intelligence that exceeded in value anything that a lower echelon might have extracted. Rob Simmons saw the issue from a good perspective. As a province-level CIA officer, he pulled up prisoners from the districts. He also watched the CIA's II Corps headquarters in Nha Trang take prisoners away from him before he was through with them, although he could normally keep the prisoners longer than non-CIA advisers could. "We usually only had seventy-two hours with prisoners before they were pulled out to Nha Trang if Nha Trang wanted them," Simmons told me. He believed that the upper echelons grabbed prisoners from below for good reasons. "People constantly complained that we had somebody really good and then suddenly he was taken away, but the higher headquarters was usually in a better position to exploit him than we were."[3]

Pacification advisers at all levels also found it difficult to get their hands on knowledgeable Communists captured by American or South Vietnamese military forces, as well as those whom the pacification forces turned over to the military. Because military units captured numerous VCI who were carrying weapons, they usually sent these cadres along with ordinary guerrillas and soldiers through the military prisoner channels. When cadres went through prisoner-of-war channels, the pacification authorities most often did not have an opportunity to interrogate them and, in many cases, never even learned of their capture. The CORDS report from Quang Tri province for the month of May 1968 notes that this problem seriously weakened intelligence initiatives against the VCI: "A lack of complete understanding on the part of US combat units still adversely affected the Phoenix program in Quang Tri Province in May. . . . Some G-2's and S-2's tended to interpret the regulations governing civilian detainees too strictly: Any person caught with a gun was automatically a POW."[4]

CIA advisers in the Province Interrogation Centers, where many important nonmilitary prisoners went for questioning, watched over the Special Police interrogations there, hired their own South Vietnamese interrogators to work in the centers, and conducted some interrogations themselves through interpreters. Soldiers in U.S. combat and intelligence units and Americans in some other organizations also conducted debriefings and interrogations through interpreters. With prisoners who did not serve in main force units, however, the Americans usually allowed the South Vietnamese to do most of the questioning. Interrogating or debriefing through an interpreter was cumbersome, and interpreters were not always reliable. The Vietnamese were not inclined to answer questions directly and immediately, particularly when foreigners were asking them. As a result, the American interrogators were less likely to know the best way to structure the sessions. In addition, the GVN often held more prisoners than the Americans could handle by themselves.

Many Vietnamese interrogators lacked the skills for effective interrogation. Some knew little about proper interrogation techniques or even what questions to ask. Others, for whatever reason, pretended to know little. The frequent assignment of inferior officers and rank-and-file personnel to interrogation positions caused these weaknesses. During March and April 1968, official CORDS evaluators John G. Lybrand and L. Craig Johnstone conducted a thorough study of the attack on the Viet Cong infrastructure in II Corps. They concluded, "Interrogation methods were usually poor. . . . At all levels there was a critical lack of qualified interrogators." Lybrand and Johnstone, who were familiar with the American pacification programs throughout Vietnam, added that their conclusions held true in the other three corps areas of Vietnam as well.[5]

As always, some organizations did not suffer greatly from these problems, at least in high-priority areas and in such important places as the Province Interrogation Centers (PICs). CIA officers who advised the PICs in all parts of the country indicated that the centers had some capable and knowledgeable interrogators who succeeded in getting prisoners to talk. "In II Corps we got a lot of low-level, tactical information from the PICs," Dean Almy said. "There wasn't a lot of high-level intelligence. Maybe that wasn't so important, though. We were trying to win the war, and we were collecting information on the VCI and tactical military intelligence, which helped."[6] Dan Mudrinich described PIC personnel in IV Corps: "The Vietnamese interrogators were not seasoned professionals, but they were not bad."[7] Special Police advisers, in addition, were not present at all PIC interrogations, so the Americans did not know about every success that the South Vietnamese achieved.

A number of other organizations interrogated prisoners, some quite successfully, so the weakness of some PICs did not impede the Allied war effort in the hamlets substantially. Many CIA advisers gained valuable information by using their own interrogators and interpreters to talk to prisoners. South Vietnamese in other organizations and U.S. military intelligence personnel successfully interrogated prisoners on a regular basis. Col. Horace Hunter knew a good deal about the Vietnamese. He served a tour as an ARVN adviser during the early 1960s, a second tour as a U.S. Army battalion commander during the mid-1960s, and a third tour as deputy province senior adviser in Chau Doc and province senior adviser in An Xuyen. "The Vietnamese had some skilled interrogators," Hunter said. "I was particularly impressed with some of our province S-2 section in Chau Doc."[8]

Allied interrogators employed a great variety of techniques to make prisoners talk. The one that captured the most attention, of course, was torture. Some people define torture as the infliction of *severe* physical pain on a defenseless person. In this book, I define torture as the infliction of *any* pain on a defenseless individual because deciding which activities inflict severe pain is an excessively complicated and imprecise business; I differentiate some activities by their severity, however, when discussing torture in detail. Under my definition, it is clear that the large majority of South Vietnamese interrogators tortured some or all of the Communist prisoners in their care. A smaller number tortured villagers suspected of collaborating with the Communists. Depending on who administered the torture, others involved in the interrogation, and the local conditions, the frequency and method of torture varied. In their study on II Corps, Lybrand and Johnstone report, "The truncheon and electric shock method of interrogation were in widespread use, with almost all advisors admitting to have witnessed instances of the use of these methods."[9]

It should be noted that a significant minority of South Vietnamese, many of them in organizations advised by the CIA, did not torture prisoners regularly. In 1971, Congressman Jerome Waldie visited Vietnam in search of Allied abuses. An opponent of the war, Waldie wanted evidence that would give more justification for U.S. disengagement. During his visit, he entered a number of Province Interrogation Centers unannounced, yet, he later stated, "I saw nothing in any of the centers to which I had access that led me to believe that abuses, in fact, did occur in the province interrogation centers," except in one center, where an adviser suspected that the Vietnamese used water torture but had no evidence of it.[10] Some Americans who regularly kept their eyes on prisoners and checked them for bruises and other signs of mistreatment could tell that their South Vietnamese counterparts seldom, if ever, tortured their prisoners. Lt. Comdr. Michael Walsh, a PRU adviser who sat in on many interrogations at the Chau Doc Province Interrogation Center, remembers, "I never witnessed any of the media horror stories that abound to this day about Phoenix interrogations at the PICs. The men I worked with were experts in their field, and they used their minds to conquer the spirit of those they were questioning."[11]

Interrogators who used force on prisoners most often resorted to beatings, electric shock, and water torture. This description of a GVN interrogator's methods gives an idea of some standard procedures:

Thanh left the fort with a strong force of PFs and police. They returned near noon, driving in their midst two men and three women, their faces bruised and their arms bound behind them. Throughout the afternoon Thanh methodically beat and slapped the captives. . . . When one woman refused to talk, he rubbed a wet cloth with lye soap and pressed it against her face. The woman struggled to breathe and sucked into her throat the stinging lye. He drew back the cloth before she suffocated, let her gasp for air once, then slapped the rag back against her face. Eventually, the gagging woman started to speak in sobs and Thanh extracted the information he sought.[12]

Some GVN personnel sexually abused female prisoners, as the Viet Cong often did and as some prisoner handlers in almost any wartime organization will do.

The Vietnamese pacification forces seldom employed gruesome forms of torture, such as breaking bones, sawing through flesh, or chopping off fingers. Although the American advisers did not see what happened to every single prisoner, they observed enough to determine the general practices of the South Vietnamese. Only on a few occasions did any of them witness particularly barbaric acts or see prisoners who had suffered them earlier. The comments of Richard ("Rick") Welcome, a PRU adviser in Binh Thuan province during 1968 and 1969, typify the observations of Americans who knew what was happening to most prisoners: "Prisoners were abused. Were they tortured? It depends on what you call torture. Electricity was used by the Vietnamese, water was used, occasionally some of the prisoners got beat up. Were any of them put on the rack, eyes gouged out, bones broken? No, I never saw any evidence of that at all."[13]

A small number of Americans have alleged that both Americans and Vietnamese regularly used heinous methods. Yoshia K. Chee, who claimed that he served as a PRU adviser while a member of the Special Forces, asserted:

One of the favorite things was popping one of their eyeballs out with a spoon. . . . You could do anything—like skinning the bottom of their feet and beating them with a bamboo rod. . . . [The South Vietnamese would] use K-bars to saw on people till they got down to the bone. One side of the K-bar is serrated, so they'd keep sawing until they got to the marrow. . . . Or chopping fingers off, that was very Vietnamese.[14]

As with many amazing tales, there is good reason to doubt Chee's testimony. One man familiar with fraudulent stories of the Vietnam War is

B. G. Burkett, who has made a name for himself by discrediting hundreds of people who have spoken falsely about the war. At my request, Burkett searched U.S. military personnel records for information on Chee. The military kept accurate records of its personnel who served as PRU advisers, despite the secrecy surrounding the PRU program. Burkett could not find a single record for a Yoshia K. Chee. Chee said that he received a Silver Star, but Burkett did not find his name on the official lists of Silver Star recipients. Burkett also found other glaring factual inaccuracies in Chee's testimony. For example, Chee had asserted that a considerable number of U.S. Special Forces soldiers were killed while operating with him on 1 April 1969 and 25 December 1969,[15] but in fact the record shows that not a single man from the Special Forces died on those days or on the preceding and following days.[16] Many other details given by Chee are inconsistent with the observations of Americans who definitely served in Vietnam. Chee's claims are not supported by any substantiated evidence, and they are contradicted by most of the evidence available.

In a significant number of cases, the South Vietnamese killed Communist prisoners whom they had questioned or Communists who were trying to surrender. At times, they executed one prisoner in an effort, sometimes successful, to scare another prisoner into talking. The killing of prisoners and potential prisoners usually occurred shortly after a firefight, before the passions of battle subsided. Col. Viet Lang noted that the main motivation of PRU members for killing prisoners was the injury or death of comrades in battle: "Sometimes the PRUs killed prisoners when the operation went bad and they took casualties."[17] American soldiers in Vietnam almost never killed prisoners except in the immediate aftermath of a battle.

In all armies of the world, torture and execution of prisoners and surrendering soldiers have occurred regularly on the battlefield. The esteemed British military historian Richard Holmes writes: "No soldier who fights until his enemy is at close small-arms range, in any war, has more than perhaps a fifty-fifty chance of being granted quarter. If he stands up to surrender he risks being shot with the time-honoured comment, 'Too late, chum.' If he lies low, he will fall victim to the grenades of the mopping-up party, in no mood to take chances."[18]

Less often, the South Vietnamese killed prisoners for reasons other than the desire for immediate information or battlefield rage. Some killed prisoners simply out of long-standing hatred or meanness. Others did so when they could not send prisoners through military prisoner channels, fearing that these people would not remain in jail for long. For a variety of reasons, the GVN set free many of the VCI and VCI suspects who went through the civilian detention system shortly after their capture. Killing these VC cadres was the only sure way to put an end to their activities, and the South Vietnamese forces wanted to make certain, at any cost, that their adversaries did not return. Usually the GVN personnel killed people for this reason only when they were positive that they were VC, and they spared some of the known VC who provided information. Some pacification forces executed people to prevent them from slipping through the jail system only if they had been released from prison previously. Jim Ward said, "Sometimes the PRUs would go out and kill a guy, and we'd ask them, 'Why didn't you capture him and bring him back?' They'd say, 'We captured him three times before in the last six months.' It was hard to blame the PRUs for doing that."[19] The problem declined somewhat during the late 1960s and early 1970s as the judicial system improved and the prisons expanded.

Allied forces, except for some South Korean Army units and ARVN main force units, did not execute prisoners as a systematic policy. Most of the South Vietnamese pacification forces executed a relatively small fraction of their prisoners. According to the observations of the U.S. advisers who talked to me, most prisoners survived captivity. The Americans also asserted that the pacification forces did not kill large numbers of prisoners to prevent their release from prison. "I don't think the PRUs were very concerned that the guys they picked up would be released from prison," Daren Flitcroft told me. "They wouldn't kill them for that reason. They may have done so in certain cases, but not as a general rule."[20] American soldiers executed prisoners even less often, and CIA and CORDS advisers rarely, if ever, did.

Some historians claim that Allied pacification forces killed far more prisoners than I contend that they killed. Most of them present as key evidence the testimony of Kenneth Barton Osborn, who served as an enlisted man with the 149th and 525th Military Intelligence Groups near Da Nang in 1967 and 1968. Osborn captured the public's attention when he appeared before a congressional committee in 1971 to condemn the "Phoenix program." One of Osborn's most serious accusations dealt with the treatment of Communists and suspected Communists in Allied custody:

> I never knew an individual to be detained as a VC suspect who ever lived
> through an interrogation in a year and a half, and that included quite a num-
> ber of individuals. . . . There was never any reasonable establishment of the

fact that any of those individuals was, in fact, cooperating with the Vietcong, but they all died and the majority were either tortured to death or things like thrown from helicopters.[21]

Osborn remains an authority—often the primary authority—on Phoenix for many opponents of the U.S. war effort. Those who embrace Osborn, unfortunately, show a disturbing unwillingness to investigate the truthfulness of his claims.

Osborn wrongly attributed to Phoenix the killing of prisoners that he supposedly witnessed. Neither the Phoenix directorate nor other pacification organizations controlled the U.S. Marines who handled the prisoners in question. Perhaps Osborn latched onto the Phoenix name because it sounded like the appropriate name for a deadly counterinsurgency program or because the mystery and rumors surrounding the Phoenix program suggested that it might be responsible for some wicked deeds. Other such flaws in Osborn's statements are readily apparent to the knowledgeable observer.

After the congressional hearings, the U.S. Army Intelligence Command investigated Osborn's allegations and uncovered a wealth of concrete information that contradicted his allegations. A brief summary of this investigation became available to the public—although few seemed to notice it—in 1973 during the confirmation hearings of William Colby for the position of Director of Central Intelligence.[22] The Army did not declassify the much more substantive text of the investigation report itself,[23] however, until 1995 at my request. Investigators assigned to the case interviewed many people who had worked with Osborn while he was in Vietnam. All of the interviewees indicated that Osborn had made false statements in his congressional testimony. They asserted, for instance, that no American soldiers received instruction at Fort Holabird, Maryland, in killing their own agents, as Osborn had alleged; that Osborn exaggerated the number of intelligence sources under his jurisdiction, as well as his level of responsibility and the importance of his achievements; that Osborn, in direct contradiction of his own testimony, worked under the close control of a superior in the military chain of command; and that Osborn received his pay not through secret monthly meetings with an army captain, as he testified, but through his team's office or through the 149/525 Battalion Headquarters.

One of the most serious accusations that the investigation disproved was Osborn's claim that an American captain had murdered Osborn's interpreter, a woman of Chinese ethnicity. Osborn described this captain, whom he refused to name, as follows: "There was an American captain who had wanted to be an agent handler himself and found only the enlisted men could do this kind of thing and found himself without a job. Officially he was in charge of intelligence contingency fund money; that is, money for the Army for agent operations. There was no money and no job for him."[24] The captain supposedly killed the interpreter on Osborn's driveway one afternoon. "His reason, his motivation for doing this," Osborn continued, "was for one thing: he had a complete disdain for the Vietnamese or any role that they might have that would be of more construction than his; and second: his rationale was when I confronted him with this, that the woman was only a slope [derogatory term for the Vietnamese] anyway and it doesn't matter."[25] In reality, this captain could have become an agent handler, and, as an officer in charge of intelligence contingency fund assets, he most certainly would have had access to money. Thus, the two causes for the jealousy that allegedly drove the captain to kill the interpreter did not exist.[26] Osborn's colleagues and his superiors, moreover, testified that no female interpreter ever worked for him, and the personnel files from his unit confirmed this fact. Relevant police records also did not mention that any person died under the circumstances described by Osborn.[27]

The investigation found no evidence to support Osborn's accusations about the execution of prisoners and other misdeeds. Osborn himself never did produce any evidence or present any witnesses to support his case, nor did he ever provide the names of the people involved. No reliable sources have ever made such incredible claims about these matters publicly or to me. The people from Osborn's unit, moreover, told the investigators that they believed that Osborn had been dishonest when he testified about the treatment of prisoners. They were certain, they said, that Osborn would have told them if he had witnessed the outrageous acts that he described to the congressional committee. For example, one of Osborn's team members, who acknowledged that Osborn had "performed his duties in a sincere and outstanding manner" in Vietnam, stated:

> I feel that much of the stories were fabricated by [Osborn]. To my knowledge, Osborn never saw anyone pushed out of a helicopter, he never saw anyone shot and he never saw anyone starved to death. I feel very sure that if he had actually observed any of these things that he would have mentioned them to someone in the Team. We lived pretty much as a family and

would discuss everything that usually occurred during the day as well as talk about things mentioned in our letters from home.[28]

Many of those interviewed for the investigation speculated that Osborn had derived his stories about the mistreatment of prisoners from rumors that commonly circulated among the American personnel in that area. They also stated in their testimony that they knew from experience that Osborn had a penchant for making fantastic statements. One of his coworkers described Osborn, who came from a family of the upper middle class, as "a 'spoiled brat', who desired to be the center of attention and to receive praise, and who frequently made exaggerated remarks in order to attract attention to himself."[29]

Most harsh critics of U.S. policy in Vietnam deplore the GVN's torture and execution of prisoners with a considerable amount of indignation. They generally state or imply that the interrogators were heartless villains who were merely doing the Americans' dirty work for money. After I examined the reasons behind the interrogators' actions, however, I found that the real reasons differed sharply from those given by the critics and that an appreciation of these reasons made the actions of the South Vietnamese much more understandable.

A comparison between American and South Vietnamese treatment of prisoners provides a good means of explaining the South Vietnamese behavior. All of the American advisers and their counterparts whom I interviewed said that few American advisers encouraged torture or tortured prisoners themselves, and none of them knew of any American advisers who had executed a prisoner or ordered a prisoner's execution. Advisers and veterans of U.S. military units said that American infantrymen were somewhat more likely to torture prisoners than were the American advisers, but they still were much less likely to do so than GVN personnel. When U.S. soldiers participated in the village war, in any case, they normally left interrogation to Vietnamese intelligence personnel. The task, then, is to explain why the representatives of two nations reacted so differently to the same circumstances.

One of the most important reasons that GVN personnel tortured and killed prisoners was the desire for revenge against the enemy. Nearly every person in the GVN had lost family members and friends to the Communists; some of them had been tortured brutally or executed in barbaric fashion. The Communists were at least as cruel to their prisoners as were their GVN adversaries, a fact unknown to many Americans. A PRU adviser talked to

American journalist Peter Kann about the great importance of retribution while troops from his unit tortured a suspect not far from the two men. "You know, it's a whole cycle of this stuff," the adviser said. "Last week in another village near Don Nhon [a district capital in Kien Hoa province] the VC marched five government sympathizers into the marketplace and beat their heads in with hammers. So we return it on this guy. It goes on and on."[30] In contrast to the South Vietnamese, the American interrogators did not lose relatives to the war, and some lost few friends and saw little or no combat. Many members of the U.S. infantry, on the other hand, lost many friends and participated heavily in combat, which helps to explain their somewhat greater willingness to hurt prisoners.

Another key difference between the Americans and the Vietnamese lay in their general attitudes toward violence. Many of the Americans currently in the media and academia believe that most non-Western cultures are as gentle and humane as they believe Western cultures to be, if not more so, and they often demonize people who suggest otherwise. An overwhelming amount of evidence in the case of the Vietnam War alone, however, contradicts this position. Most South Vietnamese and American veterans noticed that the South Vietnamese almost invariably had less humane attitudes concerning the treatment of prisoners than did the Americans. Col. Tran Ngoc Chau, a former GVN province chief who became the center of a major controversy in 1969 because of his dealings with his Communist brother, observed during the war that the Vietnamese were more likely than the Americans to treat other people cruelly. "It's a matter of culture, the way you grow up, the way you're educated," said Chau. "But it's so difficult to say exactly why."[31] Peter Scott, like many Americans who went to Vietnam, found the South Vietnamese's insensitivity to brutality shocking. Scott recounted:

> I just didn't have the stomach for torture. If we were in a fight with someone, I didn't have a problem with what we were doing, but once they had the guys tied up, I couldn't deal with it very well. So I didn't stay around to watch. I saw plenty of tortures started, and I heard them going on, but I never saw them carried out.
>
> A lot of it was motivated simply by meanness. The PRUs in my area had as much respect for humans as we Americans have for garden slugs. I was shocked by what the Khmer Rouge did later, but probably I was shocked less than some people because in Vietnam I learned there's a meanness in that part of the world that I never imagined as a boy or young man.[32]

Several factors, in addition to the desire for revenge and exposure to combat, accounted for these differences in belief. The rural Vietnamese of this era grew up in a world where pain and death occurred far more often than in the modernized West, which made them more naturally disposed to use force upon one another. Current American historians and other academics seldom explore this issue, in large part because the intellectual mainstream in recent decades has dismissed most biological explanations of human behavior as delusions of the radical right. A large amount of evidence, nevertheless, shows that intense suffering frequently activates violent animalistic instincts in humans, instincts that otherwise lie dormant for the most part. The activated instincts, even if constrained by other forces, often drive individuals to take or advocate actions that inflict pain on others. The reduction of suffering in the West in the past few centuries, the result of great medical improvements and the spread of wealth, provides a good case study. The progressive decline in levels of suffering has corresponded closely, perhaps more closely than any other factor, with decreases in the tendency of most people to inflict pain, as indicated by such phenomena as the abolition of corporal and capital punishment of criminals, the loss of the will to subjugate other racial and ethnic groups, and the reluctance to fight wars.

Witnessing violence regularly year after year during the war further eroded the Vietnamese's resistance to cruelty. Once the Vietnamese joined the GVN, they normally stayed in until the war's end, whereas most Americans spent no more than a few years in Vietnam. "When you see enough of what man can do to man in the context of warfare," explained Bruce Lawlor, "you become desensitized. It was a nasty, bloody conflict, and the people that fought it became very tough, very hard." [33]

Cultural and religious traditions also influenced the willingness of the two peoples to set free their aggressive impulses. The Vietnamese government and Vietnamese society strictly forbade both violent crime in the course of normal civilian life and crimes against one's own family, but placed no restraints on behavior beyond those bounds. American government and society imparted in most citizens a respect for the traditions of Christianity, liberal humanism, and moderate nationalism, which emphasize forgiveness and benevolent treatment of nonthreatening fellow humans. For these reasons, even most Americans who lost friends in Vietnam or who became somewhat desensitized to the horrors of the war retained a certain reluctance to hurt defenseless people, except in the immediate aftermath of a battle.

Most GVN leaders allowed or even encouraged their subordinates to torture or kill prisoners. U.S. military and CIA leaders, on the other hand, wanted to prevent both American and GVN personnel from indulging in these practices. They repeatedly ordered the Americans not to mistreat prisoners and to try to stop GVN personnel from torturing and executing.[34] In addition, they ordered all advisers to leave any scene of torture if they could not stop it. Many instructors and senior officers repeated these directions orally to the men in the field; the orders were not simply documents to be shown should outsiders start investigating the matter, although documents could prove useful in that regard. The American leaders who issued these orders argued that torture only caused prisoners to blurt out lies to save themselves and that it was immoral.

Preventing torture and execution proved to be a hard task. Leaders could not prevent mistreatment of prisoners simply by issuing a prohibition and forcing their subordinates to go along. When Vietnamese or Americans tortured or killed a prisoner, only a few people witnessed the act. The perpetrators tried to make sure that the witnesses were people—preferably not officers or advisers—whom they could trust not to complain to their superiors. The prevalence of torture, therefore, depended heavily on the beliefs of the people with immediate access to prisoners.

Even when advisers saw the South Vietnamese torture or execute prisoners, the majority of them failed to protest to the South Vietnamese or to report the torture to their own superiors, as they had been ordered to do. Some stood by and watched quietly, but the large majority of them left the interrogation area out of disgust or fear of reprimands from superiors. Lybrand and Johnstone reported, "Most advisors claimed they did not personally take part in [tortures] but 'turned their backs on them.'"[35] Non-CIA advisers had little chance of achieving anything through protest and could face formidable risks. The advisers usually lacked leverage over their counterparts, and their superiors often did not encourage them to make complaints. The South Vietnamese most frequently thought that they knew more about how to fight the war and deal with other Vietnamese than the Americans—and often they did—so they did not welcome this sort of advice.

Unless a non-CIA adviser had a close relationship with his counterpart or could make convincing suggestions to him in private, he was liable to offend the counterpart's honor if he tried to stop torture or execution on the spot. If an American reproached a South Vietnamese man in front of his subordinates or comrades, as Americans often do to each other, that man would "lose face" in the eyes of his fellow Vietnamese. His reputation would suffer seriously because he had been humiliated publicly. That a foreigner had done so increased the humiliation. The man who lost face might not say anything, but thereafter he would bear a grudge against the American who had "wronged" him and try to ignore him as much as possible.

An adviser who protested too strenuously about the treatment of prisoners put his life at risk. Col. Henry F. Dagenais, a district senior adviser in An Xuyen province during 1968–69 and the senior territorial forces adviser and S-3 adviser in Vinh Binh province during 1971–72, explained: "Let's say there are two American advisers out in the middle of the jungle with fifty or sixty Vietnamese troops. If the Americans start to get belligerent about something the Vietnamese are doing, they may be risking their own safety. They can be killed and disappear just as quickly as if they were VC."[36]

Many Americans let their South Vietnamese counterparts do as they pleased because they sympathized with them, despite their qualms about torture. The Americans understood that the South Vietnamese had lost many relatives and friends to a vicious enemy. They also appreciated their counterparts' belief that, by fighting the Communists, perhaps they could reduce Communist attacks on their families and help to ward off the dreaded prospect of Communist victory. The comments of Lee Patten, one of many U.S. Army and Marine noncommissioned officers who served as Phoenix advisers during the early 1970s, reflect the attitude of reluctant acceptance common among American advisers: "Most of the Vietnamese that we worked with on a daily basis had seen their families brutalized by the Viet Cong. Not that it makes their actions any more excusable. Where we would have reservations, they didn't, because the war had gone on for so long and they had seen their parents or their brothers or their sisters or their children killed by the Viet Cong. It was very personal. They were fighting for their lives and for the lives of their children. As much as you would hope that they would show some humanity, oftentimes they didn't show any because of their history. Could you really blame the South Vietnamese government for their hatred of the Viet Cong? No."[37]

Because the South Vietnamese gradually were assuming most of the burden of the Allied war effort, many advisers believed that the Vietnamese deserved to choose how to fight it. Many also doubted that their presence was necessary because they thought that the South Vietnamese understood each other and the war much better than they did, and thus knew best how to handle the interrogations. These Americans were paying deference to "self-determination" and "anti-imperialism," two principles that most Americans have long held dear. This deference, however, allowed the Vietnamese to fight a much more grisly war against other Vietnamese than the Americans had anticipated or wanted.

Some advisers with substantial influence over their counterparts succeeded in convincing or coercing them into stopping torture or executions. Most of these advisers worked for the CIA, but high-ranking CORDS advisers usually had some influence over the powerful district and province chiefs as well. Many believed that torture only decreased the quality of intelligence obtained, and they were not always convinced that killing one prisoner made another talk or that some prisoners had to be killed because they would escape from jail. Some advisers also opposed these practices on moral grounds or out of respect for their superiors. Master Chief Aviation Ordnanceman Mike Boynton, a PRU adviser in Ba Xuyen province, explained how he regulated the behavior of his counterparts toward prisoners: "When I had been running my PRUs, there hadn't been any problems out in the field. There were no excesses done by my men which made such great copy back in the States. I just wouldn't allow it. I kept control of my PRUs whenever I was in the field with them. And I never got any feedback that things happened when I wasn't there. The men knew that they would get paid and there wasn't any reason for any kind of excess. I told them what the rules were and they knew them. If I had people who were going overboard, killing, torturing, or collecting ears because they liked it, I would have gotten rid of them."[38] Even many advisers who had considerable influence over the South Vietnamese chose to leave their counterparts alone when they tortured someone, however, for some of the same reasons as did less influential advisers.

Most American advisers were not sure if prisoners revealed useful information when tortured. Few attended the interrogations or could understand the testimony, and the South Vietnamese often did not tell them afterward what prisoners said under duress. Even those Americans who attended and understood the interrogations were not always able to check whether the prisoners' testimony eventually proved accurate. Of those who did think that they knew enough to verify the accuracy of prisoner testimony, a considerable number echoed the claim of American policymakers that torture did not provide any worthwhile intelligence and often yielded false information. The comments of John Mullins are typical: "If you put people under physical duress, they'll tell you anything, just to get you to stop hurting them." [39]

Other Americans, however, disagreed. They acknowledged that severe forms of torture were counterproductive, but they saw situations in which limited doses of physical abuse caused prisoners to speak the truth. Bruce Lawlor subscribed to this view:

> I never saw the PRUs kill someone they were interrogating. I never saw them break anyone's bones. I did see them push some people, slap some people around to extract information that they felt they had to have. That got information. There was a certain benefit in generating anxiety in the person that you were talking to. The fear of the unknown is worse than going through it. If a guy got pushed and thought he was going to get pushed even more, that generated information. I know it did. Someone would tell you that so-and-so had a cache under his house, and you'd go to his house and dig it up. There was a point at which it did not work. If you were really hurting somebody badly, they would tell you anything to stop it. If somebody got pushed down or slapped, I wasn't going to make a big deal out of it. In the context of those operations it was not unusual. If it got much beyond that, I would usually have a sit-down with the PRU chief, and I'd tell him, "You just can't do this stuff." I think there was some degree of tension between them and me on that issue, because they knew I wouldn't tolerate it. [40]

Rex Wilson held a similar opinion:

> The worst thing I saw was people from the Special Police putting a VC's head in a pail of water and holding it there until he started sucking water down. In the cases that I saw, that method usually extracted accurate information from the prisoner, information that was acted upon. It didn't always develop information, though. I only saw them do this kind of thing when they needed information urgently for combat situations, and it was not life threatening or disfiguring, so I did not put a stop to it. I never saw my counterparts do anything that remotely resembled torture in any but urgent combat situations. There was a shooting war going on, and people needed intelligence, so people were going to get hurt when they got caught. That's war. [41]

During my interviews with people who served in the GVN, almost all of them said they knew that torture sometimes elicited valuable information quickly. Vo Van Dinh expressed this view and added that he did not care for the Americans' suggestions to avoid using force in interrogations. "The American advisers wanted us to be nice to the enemy," Dinh said. "They had bad ideas about how to treat prisoners."[42] So many American and Vietnamese interviewees testified to the effectiveness of torture that there can be no doubt that it extracted useful information in some cases.

The ability to cross-check a speaker's testimony against known facts helped all interrogators, especially when they needed information for immediate use. Many Communist prisoners lied to their captors at first, whether because of their hostility toward the enemy or because of fear of reprisals from the VC. The ability of interrogators to distinguish fact from fiction allowed them to discern lies and keep pressing for more information. Interrogators operating in their native areas, those who had been working in the same area for a long time, and former Communists typically were the best qualified to verify the statements of prisoners. Some interrogators, especially those from the Special Police and the PRUs, knew a good deal about many individual VC because they kept good dossiers on them.

When physical abuse of prisoners yielded truthful confessions, Allied forces were often able to mount successful operations against the Communists. This reality produced one of the war's most difficult, yet least discussed, moral dilemmas. Many Americans traditionally have opposed brutal treatment of prisoners, regardless of how much information that treatment might elicit, on the grounds that nothing justifies such inhumanity. This stance embodies some of the noblest moral traditions of Western civilization, and sometimes has practical advantages as well. During the Vietnam War, however, following such a policy did not necessarily yield the most humane results. Whereas the Americans often did not have direct command over operational forces and, in some cases, did not risk their own lives, GVN leaders had to consider their own safety and the safety of their men, which naturally inclined them to focus on countering immediate threats. Brig. Gen. Tran Van Nhut, one of the most successful and famous ARVN officers, explained, "When you are at the front line, you have to get information immediately, so that you can react. If you don't, if you send the prisoner to the rear, then you get the information too late to use it. If you don't get the information, your unit might be tortured or killed, because you might be ambushed a few hours later. If he gives you information, then maybe you learn enough that you won't get ambushed."[43]

Some of the Americans agreed with the South Vietnamese on this matter. Said John Cassidy, IV Corps' CIA deputy region officer in charge from 1967 to 1969, "If there was armed action involved where time was of the essence, and an interrogation was done in the field, variations of force were undoubtedly used. The force could be justified by the military situation."[44]

Interrogations that did not involve torture also produced valuable intelligence. Interrogators wielded several nonviolent carrots and sticks that convinced some people to talk. They made a variety of threats. At times, they could threaten force through subtle hints or by a fiery demeanor. At other times, the threat was quite blunt. Pointing a gun at prisoners and screaming death threats at them, for instance, worked in some cases. If such threats did not yield results immediately, another person might intervene to stop the threats and play the role of "good cop."

On occasion, the Allies threatened to walk around with prisoners in public to give the impression that they were cooperating with the GVN, or to spread rumors that certain prisoners had revealed a great deal about the Communists, which might cause the VC to hurt their families. Interrogators directly threatened the family members of prisoners from time to time. In many instances, the Allies threatened to turn prisoners over to people, such as ARVN interrogators or GVN jailers, who probably would brutalize them. Robert ("Bob") Boyke, a Special Police adviser in Kien Giang and Kien Phong during 1967–69, told me, "The biggest threat we could make to prisoners was to turn them over to the GVN."[45] Such threats brought out the truth in some cases.

By treating prisoners benevolently and offering them rewards for cooperation, interrogators enjoyed many successes, although these methods normally took time to bear fruit. Thich Van Quan, an outstanding interrogator whom the CIA and other American organizations used to interrogate important prisoners, testified, "I found that the best way to get information out of people was to make your target feel comfortable and be cooperative. It was always better to have a man willingly give you information than to have to drag it out of him. My mottos were 'Know your subject well,' and 'Treat people fairly and in a friendly manner.'"[46] Many VC were willing to betray their comrades to an extent that many Americans found remarkable; their desire to ingratiate themselves with their captors often exceeded their devotion to their old masters. Boyke recalled, "Prisoners didn't seem to have any problem whatsoever with ratting on all of their former colleagues."[47] Lower-level VC proved particularly cooperative; most of them had not committed themselves fully to the Communist cause, and self and family remained their chief interests.

Interrogators offered a variety of rewards to help loosen the tongues of their prisoners. Offers of medical treatment for prisoners or their relatives and offers of release from the dirty, cramped GVN prisons worked well. Simmons explained this and other rewards:

> When prisoners were wounded, we had a 50 percent better chance of getting them to cooperate with us than if they were not. These people knew very well that good medical treatment was scarce. Vietnamese hospitals were very primitive, and to get care you had to have money. If you were a peasant VC suspect, you wouldn't get much there. I knew some American doctors who helped me out from time to time. I'd bring in an American doctor with a big bag full of pills and devices and everything, and he'd put his gear on and listen to a heartbeat and go through a fairly elaborate routine, which seemed quite sophisticated to a peasant. Then the doctor would look at the wound and say, "Oh, that looks very bad. It could get infected. You could lose that limb."
>
> The prisoner would ask, "What can you do?"
>
> I'd usually let the doctor go, and then tell the prisoner, "We'd like to help, but it's hard to get the medicine. I can't do anything to help you without getting some sort of help in return." That tended to work well.
>
> Money was less effective in getting people to talk. Sometimes we offered prisoners reduced prison sentences. Sometimes we'd let them go in exchange for their cooperation. Of course, we had to arrange bribes for them. If you just let a guy go, the VC would think he was a spy and might kill him. It was a lot easier for the guy to say, "I beat the rap because we bribed the cop," than to say, "I gave a lot of information and cooperated and the GVN let me go." We'd have him send a letter out to his village to ask for money. The relatives would come, if he had visitation privileges, and give him the money, and a week or so later he would be released.[48]

Many captured documents showed that the Communists feared the release of prisoners in exchange for information. One such document, concerning the first four months of 1969, reads: "After our attacks against cities, district seats, and province capitals, [the Allies] would persuade captured cadre and guerrillas, defectors, and ralliers to work for them and then plant them in our agencies and units by giving them a chance to escape from prison to return to their local areas. They even used relatives of our cadre and troops to convince the latter to work for them."[49]

Skilled interrogators manipulated prisoners with psychological pressure and a variety of tricks. The CIA's preferred methods at the Province Interrogation Centers, as described by senior CIA officer Douglas Blaufarb, included "painstaking, patient questioning, checking and requestioning in circumstances calculated to emphasize the prisoner's helplessness and dependence on his captors."[50] Interrogators tried to show their interrogation subjects that they knew so much about them that continued silence would accomplish nothing except prevent them from receiving the rewards offered for cooperation. CIA interrogation techniques, in the words of William Colby, "stress the value of cross-checking a prisoner's story with other known facts and gradually convincing him that the interrogator already knows the basic story, and is merely filling in the details. Combining this with the 'good guy–bad guy' alternate team challenging and sympathizing with the subject can often lead to the first confidences, which then can be built upon to produce more, and certainly produces more accurate information than torture ever can."[51] More furtive means of obtaining information included bugging the holding cells of prisoners and inserting Allied personnel or agents into the cells in the event that unsuspecting prisoners might speak the truth to them.

Interrogators tried to convince some prisoners that they had been fighting for the wrong side. By treating prisoners decently, the GVN could show that it was not the evil monster portrayed in VC propaganda. Taking prisoners, especially those from North Vietnam, into the bustling and prosperous cities of South Vietnam gave them cause to doubt the Communists' claims that the South Vietnamese government so terribly oppressed the people. A visit to a large military installation might convince a prisoner that the Communists stood no chance of winning the war.

Although torture sometimes elicited useful information from prisoners more quickly than gentler methods, it often restricted the amount of information that a prisoner ultimately gave. Tortured prisoners tended to cooperate only as much as was necessary. Nonviolent methods of interrogation generally caused more prisoners to talk and drew better information from them. Col. Viet Lang said, "By treating prisoners well, if you put them in a nice place and gave them good things, you got better results. If you hit them, you didn't get all of the information they knew."[52] When interrogators questioned low-level prisoners, the benefits of using force generally outweighed the negative consequences because these prisoners usually knew relatively little of importance beyond tactical information that quickly became outdated. With more knowledgeable prisoners, however, the use of torture blocked access to a great many valuable pieces of information. The South Vietnamese undeniably used more force than was effective in many cases, and they killed prisoners who might have been valuable sources.

It is fortunate that the harshest forms of torture did not work well as interrogation tools. Had they been effective, their usefulness on the battle-field would have led more soldiers and policemen to brutalize prisoners when they desperately needed information. As it was, the limited usefulness of lesser forms of torture, along with the general viciousness of the war, ensured that force would remain a favorite resource of some interroga-tors, one that the U.S. leadership was incapable of eradicating even had it put more effort into doing so.

9 Ralliers, Documents, and Photographs

risoners were not the only prizes that the Allies took from the Communists and used against them. Ralliers, who defected to the GVN through the Chieu Hoi program, sometimes provided excellent information about the shadow government. Some ralliers were VC who were captured and then chose to defect; GVN interrogators offered that option in some instances in return for their cooperation. Most ralliers, however, turned themselves in to someone from the GVN, frequently to a person they knew and trusted or, in areas dominated by the VC, someone in a nearby Allied unit.

The Communists tried to impede defection in a variety of ways. They threatened to terrorize ralliers and their families, but they seldom carried out these threats. Would-be ralliers faced a significant danger of dying at the VC's hands only during their attempts to leave the other Communists and move to a GVN area. Ralliers usually stayed in GVN-controlled areas after defecting, and their families moved to safe areas as well unless other family members, whom the Communists would not want to anger, remained in the VC. Considering the high numbers of ralliers during certain periods, moreover, the Communists would have had to torture or kill so many people that they would have spawned tremendous resentment. The VC spread rumors that the GVN tortured or killed people who rallied, but most VC sooner or later heard about ralliers who had not endured mistreatment. Communist leaders also tried to convince their followers to persist despite the difficulties they faced. Although these appeals helped considerably, even fine leaders could not always stop defection, and the quality of VC leaders declined after the Tet offensive. In spite of all the VC's countermeasures, tens of thousands of Communist cadres, soldiers, and guerrillas rallied each year during the late 1960s and early 1970s.[1]

Ralliers had the same sort of information that the prisoners had, but they told most or all of it willingly. The majority of ralliers had served the VC in low-ranking positions—the higher ranks of the Communists tended to rally and confess less often because of greater dedication to the movement—and their knowledge of the shadow government usually did not go beyond the village level. Numerous ralliers, including many who had served the Communists fervently for years, provided details that led to the arrests or deaths of former buddies. Once they had switched their allegiance to a new master, the ralliers usually turned their backs on the VC. "I couldn't believe how cooperative some of the guys were," said Felix I. Rodriguez, a III Corps PRU adviser during the early 1970s, the same CIA officer who talked with the captured Che Guevara in Bolivia during the last hours of his life. Rodriguez, like many advisers, witnessed numerous operations, based on rallier intelligence, that led to the death of the ralliers' former comrades. In some cases, the ralliers even rejoiced at the killings.[2] The Communists regularly observed that intelligence from ralliers led to many Allied triumphs. The author of a 1970 VC document on Sub-Region 1, for example, comments that "the enemy obtained considerable success in attacks guided by our former personnel who surrendered to him."[3]

The Viet Cong rallied for a large variety of reasons, and each person usually rallied for more than one. Those who were prisoners of the GVN often rallied simply to regain their freedom and avoid torture and imprisonment in sordid jails. A few of them returned to the VC fold as soon as they could, but Communist fears that the GVN had converted them and sent them back as spies made the returnees rather unwelcome.

The shadow government, on occasion, ordered loyal VC to rally so that they could become legal cadres or infiltrate GVN organizations that employed defectors. Many Vietnam War commentators assume that the Communists used this tactic regularly and with great success. In reality, the VCI did not send many people to rally falsely and gained little from those they sent. They feared that false ralliers might decide to become true ralliers once they experienced the comfort of the provincial capital and would never come back, or that the Allies would convince them to spy on the VC upon their return. The deputy secretary of COSVN, according to a report from Hackle, stated: "The use of false ralliers to gain legal documentation was quite insignificant in relation to the emphasis placed upon proselyting the mass of the population. This was because most false ralliers were immature and almost always possessed aberrant behavioral characteristics. The Party selected these people to rally falsely only because the Party did not completely trust them nor did it consider them to be potentially loyal and stable cadres within a long-range stabilized infrastructure."[4] Donald Colin, a Vietnamese-speaking U.S. State Department Foreign Service officer who served as a IV Corps Phoenix adviser and as Vinh Binh deputy province senior adviser, commented, "VC-directed ralliers who falsely pretend to love the GVN are never sure bets; sometimes that is the order they have been awaiting and they scamper off never to be heard from again. Sometimes they make down payments on the TV set and the Honda before the VC approach them again and it is too late."[5]

A large number of Communist soldiers, and a much smaller number of cadres, decided to quit the Communists and rally because their lives had become too difficult and terrifying. They desired an end to food shortages, malaria, leeches, Allied ambushes, and attacks from B-52 bombers and other deadly weapons. American advisers noticed that rises and declines in the level of Allied military activity tended to produce rises and declines in the rates of Communist desertion in an area and observed that Allied military pressure caused more defections than any other factor. The absence of prospects for a Communist victory in the near future and the success and strength of the Allies also caused many VC to quit fighting.

Often, a group of VC rallied together. When a single VC rallied, moreover, he or she sometimes triggered a chain reaction of other defections. Some VC joined their fellow VC in rallying because they learned that the initial ralliers had received good treatment from the Allies. Others decided to follow suit because the very decision of those comrades suggested that the will of heaven was changing in favor of the GVN, and they had better obey. Defecting VC leaders proved particularly effective in persuading other VC to join them. The author of a VC instructional document covering the year 1970 remarks, "Especially, in some areas, one half of the total number of village guerrillas and even the entire village guerrilla platoon (including its command committee) surrendered to the enemy. . . . Collective surrenders have often occurred among our ranks."[6]

As the war progressed, many Southern Communists rallied because they realized that life in the VC no longer offered them and their families better prospects for prosperity than did cooperation with the GVN. Rivers of American aid money and a massive GVN land reform program during the early 1970s, on the one hand, and economic decline in VC areas, on the other, provided a much higher standard of living for most villagers in GVN hamlets than for those in VC hamlets. One man explained his decision to rally: "My father was dead then, and I felt that I had the duty to take care of my wife and my two young sisters. If I continued to stay with the VC, I could not fulfill my duty as the man of the family. . . . As a guerrilla, I did not have enough food to eat, so how could I support my family?"[7] Some simply missed their families tremendously and wanted to rejoin them.

Sometimes the encouragement of GVN personnel convinced the hesitant to rally. People from the Chieu Hoi program, the armed propaganda teams, and other programs assured potential ralliers, often through relatives, that the GVN would keep them safe from VC assassins and unforgiving GVN officials. In some cases, they offered to bring families to safe areas to protect them against possible VC retribution. Many GVN proselyting cadres were also former VC, so they served as proof that the system worked. A captured document from the VC's Can Tho province relates, "The enemy's propaganda has much effect. Some of our Party Chapters and people think that the enemy is still strong and that the life of our revolutionary cadre is endangered so that they do not believe in the final victory of our Revolution. Some were so disturbed that they defected, especially those in villages recently taken over by the enemy."[8] The Allies sometimes offered monetary rewards to ralliers. On occasion, the GVN turned to more coercive measures. It warned cadres via their relatives that they should rally or else face a less pleasant fate, and it put up wanted posters of particular cadres, thus increasing those individuals' fear of capture or death.

Some ralliers, including quite a few cadres, quit the VC or were forced to quit because of conflicts with other Communists. Disagreements over promotions or demotions, mistreatment of one's family members, accusations about collaboration with the GVN, and animosity between subordinates and superiors were typical examples. Tension between the Southerners and the Northerners who had come South also caused many to defect. The animosity was most prevalent among the VC who were natives of the III Corps and IV Corps provinces; those from the northern provinces of South Vietnam did not differ as much culturally from North Vietnam's people, especially those from the southern part of North Vietnam, with whom they shared an Annamese heritage. Some VC, primarily those from wealthier backgrounds, left out of frustration because the Party promoted poor people over better-qualified people from higher social classes. A small but important minority rallied because, like some of the Allied agents in the VC, they had discovered the bankruptcy of Communist political ideology.

The Allies' proficiency in obtaining information from the ralliers varied widely. South Vietnamese military intelligence officers debriefed most turncoats first in order to get tactical military information, then sent them to the Chieu Hoi centers. There, personnel of the Special Police, PRUs, CIA, and other organizations could debrief ralliers at their leisure, unless officers at higher levels snatched them away, as they did with prisoners. Sometimes, these organizations did not have, or did not assign, enough qualified people to debrief all of the incoming ralliers. The effectiveness of debriefers depended on the quality and quantity of the questions that they asked. Experienced debriefers and those with considerable knowledge of the local situation thus enjoyed a distinct advantage. Good debriefers, in addition, gained the confidence of ralliers by keeping their collaboration secret, should their families still be in jeopardy or the VC later have access to them, and gave the information obtained only to the necessary people in the organization. If they asked ralliers to identify prisoners, new defectors, or legal VCI in a public place, they put the ralliers in a concealed position so that the suspects and other onlookers did not know what they were doing, or photographed the people in question and showed the pictures to the ralliers.

Some ralliers joined the PRUs, Chieu Hoi program, Kit Carson Scouts, or other organizations. Before joining, they had to help the Allies hurt the Communists in order to demonstrate their loyalty. Col. Viet Lang said, "We used the ralliers to get information and tested them many times to find out who was reliable before we let them in."9 Once they joined, they continued to make use of their knowledge of VC personnel and modes of operation. "In my unit," Le Van Thai told me, "there were about five Hoi Chanhs [ralliers]. They helped us a lot. They told us about the Viet Cong activity in the area, and they knew some of the VC."10

Documents provided a wealth of information on the VCI. The Allies found numerous documents in the possession of dead and captured VC and discovered many others in hidden VC base areas. Documents provided names and positions of many cadres and other VC and comprised one of the best tools for filling in the blanks on the Allies' charts of the shadow government. Some documents implicated legal cadres by their real names or revealed the names of the shadow government's spies. A few documents even gave the time and place of VC meetings, tax collections, and other activities.

Another major intelligence asset that the Allies captured during their operations was photographs. The Allies often found photographs of Communists or Communist sympathizers on the person of prisoners and Communists killed in action. Some Allied organizations, especially the Special Police, PRUs, and other sophisticated intelligence groups, amassed large collections of photographs. They matched photos with the faces of ordinary villagers in order to locate legal cadres, but, more often, they matched them with those of suspicious people detained during Allied searches and of armed VC captured by the Allies. Ralliers, agents, and cooperative prisoners helped with identification. "We had pictures of a lot of the key cadres," Rex Wilson recalled. "All the Vietnamese had their pictures taken—it was a cultural thing. Even the VC in the VC areas had their pictures taken on a pretty regular basis, posing with their weapon, and they all carried the pictures around. We got pictures from prisoners and bodies and we'd try to match them up with other people. We'd ask ralliers who they were."[11]

Misinformation

ne of the dangers inherent in revolutionary warfare is that combatants or their sources of information will accuse nonparticipants of serving the opposing side in order to have personal adversaries arrested, tortured, or killed. A good measure of an efficient government during a revolutionary war is its ability to prevent its members from using their powers in this fashion. The Viet Cong shadow government employed procedures that, for the most part, prevented such abuses of power. The Allies had many more organizations involved in eliminating the enemy apparatus than did the VC, and they differed considerably in the ability to avoid inappropriate targeting.

The people who identified members of the shadow government often had many types of non-Communist enemies in their area of operation, particularly if they worked in their native areas. Like most people, they had personal enemies: the men who had insulted their sisters, the men who had stolen their sweethearts, the farmers who had borrowed money from their families and failed to repay it, and even the GVN officials who had beaten their cousins. Family members of these enemies also could be fair game, especially when previous offenses had involved relatives. In some areas, GVN personnel and villagers from various religious groups disliked and schemed against one another. Vietnam's racial minorities, as mentioned in chapter 3, had little regard for the ethnic Vietnamese, and the animosity was mutual. "We Vietnamese are very prejudiced," said Vo Van Dinh. "The Vietnamese don't like the Chinese, or the Cambodians, or the Montagnards. There is a popular saying, 'It is better to die than to have my daughter marry a Cambodian.'"[1] Because members of the Vietnamese race held almost all of the leadership positions in both the GVN and the VC shadow government, they could attack members of minority groups in the name of prosecuting the war, whereas the minorities lacked the influence to commit such abuses.

Non-Communist political factions in certain parts of the country often quarreled with one another. Some people in the GVN belonged to these groups. GVN leaders who did not belong to any of the strong non-Communist opposition groups often felt threatened by these groups and wanted to subvert them. Saigon often encouraged them to do so, although President Thieu did not try to destroy every movement that had its own independent leadership and often assigned leaders of certain political and religious sects to important posts.

Within many specific areas, certain families, religious groups, races, and non-Communist political factions favored the GVN, whereas others supported the VC. The GVN and the VC exerted covert influence or control over some of these groups. Indeed, a group might have aligned itself with the VC or the GVN simply because its enemies supported the other side. The distinction between the VC and private enemies became nebulous in such cases.

Author Monika Jensen-Stevenson suggests that the United States tried to use Phoenix to assassinate American soldiers who had defected to the Communists, and that U.S. leaders labeled suspects as defectors without sufficient evidence. She cites Robert Garwood, who spent the years 1965–1979 with the Communists, as an example of an American POW whom the United States unfairly classified as a defector and tried to assassinate.[2] Jensen-Stevenson's charges lack any basis in fact. She provides no evidence showing that Phoenix ever played a role in the hunt for Garwood or any other American. I have never come across any evidence that the Americans deliberately used Phoenix or other elements of pacification, rather than the U.S. military, to mount operations against American defectors. It also should be noted that only a handful of American servicemen—probably no more than a dozen—are generally believed to have defected to the Communists. Garwood is the only member of this group whom the U.S. government unequivocally identified by name as having fought against U.S. forces, and he is the only one whom it prosecuted for having done so. The U.S. military, moreover, had a wealth of compelling evidence indicating that Garwood did indeed defect and participate in combat alongside the Communists.[3]

Anyone who provided information to the Allies about the VCI might try to claim that a non-Communist enemy was a VCI. Informants, agents, ralliers, cooperative prisoners, and villagers who volunteered information could tell their GVN contacts that certain people were VCI and perhaps receive some sort of reward in return. To complicate matters, such people might have been secretly providing misinformation to more than one Allied intelligence agency. If each agency sent the information to Phoenix centers without mentioning the source's identity, the information would seem to have multiple confirmations and a higher level of reliability. Edward ("Ed") Brady, a Vietnamese-speaking adviser to the South Vietnamese military during the mid-1960s and a member of the national Phoenix staff under the CIA and CORDS from 1968 to 1971, recalled, "It sometimes happened that three independent sources were, in fact, the same agent. He might be an agent in your network and an agent in two other networks and you don't tell each other. You then had three reports but you didn't know if they were from three sources, two sources, or one source."[4] If one person made similar reports to different agencies, the recipients might discover the trick because they sometimes compared notes. If more than one agency tried to act on the information and it was time sensitive, the second agency to inform the tactical operations center would find its operational area taken and might suspect something.

Dishonest GVN intelligence personnel and their leaders could assert that their sources had fingered a personal adversary as a member of the shadow government. Col. Nguyen Van Dai, NPFF commandant from 1968 to 1970, mentioned a couple of instances where he suspected the PRUs of putting personal enemies on the list of VCI: "The PRUs saw a man throw a hand grenade into someone's pond to get the fish. They reported back that he was a VCI. If they saw a beautiful girl, they tried to be her boyfriend. If they got turned down, then they accused her of being a VCI."[5]

VC agents in the GVN and VC supporters in the villages also tried to misinform the Allies. On occasion, they claimed that GVN employees and supporters were really VCI. The GVN, however, might investigate the accusations, prove them false, and perhaps even arrest the sources for spreading the information. The VC, therefore, generally chose to abduct or kill their enemies themselves.

Private and group animosities were not the only reasons why people would accuse someone falsely of serving in the shadow government. The Americans gave some GVN units quotas of VCI to be neutralized per month or pressured them in other ways to neutralize certain numbers of cadres. They also paid rewards to some forces for capturing or killing VCI. Further, GVN leaders arrested villagers and forced them to pay bribes for their release. Consequently, anyone who needed to show higher neutralization numbers to a superior or who wanted more money might try to accuse someone of being a VCI without any real evidence. These factors, however, did not lead to much misbehavior, as chapter 16 explains.

The extent to which the Allies wrongly identified villagers as VCI is one of the most controversial issues of the war against the shadow government.

Many critics of the Allied war effort argue that it occurred frequently and base their claims on statements from such people as Kenneth Barton Osborn and Yoshia K. Chee. Osborn said that the Allies, particularly the PRUs, regularly obtained information alleging that someone was a VCI and then killed the person without trying to verify the information. "It was completely indiscriminate," Osborn said. "There was no cross-check; there was no investigation; there were no second opinions."[6]

Those who argue that the Allies did not try to verify their information do not recognize that U.S. military intelligence organizations were not normally involved in attacking VCI. Organizations staffed by the South Vietnamese had the primary responsibility for the war against the shadow government. The critics also do not understand much about the South Vietnamese organizations that had this responsibility and do not appreciate the crucial differences among them. They mistakenly assume that the less capable and sophisticated organizations, such as the territorial forces and the National Police Field Forces, followed the same procedures as better organizations, such as the PRUs and the Special Police.

The less sophisticated organizations typically based their arrests of VCI suspects on information gathered from informants by word of mouth. The CORDS and U.S. military advisers who tried to monitor these organizations seldom had good access to this process. Most of these advisers also were not present when the Vietnamese interrogated prisoners and did not always attend rallier debriefings. When they did witness these transfers of information or when people in the GVN discussed such matters, only a few of the Americans could follow the conversations because most advisers did not understand the Vietnamese language and many lacked competent interpreters. As Masayoshi Riusaki, a district senior adviser in Vinh Binh, states: "Where no common language is available between advisors and counterparts, the level of cooperation and understanding is reduced to the ability of the interpreter, who for the most part is not qualified."[7]

When American advisers observed the target selections of the South Vietnamese, few knew enough about the local society to detect whether the targets were VCI or enemies of a different type. Again, the language barrier contributed greatly to this problem, as did several other factors. Most of the advisers knew little or nothing about Vietnam or about revolutionary warfare prior to their arrival in Vietnam. They had to find out for themselves which people and groups were likely to slander other people and groups. Their GVN counterparts, the interpreters, and the local populace seldom saw any need to educate the Americans in local intrigues. Many

South Vietnamese were especially reluctant to talk because they feared that an American's interpreter might be working for someone else in the GVN or for the VC, as indeed was often the case.

Their GVN counterparts, in fact, encouraged many American advisers to discount the existence of any hidden truths that might have helped them in their jobs. Typically, the South Vietnamese told the advisers that they knew a great deal and that they gave good advice, even when the counterparts seldom heeded the Americans' suggestions. Many CORDS and military advisers, especially those who were gullible or unmotivated, wanted to believe what they were hearing. They could take satisfaction in having good relationships with their counterparts and a firm grasp on the situation. Because of their confidence, they saw no need to learn anything else. They could also please their American bosses by reporting that all was well, and their South Vietnamese counterparts were pleased because their advisers seldom gave them orders.

Advisers also faced a time constraint. Most CORDS advisers and other military personnel stayed in South Vietnam for just one year and often changed jobs every six months or less. A great many advisers complained that a large portion of their time in country had elapsed before they understood the Vietnamese environment. "If we could have kept people in the field for four years," Peter Scott commented, "we could have done some real damage. But four or five months at a time in an area? When I was moved from one province to another, I had to learn a lot of things again, and by the time I had, it was time to go home."[8]

Some CORDS and other military advisers lacked the skills or the interest to acquire the information needed. The comments of Col. Henry Dagenais typify those of many seasoned advisers:

> American advisers from the military, especially the younger officers, in many cases were not suitable for the job. Many of them would rather have been in a big U.S. military unit where there was more recognition and awards, not with the Vietnamese out in the bush getting little recognition. Very few of these people made any effort to learn the Vietnamese culture, or Vietnamese history, or any of the problems between the racial groups or the religious sects. They probably never understood most of what was going on during their tour. I'd say that 50 percent or more of the younger officers didn't make any effort to increase their understanding of the environment they were in.[9]

In the end, these U.S. advisers could not prevent most attempts to label personal enemies as VCI. Other elements of the war against the VCI, however, could prevent them. Some inherent characteristics of the GVN hindered anyone in its organizations who thought about misusing the system for this purpose. Volunteer informants and VC prisoners and ralliers were least likely to succeed in identifying non-VCI as members of the shadow government, for the GVN was apt to regard anything that these individuals said with considerable suspicion. GVN commanders feared that unknown sources might be VC supporters sending their forces into ambushes or that they might lose men to mines, booby traps, and chance encounters with the VC. In addition, most leaders preferred to avoid offending the villagers through unjustified arrests. They checked particular statements against established facts to test the validity of both the statements and their sources.

Informants, agents, and rank-and-file intelligence personnel had somewhat better chances of misusing the system, but the GVN leaders had to sanction any intelligence before a unit acted on it. These leaders seldom had any interest in using their own resources to carry out other people's vendettas, and again they feared VC traps. Good leaders most often discovered such subterfuge. They had a fairly good idea of which subordinates and sources were reliable, especially because the GVN so often exploited family ties and other relationships of trust to get information. They normally investigated or cross-checked questionable information before acting on it. Brig. Gen. Tran Van Nhut stated, "We learned someone was a VCI from many sources, not one source. If you trusted only one source, maybe sometimes you'd make a mistake. If we had one source, we asked other people to collect more information about that person."[10] All operations against VCI ostensibly required identification of the target by three independent sources, but few South Vietnamese always adhered to this rule because it curtailed their freedom of action unnecessarily. In some cases, they targeted someone as a VCI on the basis of a single source if that source had proved reliable in the past or if the source was an informant who had a family member in the organization. As John Tilton said, "The three source rule may have been in the instruction books, but three sources can be less reliable than one good source."[11]

American advisers confirmed that good, vigilant GVN leaders of organizations not affiliated with the CIA detected and stopped attempts to misuse the system. Col. Horace L. Hunter, for example, told me:

> Reprimands for failure to build proper dossiers or otherwise not adhering to *an tri* [emergency detention] procedures were not uncommon in Chau Doc. This was in part due to a good adviser or two, but also to the fact that

two successive province chiefs and a province chief justice gave serious attention to Phung Hoang and supervised it closely. Falsification of data and targeting of personal enemies did occur, and when discovered usually resulted
in some form of disciplinary action.[12]

A large number of the GVN leaders in question were weak leaders and permitted some abuses, but their forces usually preferred inactivity to targeting
anyone.

GVN leaders—province chiefs, district chiefs, police chiefs, and others—
had the best odds of success for targeting non-Communists because their
own superiors often did not pay close attention to them. Only when they
tried to get another GVN leader to act on their misinformation were others
in the GVN likely to scrutinize the information. The national leadership of
the GVN, however, usually avoided assigning district- and province-level
leaders to their native districts and provinces, in part because it prevented
them from having many personal or familial enemies in the area. These
leaders generally limited their bogus accusations of complicity with the VC
to independent non-Communist political groups.

The operations of the CIA-sponsored PRUs and Special Police targeted
specific villagers much more often than did those of the territorial forces,
National Police Field Forces, and other non-CIA pacification forces. The intelligence verification methods of these two organizations, therefore, had a
much more significant impact on the war. Their methods proved to be considerably more effective than those of the other organizations. The CIA generally assigned or helped to assign superior leaders to the PRUs and, to a
lesser extent, the Special Police. These leaders prevented many misuses of
intelligence, as good leaders did in other organizations. "Good PRU leaders
checked the intelligence carefully," Le Van Thai noted. "As a result, their
units usually did not go after the wrong people."[13] The province chiefs had
to approve PRU and Special Police operations against the VCI and thus served
as another check against abuse.

The CIA believed, nevertheless, that misuses of the attack on the shadow
government for personal reasons could occur despite the efforts of these
leaders. CIA advisers, unlike most CORDS advisers, had assets of their own
that they used as additional means of keeping the Vietnamese from acting
on unsubstantiated information. PRU and Special Police advisers generally
had better access to their counterparts' intelligence-collection processes
than CORDS advisers, and more of them could understand it because they
spoke Vietnamese or had good interpreters. They also had more experience

in and knowledge about intelligence matters. For these reasons, they could distinguish better between good intelligence and bad intelligence.

When the CIA officers did not themselves know enough to discern whether their counterparts were targeting the right people, they questioned their sources about whom the GVN was targeting and whether or not they were VCI. Villagers, ralliers, and prisoners sometimes had the answers. Informants and agents in the counterpart organization also provided information about targeting. The CIA had to employ these GVN sources carefully and in moderation because their counterparts did not like having CIA informants working for them. PRU advisers also gave polygraph tests to the PRUs and their Vietnamese chiefs. Jack Harrell, who advised a team of Kit Carson Scouts in Kien Hoa during the late 1960s and served as a region-level PRU adviser in II Corps and III Corps during the early 1970s, said: "I had some PRUs that reported to me independently. It was helpful. You had to be very careful. For the extra money, just about anyone in the organization was willing to share with you information on any target. I only recruited a few. I tried to recruit those with whom I had already established a good rapport. Actually, it was stronger than a rapport, it was friendship. I didn't use the polygraph on a regular basis. In some cases, if the PRUs had claimed a really good operation and I just had to be absolutely sure that they had pulled the guy in, I polygraphed the PRU chief."[14] Dean Almy told me, "We used the polygraph on the Vietnamese from time to time. The polygraph was generally considered to be less accurate when used with Asians than with Caucasians. In order to be effective with the Vietnamese, the polygraph operator had to have an excellent understanding of the Vietnamese culture. Certain statements, certain phrases that ordinary Americans would consider to be lies would not strike the Vietnamese as lies. Few of our officers had been in Vietnam long enough to understand these subtleties fully."[15] A few CIA advisers bugged GVN offices to gain access to some of the information that the South Vietnamese hid from the Americans, but this method generally required more time and effort than the CIA wanted to invest. American influence, when it was used, usually forced the Vietnamese to conduct their war in a more civilized fashion, as it did with interrogations.

The CIA advisers had to approve of all PRU and Special Police operations against the VC and the VCI, and many of them rejected Vietnamese operational proposals because of insufficient intelligence. If the advisers found the Vietnamese misusing or fabricating information to an alarming extent, they could warn them and, if necessary, replace them. Said John

Mullins: "I had my own informants in the province. There were times when I questioned a name on the blacklist of VCI. 'Is this guy actually VC infrastructure, or is he a political enemy or a business enemy of the province chief or district chief or somebody else?' I'd do my own checks with my sources, and there were times when I flat out refused to pick up people because they obviously were not put on the list for the purpose of rooting out the VC infrastructure."[16]

In many cases, CIA officers gave the PRUs intelligence that they had collected themselves, which made assessing the validity considerably easier. They did not have to rely on the integrity of their counterparts, and they had better means of verifying their own information. The CIA gave polygraph tests to some informants, agents, cutouts, and interpreters. The ability of CIA officers to meet with or test the agents and cutouts in the CIA or Special Police operations varied greatly. "We were always trying to get our people to move along the chain towards the source," said Don Gregg. "It depended on whether they were trying to sell a fabrication or not. If the Special Police were putting out a fabrication, it was usually harder to get further up the line than if it was genuine."[17]

CIA advisers could evaluate the general reliability of their own sources more thoroughly than they could the reliability of their counterparts' sources. Like the South Vietnamese, they tested the sources and checked other information that the sources had given against known facts. Bob Boyke explained how this process worked with informants: "When you recruited an informant, the first thing you said to him was, 'If you expect me to pay you for your information, you've got to verify the fact that you've got access. So, here's twenty bucks. That's just for the first time. Now, go out and bring me back something I can verify as authentic.' After one or two reports from them, you got to know who was serious and who wasn't."[18]

The CIA advisers did have their limitations. Some chose to ignore their counterparts' faults in order to maintain smooth relations and avoid trouble with the South Vietnamese or their own bosses. Many wished they could have stayed in one place for longer; the maximum tour of field duty for most was two years. By the late 1960s, shortages of staff officers forced the CIA to hire many people, known as "contract officers," for short-term duty. Some of the contract officers lacked the natural talents that most career people possessed, and none of them went through very extensive training. "The contract officers were a mixed bag," Gregg commented. "Some were excellent while others were mediocre at best."[19] Many CIA staff officers in Vietnam also were not of the highest caliber because of

CIA personnel policies. To meet the staffing needs of the Far East Division in Vietnam, the CIA asked its other divisions to send some of their staff officers to Vietnam. "If you're a division chief," Daren Flitcroft explained, "and you're told to come up with fifty officers to go to Vietnam, do you send your fifty best officers? No way."[20] Again, because of personnel shortages, the majority of CIA advisers did not receive substantial instruction in the Vietnamese language. Although those who did not speak Vietnamese generally had good interpreters, the interpreters did not tell them everything they heard, and some people chose not to speak to the advisers because of their interpreters' presence.

The CIA's African American advisers experienced great difficulty in getting information from people in the GVN and from other South Vietnamese, much more than the white advisers experienced. "I overheard so many insults about Americans from Vietnamese who didn't think I understood Vietnamese," Bruce Lawlor said. "They called the whites gorillas, because we have hair on our bodies, that sort of stuff."[21] Lawlor, who is white, enjoyed much better relations with the South Vietnamese than did his African American colleagues. He described the plight of the typical African American case officer:

> The guy walked in the door and already, without saying a word, insulted this Vietnamese beyond belief. . . . The Vietnamese would come to me and say, "Can't we get somebody else?" and they wouldn't tell you why. "Well, we don't like so-and-so. He doesn't understand us." And you'd try to explain to them he's really a good guy and he's got the ears of the highest man in our organization and it never took.[22]

John Cassidy also commented on the problems that the African American advisers faced. He said, "Our black operations officers and province officers reported strong prejudice against them among the Vietnamese, often prejudice that was more severe and overt than they had ever experienced in the U.S."[23] During my interviews with former GVN personnel now living in the United States, some conceded that they preferred working with whites over African Americans, although they were reluctant to explain why.

In discussing the target selections of the CIA and the GVN organizations that it sponsored, almost all CIA advisers and their counterparts said that they usually targeted people only when they had strong evidence that they were full-fledged Communists. Command Sgt. Maj. Michael N. ("Mike") Martin, who served as an adviser to the South Vietnamese Rangers, the PRUs, and the territorial forces, said that he knew of cases where the PRUs arrested people for trivial offenses, such as flying the VC flag to appease the VC, but he added that the PRUs made only a few arrests on the basis of such flimsy evidence. "When we went out and arrested a guy, we were pretty sure he was a VCI," said Martin. "The PRU chief and the deputy PRU chief sat down with the PRU adviser and went over all of the intelligence with him. The adviser cross-checked the information with other sources. He could check it with other intel [intelligence] people in the area, with the district and province chiefs, or the local police. We verified all information independently before we used it." [24]

The Special Police, who spent less time going after low-level VC and VCI than the PRUs, tended to be even more demanding than the PRUs. "I always differentiated between thick files and thin files," Rob Simmons remembered. "The thin files only had a few reports about a person. We didn't take a lot of interest in the thin files. If we got a single report through an agent network that someone was a VC, we probably weren't going to try to arrest him. We might have gotten shot. It just wasn't worth it. We'd go after the people with thick files, the ones we were reasonably confident were VC. We'd have a number of agent reports, interrogation reports, or captured documents in which they were mentioned. Sometimes we'd use the DIOCCs and PIOCC as libraries, to run a cross-check on somebody." [25] Lt. Col. Dao Quan Hien, who, as a National Police chief, had authority over the Special Police in his corps area, said: "The PRUs and the Special Police seldom tried to get the wrong people because, before arresting or destroying the infrastructure, we had to work closely with the U.S. advisers and discuss it with them. They had to agree on the operation." [26] The safeguards were not foolproof, but they prevented most potential abuses.

The misuse of power in the attack on the shadow government depended on factors besides those cited thus far. When people within the GVN had grudges against other people, they sometimes simply set off alone or with comrades and tried to arrest or shoot them. In some instances, if their superiors tolerated it, they tried to do the same during the course of a normal operation against the VC. Thus, they bypassed the intelligence systems that the Allies used to identify and locate the Viet Cong cadres. At the same time, mechanisms besides those built into the intelligence systems impeded improper targeting. These considerations and the general prevalence of neutralizing people for the wrong reasons are discussed in chapter 18.

PART THREE: Coordination

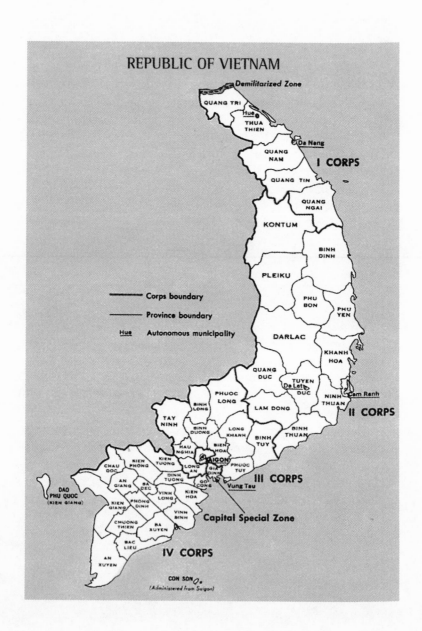

REPUBLIC OF VIETNAM

11   The Challenge: Phoenix Centers

he Phoenix concept of intelligence and operations coordination was more ambitious than it might have seemed to the
casual observer. ICEX and Phoenix, which I collectively call
Phoenix for simplicity's sake, and the parallel South Vietnamese Phung Hoang program had to overcome formidable obstacles in
order to achieve anything. The greatest obstacle, by far, was the reluctance of the intelligence agencies to share intelligence.

Through the District and Province Intelligence and Operations
Coordination Centers, the Phoenix program tried to coordinate
intelligence and operations against the shadow government and to
neutralize as many VCI as possible. In some places, especially at the
provincial level at the beginning of the program, Phoenix and Phung
Hoang were merely committees with no separate centers of their own.
To simplify the discussion, however, I refer to these committees, along
with the coordination centers, as Phoenix centers. The Phoenix centers varied considerably in their methods of operation, and these methods often affected the coordination capacities of a particular center.
The Americans and South Vietnamese in Saigon and at the regional
level gave their subordinates some freedom to organize the Phoenix
centers and assign personnel to suit local situations. In certain areas
with intense military activity and little opportunity for police work,
Phoenix centers concentrated exclusively on collection of tactical military intelligence, even though the Phoenix concept envisioned this
function as secondary in importance. Henry McWade, a Phoenix
adviser in Gia Dinh and Hau Nghia provinces from 1968 to 1970,
stated, "When the ground war heated up to the point where an NVA
regiment was slugging it out with elements of a U.S. division and an
ARVN division, then order of battle and tactical intelligence had the
highest priority."[1] Conversely, in some places where large-scale military activity was minimal, Phoenix center personnel spent most of
their time in trying to identify and locate the VCI.

Phoenix functioned differently at the district and provincial echelons within the same province. Usually the province chief or the province Phoenix coordinator chose whether the DIOCCs or the PIOCC would do most of the work. The individual making the choice usually based it on considerations of geography and demography—whether operations could be run more efficiently from the provincial capital or district capitals— and on the capabilities of the intelligence and operations agencies at each level. The best GVN organizations tended to have their advisers and top people, or their only people, at the provincial level, and the CIA's advisers normally worked at the provincial level. As a consequence, the province became the preferred echelon during the first years of Phoenix. Later, when the CIA scaled back its involvement in Phoenix, a much larger proportion of coordination occurred in the district centers. Starting in 1969, village-level Phoenix centers came into existence, but they never accomplished much.

The emphasis of many Phoenix centers, on the other hand, did not reflect a concern for local conditions. The South Vietnamese sometimes geared the Phoenix centers strictly toward tactical military intelligence when enemy military units did not pose a serious threat. In most of these cases, South Vietnamese military intelligence officers controlled the centers and chose their focus. Lybrand and Johnstone note, "When the S2 [military intelligence officer] heads either the province or the district Phung Hoang Committee, the emphasis of the program at that level tends to be on tactical or order-of-battle intelligence rather than on matters of infrastructure."[2]

Military intelligence officers understood tactical intelligence best, and their primary job was to collect it. They usually had few incentives to pay attention to the VCI. The policemen in such Phoenix centers normally were powerless to get the military to change its stance because the senior military officer typically enjoyed the favor of the province chief and outranked the senior police officer. The province chiefs, who had ultimate control over the personnel of their respective centers, tended to favor the military because all of the chiefs had military backgrounds and most were concerned primarily with military affairs, rather than the attack on the VCI. If they paid attention to the Phoenix centers at all, they generally wanted to use them only to improve military intelligence efforts. In the words of Col. Hoang Ngoc Lung, one of South Vietnam's top intelligence officers, "Province police chiefs were only second lieutenants. . . . Yet in the administration of the Phoenix Program they were supposed to direct the activities of ARVN officers, usually experienced captains who were province intelligence and operations officers. Even at the district level the police officer was outranked by the ARVN intelligence and operations officers. The result was that the police official had very little influence over policy or operations."[3]

Some American advisers also contributed to this situation. They too were more interested in tactical military matters than in the shadow government and did not press the South Vietnamese to put more effort into Phung Hoang. Ed Brady, who encountered many such people, said:

> Some battalion commander or brigade commander would say to the U.S. Phoenix adviser, "I don't know why you're not giving me anything that I can use. What the hell are you doing all this police stuff for? I want to know where the VC units are." The Phoenix adviser would try to help him. That was a perversion of what Phoenix was supposed to do.
>
> One time I went to a province in I Corps and after half a day of investigation, I concluded that the province adviser had no concept of what Phoenix was about. The PIOCCs and the DIOCCs were doing nothing worthwhile. I told the province senior adviser on my way out what my conclusions were, and he said, "I'll fix your career. I'm going to have you court-martialed." By the time I got to Saigon, he had called a three-star general to have me arrested for insubordination because I had challenged his authority. That colonel was one of the commander of MACV's favorite colonels, but he had no interest in what was going on with the Vietnamese or in a program like Phoenix. He had an interest in his own career and in U.S. units.[4]

Neither the Americans nor the South Vietnamese allocated personnel to the Phoenix centers as efficiently as they might have. By the end of 1969, despite the objections of Evan Parker, Jr., and other Americans, the South Vietnamese had established Phoenix centers in every province and in almost every district. Bureaucratic rigidity dictated that the program function in every administrative area, rather than in only the more important areas. As a result, in areas of low VCI activity or heavy main force unit activity, many personnel in the new Phoenix centers had almost nothing constructive to do, whereas Phoenix centers in other areas with higher levels of activity in the village war could have benefited from their services. Although less important districts and provinces generally received less capable people, some of the assigned personnel, particularly the U.S. advisers—of whom few were truly incompetent—could have contributed to the war effort in other significant ways. Parker explained:

> One of the unhappy things about the way that Phoenix was set up was that instead of concentrating on areas where there were a lot of people on our side and a large amount of VCI activity, the same structure was applied to every province and district. In some of these places, there weren't many

Americans or South Vietnamese because the areas were under enemy control or because there wasn't enough VC activity. There just wasn't very much to coordinate.[5]

By far the most important weakness of the Phoenix centers, however, was the unwillingness of the GVN intelligence agencies to share their information. Suspicion of the people in the centers and in the other participating organizations frequently accounted for this lack of cooperation. The officials of each agency believed or suspected that Phung Hoang and the other participating organizations had VC spies or other untrustworthy people in their ranks. They feared that, if their agency revealed its sources to others, someone might betray them to the VC, thus compromising its informants and agents and rendering its information useless. They also worried that another intelligence agency, after learning the identities of their agency's sources, might try to recruit them for its own purposes. Even if their agency provided information but did not disclose a source or gave only the source's code name, someone still might discover the person's identity.

Agencies sometimes claimed that fear of compromising their sources kept them from sharing intelligence in order to hide the fact that they had not collected good intelligence. Nevertheless, considering the numerous VC informants and agents within GVN organizations, GVN intelligence agencies had good reason to be cautious about sharing their information. An extensive 1971 study of Phung Hoang, titled *Phung Hoang Reexamination (PHREEX) Study,* concludes:

> The Phung Hoang Center, by its organizational nature, is not a secure repository for intelligence information. Most of the personnel in the center have no real feeling for the strict security measures necessary for the proper functioning of the program. The resultant high probability for compromise of sensitive sources and information makes professional intelligence gathering organizations, such as Police Special Branch and MSS [Military Security Service], reluctant to share their intelligence with the Phung Hoang centers.[6]

Intelligence agency officials also feared that the Phoenix centers would not make good use of intelligence. Phung Hoang might give the intelligence to a unit that would botch an operation that the intelligence made possible, squander the intelligence, and perhaps compromise the source of the intelligence. A considerable number of South Vietnamese and Americans avoided sending information to Phoenix centers because they did not have much confidence in the abilities of the National Police Field Forces, a primary Phoenix action arm. The following excerpt from a report on Quang Tri province exemplifies the widespread disdain of the NPFF:

> The biggest problem of the NPFF was said by the police advisor to be the availability of timely intelligence. Coordination between the NPFF and [Special Police] is a problem as the [Special Police] prefers to provide intelligence for the PRU rather than the NPFF.[7]

In addition, Phung Hoang often could not pass timely intelligence to a reaction force soon enough to be useful. By the time the Phoenix centers assembled the intelligence and helped arrange an operation, the intelligence might be out of date.

Officials of the various organizations often disliked one another, which made them reluctant to work together. Personal conflicts, organizational rivalry, or animosity between indigenous and nonindigenous personnel typically caused this problem. The military and the police had the most extensive record of mutual hostility. In a Phoenix center, the different intelligence targets—tactical military intelligence for the military, VCI intelligence for the police—provided grounds for disagreement. The inferior rank or skills of many police officers produced additional tensions. The Binh Duong Province senior adviser reported that "an atmosphere of jealousy and suspicion, if not distrust and hostility, exists between the various agencies, particularly between the military and the police. Under these conditions cooperation between the various elements has been little more than superficial."[8]

One of Phoenix's most significant problems, according to Lybrand and Johnstone, was "the generally poor relations between the National Police and the sector or subsector S2's. The rivalry and resultant lack of cooperation between the two are traditional. The ramifications of this rivalry are apparent at all levels from corps to district. Only in exceptional circumstances could the two elements be found working together productively. . . . As a general rule, if the Phung Hoang Committee were under the control of the S2, the police would not cooperate . . . whereas if it were under the control of the police, the S2 would not respond."[9]

Self-centered attitudes also stood in the way of intelligence sharing. The officials of each agency were concerned about getting the maximum credit for their agency's work in order to score points with their superiors. If the agencies shared their intelligence, the Phung Hoang staffs or the action arm that exploited the intelligence would get at least some of the credit. American advisers repeatedly complained, usually to no avail, that the people in intelligence organizations refused to share because they cared more about their personal and organizational prestige than about improving the overall attack on the VC shadow government. In August 1968, the Phu Bon province senior adviser noted:

> Reporting agencies are more concerned over who is going to get the credit than they are over how to negate the influence of the VC infrastructure in the Province. This is having a very serious effect on the operational effectiveness of the combined intelligence community. Confidence must be built up to the point where the various agencies are not competing with each other for recognition.[10]

The reluctance to share intelligence because of suspicion and jealousy afflicted the CIA and the U.S. military to a lesser extent. Generally, the Americans were more willing to set aside petty rivalries and share information. Initially, the CIA controlled Phoenix at the provincial level, so most Americans had little need to fear VC spies. The primary aim of Phoenix and Phung Hoang, though, was to stimulate sharing by the South Vietnamese; the Americans were a secondary consideration. Intelligence sharing among the South Vietnamese, in the long run, greatly exceeded in value the sharing among Americans. The GVN had more organizations and less interorganizational cooperation than the United States, and the Vietnamese ultimately would have to fight the Communists in the villages without American intelligence.

12 Attempts to Make Phoenix and Phung Hoang Work

ureaucratic discord prevented the South Vietnamese intelligence agencies from contributing to the Phoenix centers during most, but not all, of the program's history. The one major exception came at the provincial level during the years that the CIA managed the program, when the CIA used its unique assets to make the program work. CIA case officers contributed large amounts of their own intelligence to Phoenix. They controlled or exerted considerable influence over some of the key South Vietnamese organizations involved, and they had ways to find out how much intelligence these organizations had. As a result, they were able to persuade or force the organizations to share much, if not most, of their information. These advisers, however, did not have much influence over other GVN organizations. Phoenix worked better at the provincial level than at the district level during this time because the CIA advisers, the Special Police, the PRUs, and the other South Vietnamese at the provincial level usually had more influence and better skills than did CORDS advisers and the South Vietnamese at the district level. According to Daren Flitcroft, "Phoenix was more effective at the province level than at the district level because you had more senior people and more capable people there."[1]

In some provinces, nevertheless, CIA advisers did not try to stimulate much intelligence sharing during the years of CIA control over Phoenix, or they used methods different from those designed by the Phoenix directorate. Some CIA officers at the regional level and in Saigon did not require province-level officers to put much effort into the program, thus allowing those not interested to ignore it for the most part. Lt. Col. Robert Inman, who worked on the Phoenix staff in Saigon, commented:

> It didn't matter too much to the province officers what Saigon said. If CIA headquarters said, "This is our number one priority," some guy in a province could say, "To hell with that, this is what I'm interested in," and that's what he'd do. That happened in almost every program

in Vietnam. Sometimes the CIA adviser who ran the PRUs, the RD Cadres, and Census Grievance wouldn't even cooperate with the CIA Special Police adviser, and we at Phoenix couldn't do anything about it. You had a whole bunch of individuals doing whatever they wanted to do to get their time in, as well as some who were really sincere and thought that their program was the one that was going to win the war.[2]

The CIA's coordination efforts also did not function well where the province chiefs did not give Phoenix their blessing. "If the province chief was against the program," Ed Brady said, "it didn't work, because he was in a position to keep it from working if he wanted to."[3] Disapproving chiefs prevented many of the relevant organizations from participating in Phung Hoang. The province chiefs often did not have complete control of the Special Police, Census Grievance, and RD Cadre programs, and they usually had even less influence over the PRUs, but they normally had enough power to keep the program from working. If the province chiefs obstructed the Phoenix program, only the Americans shared much intelligence with the Phoenix centers. In most provinces, however, the province chiefs did not actively oppose Phung Hoang or the CIA convinced them not to oppose it.

During the years of CIA management, Phoenix center coordination at the district level did not achieve nearly as much success as at the provincial level because CIA advisers did not work at the district level nor did they usually try to exert much influence there. Most CIA case officers concentrated on working with the considerable assets of the CIA and its counterpart organizations at the provincial level, rather than working closely with the CORDS advisers and the South Vietnamese in the DIOCCs, who frequently lacked training, experience, or sources of information about the VCI. At the beginning, CIA officers helped to acquaint the DIOCC advisers with the local intelligence apparatus and counseled them on intelligence techniques, but they channeled specific pieces of intelligence to the DIOCC advisers in only a few cases. Peter Scott said:

> The CIA guys would recommend who to talk to. They knew the intel networks pretty well, and I was a new guy. So they'd say, "Go to the Special Police if you want, or go to the NPFF if you want, but don't believe anything Captain Hung tells you, because he's working both sides," or "That guy doesn't know a damn thing," or "He's stoned all the time," or something like that. They were basically just trying to help a kid learn the ropes. After I was there about half a year, the CIA people started becoming less and less involved.[4]

When the CIA disengaged in mid-1969, the main impetus for Phoenix disappeared and the program never recovered. In most cases, Special Police advisers no longer put much pressure on their counterparts to participate in Phung Hoang, and CIA advisers stopped giving much of their own intelligence to the centers. Chief of Station Shackley's emphasis on penetrating the VC diminished the interest of the Special Police and CIA case officers in tactical intelligence concerning the VCI and the village war. CIA advisers also lost their interest in the program because CORDS did not have the power or the knowledge needed to maintain the previously high levels of effectiveness and security. "After the CIA pulled back from Phoenix," Henry McWade recounted, "CIA personnel in the field would stiff-arm anyone from Phoenix as if he had leprosy."[5] As the CIA exited from Phoenix, the South Vietnamese military gained greater control over the Phoenix centers, which reduced the emphasis on attacking the VCI. In 1970, Robert Komer reported, "Shifting the U.S. advisory effort from a joint MACV/CIA affair to a wholly MACV responsibility was costly. One very senior and experienced U.S. official called it frankly a 'disaster.'"[6] The CIA maintained close ties with the Special Police and the PRUs, still two quite effective weapons in the village war, but used them independently of Phoenix. Conveniently fleeing the bureaucratic complications and the negative publicity that accompanied Phoenix, the CIA continued to fight the shadow government.

Without CIA help, the CORDS advisers in the Phoenix centers held unenviable positions. They had little intelligence of their own. The advisers most often could tell when the South Vietnamese were making token gestures without sharing intelligence, but they seldom could prod the South Vietnamese into participating in Phung Hoang because, unlike the CIA, they had no direct influence over the GVN intelligence organizations. Appeals to higher-level Americans to encourage GVN participation or direct appeals to South Vietnamese counterparts usually achieved little aside from encouraging more token gestures. The limited knowledge of the CORDS advisers in intelligence matters, moreover, restricted their ability to offer much valuable guidance to the South Vietnamese. Evan Parker, Jr., said of the CORDS advisers, "My biggest regret was that we had so many people involved as Phoenix advisers who hadn't been involved in intelligence as a career. I'm not saying they weren't good, because lots of them were very good. I only wish that our advisers had had a consistently higher level of experience and training."[7]

CORDS Phoenix advisers, however, did gain the cooperation of some U.S.

military units. As mentioned in chapter 10, some Phoenix centers gave U.S. units tactical military intelligence. The U.S. units often returned the favor. "I spent some of my time working on purely tactical military operations," said Lt. Col. John Cook, "so I coordinated with the S-2s of the surrounding U.S units. We got some good information from the battalions of the 1st Infantry Division in our district."[8] The U.S. military units and the Phoenix centers also shared information on the VCI, and the U.S. units provided some military support for operations in the villages.

A few of the South Vietnamese had the power to make the Phoenix centers work. Foremost among them were the district chiefs and province chiefs. They could make many of the agencies share intelligence and could order action forces to mount operations with Phung Hoang intelligence. The province chiefs were especially important because they appointed and fired the district chiefs and told them what to do. Once the CIA pulled out of the program, the ability of the Phoenix centers to function, and especially to stimulate intelligence sharing, depended mainly on the efforts of these chiefs. The Phoenix yearly report for 1969 states, "Improvement of exchange of information between agencies responsible for PIOCC and DIOCC operations occurred only where strong Province Chief or District Chief interest and pressure was applied."[9] On occasion, other district- and province-level GVN leaders made Phung Hoang work because their respective district or province chiefs, although they did not care about the program, gave them the authority to implement it.

Certain circumstances suggested that the district and province chiefs would support Phung Hoang. Following the Communists' Tet offensive of 1968, the overall quality and initiative of the GVN leadership in the districts and provinces improved greatly. Many more district and province chiefs were making bold attempts to fight the VC. When President Thieu issued a decree in July 1968 that ordered the chiefs to support Phung Hoang, GVN officials suddenly began taking an interest in the program. Most district and province chiefs, however, stopped paying attention to Phung Hoang soon after the decree's issuance and ignored it for the rest of the war. A number of factors account for their indifference. Some of them found the program too complicated or its objectives too difficult. With many other responsibilities and many committees to chair, the chiefs did not have time to work on all of the programs that the Americans wanted them to run. A few American advisers thought that the Vietnamese had ulterior motives for not supporting Phung Hoang, but it was hard to prove their suspicions. An effective Phung Hoang program might reveal the VC in a district or province to be stronger than the chief had claimed, which could make him look bad. Some district and province chiefs did not want to coordinate operations against the shadow government because they feared such operations would have negative consequences (see chapter 16).

Many knowledgeable Americans and Vietnamese believed, however, that the most important reason why district and province chiefs did not put any effort into Phung Hoang was the unwillingness of President Thieu and the powerful ARVN corps commanders to pressure their subordinates to make the program work. The district and province chiefs would have worked on the program if their superiors had ordered it. As one province senior adviser observed, "High level GVN pressure on Province and District Chiefs is an essential ingredient in ensuring the success of the Phung Hoang program. This point cannot be overemphasized."[10]

Although Thieu and other top GVN officials always assured the Americans that they ordered the district and province chiefs to make Phung Hoang a top priority, real GVN command emphasis faded soon after its initial surge in July 1968. The high-level GVN commanders decided that other activities, especially military operations of a more conventional type, deserved the chiefs' attention more than did Phung Hoang. They, as well as many American generals, reasoned that the military units would ultimately decide the war's outcome, which was true, and that the Viet Cong shadow government, therefore, was not very important, which was not entirely true. Many commanders also understood that the most important VCI by now tended to travel alongside the armed VC units; by destroying the military units, they would eliminate many of the cadres anyway. Throughout the period 1968–72, American advisers in most districts and provinces made reports similar to this one from Bac Lieu province: "The Phung Hoang program is not functioning at an acceptable level. Despite repeated efforts by responsible advisors, Vietnamese officials, including the Province Chief, are not implementing the program according to concept. If any progress is to be made, higher GVN echelons must bring pressure to bear on the Province Chief."[11]

An examination of the Phoenix centers themselves manifests the failure of Phoenix and Phung Hoang to collect VCI intelligence from Allied intelligence organizations and to mount operations against the VCI in most of South Vietnam. Almost all Phoenix advisers complained that Allied intelligence agencies, absent the direct involvement of the CIA, kept their own separate files on the VCI and refused to share much information from those files with the Phoenix centers. "The Intelligence and Operations Coordination Centers were not too effective," Colonel Inman said. "The problems existed on both the American and Vietnamese sides. Nobody shared their resources. The most common reason given was concern for security, but that could be a pretty handy excuse for anything else."[12]

The GVN intelligence agencies often sent their least competent personnel to serve as representatives in the Phoenix centers and normally withheld their good intelligence from these representatives lest they should make it available to the centers. Donald Colin reported, "When the Vietnamese intelligence services were approached to contribute personnel to staff the Phung-Hoang program, they sent their most marginal members and took immediate steps to ensure that these members would no longer receive any meaningful intelligence from their parent agencies."[13] These representatives, moreover, often spent little time at the Phoenix centers, especially at the district level, except when inspection teams or commanders made visits to check up on them. The individual GVN agencies, however, sometimes had justification for these actions. The Phoenix centers often had little meaningful work to do because the intelligence agencies provided minimal information. Therefore, an agency stood to lose by assigning a representative, especially one of its better people, to waste most of the day sitting around in an idle Phoenix center. The Phoenix center chiefs and advisers, indeed, often allowed the representatives to work only part time because of the centers' inactivity. Scott said of his district Phoenix center, "There just wasn't enough intelligence coming into the DIOCC for us to hold people there."[14]

According to official policy, the duties of Phoenix center staffs included determining where the organizations were getting their information and using that knowledge to evaluate the quality of intelligence and to prevent multiple agencies from using the same source. Staff members rarely accomplished this mission. Allied intelligence organizations refused to reveal their sources, most often because of the fear that VC spies in the centers would learn the identities of sources, or the fear that other intelligence agencies would recruit their sources. Each of these fears was legitimate. Lybrand and Johnstone note:

> One of the complaints most often voiced by DIOCC and Phoenix advisors in the field was the lack of a control system for agents of the various groups having an input into the DIOCC. The results are often that a piece of intelligence information will be reported by one agency and confirmed by two or three others, giving it a high credibility rating. In fact, the information may come from only one agent who reports it to several different agencies. ...

The problem, it is felt, is as bad among the US intelligence sources as among the Vietnamese.[15]

Phoenix and Phung Hoang generally enjoyed moderate success in identifying VC cadres by name. When the CIA managed Phoenix, it amassed a large amount of information about the identification of specific cadres, considerably more than when CORDS ran the program. Under CORDS, the Phoenix centers regularly calculated the number of VCI that they had identified and compared it with total estimated VCI strength. In 1970, for instance, the Phoenix centers claimed to have identified 57 percent of the VCI, on average, in their provinces.[16] Their calculations, however, were both inaccurate and misleading. Many of the identified VCI had not been confirmed. Binh Thuan province, which had one of the best Phoenix programs in Vietnam in 1971, reported 722 identified VCI out of an estimated VCI strength of 950 during that year, but only 300 of those identified had been confirmed.[17] Given the difficulties inherent in counting the members of the shadow government, moreover, the total number of estimated VCI, as well as the number supposedly identified, might have been well off the mark.

Another potential indicator of the success in identifying the VCI was the fraction of neutralized cadres who had been identified as VCI before neutralization. CORDS statistics typically showed that about one-half of captured and killed VCI had been identified as such beforehand, although the proportion varied considerably from one area to the next.[18] Again, the numbers were deceptive. Some reports from the provinces differed sharply from the official CORDS reports. The province senior adviser in Binh Duong, for example, stated that the figure in his province was only 20 percent, whereas CORDS listed it at 64 percent.[19] Detailed inspections of Long An and Phu Yen provinces revealed that only 16 percent of neutralized VC cadres who held village leadership positions—crucial VCI targets—had been identified prior to neutralization. Official CORDS statistics from about the same time listed the VCI identified before neutralization at 83 percent for Long An and 97 percent for Phu Yen.[20] The CORDS statistics also suffered from flawed means of collection. As parts IV and V explain, the Allies often misidentified certain prisoners and dead bodies as VCI. They called some of these people previously identified VCI and some previously unidentified VCI.

A few Phoenix centers contained fairly good dossiers on the cadres about whom they had some information, usually in provinces where the province chiefs or the CIA exerted pressure to make the centers work. In most districts and provinces, however, dossiers contained little information from intelligence reports or other hard evidence about the cadre's identity, personal life, and modus operandi. Brady described his experience:

> I spent an awful lot of time touring the country and inspecting VCI dossiers and other things in DIOCCs and PIOCCs throughout South Vietnam. It was very routine for us to go into center after center and go through hundreds and hundreds of file folders, and find virtually nothing in them. Or we'd find that what was in them was very superficial and not useful to the purposes of targeting someone. I saw hundreds of dossiers in which the main piece of intelligence was that an unspecified person in the marketplace said the guy was VC. Maybe he was and maybe he wasn't. How would anybody know? You had no way to check on the veracity of the source. A great deal of what was in the dossiers was trash. People did it because they were under bureaucratic pressure to build dossiers and put pieces of information in them. It was just like a U.S. government agency—if you ask them to do something, they do it, and a lot of the time it isn't high quality.[21]

Not all operations depended on dossiers. As the result of tips or other timely information, the centers sometimes acted immediately against particular cadres or other VC for whom they lacked adequate dossiers or other information. Almost no Phoenix centers, however, ever coordinated a significant number of operations against particular VCI or VC on the basis of either this type of intelligence or dossiers. Many centers coordinated no operations at all, and those that did usually coordinated only regular military operations or random searches of villages, rather than attempts to capture specific people at particular times and places. In most cases, Phoenix centers had less information suitable for operational use in the village war than the Special Police, the PRUs, and the CIA each had by themselves. One typical report, from Thua Thien province, states, "In all cases [Special Police and Phung Hoang] are found to possess the same mission and virtually the same information with one exception, that the [Special Police] has more and better information in almost every case."[22]

In the end, most Phoenix center personnel spent their time on data processing and record-keeping tasks of marginal value. The South Vietnamese in the centers often produced reams of seemingly impressive paperwork and organized it neatly in their efforts to satisfy the American advisers, who generally cared more about the success of the Phoenix centers than did the South Vietnamese. The centers often impressed inattentive advisers and inexperienced visitors, but perceptive advisers invariably saw through the charade and realized how meaningless most of the paperwork was. Stephen Dukkony, the deputy province senior adviser of Go Cong province at the end of American involvement in pacification, asserts in his completion of tour report, "The results of the program are extremely poor for the number of people involved and the vast amount of energy expended. The system may be acceptable as a record keeping and data collection point, but the ability to conduct targeted operations is practically nil."[23]

The absence of intelligence sharing and coordination of operations after mid-1969 frustrated the Americans so much that many advocated overhauling or eliminating the system. During late 1971, in response to these criticisms, CORDS finally decided to rebuild it. During the next six months, CORDS and the GVN transferred the tasks of the Phoenix centers to the Police Operations Centers. The National Police then established new interagency Phung Hoang committees in the districts and provinces, and the intelligence agencies sent representatives to these committees. Because the CIA-supported Special Police assumed responsibility for coordination, the CIA renewed its involvement in a centralized attack on the VCI, which it had abandoned a few years before. By this time, however, the CIA had withdrawn from its role in the Census Grievance and RD Cadre programs and had become less concerned with the VCI than with other matters, so it did not put as much effort into the program as before. In most places, the volume of intelligence sharing did not change appreciably after the Special Police took over Phung Hoang.

Considering the inactivity of the Phoenix centers, it might seem that the program wasted valuable GVN human and material resources. Most GVN agencies, however, assigned only their least competent personnel to the centers, and many of these representatives did not work full time in the centers. Compared with other Allied programs, Phoenix centers did not cost much to construct and operate.[24] Phoenix centers that did not work well, however, squandered the services of some capable young American officers.

13 Other Intelligence and Operations Coordination

hroughout South Vietnam, intelligence and operations coordination occurred independently of the Phoenix centers much more frequently than it did through the centers. Intelligence agencies regularly passed information directly to operational forces, as they had before the initiation of Phoenix. This sharing transpired in the tactical operations centers and Police Operations Centers or via interagency meetings and informal contacts elsewhere. An American report from Ba Xuyen province describes a common intelligence-sharing arrangement: "The PIOCC continues to be a storehouse for inert intelligence rather than an exploitation center. Presently, the [Special Police] is providing targets for the NPFF and the PRU without the knowledge of the PIOCC."[1]

Bypassing the Phoenix centers gave intelligence and operations organizations several advantages. Intelligence services knew which forces would exploit the intelligence and whether or not they were reliable. Knowing the organization or source that provided a piece of intelligence gave operational forces a good indication of its validity. Both parties also avoided the risk that VC informants or agents in the Phoenix centers would learn who was furnishing what information or what operations would take place soon. In addition, direct coordination eliminated the time interval needed for the intelligence to go through a Phoenix center on its way to an action unit, which could make time-sensitive intelligence useless.

Such cooperative relationships between organizations often depended on organizational relationships or the personal relationships between their leaders and advisers. In the large majority of cases, the South Vietnamese shared among themselves, and the Americans shared among themselves. Each group could more easily establish personal rapport and mutual trust within itself because of common language and culture. Sharing between Americans and Vietnamese occurred regularly only in the cases of the PRUs and the Special Police, which enjoyed uniquely close relationships with CIA advisers.

Most CIA province officers frequently fed useful intelligence about the VC shadow government to fellow CIA officers who worked with the PRUs or to the PRUs themselves. CIA officers at the regional level also gave substantial amounts of valuable intelligence to the PRUs and helped to organize some PRU operations. Le Van Thai, a deputy province PRU chief, said, "The PRUs got most of their information from the CIA or from themselves."[2] Members of the Special Police, as discussed in chapter 6, consistently provided information to their advisers.

Within the South Vietnamese group, district and province chiefs, if so inclined, could pass information or direct organizations to pass information without going through the Phoenix centers. Because of their power over a variety of organizations, they could stimulate a great deal of intelligence sharing without the assistance of Phung Hoang. Most low-ranking officers of the various organizations seldom shared information with each other, unless they had help from the higher ranks, for the same reasons that they did not contribute information to Phung Hoang.

After removing itself from Phoenix, the CIA continued to facilitate intelligence sharing among CIA-sponsored organizations through its advisers to the respective organizations. Except at the beginning of the Phoenix era, CIA advisers at the provincial level worked under the same superior, who, in some cases, forced them to share. They usually lived and worked together, which made cooperation easier. Col. Viet Lang said, "Sometimes the PRU adviser got information from the Special Police advisers for us. We alone had no power over the Special Police, no way to get the information."[3] CIA officers also worked closely with some of the Chieu Hoi advisers and, to a much lesser extent, with other CORDS advisers.

The CIA and U.S. military intelligence organizations often shared information directly with each other. CIA officers provided intelligence concerning the VCI and their protectors to U.S. units, particularly the SEALs (Sea-Air-Land teams) and the Special Forces. The CIA called on these units when the PRUs were otherwise occupied or lacked the necessary mobility and firepower. "If we had an important target and the SEALs weren't already out on a mission," Rex Wilson said, "we'd give it to them."[4]

Some American intelligence personnel generally avoided sharing information with anyone either because they disliked or distrusted other advisers and organizations or because they did not want others to get the credit. PRU adviser Jack Harrell said, "Very seldom would Special Police advisers want to coordinate operations with me. It was a matter of not wanting to share assets, and of worrying that there were penetrations in various organizations. If I had a contact that I wanted to work myself, I wasn't about to share the information with the Special Police or anyone else, and that's about the same feeling that Special Police advisers and other advisers had."[5]

American advisers coordinated many joint operations between their South Vietnamese counterpart units and American forces. These operations took place most commonly in areas where light GVN forces stood a good chance of being overrun by larger Communist forces and where the American military units needed intelligence from local personnel. "We had a brigade commander from the 101st Airborne in my area who recognized the importance of the PRUs and the Phoenix Program," John Mullins recalled, "and he cooperated with us 100 percent. When we needed helicopters to go into a place, when we needed soldiers to secure a village, he would provide that. We provided the intelligence and the specifics. They provided the muscle."[6] The unit with the intelligence normally could avoid divulging much about its source and merely give operational directions to the partner unit. Both units received credit for successful operations.

In some instances, the Phoenix centers facilitated direct coordination between action forces although they did not carry it out. By bringing together representatives from different organizations, the centers increased the likelihood that two agencies would decide to work together in attacking the VCI. Phoenix advisers themselves sometimes helped to arrange such coordination, especially the CIA Phoenix coordinators, because they had close contact with certain organizations. At times, Phung Hoang and the Phoenix advisers also prompted better GVN coordination of attacks on the VCI that did not involve the Phoenix centers simply by making GVN leaders more conscious of the VCI threat.

Frequently, action units operated according to intelligence that they generated themselves and avoided intelligence sharing altogether. Some units almost always used their own intelligence because they were more certain of its veracity and, of course, of the reliability of the action arm than if they had worked with the Phoenix centers or other organizations. In addition, because they knew the identities of all their sources, the units could force those individuals who produced intelligence to participate in the operations, thereby deterring them from supplying information that would lead the unit into a Communist ambush. John Wilbur, a Yale-educated SEAL officer who headed the PRU advisory effort in the Mekong Delta during 1967 and 1968, explained:

A lot of what the PRUs did was internal. They produced their own intelligence, and they set up and planned their own reaction responses. We thought these methods ensured the security and integrity of the operation. If you were working for someone across the street and you came over to me with a hot tip, and I told my guys, "Joe over there has a hot tip," they would have said, "Who's Joe? How do we know if he's right or wrong?" We knew how reliable our own sources were, so there was a strong bias against setting up operations that relied on an external, unknown source.[7]

Further, a unit could react more quickly to its own intelligence than to intelligence from other sources.

The overall success of Allied organizations in obtaining intelligence to use in neutralizing the VC shadow government and other VC in the villages followed the same patterns in many places at many times. GVN intelligence agencies not affiliated with the CIA generated anywhere from no intelligence to a very large amount of intelligence. They could obtain plenty of information if they had good leaders, but some of their leaders were poor. Some agencies lacked indigenous personnel, which prevented them from obtaining information from relatives in the hamlets or in the VC. The two main action arms under the CORDS aegis, the National Police Field Forces and the territorial forces, generally fared quite differently in obtaining this type of intelligence. The National Police Field Forces, which usually had neither good leaders nor native personnel, generated little intelligence on their own. Intelligence agencies were supposed to feed the NPFF large amounts of information, through the Phoenix centers or directly, which they could use to neutralize the VC cadres. The NPFF, however, seldom received much intelligence in most of the provinces, except during the last years of the war. For all of the reasons mentioned in chapters 12 and 13, the intelligence agencies were reluctant to share their intelligence with such an unimpressive organization as the NPFF. In a typical report, senior adviser to the NPFF William Grieves states:

> The most consistent comment on intelligence contained in NPFF Operational Reports by US Public Safety Advisors during 1969 was that the intelligence and targeting furnished NPFF by the [Special Police], the PIOCCs and the DIOCCs were slow, inadequate or non-existent.[8]

The Regional Forces and Popular Forces generally had better access to information. They had many good leaders and they worked in their home areas. District and province chiefs often gave the territorial forces information from other sources. Because the GVN high command emphasized military action over attacks on the VCI, the Regional Forces and Popular Forces generally paid less attention to the shadow government than they did to the enemy armed forces. The VC and the VCI were so closely inter-connected, however, that information about small enemy units usually contributed significantly to attacks on the VCI.

South Vietnamese organizations that the CIA funded—PRUs, Special Police, and, for a time, RD Cadres and Census Grievance—produced, in most cases, substantial amounts of intelligence concerning the VCI and their VC co-conspirators. These organizations, particularly the PRUs, had better leadership on average than other GVN organizations because of the CIA's influence, although some leaders were nonetheless weak and unproduc-tive. With the exception of the RD Cadres, furthermore, these organiza-tions drew many of their employees from the local population.

CIA personnel at the provincial and regional levels usually amassed this same type of intelligence in considerable quantities. Together, the CIA offi-cers and their South Vietnamese counterparts, even when the CIA no longer controlled Phoenix, identified a large fraction of the VC shadow government in most places. Rex Wilson, for instance, recalled, "I'd say we had maybe 65 or 70 percent of the VCI in the province identified. We knew the structure, and so we could do wiring diagrams of the different levels and fill in the names. If we had good coverage, we had 75 percent of the key cadres named. We had pictures of a lot of them."[9]

The CIA and the South Vietnamese whom they advised also developed plenty of intelligence that located the VCI and other VC involved in the vil-lage war. The Special Police hoarded some of the intelligence, but the bulk of it went to the PRUs. Most PRU members and CIA advisers testified that the PRUs had an abundance of intelligence that helped them to find the local VCI and small VC units. James Watson, PRU adviser in the Rung Sat Special Zone during the late 1960s, notes, "With the Agency feeding me intel for the PRUs, I had all the information I could handle."[10] Bob Boyke told me, "The PRUs had more than enough intelligence to keep them busy all the time. There was always something for them to do, and they were very, very active."[11]

PART FOUR: Operations

14   The Nature of Operations

A common image of the "Phoenix program" involves South Vietnamese commandos sneaking into village huts at night and arresting or killing people. In reality, the Allies neutralized VC political cadres or alleged cadres in many different types of situations, most of which bore little resemblance to this scenario. Allied forces did arrest or kill most of the cadres they neutralized, but, in a few cases, they asked cadres to remain in place and spy for the GVN or encouraged them to rally through the Chieu Hoi program. The type of operation that the Allies ran depended on their operational mission and capabilities, the behavior of the VCI, the local military situation, and, above all, the intelligence available. Even for elite forces, whose fighting skill and stealth are often considered their most important assets, intelligence largely determined the circumstances under which they would come into contact with the shadow government.

With "rifle-shot" operations, the Allies tried to neutralize VCI who were reported to be at a certain place at a certain time. Rifle-shot operations succeeded much more often than other operations, but they required the most specific—and hence the most scarce—types of intelligence. In some cases, the Allies ran rifle-shot operations based on intelligence indicating the location of illegal cadres on a specific night or at a specific time of night while they were visiting a hamlet or traveling to a hamlet. Most of these cadres were trying to perform the functions of the shadow government or to see their families, and they usually had other VC with them. In a smaller number of cases, the Allies discovered the trails or canals, remote from the hamlets, on which the cadres and their fellow VC would travel on a particular night or at a specific time. Still less often, they pinpointed VCI in the wilderness at stationary targets, such as secret bases or supply depots.

Another common form of rifle-shot operation resulted from the identification of legal cadres. When the Allies identified certain citizens as legal cadres and wanted to neutralize them in one way or another, they merely had to go to their homes or wait for them to show up at a central marketplace. From time to time, in the diminishing number of hamlets under VC control, the Allies located illegal cadres living full time in the hamlets, who did not suspect that the Allies might come after them. These people were dealt with in similar fashion. If an intelligence source identified a considerable number of cadres living in hamlets, however, Allied units tried to neutralize them simultaneously; otherwise, word of the security leak would spread and some cadres would hide from the Allies.

With less precise intelligence, the Allies mounted "shotgun" operations. Allied units that had intelligence on the identity, but not the location, of VC cadres often ran a type of shotgun operation known as "cordon and search." Armed troops surrounded a hamlet suspected of harboring VC to prevent anyone from leaving, and a search party, frequently composed of intelligence or police personnel from other organizations, combed the hamlet for VCI and VC. To identify cadres, the searchers relied on information already obtained by Allied intelligence agencies, on interrogation of villagers and any captured VC, and on ID card checks.

Some cordon-and-search operations fit better into the rifle-shot category because the Allies conducted them when they knew beforehand that certain illegal cadres or Communist soldiers would be in a particular hamlet at a given time, or when they had already identified cadres living in a hamlet and simply were rounding them up. More commonly, however, the Allies cordoned off a hamlet on a hunch that some local VCI and VC might be there. The Allies often executed these haphazard cordon-and-search operations poorly. In some cases, they did not establish a cordon tightly enough and the Communists escaped. At times, they did not have adequate intelligence. To make matters more difficult, the illegal cadres and other VC spent less and less time in the hamlets as the war progressed. A typical evaluation report of the National Police Field Forces, which normally lacked both good operational and intelligence capabilities, states: "The present technique of operating in a cordon and search seems rather fruitless. Immense numbers are used with paltry results. Most VCI suspects detained are later released."[1]

On occasion, when the Allies could identify cadres but could not find them, they disseminated false information in order to discredit them in the VC's eyes. In some instances, they tried to spread rumors that cadres spied for the Allies. The Allies used this method only sparingly because it required skill and patience, and the VC sometimes tracked down and punished those who participated. Less risky methods of deceiving the enemy included showering cadres' families with gifts to encourage neighbors to suspect that they were working for the Allies. Col. Viet Lang gave another example: "If we tried to kidnap someone and we failed, we left something for him that damaged his career with the Communists. We put a radio or a cassette with a note saying, 'Dear so-and-so, we came to see you, but unfortunately you were not here and we could not talk to you. We are giving you this as a present.' When the Communists came, they thought, 'Maybe this guy changed his mind and decided to work for the enemy.'"[2]

If the Allies knew when and where certain VCI frequently traveled but did not have exact times and locations, they often resorted to another form of shotgun operation, in which they set up ambushes along their routes of travel. To cover more extensive areas, Allied troops patrolled in various strengths—large groups when firepower was the main concern and small groups when stealth was most important. Ambushes and patrols succeeded most often at night, when the Communists usually moved and worked, but effective night operations required aggressive leaders who disciplined their troops well, a scarce commodity in some GVN organizations.

In many cases, the Allies neutralized VCI even though they had no intelligence about particular cadres. Because the VCI usually traveled with armed guards, small Allied operations against the VC and larger main force operations inevitably netted some VCI in the process. Many commentators and historians overlook the role of the military forces and presume that the Phoenix program or other elements of pacification were responsible for neutralizing most of the VCI.

Most of the Allied units that ran operations aimed specifically at the VCI conducted more shotgun operations than rifle-shot operations. They did not have the intelligence necessary for rifle-shot operations against identified VCI, and they were often unwilling to operate at night or in dangerous areas. The only forces that knew the location of many particular VCI and targeted them were the PRUs, and even they spent the bulk of their time on regular small-unit military operations. The Special Police and elite units, such as the SEALs and the Kit Carson Scouts, targeted specific VCI somewhat less often. This 1968 report is similar to many that preceded and followed it:

> The "rifle as opposed to the shotgun" approach of the Phoenix program has not yet materialized in the field. The majority of anti-infrastructure operations are of the cordon and search variety where anything that might fall into the trap is picked up. . . . The two principal reasons [rifle-shot] targeting is not being done are, first, a lack of good intelligence on the activities of the VCI and, second, a lack of an effective targeting force at the district level. . . . The only effective reaction force with a targeting capability is the PRU.[3]

Statisticians tried to quantify how many operations targeted specific VCI, but their efforts were unproductive because they did not have access to all of the PRU operational information. They also provided unsatisfactory definitions of "specific targeting" and "general targeting."[4]

When choosing whether and how to operate, the action units had to consider the local military situation. In areas where Communist military forces were strong and active, the Allied main force units and the territorial forces had to direct many or most of their operations toward destroying the Communist forces and defending district and provincial capitals and military installations. They often had little time for cordon-and-search or other operations aimed directly at the VCI. Inspectors who surveyed Dak To district in Kontum province during 1969 reported: "The feeling of the district chief and the DSA seemed to be that they had their hands full with a regimental sized enemy threat and intense small and medium-sized contacts with the enemy. That just did not leave much GVN time or energy for other programs such as the attack on the VCI."[5]

At times, particularly during large-scale Communist offensives, such as the Tet offensive and Easter offensive, even the PRUs, RD cadres, and police had to commit themselves to fighting the Communist main and local forces. "The PRUs weren't meant to be frontline soldiers," Dan Mudrinich said, "but on occasion, when an area was badly hit by the Viet Cong, they joined the regular military forces. A couple of times at Moc Hoa [the capital of Kien Tuong province] the only thing that kept the Viet Cong from taking the town was a unit of a hundred PRUs."[6]

In areas with high levels of military activity or in quieter areas where the VC possessed formidable military forces, pacification forces usually avoided operating against the VCI unless accompanied by military units. These areas declined in number as the war progressed, and few of them existed in the Mekong Delta throughout this period, but they remained in some parts of I Corps for most of the war. In such areas, the VC typically had enough information from their sources in the GVN and the rural population, as well as from their own patrols and reconnaissance missions, that they could usually locate GVN pacification forces rather quickly and defeat them with overwhelming strength. Lt. Gen. Ngo Quang Truong, whom most observers deemed one of the most capable of the ARVN's top officers, describes this matter in reference to the Regional Forces (RF) and Popular Forces (PF):

> Given their organization and mission, RF and PF performance depended primarily on the effectiveness of the regular units which provided the protec-

tive shield against invading forces. When this shield was solid, the RF and PF could easily defeat adversaries of the same size. But when enemy main force units succeeded in penetrating this shield in large numbers, there was no way the RF and PF, with their limited capabilities, could defend themselves. Unfortunately, this happened often in South Vietnam because geographical configuration and terrain were not conducive to effective defense against infiltration.[7]

Territorial forces themselves contributed to the shield for smaller forces in areas of lower military intensity.

The PRUs and the best of the GVN Regional Forces sometimes ventured into areas where the enemy had substantial armed strength and controlled the hamlets, yet even they tended to stay away from areas where the Communists had large military units. "There were quite a few areas in Quang Nam where we didn't operate," Bruce Lawlor said, "because you'd have to fight your way in and fight your way out, and the PRUs weren't designed to do that. The amount of force that the enemy had in those areas was more than we would want to deal with. The U.S. Marines patrolled in those areas, but they'd go in with a company or a battalion, with air or artillery support."[8] Several former PRU advisers told me that their most frightening experiences with PRU units involved unintentional contacts with Communist main forces. The PRUs, they recalled, fought well but tried to get away as quickly as they could.

In the many areas where the VCI were active and the Communists did not have enough conventional military power to threaten the district and provincial capitals seriously, a particular Allied unit could help the Allied cause by participating either in military operations against armed Communists or in operations designed specifically to neutralize the shadow government. This distinction, however, was misleading, for emphasizing the attack on the VCI did not necessarily lead to greater success in the war against the shadow government. VC military forces usually escorted the illegal cadres, who were the most important VCI. As a result, effective military operations, such as ambushes near contested hamlets, frequently netted more VC political cadres than random cordon-and-search operations and other so-called anti-VCI operations. In addition, a clear dichotomy between the types of operations did not always exist. Information about a VCI who happened to be traveling with an armed unit often led to an ambush or other operation that could be termed a "military" operation.

Some commanders in these areas could choose to focus on certain types of military operations that damaged the shadow government more than did other types, an important consideration that the distinction between military operations and anti-VCI operations does not take into account. On the one hand, they could run small military operations in the village areas, which, in all probability, would neutralize some illegal political cadres. On the other hand, they could concentrate on undermining the Communist main forces with conventional military operations in regions remote from the population, which were unlikely to neutralize many political cadres because few of these cadres normally served alongside the Communist military forces in such places. When deciding how to use his forces, the responsible commander had to assess the relative importance of the shadow government and of the Communist military forces in the area, along with the capabilities available for dealing with each threat.

One of the greatest difficulties inherent in any operation was keeping it secret from VC agents and informants who worked for the GVN or the Americans and who had access to plans for upcoming Allied operations. The planning for many GVN operations, especially those requiring large units and air and artillery support, involved significant numbers of South Vietnamese, and American operations often included interpreters. In addition, all operations were reported to the local tactical operations center (TOC), which coordinated the various Allied forces in order to prevent them from operating in the same area and attacking each other. VC spies often infiltrated these centers. Spies with access to Allied intelligence work also watched for concerted efforts to collect information in any particular area, because such concentration suggested that the Allies were preparing to target that area.

After VC spies in GVN organizations obtained information about upcoming operations, they sent it from person to person until it reached the appropriate people. When forewarned of an Allied operation, the targeted Communists either fled the area or tried to ambush the Allied forces. Some GVN units regularly failed to maintain operational secrecy and either found nothing or ran into ambushes on their operations.

In most cases, however, competent Allied forces that operated in small units found ways to keep the VC from discovering their intentions ahead of time. To prevent traitors from identifying the focus of intelligence collection, the Allies investigated a multitude of areas instead of only the target area. They kept radio communications to a bare minimum. As chapter 7 explains, the Allies succeeded in keeping a number of VC informants and agents out of sensitive positions and in concealing secret information from some suspected VC collaborators whom they could not remove. Allied commanders also went out of their way to minimize the total number of people who knew about operational plans, whether or not they detected the presence of traitors. Many GVN leaders did not even tell their own staffs about future operations. Col. Walter B. Clark, the Vinh Binh province senior adviser in 1971 and 1972, recalled that his counterpart employed extreme measures to hide information from his own people. Clark described a meeting between this province chief, Col. Chung Van Bong, and an ARVN division commander:

> They conferred openly in front of their respective staffs in Colonel Bong's headquarters, but then to conduct their real business, they got in Jeeps with a few of us and drove to a large open field. The two men walked to the center of the field and conducted their business while the rest of us stood hundreds of yards away, unable to hear anything. That's a difficult way to run an army.[9]

If an action unit leader suspected one of his men of passing information to the VC, he made sure to take the suspected collaborator on any operations that he might have compromised so that he would face death if the Communists ambushed the unit. "We had two guys who I thought were working both sides," said Peter Scott, who worked closely with a team of Kit Carson Scouts in Chau Doc province. "We'd take them with us on operations, so we'd know that they hadn't squawked, because if they had, they'd be killed too."[10] The Allies adopted a similar policy with some ralliers, prisoners, guides, and informants whom they did not trust entirely. They often persuaded or forced these people to escort them to VC hideouts in order to ensure that the sources did not lead them into ambushes.

Lt. Comdr. Frank Thornton, Jr., a PRU adviser in the Rung Sat, explained how the SEALs and the PRUs treated guides:

> If the operation the SEALs would go on was more than a regular ambush, I would have a couple of PRUs go along with the guide and he would take the squad in. That way the squad could concentrate on the area around them and the PRUs would watch the guide. If it turned out the intel was bad and the guide was leading us into a trap, he would be the first one to go. Hard as this system is, it cut way down on bad intel and bogus guides.[11]

If forced to go on operations, VC informants or agents who worked for the GVN could tip off the Communists with the understanding that the Communists would dodge the Allied forces but not try to ambush them. To minimize this problem, GVN commanders waited as long as possible to tell their units about a coming operation. Once they went over the operation with their troops, they denied them any opportunity to communicate with the Communists. If any people who did not go on the operation had to know about it, the commander also informed them at the latest possible moment. Le Van Thai said, "Maybe the PRUs had someone working for them who helped the VC, but it was very difficult to find out who they were. When we got information, only my company commander and operations officer and the intelligence officer and I knew, and we planned the operation. Sometimes we let the district leaders know. Then we told the men about the operation one or two hours before, and we didn't let them go anywhere."[12]

The Allies had several means of preventing the VC from learning about operations through sources in a tactical operations center. Some PRUs and a few other forces with political clout would not inform the TOC where they would be operating. Instead, their representatives visited the TOC and checked the location of other current Allied activities. Then, the units chose areas of operation in places free of friendly action. If they had to tell the TOC where they were going, they might be allowed to wait until shortly before the beginning of the operation to reveal the location, so that any VC collaborators in the center would not be able to pass the news along in time. When local authorities insisted that a unit report its operations well in advance, they might at least let the unit claim that it was operating in several sizable areas at once. Should the VC hear about the different targeted areas, they could hope to dodge the operation only by evacuating all of them. The evacuations might disrupt their activities or expose them to other military operations. Another method used when a unit had to report its operations to the TOC well in advance relied on Viet Cong penetration of the TOC. Rear Adm. Irve C. LeMoyne, who as a junior SEAL officer replaced John Wilbur as IV Corps PRU adviser in 1968 and later became one of only three SEALs to attain the rank of admiral, saw this method at work. "One of the PRU advisers," LeMoyne explained, "would tell the TOC that the unit was going one place and then set up ambushes on the avenues of escape from that area. Word would filter out from the TOC to the VC, and they would start leaving along those avenues."[13]

The Viet Cong's surveillance system around the hamlets also gave the VC warning of Allied operations. Sentries, as well as villagers assigned to lookout duty, tried to signal the approach of Allied forces to Communists in a hamlet. Unless they had enough people to put up a good fight, the VCI and VC tried to flee the hamlet or to hide in secret bunkers or tunnels.

Sometimes, a VC or VC sympathizer saw Allied forces pass by on their way to another area and attempted to get a unit together to follow and attack the Allies. By the time the unit was assembled, however, the Allies usually had moved too far away for the VC to pursue them. The unit waited at the location of the sighting should the Allies return along the same route.

Local VC surveillance became less effective during the late 1960s and early 1970s as the shadow government's presence in the hamlets declined. No longer did the cadres employ the farmers in a daily routine of lookout duty and maintain a regular system for reporting the presence of enemy forces. Instead, they had to gather together a group of villagers to help them when they came to a hamlet. As the villagers became less willing to help them, the cadres relied more heavily on VC guerrillas and members of local forces to watch the roads, trails, and canals. These groups also decreased in number over the years. Allied use of helicopters to move troops further reduced the effectiveness of local Viet Cong surveillance. One cadre described how an ARVN operation employing helicopters captured him: "It was very difficult for the cadres to escape, and whoever was seen fleeing was shot down by the 'copters. This strategy made our alarm system void, and the former 'hour precaution' set up by the Front to help us flee from sweeps was no longer effective."[14]

By the late 1960s, small, disciplined Allied units operating in familiar territory usually could avoid enemy units when moving through the countryside until they reached their targets, except in areas of intense conventional military activity. They could return safely in most instances if they did not take the same course they had taken to get there. "We could go right through supposedly Viet Cong areas without being bothered," Jack Harrell recalled, "as long as we didn't let anybody know where we were going, and as long as we went at high speed and didn't return the same way we came."[15]

15   The Birds of Prey

ll Allied operational forces that sought battle with the enemy
in the countryside participated in the war against the Viet Cong
shadow government in some way. The many types of forces
differed greatly from one another in their activities and achievements. Some focused on neutralizing the VCI or fighting the village
war; others caused problems for the VCI only as incidental results of
their other efforts. The most important forces that fought the war
against the shadow government operated in most or all of the districts and provinces, and they usually engaged in similar activities in
most areas. This chapter focuses on the forces that made major contributions nationwide.

Some of the many nationwide forces, such as the Kit Carson Scouts,
U.S. Special Forces, U.S. Navy SEALs, Armed Propaganda Teams, and
South Vietnamese Military Security Service, conducted operations
that neutralized the VCI or attacked the VC in the village areas but,
on the whole, made relatively minor contributions because they
focused on other missions. The methods used in these operations differed little from those of some of the more prominent forces, so examination of these methods is not necessary. In some districts and
provinces, local leaders created unique units, usually small in size and
significance, to carry out particular types of operations against the
VCI and other Communists. These units usually drew their personnel from nationwide units and operated in similar ways.

American, South Vietnamese, South Korean, and other main force
military units contributed to the war against the shadow government
mainly by killing or capturing illegal cadres in the course of their regular military operations. Some of their operations, such as those aimed
at interdicting Communist lines of communication and small unit
operations near the villages, caused considerably more damage to
the shadow government than did their standard main force activities.
On occasion, the CIA and other intelligence organizations passed information about the location of VC cadres to main force units if the cadres
had substantial military protection.

As strangers to their areas of operations, even most of those who
served in the ARVN, the main force soldiers normally lacked the

familiarity with an area that facilitated small unit operations and hamlet searches. Few main force units remained in an area long enough to know it well. Lt. Gen. Ngo Quang Truong explains:

> Territorial security required the ability to recognize and identify the enemy among the masses, familiarity with all accesses, hiding places in the hamlets, a working relationship and close touch with the population and, above all, the people's cooperation and support. All of these requirements could hardly be met with satisfaction by regular ARVN units whose strengths were conventional in nature and whose primary target was the enemy's main force, not his local or guerrilla units.[1]

The ARVN troops did enjoy some advantages over the non-Vietnamese soldiers because they could speak directly with the villagers, they had fought longer in the country, and some had grown up in rural Vietnam. Many main force units employed local GVN personnel to provide the knowledge that their troops lacked, which allowed these units to perform reasonably well when they chose to do so.

The GVN territorial forces, consisting of hundreds of thousands of Regional Forces and Popular Forces troops, also netted many VCI during their operations. They set ambushes and conducted patrols and hamlet searches that caused many problems for the VC. Some spent most of their time guarding lines of communication, bridges, and installations, but, as the war moved along, an increasing number fought in the populous rural areas to drive out the Communists. They frequently lived in outposts near the hamlets with their families when they fought the village war. Dispersed widely, many of the outposts were vulnerable to large-scale Communist attacks, and the Communists assaulted them over and over. The territorial forces often suffered more casualties from these attacks than they did when they left the outposts. "The RF/PF had mud forts all across the Delta, and they were death traps," Jim Ward recalled. "Once the enemy got RPG-2s and RPG-7s [Soviet antitank grenade launchers], they could go right through any one of those forts. They could throw hand grenades over the top of them. It was much better to have concealed positions, and to change your positions every night, so the enemy didn't know where you were."[2]

The territorial forces, nevertheless, seldom abandoned their reliance on outposts, although some units spent a large portion of their time away from the outposts and many operated with considerable mobility from district or provincial capitals, where the enemy could not overrun them. In some cases, weak leadership prevented them from operating without the outposts.

In others, commanders feared that too many soldiers would desert if separated from their families and forced to endure additional hardships. Further, some leaders highly valued the outpost system's advantages. The outpost provided a place to rest and store supplies and gave the villagers a sense of a permanent, reliable GVN presence to which they could turn for help.

Active territorial forces units enjoyed considerably more success in defending the hamlets than their outposts. Because many units sent out patrols day and night and set up ambushes in various places around the hamlets, the VC had to fight them unexpectedly and withstand their ambushes in order to maintain access to the population. For example, after studying Kontum province in early 1970, CORDS inspectors wrote:

> Observation in several hamlets at night and questioning during the day indicated that the PF do deploy at night and that in many instances they go beyond the village perimeter into night ambush positions. There have been several recent occasions in which the PF have successfully defended themselves and inflicted enemy casualties against superior local forces and NVA units.[3]

The Regional Forces served in their native provinces and the Popular Forces in their native districts. Their observations and information from relatives and other villagers gave them knowledge about the local shadow government and the local situation that foreigners or Vietnamese from other parts of the country did not have. During their searches of the hamlets, they had a good sense of where to find the VC, and they could identify the VC who posed as ordinary citizens. They knew where the VC operated most often, where they set their ambushes and placed their mines, and what their most likely escape routes would be.

Because they served in their native areas, the territorial forces had a more tangible stake in their own combat operations than did ARVN forces. They were fighting to protect their families, homes, and villages, as well as themselves. The effectiveness of the territorial forces, nonetheless, depended primarily on the quality of their leadership, not on the attitudes of the mass membership. One province senior adviser reported: "The effectiveness of the RF companies in the province is almost always a reflection of the commander's ability, motivation, and leadership."[4] Some CORDS inspectors, after studying Quang Nam province in great depth, noted that the territorial forces units did not have secondary leaders who could make the unit function if the commander were weak, as U.S. noncommissioned officers can do. Their report states: "The quality of [the Popular Forces'] performance turns upon the quality of the platoon leader. If the platoon leader is competent and aggressive he carries the platoon; if he is inept, there is no secondary level of leadership which steps in to fill the vacuum."[5]

The competence and aggressive spirit of most territorial forces units increased tremendously in many places after the Tet offensive of 1968, even as the forces grew rapidly in size, mainly because of a considerable improvement in leadership. Pressure from U.S. advisers, who accompanied operations more often from 1968 to 1972, and the distribution of M-16 rifles to most units in 1968 and 1969 also improved performance. Joint operations between the territorial forces and American units, including the CAP platoons, worked well. The Americans had control over the operations, but many American commanders declined to conduct joint operations because they distrusted the territorials too much or had other reservations. The Americans, aggressive as American soldiers usually are, inspired the Vietnamese and prodded those they could not inspire. As one Popular Forces soldier said of his experience with a Combined Action Platoon, "The Americans were so brave that we became brave, too."[6]

The improvement of the territorial forces was one of the most important developments of the post-Tet period, but, like many other aspects of this era, it went largely unnoticed in the United States. Many American advisers who served between 1968 and 1972, however, took note of what happened. Jerry Dunn, deputy province senior adviser of Quang Tin province, called the Popular Forces in Quang Tin in 1970 "a tremendous success story."[7] Lt. Col. Cecil Simmons, who served as deputy province senior adviser in Dinh Tuong province, commented at the end of his tour in July 1972 that "the overall combat effectiveness of the RF/PF is absolutely remarkable. Day after day, night after night, these units are on combat operations. And to those critics who think they won't fight, I say 'go to the hospitals and see for yourself.'"[8]

In some places, most of minimal strategic importance, all of the territorial forces remained ineffective because of poor leadership. In others, the Regional Forces performed well but many of the Popular Forces did not. Col. Walter Clark said of his experiences in Vinh Binh province during 1971 and 1972: "The Regional Forces battalion in the province was pretty good. The Popular Forces were not very valuable. Some of them were aggressive and fought very well, but for the most part they were passive, poorly disciplined, poorly trained, and poorly equipped."[9]

In 1968, at the urging of Robert Komer, President Thieu created another local defense program called the People's Self-Defense Forces (PSDF). The

GVN required that all able-bodied males, ages sixteen and seventeen and ages thirty-nine through fifty, join the PSDF (those eighteen through thirty-eight years old had to serve in regular GVN organizations) and encouraged other villagers to enlist. Each PSDF member had to stand guard with a weapon or serve as lookout one night per week. Village chiefs distributed the weapons in the evening and took them back in the morning to deter theft and misuse. The leadership, training, and equipment of the PSDF were usually poor, and even the good units seldom did anything except shoot at small groups of VC that came to their hamlets. Lt. Col. James C. Cloud, who served in Tay Ninh province, said concerning the PSDF: "In a few cases they have fought well and in others they have failed miserably."[10] Where the village and hamlet leaders made the program work, it had political effects, more important perhaps than its military effects. It forced villagers to take sides with the GVN, which made them more likely to provide the GVN with intelligence information, taxes, and recruits.

The Revolutionary Development Cadres did not usually function well as a paramilitary entity. Americans and South Vietnamese have offered a variety of reasons for the program's failure to live up to expectations: the prominent role of the South Vietnamese at the top of the program caused a politicization of leadership selection, many of the cadres were young city residents who did not care much about the hamlets in which they worked, unit quality declined because the program expanded too rapidly to allow sufficient time for leadership selection, and the program did not provide adequate training for the cadres. Leadership politicization probably weakened the program the most, but each of these factors played some role.

The first RD Cadre units each consisted of fifty-nine people, the majority of them males. A unit was supposed to be strong enough to stay in the hamlets at night and defend itself against small-scale Communist attacks, with help from the villagers. The Communists knew that the RD Cadre units blocked their access to the population, however, and often mounted attacks large enough to overwhelm them before help from other Allied forces could arrive. Some RD Cadre units repeatedly tried to resist the Communist nighttime assaults and usually found themselves engaged in bloody battles, but most of them, once they had encountered resistance, chose to stay in secure outposts away from the hamlets at night. Although attacking the local VC shadow government was supposed to be the top priority of RD Cadre units, they rarely succeeded. Poor leadership and unwillingness to operate at night contributed to their lack of success. The very presence of RD cadres in a hamlet, however, forced the VCI in that hamlet to reduce their activities, thereby making them more difficult to neutralize.

A 1968 CORDS evaluation of the RD Cadre units in Quang Nam province, which likened the units there to those in other parts of Vietnam, concludes: "Very little success had been achieved by any of the teams against the VC infrastructure in the hamlets."[11] From late 1968 through 1969, the RD Cadre unit was reduced in size to thirty people and, later, to an even smaller number. From then on, the RD Cadre units joined with Popular Forces units for protection when working in insecure areas. In 1971, the GVN dissolved the program for lack of funds.

The National Police Field Forces seldom lived up to their billing as a leading element in the attack on the VC shadow government. The NPFF usually proved incapable of targeting specific cadres or groups of VC because, as noted in chapter 13, they seldom had access to good intelligence and because they lacked the discipline necessary for nighttime operations and other operations requiring stealth. NPFF troops searched and patrolled village areas somewhat more effectively, when they made the effort. If they went alone, their proficiency was fairly limited because they did not know much about the VCI and because most of them were not native to the areas where they worked. Lt. Col. Mebane Stafford explained the situation in his province: "Over eighty percent of NPFF forces in Quang Tin are non native to the province. . . . In cordon and search operations the NPFF are aliens to the villagers which also reduces their effectiveness, and their own spirit and motivation are also foreign and alienated [sic] to these areas."[12] In some cases, the NPFF mainly served as the cordon force for Special Police or other people who knew better what to look for. Some of the district and province chiefs merely used the NPFF for simple tasks, such as static guard duty in provincial capitals, especially near the beginning of the new attack on the shadow government. Even in 1970, half of all NPFF units were serving in such capacities.[13]

The quality of NPFF units varied considerably and depended mainly on leadership. On average, they functioned better during the early 1970s than they had during the late 1960s. Dunn described the NPFF that he saw as "Beset by poor training [and] low morale, badly led, and lacking motivation. As someone recently remarked, 'They're more trouble than they're worth.'"[14] Peter Scott, by contrast, said of his experiences in a district of Chau Doc province, "The NPFF were good because of their captain."[15] The NPFF leadership did not benefit as much from U.S. advisory pressure as did that of many other pacification units because the advisers from the

CORDS Public Safety Division who worked with them seldom knew much about the NPFF or cared about it. Col. Doug Dillard's assessment of NPFF advisers exemplifies those of many independent observers:

> I think that, predominantly, they had a pretty sorry group of people. They were very unproductive. Most were very inept because of a lack of experience in foreign countries. They had retired from city, county, or state police in the U.S., and they had an opportunity to go over to Vietnam in a post-retirement mode and earn a lot more money on those contracts. I rarely ever met one, because they were either in Saigon on R and R [rest and relaxation], or they were on one of the short R and Rs out of country to Hong Kong or to Australia or to Hawaii, or they were shacked up with their girl-friends in the province capital.[16]

The Special Police apprehended significant numbers of VCI. Because of their superior intelligence capabilities, their neutralization totals included a larger percentage of higher-ranking cadres than those of other organizations. Members of the Special Police arrested suspected VCI in cities and towns and in relatively safe rural areas. When they stood a good chance of encountering armed resistance, they usually conducted joint operations with more powerful action forces. During the last few years of the war, however, the Special Police built up their operational capabilities in some areas by absorbing PRU members and recruiting other people for that purpose. During the early 1970s, improvements in the quality of Special Police leadership and the expansion of the Special Police also enhanced performance.

The General Duty policemen, who served under the National Police umbrella, concerned themselves mainly with such tasks as directing traffic, finding draft dodgers, and preventing the VC from smuggling supplies out of the towns and cities. They arrested a few legal cadres and other VC posing as ordinary citizens in the towns and cities and at checkpoints on roads. They almost never went out of their way, however, to capture VC cadres.

The forces most successful in operating against the VCI and their VC cohorts in the villages were the Provincial Reconnaissance Units. Because PRU activities were likely to stir up controversy in the United States, the CIA kept information about these forces top secret; as a result, the American public has learned little about them to this day. This secrecy, combined with the intensity of the debate in the United States over the Vietnam War, inevitably caused a host of myths to arise concerning the PRUs, which obscured them further. Substantive documents on the PRUs remain unavailable even now. By interviewing many Americans and South Vietnamese who took part in the PRU program, however, I was able to discover the methods of the PRUs and the reasons for their success.

The PRUs were among the few Allied forces that regularly operated at night and in VC-controlled territory. Only the U.S. military and some ARVN and RF units could make the same claim, and they usually worked in larger units and with heavier weaponry than the PRUs. The PRUs infiltrated into hamlets in small numbers and captured or killed VC, set up small ambushes across the countryside, and swept through hamlets to find hidden VC. A wealth of accurate intelligence allowed them to surprise the enemy again and again. Operating in areas known to be clear of other friendly forces, the PRUs sometimes dressed like the enemy and carried the enemy's weapon, the AK-47. When firing erupted, the sound of their AKs confused the Communists, who usually, for at least a few moments, mistook the PRUs for Communist soldiers shooting at them by mistake. In some provinces, the PRUs participated in conventional military operations during emergencies, served as scouts for main force units, collected information about all sorts of Communist activities, and rescued downed pilots and prisoners. The PRUs concentrated most of their efforts, however, on eradicating the VC cadres and small groups of VC soldiers and guerrillas in the rural areas.

The PRUs served in their native provinces, so normally at least one PRU member knew a given village, its local VC, and the best ways to operate unobserved in the area. To acquaint themselves with operational areas and the enemy, some PRU members scouted places or people in small groups or in the helicopters of Air America, the CIA's secret air fleet. PRU intelligence, local knowledge, and operational skill were so good that the units endured remarkably few casualties. Many American advisers said that their PRUs captured or killed hundreds of Communists in six months or a year without suffering any fatalities. Rick Welcome, for instance, recalled, "During the six months that I was operational with the Binh Thuan PRUs, we killed or captured over six hundred Viet Cong and NVA. Only two of us were wounded, and none were killed."[17]

The CIA always controlled the PRUs, as it had the Counter-Terror Teams before them, although at times, other American and Vietnamese entities nominally controlled the units. CIA case officers at the provincial and regional levels selected, supervised, and funded the South Vietnamese provincial and regional PRU chiefs. The CIA trained the PRUs on the Vung

Tau peninsula, and the units received on-the-job training from PRU leaders and CIA advisers. For a time during the late 1960s, some soldiers on loan to the CIA from the U.S. Army Special Forces, the U.S. Navy SEALs, and the U.S. Marines served six-month tours with the PRUs. They accompanied the PRUs during their operations and verified that their reports corresponded to the actual operations. Fearful of adverse publicity, the military stopped assigning its personnel to the PRUs at the end of 1969. Thereafter, the CIA prohibited Americans from going into the field on PRU operations. Dead Americans would have drawn more attention to the program; captured Americans might have divulged information to the enemy, and their presence would have helped Hanoi's propaganda machine. Some CIA advisers ignored the prohibition and continued to go on operations.

From time to time, the U.S. military expressed a desire to take over the PRU program. In previous cases where it had taken control of such unconventional programs, the military had used them for conventional military purposes, so the CIA never granted this request. Many South Vietnamese province chiefs also wanted complete control over the PRUs, and the CIA refused them as well. The CIA knew that they too preferred employing forces in conventional missions over employing them in the village war and that some province chiefs would have appointed PRU chiefs on the basis of political connections, money, kinship, or friendship, rather than on the basis of competence. The province chiefs, however, did have some influence over the PRUs. The PRUs could not operate without their approval, and many chiefs demanded that the PRUs seek approval for every mission. Some province chiefs insisted on choosing chiefs for the PRUs within their provinces, but, in such cases, an individual so chosen received only the title of PRU chief; someone else, who was picked by the CIA, actually led the unit. On occasion, the province chiefs did not want the PRUs operating in their provinces, so the CIA bought their support. The Kien Phong province chief refused to allow the PRUs to operate during Bob Boyke's first months there. "We finally gave him a snub-nosed .38," Boyke told me, "because he always wanted a revolver like the ones we carried. That finally tipped the scale in our favor, and he gave us the green light to start operating."[18]

In 1972, the CIA integrated the PRUs into the Special Police, but it maintained a considerable amount of influence over them because of its close relationship with the Special Police. This transition did not occur very smoothly in many provinces, for GVN officials did not like the CIA's terms. Many province chiefs suspected that the CIA had hired some of the PRUs to keep it informed of the Special Police's activities, and they wanted to avoid informational leaks. Some also feared that they would have trouble controlling such aggressive and heavily armed troops. "As whole units, the integration of the PRUs into the Special Police was not successful," Jack Harrell said. "The GVN didn't want the PRUs, because they didn't know how many were recruited by us to report on them. There was also tremendous suspicion because the PRUs had a lot of weapons and firepower, and the GVN didn't know if it could trust them."[19] Where the former PRUs did join the Special Police, according to Col. Viet Lang, "the province chiefs and Special Police chiefs sent them on dangerous operations and didn't give them important information, because they were afraid the former PRUs still worked for the CIA."[20] Some of the PRUs disliked these arrangements so much that they chose to serve in other units or to desert instead of serving in the Special Police.

Because the PRUs performed well but numbered only between four and six thousand men countrywide at any one time, many observers have wondered why the CIA did not make them larger. The CIA did not lack the necessary funding or authorization to expand them. When someone suggested a budget cut for the PRUs to President Nixon in late 1969, according to one of Secretary of State Henry Kissinger's senior aides, Nixon said, "No. We've got to have more of this. Assassinations. Killings. That's what they're doing [the other side]."[21] The CIA decided not to enlarge the PRUs because of fears that the task would require the recruitment of more, hence generally less capable, leaders and advisers and overextend the CIA's supervisory capabilities. "We put all the resources into the PRU program that we thought we could put into it," Lew Lapham explained. "If we had expanded the program, it would have meant going to the military and asking the Special Forces and SEALs to take over. The CIA is able to handle activities like the PRUs on a selective and highly targeted basis, but when it comes to doing it on a massive scale, we just don't have the personnel resources to do it."[22] CIA leaders also thought that expansion would greatly reduce its ability to maintain the secrecy that obscured the PRUs from Americans who would have disapproved of the program.

The CIA took several steps to make the rank-and-file PRU members more likely to work hard and effectively. CIA advisers and the PRU chiefs tried to recruit South Vietnamese who hated the Communists, for they generally would be the most dedicated and reliable. Many PRU members and most of the PRU chiefs fit this description. A large number of these anti-Communists were men of strong passions who had served the Communists in former days. The Saigon regime did not allow them to serve in most other

GVN units because it suspected them of maintaining loyalty to the Communists. Jim Ward explained:

> Some of the PRUs had been members of the VC, but for one reason or another they turned against the VC. It was usually because of a grudge against some particular individual who mistreated them or their family, because they wanted to be with their family, because a brother had joined the GVN forces, or something like that. The reasons were usually personal rather than ideological. Then they needed a job, and when they came over all they knew how to do was fight. They didn't want to be farmers, so they tried to join the PRUs.[23]

Recruiters often could not find enough capable people who deeply despised the Communists to fill the PRU ranks entirely, so they had to find other sources of personnel. One was the ARVN. Significant numbers of ARVN soldiers deserted to join the PRUs, and the CIA had enough power to keep the GVN authorities from returning them to their ARVN units. The CIA had an excess of applicants from ARVN units, and it took only the best of them. A small number of the PRU soldiers in some provinces were former criminals who had penchants for aggressive and violent behavior and preferred fighting to sitting in jail. PRU chiefs and other PRU members had to maintain close watch over them to prevent them from committing criminal acts. When asked about these ex-criminals, Col. Viet Lang commented: "Those people were very tough. You had to control them carefully. Once you guided them onto a target, they were better than ordinary people, because they were very courageous and weren't afraid of being killed."[24]

The CIA offered material incentives, primarily money and superior living conditions, to PRU members. They received far higher salaries than the South Vietnamese who worked for the GVN, and they were among the few South Vietnamese who received U.S. medical treatment. The CIA often rewarded them for VCI captured or killed and for weapons captured, and many American advisers and PRU chiefs also allowed them to keep money captured during their operations. PRU soldiers resided in provincial capitals, where they were relatively safe from Communist attack. They enjoyed good food, drink, and other amenities, and their families lived with them or nearby. The conditions of the PRU job itself also appealed to members. Although their operations often involved long treks through dangerous territory, the PRUs sustained far fewer casualties than most units. The high level of dedication throughout the units strengthened the warrior bonds that members formed with each other, bonds that made them willing to work hard and to risk their lives for each other.

For PRU members, nevertheless, the most important motivator by far was leadership. CIA advisers accompanied PRU operations and participated heavily in operational planning and coordination, but they usually left direct command of the PRU units to the South Vietnamese province-level PRU chiefs. The CIA knew that the South Vietnamese could lead each other better than Americans could lead them and that charismatic South Vietnamese leaders drove the PRU members to perform extraordinarily well. Once the PRUs had the necessary intelligence, their operational capabilities as a whole depended primarily on good leadership, for strong leaders could make the PRU members carry out all of the necessary tasks as effectively as was humanly possible. CIA training and funding, rank-and-file enthusiasm aside from that produced by the leaders, and the fighting skills and advice of CIA advisers played much smaller parts in determining PRU operational capabilities. All of the regional PRU advisers whom I have met echoed this statement from John Wilbur: "The unit was as effective as its leader. A good PRU unit was run by a strong, aggressive leader who had natural leadership qualities. If the PRU chief was a weak or passive leader, the unit was ineffective."[25]

The Americans monitored the performance of the PRU chiefs by accompanying their operations and paying PRU members to keep them informed. Most of the PRU chiefs were aggressive and effective, and they normally ran their units according to the CIA's guidelines because they knew that the CIA had authority over them. When, on occasion, a PRU chief performed poorly, the CIA advisers told him to perform better; if he did not, they removed him. During the later years of the program, they had more difficulty in replacing ineffective PRU chiefs because they had to get the agreement of the South Vietnamese PRU directors at the regional level, whom the CIA station chief in Saigon appointed. The CIA advisers and the regional PRU directors, nevertheless, managed to maintain a fairly high level of leadership quality.

The ability to control the PRU leadership and keep it free of the weak officers who held so many leadership positions within other South Vietnamese organizations was the key reason why the PRUs, on average, performed much better than other South Vietnamese forces. Rudy Enders gained an unusually good understanding of the PRUs by working with them for many years. He supervised the RD Cadre program, the Counter-Terror Teams/PRUs, and Census Grievance in Bien Hoa during 1966, the same programs in all of I Corps from late 1966 to 1969, and the III Corps PRUs from 1970 to 1972. Enders said: "The crucial difference between the PRU program and any other program was that we, not the Vietnamese, selected the leadership. The main reason the program succeeded was that we were able to put competent people into the leadership, instead of politicians as the Vietnamese would have done. That made all the difference in the world. The Vietnamese themselves were very good fighters, they just needed to be led."[26]

In most provinces, the PRUs enjoyed considerable and sometimes spectacular success in their activities against the VC because they had large amounts of intelligence and outstanding operational capabilities. The PRUs operated behind a wall of secrecy so thick that almost no Americans in Vietnam outside of the CIA, not even those in CORDS, knew about all of their activities. When the PRUs in a province neutralized a certain number of VCI in a particular month, they did not have to—and usually did not—report all of their results to the local CORDS advisers. Brig. Gen. James A. Herbert spent most of the 1960s and early 1970s in Vietnam. He was the province senior adviser of Long An and Gia Dinh during the late 1960s and deputy assistant chief of staff of CORDS during the early 1970s. His remarks typify those of most CORDS advisers whom I interviewed: "The PRU handlers weren't allowed to give us anything but general information. We did not get all their reports, only occasional, anecdotal reports. We never got the full picture."[27]

Some CORDS province senior advisers tried to find out more about the CIA activities in their provinces, and some even tried, unsuccessfully, to gain control over them. William Colby had a good view of this conflict after he succeeded Komer as head of CORDS in 1968. Although he did not interfere with CIA activities at that time, he maintained a low-key affiliation with the CIA. "A lot of CORDS people," Colby told me, "were always jealous of the fact that the CIA people had some secrets. Some of our province senior advisers would want to control the CIA people in their province. They'd be mad at them. I would have to tell the CORDS people, 'The CIA people are entitled to have some secrets. That's the CIA's business. Don't worry about them.'"[28] CIA advisers usually became less communicative when the CORDS advisers tried to meddle in their affairs. CIA adviser Gary Masters described his experiences with one CORDS province senior adviser: "He was obsessed with getting the PRUs under his control. He was a political hack and an idiot. He had all the forces that belonged to the province chief except the PRUs, so I didn't see any point in turning the PRUs over to him. I never told him anything about our activities."[29]

Some attentive CORDS advisers were able to gauge the general proficiency of the PRUs, but few knew the extent of their achievements. As a result, in reports and postwar interviews, most CORDS advisers either did not mention the PRUs or gave them credit only for relatively minor successes. CORDS advisers, on the other hand, knew that most programs besides the PRUs seldom neutralized VC cadres by targeting them specifically, because they worked more closely with these other programs. Some of these advisers said that no Allied organizations damaged the VCI significantly, as they lacked evidence to the contrary, whereas others stated that the attack on the VCI generally was a failure, even if they did not mean to include the PRUs. In either case, their testimony helped to convince many journalists of the day and subsequent commentators that no Allied forces, not even the PRUs, made much headway in attacking the shadow government.

The CIA submitted neutralization statistics for the PRUs to CORDS headquarters in Saigon for only one complete year, 1970. According to these statistics, the PRUs captured or killed 1,683 VCI that year, about 140 per month.[30] On the basis of this figure, CORDS calculated that the PRUs accounted for only 6.7 percent of all the VCI whom the Allies captured or killed during that year.[31] These statistics helped to persuade many people that the PRU contribution to the attack on the VCI and the war in general was fairly small.

The CORDS figures are far less informative than they appear at first glance. The average figure of 140 VCI per month does not include the many Communists who were captured or killed by the PRUs and who were not considered members of the Viet Cong infrastructure. The CIA's PRU reports list both "VC"— which include some NVA as well—and "VCI" captured and killed, and their totals of "VC/VCI" neutralizations are much higher than the VCI numbers alone. A few available documents list the "VC/VCI" totals. During the first ten months of 1969, according to one document, the PRUs captured 741 VC/VCI and killed 441 VC/VCI per month.[32] A document from national-level PRU adviser William Buckley states that the PRUs captured 534 and killed 129 VC/VCI per month during the first six months of 1971.[33] The Allies often had trouble differentiating between the VC and the VCI, so some of the individuals listed as VC undoubtedly were VCI. Some people in the CIA, indeed, used the number of VC/VCI neutralized when discussing how many members of the shadow government the PRUs had neutralized. Even station chief Ted Shackley referred to all of the VC and VCI captured or killed by the PRUs as "VCI."[34] In addition, the VCI in the village areas relied heavily on the assistance and protection of other VC. Many, if not most, PRU neutralizations of VC occurred in and around the villages, and these neutralizations thus weakened the shadow government. Finally, comparing the CORDS statistics for the PRUs to those of other units is misleading because all of the neutralization statistics are inaccurate, as this and subsequent chapters explain.

The CIA will not release its own statistics, but the statements of certain CIA officers strongly suggest that the CIA actually understated the numbers of VC/VCI captured or killed in the documents made available to other U.S. government organizations and to the public. The CIA did so, in all probability, to avoid negative publicity. The figures in these documents, especially the 1971 figures, have a high ratio of captured to killed. Some Americans who were in Vietnam during the years in question, however, have stated that the PRUs consistently killed more Communists than they captured. Enders spoke of his years as regional PRU adviser in both I Corps and III Corps: "It was very hard for us to bring the number of captures above the number of kills—we tried hard to do that—because it was difficult to capture people. I'd say that the ratio of killed to captured generally was about two to one."[35] Jack Harrell stated, "In II Corps and III Corps, when I was in those areas, the ratio for the PRUs was probably two Communists killed to one captured.[36] In the documents, the CIA did not wildly exaggerate the numbers of VC/VCI captured; doing so might have attracted unwanted attention. The number killed, therefore, must have been much higher than the documents state.

A number of CIA advisers have indicated explicitly that they thought the PRUs generally captured or killed more VC/VCI per month than the available documents list. The most precise estimates from these advisers concern the period before 1969, which the documents do not cover. The comparison, nevertheless, is still valid, for the CIA advisers whom I interviewed said that PRU results from 1969 onward did not differ greatly from previous results. PRU National Director William Redel, for instance, told CIA officer Orrin DeForest at the end of 1968 that the PRUs had been responsible "for approximately seven thousand Vietcong killed per year for the past four or five years,"[37] which averages out to 583 per month. Rear Adm. Irve LeMoyne gave a figure that suggests even larger nationwide neutralization totals: "We were capturing, in the delta, a thousand to twelve hundred VCI monthly."[38]

My best estimate, based on my own conversations with many PRU advisers and on other sources, is that the CIA leadership believed that the PRUs captured or killed anywhere from 700 to 1,500 Communists during most months from 1967 to 1972. These CIA figures themselves are not entirely reliable, but they are more accurate than the neutralization figures given for most other forces because CIA advisers generally inhibited falsification better than other American advisers. Knowledgeable CIA advisers told me that the PRUs in most provinces went on many operations every month and that each unit regularly captured or killed at least 10 or 20 Communists per month. Some advisers remembered specific PRU operations that resulted in 100 to 500 Communists captured or killed during a single day. Success of this magnitude, of which few people outside the CIA have been aware, translated into serious losses for the Communists. Chapter 21 investigates the severity of these and other losses.

Because the CIA controlled the PRUs and used money as a principal motivational tool, American opponents of U.S. involvement in Vietnam contemptuously call the PRUs "mercenaries." They describe them as armed thugs hired to carry out the Americans' dirty work and contrast these mercenaries with VC "idealists." Georgie Anne Geyer, one of the very few journalists who accompanied a PRU operation, wrote a detailed article on the PRUs in 1970 entitled "The CIA's Hired Killers." She accused the PRUs as well as the VC of engaging in terrorism, and compared the "terror" of the PRUs to that of the enemy: "The major difference was there was no real political organization—no political ideology—behind our terror. Their boys did it for faith; our boys did it for money."[39] Many PRUs, it is true, joined mainly for the money and other personal benefits, but many others enlisted primarily because they loathed the Communists, liked the PRU leaders, or simply enjoyed fighting. Thus, if a mercenary is defined as a soldier who works for a foreign country strictly to obtain tangible personal benefits, it is fair to say only that some of the PRUs were mercenaries. In fact, according to this definition, some people in all GVN organizations were mercenaries. Although many GVN employees were conscripted or served for reasons other than self-interest, others served primarily to receive money and other personal rewards. They could receive a salary, work close to home, and fill their pockets through corrupt activities. They could also gain the favor of a powerful political entity and prevent the VC from confiscating their land and other possessions. The United States indirectly and directly provided most of the bounty available to GVN employees, and its funding kept the GVN afloat until its last years. For most of the war, therefore, these people worked for the GVN because the United States gave the GVN money.

The alleged difference between GVN mercenaries and VC idealists did not exist, for most of the VC were mercenaries as well. The most common personal benefit for those who joined the VC or forced their children to join was acquiring land. Other benefits included ridding themselves of tyrannical GVN officials or landlords and obtaining the favor of the strongest local authority. They worked for the foreign North Vietnamese. North Vietnam's politics and culture differed historically from those of the South Vietnamese to the extent that North Vietnam and South Vietnam each justifiably could claim its own nationhood. The Northern Communists, moreover, espoused a collectivist philosophy more alien to the individualistic mentality of the South Vietnamese than was American free-market capitalism. As North Vietnam's rough treatment of almost all Southerners after the war would show, even the North Vietnamese at some point came to view themselves as conquerors of South Vietnam, not as unifiers of a single country.

North Vietnam itself was hardly free of financial dependence on foreigners during the war. It received major material contributions from two nations that wanted to influence the war's outcome—the Soviet Union and China. Col. Bui Tin, the NVA officer who took the GVN's surrender in Saigon's presidential palace on 30 April 1975, recently criticized North Vietnam for the hypocrisy of its attacks on the GVN's nationalist credentials. After noting Hanoi's dependence on foreign aid, he comments, "During this war we were quick to condemn the regime in the South for relying on the Americans as foreign interventionists. What we did not then realize in the North was that the Chinese and the Soviets were also foreigners."[40] Had either the GVN or the VC leadership failed to obtain the assistance of many mercenaries, it would have had too few personnel to offer any serious resistance to the enemy.

16   The South Vietnamese

The operational prowess of the territorial forces and some of the other pacification forces generally reflected the leadership capabilities of the district and province chiefs. Excellent district and province chiefs presided over units whose skill and aggressive spirit rivaled those of the PRUs. As explained in chapter 15, the effectiveness of an individual unit depended on the quality of the unit's leader. The district and province chiefs selected and motivated the leaders of the most important pacification units, except for the PRUs, and the chiefs tended to select subordinates of a caliber similar to their own and to drive them as hard as they drove themselves. Bruce Lawlor explained:

> The Vietnamese private was a great soldier. You gave him a bowl of rice and a canteen of water and sent him out, and he was fine. The conditions under which he could live were a hell of a lot worse than what the Americans could stand. But to be effective, he needed a good leader. If the leadership was poor, it negated the strengths of the soldier. The leadership came from the top down, so for the RF/PF it came from the province chiefs.[1]

For part of the war, GVN village chiefs ostensibly held command positions of considerable importance as well. On 1 April 1969, the GVN officially gave control of village-level Popular Forces, RD Cadres, People's Self-Defense Forces, and police forces to the elected village chiefs. In reality, however, these forces usually remained under the control of the district chiefs. The authors of a 1970 CORDS study of Quang Nam province conclude: "Village/hamlet chief authority—which is unprecedented—is generally overridden by the established authority of the District Chief over all programs within the District."[2] District chiefs could influence village elections and, with relative impunity, compel the village chiefs to obey their commands. They could withhold artillery and reinforcements from village chiefs who would not yield control of local units. Some district chiefs, no doubt, were power hungry, but most did not cede control of the pacification forces because they believed—correctly, in most cases—that village chiefs lacked the requisite knowledge of military affairs. Brig. Gen.

Tran Van Nhut said, "The village chiefs did not control the territorial forces militarily. They were civilians, so they didn't know anything about the military. The district chiefs had the military control."[3] Many village chiefs appreciated their underqualification and also knew that the VC tried to kill aggressive village chiefs, so they were quite willing to let the district chiefs keep their powers.

District and province chiefs who wanted to attack the shadow government usually succeeded in getting the Allied operational forces, aside from the PRUs and foreign military forces, to mount legitimate operations of some sort against the VCI. The PHREEX study states that "where [district and province chiefs] show genuine concern and understanding, the program generally performs effectively."[4] Where the chiefs did not emphasize the attack on the VCI, these forces tended not to conduct anti-VCI operations or they conducted bogus operations that stood no chance of making contact with the enemy.

The large majority of the district and province chiefs seldom organized operations aimed directly at the shadow government. Wilbur Wilson, the head of CORDS in IV Corps, made a typical complaint in 1971: "There is a definite lack of interest or motivation on the part of the GVN leadership which will make this program a success and which will eventually result in the elimination of the Communist Party apparatus in MR 4."[5] In some districts and provinces, the subordinate commanders, such as the police chiefs, territorial forces leaders, and S-2 officers, could lead operations against the shadow government as long as the district or province chief did not do so and did not order them to use their men differently. In most districts or provinces where the chief was so weak, however, his subordinates shared his taste for inactivity.

The most important reason for the GVN's general apathy toward operations aimed at the VCI was that Thieu and his highest-ranking generals did not encourage district and province chiefs to conduct them, the same reason that many chiefs did not order organizations under their control to share VCI intelligence with Phung Hoang. District and province chiefs received high marks from their superiors for conventional military successes but not for neutralization of the VCI. For example, Robert Komer reported in 1970:

> Most corps commanders and middle-level officials don't pay much attention to Phung Hoang. Few corps commanders or province chiefs would even rate it among their first six priority tasks. As Colonel Than in Hue (proba-

bly the best GVN province chief) told me: "Province and district chiefs are still graded mostly on how many enemy KIA [killed in action], how many weapons captured, etc. If we want to change their attitude on Phung Hoang, Saigon and corps must give them a real feeling that it is top priority. They must change their whole philosophy as to priorities."[6]

Some district and province chiefs preferred channeling their energies toward regular military activities because they had much more training or experience in military operations than in police and paramilitary matters. Lt. Col. Dao Quan Hien, who was a military officer as well as a police officer, explained:

> The province chiefs were military officers, so they leaned towards the military side. The province chiefs only organized military operations to follow and destroy the military units of the Communists. They did not put much effort into the destruction of the Communist infrastructure. To destroy the infrastructure was very difficult, more difficult than destroying the armed units, because the Communist armed units were something we could easily find. They were visible, easy to collect intelligence on, and it was easy to verify where they were located. But the infrastructure had good security. They had organizations among the population, inside the population, and it was difficult to distinguish some of the Communist cadres from the inhabitants.[7]

Many GVN leaders also believed, as mentioned in chapter 14, that they could hurt the shadow government substantially with military operations and thus did not need to pay closer attention to the VCI.

The desire to concentrate on other aspects of the war was not the only reason why most GVN leaders did not press the attack on the shadow government. Some did as little as possible to hurt the Communists without risking their jobs because they were lazy or corrupt; some did so because they knew that the VC tried, often successfully, to kill GVN leaders who got in their way. Brig. Gen. Stuart A. Herrington, at the time a young Phoenix adviser in Hau Nghia, remarks that "district chiefs could hardly be expected to embrace the Phoenix concept enthusiastically in an environment where effective district chiefs often found that the reward for their efficiency was assassination by the Vietcong. It was considerably safer to do an average, status quo job, avoid any heroics, and live to fight another day."[8]

A fair number of GVN officials also feared that, if the war itself did not kill them, the Viet Cong would take revenge on them in the event that the Communists won the war. Col. Carl Bernard, in reference to four South

Vietnamese officers who recently had become less aggressive, observed that "they do not want to 'offend the VC' any more than is absolutely necessary to maintain their positions." He reasoned: "They are trying to become candidates for something besides elimination in the event of a VC take-over."[9] On the other hand, many GVN leaders suspected that the Communists would kill them and their families if the GVN fell, regardless of how effective their efforts against the Communists had been, unless perhaps they risked becoming VC agents. Fear of the future, therefore, encouraged these people to attack the Communists fiercely.

GVN leaders also were reluctant to neutralize VC political cadres to whom they were bound by blood, friendship, or other group affiliations, and they tried to prevent other Allies from identifying and targeting those people as VCI. The GVN limited this problem rather effectively by making sure not to appoint district and province chiefs to their native areas. A good chief could not always stop his subordinates from trying to protect their relatives or others in the VC, but he could convince them to run enough operations against the enemy that the guarding of certain individuals did not significantly undermine the war effort.

American observers offered other reasons for the unwillingness of GVN leaders to arrest or kill certain cadres. Some of these reasons motivated leaders to a lesser extent than those mentioned above, whereas others had little effect. The most influential was the VC's payment of bribes to corrupt GVN leaders in return for the safety of certain cadres. Col. Viet Lang said, "Sometimes it happened that a cadre paid the province chief one hundred thousand piasters so that the province chief would leave him alone and not let anyone get him."[10]

Some observers speculated that certain GVN leaders left the VC alone because these leaders actually were Communist agents. In reality, only a few GVN leaders were VC agents; numerous North and South Vietnamese witnesses have stated that at the end of the war, almost all GVN leaders either fled the country or suffered execution or imprisonment. Most who were agents had to inflict considerable damage on the Communists in order to keep their jobs. Various Americans also thought that some GVN leaders avoided neutralizing many low-level VCI because such actions would arouse too much popular resentment, usually because GVN leaders said as much.[11] This charge contains some truth with respect to a small number of GVN leaders, but its importance has been exaggerated. Many Americans overestimate the popular resentment resulting from attacks on the VCI (see chapter 21). The reliability of GVN leaders who claimed they did not want to anger the people is also questionable. Few GVN leaders would divulge to Americans their true motives for not targeting VC cadres. Many knew that it would be unwise to say, for example, "I'm leaving most of the important VC cadres in Trang Dinh district alone because they have agreed to pay me a million piasters to ensure their safety." The GVN leaders realized that claiming they did not want to alienate the people, whether it was true or not, seemed to be a much more legitimate excuse for inactivity to most Americans.

Where the Government leaders did not want to prosecute the war as best they could, they sometimes made nonaggression pacts, tacit or express, with the Communists. The GVN forces allowed the Communist cadres and soldiers to do as they pleased by purposefully avoiding them on patrols or by leaving them plenty of opportunities to flee. The Communist forces, in return, did not harm the GVN forces or their commanders. In this type of situation, a GVN leader could point out that his forces went on numerous operations—a large quantity of operations impressed some people regardless of the quality—and seldom encountered the Communists, which seemed to suggest an absence of Communists in the area. "Vinh Binh was rated 'secure' in most places when I got there," Colonel Bernard recalled. "The deal was that the locals didn't disturb the VC, and the VC didn't disturb them. Normally, a PF platoon would go on a patrol playing loud music and walking along set routes, and they never got ambushed. Essentially, the VC ran the place without annoying the local people."[12]

This acquiescence to Communist rule in rural areas occurred much less often during the late 1960s and early 1970s than it had earlier in the war. The main reason for the change lay in a remarkable improvement in the caliber of district and province chiefs across the country. During this period, the Thieu regime replaced many unmotivated and incompetent chiefs with ARVN officers eager to clash swords with the Communists. The ARVN had always contained considerable numbers of capable officers who wanted to fight hard, primarily for nationalistic, religious, or political reasons or to avenge family members killed by the Communists. Now, however, more of them received important command positions than before. Komer explains why the Thieu regime began appointing better leaders:

> Most experienced observers on the scene noted a marked improvement in overall GVN administrative performance beginning with Tet 1968. In part this was attributable to increased US advisory influence and occasionally pressure. In part it was simply that the earlier efforts of 1965–1967 began

to bear more fruit over time. But even greater influences on GVN behavior were the twin shocks of Hanoi's Tet and post-Tet offensives and the resultant clear beginning of U.S. deescalation.[13]

Many of the newcomers did not pay much more attention to attacking the shadow government directly than had their predecessors, but they drastically improved the performance of GVN armed forces and administrative personnel, especially the territorial forces, in the fight against Communist soldiers and guerrillas. Donald Colin, for instance, wrote at the end of his tour in August 1971:

> Thirty months ago, the number of good leaders in MR IV could be measured on one hand. Even the Corps Commander, while he was a good, honest and fairly capable leader, was shy, unimaginative and not capable of stirring his subordinates to aggressive and positive activity. Division commanders were largely incompetent and most Province Chiefs were both incompetent and corrupt. Subordinate commanders not only mirrored but in most cases magnified these faults. Now, the overall level of competence, honesty and dedication has risen to levels I would previously have thought unimaginable.... This particular change has made me more sanguine regarding the ultimate ability of the Government to fully control Vietnam and establish a stable Government.[14]

Communist sources acknowledged that the GVN leaders responsible for pacification were prosecuting the war much more vigorously and effectively than before. An October 1970 Communist document, from an area where foreign troops did not participate in pacification, states: "From July 1970 to September 1970, the enemy surged forward and implemented his special pacification program to encroach upon land. He succeeded in seizing portions of Ca Mau, U Minh, and penetration bases in districts and provinces. The general enemy scheme remains basically the same, although recently the land policy has been added, but it is now implemented more energetically, more skillfully, and more bluntly."[15]

The rise in quality among district and province chiefs was one of the GVN's finest achievements and one of the most important factors in altering the course of the war after the Tet offensive. Some opponents of the American war effort have tried to deny that this change occurred in order to support their claims that the GVN was completely worthless. Renowned journalist and author Neil Sheehan, for instance, writes that, after Tet, John Paul Vann did not "find himself working with the kind of province and district chiefs he had originally hoped Tet would shock the Saigon regime into appointing." Sheehan presents an exceptionally bad province chief, who had kept his job only because he was President Thieu's first cousin, as a typical example.[16] Many American advisers with whom I talked, in fact, bitterly criticized the American media for depicting the GVN leadership as universally inept. "The picture of all the Vietnamese as being corrupt or not caring is simply not true," Dean Almy said. "There were some who were outstanding."[17] Brig. Gen. James Herbert told me, "I have never read a book about capable GVN leaders in this long war, but I served with quite a few. I walked in too many funeral processions for courageous and able field commanders. Some GVN leaders were total duds, but some were really top notch."[18]

Some South Vietnamese commanders received quotas, or goals, of VCI to be captured or killed; both had essentially the same effect. Some commanders received monetary rewards for neutralizations. The Americans had designed these incentives to stimulate GVN operations, and the South Vietnamese had to deal with them in one way or another. CORDS relied mainly on quotas to encourage activity against the VCI, but some CORDS advisers also paid rewards. In August 1968, over the objections of Phoenix Director Evan Parker, Jr., Komer persuaded Thieu to begin assigning quotas. Because Komer had used quotas successfully in other pacification programs, such as refugee handling, construction projects, and education, he thought that they would produce better results in the attack on the VCI.[19]

A few of the advisers whom I interviewed and a few of the others who are on record observed that the quotas spurred meaningful South Vietnamese operations against the VCI. Said Lloyd Pomeroy, "There was a problem in getting province and district officials to pay attention to Phung Hoang, because they were focused on the enemy military units. I think the quota system helped bring their attention to the program. Numbers were a valid indicator of performance, when considered with other indicators."[20] Most, however, thought that the Phoenix quotas and rewards did not work well. Some skeptics thought that the quotas were not suitable for the situation in question. In a number of areas, they noticed, the Americans assigned unrealistic quotas because they did not take into account all of the conditions in these areas. Others complained that the quota system encouraged action units to target low-ranking VCI, rather than more important cadres. The quota system gave equal credit for neutralizing all types of VCI, and low-level political cadres operated more often among the population, had less protection, and were more numerous than mid-level and high-level VCI. South Vietnamese units that wanted to meet the quotas without much exertion, the critics contend, were likely to try neutralizing low-level people instead of cadres of greater significance. In reality, the quotas seldom caused this problem. The Allies usually had little choice as to the importance of the cadres they captured or killed. The South Vietnamese who wanted to eliminate enemy personnel went after any Communists they could find, and the only ones they had much hope of finding were the legal cadres, who did not rank high in the VC hierarchy, and low-level illegal cadres plus their armed companions. The higher-level cadres were extremely hard to find and well protected. On the few occasions when the Allies had the opportunity to hit important targets, they usually jumped at it, for they could impress their bosses and many other people if they succeeded.

Some historians and other outside observers contend that the quotas caused the South Vietnamese to target people who did not belong to the VCI or the VC armed forces. One group claims that the GVN, in order to meet the quotas, arrested large numbers of people who provided relatively minor assistance to the Communists. Another group believes that the GVN arrested many people without any evidence of involvement with the VC merely to satisfy quotas. Among the most prominent members of the latter group was the American scholar Allan Goodman, who surveyed sixty deputies from the Lower House of the South Vietnamese National Assembly from August 1969 to January 1970. The deputies told him that 40 percent of complaints from their constituents concerned "injustices related to the Phoenix program" and that more citizens complained about this issue than any other. Goodman suggests that the arbitrary arrest of civilians to meet neutralization quotas produced most of these grievances.[21]

Goodman's list of injustices related to the Phoenix program includes "illegal arrests made by police and security forces," acts for which Phoenix conceivably could have been responsible. Other injustices on his list did not fall under the jurisdiction of Phoenix, such as "torturing of suspects, imprisonment without charge or trial for longer than two months, [and] imprisonment under substandard living, dietary, and sanitary conditions."[22] Such injustices were actually more widespread than Goodman suggests, so "illegal arrests" of any kind under the aegis of "Phoenix" could not have been as prevalent as he believes. Only about one-fourth of villagers questioned in a 1970 survey, moreover, knew that Phung Hoang was a program designed to destroy the VCI.[23] Obviously, Goodman or the assembly deputies, rather than the villagers, identified these problems as related to the Phoenix program in many cases. This fact casts further doubt on the culpability of Phoenix. One must also question the reliability of the deputies' constituents. The Viet Cong cadres regularly convinced ordinary citizens to complain to the GVN about policies that hurt the Communist cause, so this clever tactic probably accounts for a sizable percentage of the purported grievances. A small landowner from Dinh Tuong province, for example, recounted that the VC political cadres "forced the people to write requests to ask the GVN not to bomb or fire mortars into the village, not to arrest young people for the draft, not to have military operations in the village, and not to take away the innocent villagers and beat them to death."[24] Further, the families of VC cadres and guerrillas whom the GVN arrested undoubtedly approached GVN officials and claimed that their loved ones had been imprisoned unfairly, in order to obtain their release. Admitting that their relatives belonged to the VC would have hurt their cause.

The biggest oversight of the critics relative to the quota system is that the quotas lacked the power to provoke unwarranted arrests. Numerous advisers said in their reports and to me that the South Vietnamese filled the quotas with bogus neutralizations. Cadres neutralized in military encounters not directed at particular members of the shadow government, as well as those neutralized by anti-VCI operations, counted toward quota totals. Not surprisingly, therefore, many South Vietnamese claimed that ralliers, prisoners, and corpses of all sorts were VCI, regardless of whether or not they could identify the individuals.

The fraud succeeded most easily with corpses. The South Vietnamese frequently claimed that dead Communist soldiers were VCI, a quite plausible claim because many VC political cadres bore arms and served alongside armed forces. Innocent civilians killed in battle often were labeled VCI as well. Many Americans who searched battle sites after the fighting ended told me that, in some instances, the dead bodies greatly outnumbered the weapons recovered, and yet the South Vietnamese units present reported that most or all of the bodies were VC or VCI. Although some of the dead were Communists whose comrades had taken their weapons, others were Communist supporters, villagers conscripted for forced labor, or villagers caught in the cross fire. On some occasions, the South Vietnamese reported that they had killed VCI, but they had no bodies to prove it and claimed that they had not been able to retrieve the dead for one reason or another. Komer reported in 1970, "John Vann points out that around 50–60 percent of all VCI neutralizations in IV Corps provinces are kills—to him this clearly means fakery; he thinks half the kills are falsely listed as VCI just to meet

Phung Hoang goals, and the rest are the product of ex post facto identification after normal military operations."[25]

The misidentification of corpses had occurred regularly long before Phoenix began. Throughout the war, any GVN forces that found the bodies of civilians killed during battle were liable to count them in their total of enemy soldiers killed. Perhaps they could not tell the difference, or they wanted to increase their body count of enemy soldiers, or they wanted to hide the fact that civilians had died. Although GVN units did not always get away with calling every unknown corpse a VC soldier, they received credit throughout the war for many of the unidentified bodies.

Phoenix advisers and other CORDS advisers were supposed to prevent these sorts of deceptions. They had some means of confirming that a person was a VCI. Many went on operations and thus could see whether the captured or killed people had offered resistance. If they visited a battle site after an engagement, they could count bodies to determine whether the number of enemy personnel that the South Vietnamese had reported as killed actually exceeded the number of bodies. Weapons, photographs, documents, letters, and ID cards, especially those found on alleged VCI, implicated quite a few people. The age and sex of an individual also provided good clues. Americans could, and did, question some prisoners and ralliers about identities of the dead, and they used confirmed ralliers to identify supposed VCI of all types. The Americans disallowed a considerable number of South Vietnamese neutralization claims. During the first years of Phoenix, when the Phoenix advisers and the South Vietnamese made separate neutralization reports, the Americans were able to reject, on average, about 30 percent of the GVN's neutralization claims.[26]

In a great many cases, however, the Americans did not detect incorrect reporting. When the South Vietnamese allegedly killed VC cadres, CORDS advisers were not always present at the battlefield nor could they always arrive in time to identify the bodies. If Phoenix advisers and other CORDS advisers did have access to alleged VCI, living or dead, they frequently could not tell whether their counterparts had identified the people correctly. Some prisoners and ralliers did not say much to the Americans or to anyone else, and the Americans did not recognize most bodies found on the field of battle. The advisers could not gauge the veracity of reports by comparing bodies found to weapons captured because some VC cadres did not carry weapons because the survivors of a battle often took the weapons of their fallen comrades. Peter Scott's experience was similar to that of many American advisers:

I was supposed to corroborate and confirm neutralizations, but the more I learned the less I cared about it. I'd go to the aftermath of a firefight with Phung Hoang representatives from a couple of the branches. We'd turn over the bodies, and sometimes one of them would say, "Well, I'll be damned if it isn't Nguyen Van Dang!" He'd hold up the guy's head and another guy would say, "That's him for sure." I'd look on the VCI list and there'd be a Nguyen Van Dang. Of course there was. Every village had a Nguyen Van Dang. They'd point to Nguyen Van Dang on the list, who was said to be a village propaganda cadre, and say, "That's him." How the hell would I know? He wasn't carrying any paperwork. It looked to me like he was just a regular foot soldier because he'd been mowed down here on the battlefield in a stupid night attack. I couldn't have known the difference unless I had been there for years and years, and known Nguyen Van Dang from Luong Phi, Nguyen Van Dang from Tri Ton, and Nguyen Van Dang from Olam. But these guys said it was him, and I had looked at the body. Maybe the Vietnamese were telling the truth.

Sometimes we'd get a second opinion from someone we trusted, but you could never really be sure. Occasionally I'd find out that this Nguyen Van Dang or whoever it was had been reported killed two months ago, but then the Vietnamese would just say, "That was a different Nguyen Van Dang." I'd go along with them because it made them happy, and it made me look better. Besides, it seemed sort of ridiculous to a lot of us that we'd think we could win the war because we'd found the name of a VC who'd been killed on some list. Later, my bossman would ask, "Did you look at the body?" I'd say, "Yes." The bossman, who wanted it to be true, would report, "The American on the ground corroborates."[27]

In many, if not most places, the South Vietnamese did not even have to match a body with a name from a VCI list. As indicated in chapter 12, at least half the cadres reported captured or killed nationwide had not been identified previously as VCI. In a study sponsored by the U.S. government, the investigators note the ease with which the South Vietnamese could make false VCI neutralization reports: "Many US advisory personnel in the districts question the accuracy of the neutralization claims, pointing out that it is quite an easy matter to claim that individuals killed in the course of military action are members of the VCI when in fact they may well be simply local guerrillas without rank or responsibility."[28]

The South Vietnamese charged with carrying out the Phung Hoang program could meet almost any quota without arresting or killing more people than they had normally arrested or killed before the program started. To meet the quotas, they could simply dub some of the prisoners, bodies, or ralliers "VCI," regardless of their true status. The top GVN leaders did not care about the quota system and tolerated these reports. Many CORDS advisers knew that the South Vietnamese were meeting their quotas without running new anti-VCI operations and disapproved of the falsifications, but their ability to correct the situation was rather minimal. An adviser's report from Ninh Thuan province describes what typically happened when the Vietnamese were told that they should neutralize a larger number of VCI:

> A recent attempt by MR 2 to make inspection results more meaningful has fallen far short of expectations. A checklist which heavily weighted neutralizations, but did not stipulate that they be "targeted" neutralizations, completely distorted the inspection. An Phuoc, which has long been our worst DIOCC ranking 39 out of 52 on the last quarterly inspection, jumped to the best in the province and sixth best in MR 2 without any improvement in their procedures. They simply got credit for a number of VCI killed by Sector-controlled troops.[29]

Some CORDS advisers said that their counterparts simply ignored the quotas; the indifference of South Vietnamese commanding officers and the advisers' lack of authority allowed them to do so. "Quotas were assigned for the Phoenix program," Brig. Gen. James Herbert said, "but I didn't see them being filled by just bringing in anybody, or by labeling civilian casualties as VCI. After the Phung Hoang program got going in my provinces, Long An and Gia Dinh, the Vietnamese didn't meet their quotas. The province chiefs refused to have anything to do with quotas. They wanted the effort to succeed, but they said, 'Don't get too anxious about quotas.'"[30] Most CORDS advisers also noted that the rewards that the Phoenix program offered for neutralizing the VCI generally were too small to invite many dishonest arrests.

The CIA did not usually assign specific quotas to PRUs, the Special Police, and other forces that it sponsored. Many advisers told me that, in their experience, the CIA did not put any pressure on the South Vietnamese to achieve high numerical results. In a limited number of cases, however, CIA officers told the unit leaders that they needed to show better results in the future; in other words, they had to achieve higher neutralization totals to keep their jobs or to get promoted. The CIA also offered money to these forces for specific neutralizations or for general success in neutralizing members of the shadow government. These organizations sometimes submitted bogus reports, as did other South Vietnamese organizations. Gary Mattocks offered the following example: "Let's say you decided to go after a guy in a given hamlet. You went into the hamlet, and he happened to have a squad of Viet Cong protecting him, and they resisted. A firefight would ensue, and there could be villagers in the surrounding huts who got hurt or killed. The PRUs would report those people as VCI. It would be naive to think otherwise."[31] On occasion, CIA-sponsored forces also arrested civilians who supported the VC and reported that they were VCI.

CIA advisers, however, detected and prevented falsification by the South Vietnamese much more often than did CORDS advisers because they had access to more relevant information and could take disciplinary action, if necessary. Their informants within these organizations reported to them about the quantity and identity of people whom their units captured or killed. CIA advisers devised other methods of detecting falsification, such as monitoring the serial numbers of captured weapons. "There was a case in An Xuyen province," John Wilbur recalled, "where it turned out that the same rifle was captured four times." Wilbur doubted that some of the operations during which the PRUs reportedly captured the weapon ever occurred. As a result, he said, "We had to go down to An Xuyen and clean house."[32]

Most American noncommissioned officers who worked with the PRUs, as well as some other PRU advisers, went on PRU operations, which allowed them to see the operational results firsthand. When these advisers stopped going on PRU operations, their ability to prevent statistical falsification declined significantly. Jack Harrell thought that the South Vietnamese frequently inflated neutralization statistics once the Americans stopped accompanying them on operations. Harrell recounted, "The people in Saigon pressured the PRUs to get better neutralization results, but it only led to more falsified reports. A lot of times, without question, a sympathizer or a person who was coerced to cooperate with a VCI was killed, and those people were all classified as VCI once they were killed. In fact, they weren't VCI at all, but it looked good on the reports. We also had a lot of bogus reports because operations were fabricated. The statistics were so inflated that they lost their meaning." Most PRU chiefs in the regions where he worked, Harrell added, still ran enough legitimate operations to keep their jobs. Only in one exceptionally troublesome situation did he take action: "I took it upon myself to investigate the PRU chief in one province because the unit was getting a lot of money from a bonus program. I found out that 90 percent of what the chief was reporting was bogus."[33]

On average, PRU chiefs were more honest and hardworking than other

South Vietnamese chiefs, and the Americans usually disciplined or removed
them if they fabricated too many reports or if they deliberately captured
or killed more than a few people without evidence of their collaboration
with the VC. Special Police advisers could not check on their counterparts
as effectively as the PRU advisers because they accompanied them on operations less often and had less influence over them, although they had more
influence than CORDS advisers.

A typical hamlet in the Mekong Delta, ca. 1969. (Courtesy Peter Scott)

A hamlet in the sparsely populated highlands of II Corps, 1970. (National Archives)

A Viet Cong leader speaks at a meeting in a wooded area. (COURTESY FRANK C. BROWN, CAPTURED VC PHOTO COLLECTION)

A meeting of Viet Cong cadres. (COURTESY FRANK C. BROWN, CAPTURED VC PHOTO COLLECTION)

Members of the Viet Cong show their approval of a leader's speech.

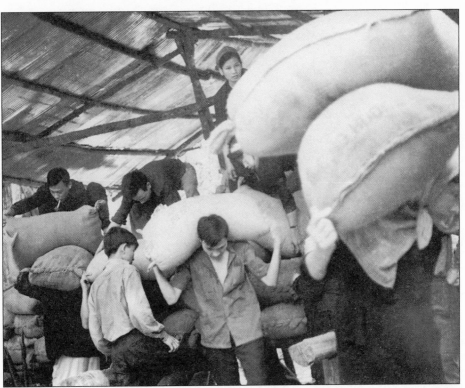

The Viet Cong shadow government uses villagers to transport rice that it has collected from the villagers.

An outpost of the GVN's territorial forces in Duc Hue district, Hau Nghia province, 1963. (NATIONAL ARCHIVES)

In Binh Dinh province, a member of the South Vietnamese National Police (left) questions a man suspected of supporting the Viet Cong. (NATIONAL ARCHIVES)

Soldiers of the ARVN 21st Division move toward a hamlet in search of Viet Cong, 1963. (NATIONAL ARCHIVES)

Members of the Viet Cong on the move. (COURTESY FRANK C. BROWN, CAPTURED VC PHOTO COLLECTION)

A group of VC show off their weapons. (COURTESY FRANK C. BROWN, CAPTURED VC PHOTO COLLECTION)

A member of the National Police (second from right) serves as an interpreter for Americans from the Americal Division who are questioning a VC suspect. (NATIONAL ARCHIVES)

South Vietnamese refugees leave their village, 1967. (NATIONAL ARCHIVES)

Meeting between CIA officers and the II Corps Special Police. The Special Police chief is fourth from right, and Dean Almy, the CIA's region officer in charge, is fifth from right. (COURTESY DEAN ALMY)

Col. Douglas Dillard, USA, deputy Phoenix coordinator in IV Corps (left), with Brig. Gen. Vu Duc Nhuan, head of the South Vietnamese Military Security Service. *(Courtesy Douglas Dillard)*

A rare photo of the CIA compound at Cao Lanh, the capital of Kien Phong province. *(Courtesy Robert Boyke)*

A district-level Phoenix center, technically known as a District Intelligence and Operations Coordination Center, in the Mekong Delta.
(COURTESY DOUGLAS DILLARD)

A Provincial Reconnaissance Unit in An Xuyen province, 1967. (COURTESY HENRY F. DAGENAIS)

John Wilbur, SEAL officer and IV Corps PRU adviser (right), with a PRU member. (COURTESY JOHN WILBUR)

Peter Scott, a Phoenix adviser who served in Chau Doc and Chuong Thien provinces, with ethnic Cambodian Kit Carson Scouts in Chau Doc. (COURTESY PETER SCOTT)

PRUs of Quang Tri province before an operation against the Viet Cong. (COURTESY WARREN H. MILBERG)

Quang Tri PRUs move in a column during an operation. (COURTESY WARREN H. MILBERG)

An interrogator from the South Korean Tiger Division questions VC suspects in Qui Nhon, the capital of Binh Dinh province, 1967. (NATIONAL ARCHIVES)

A Vietnamese Ranger (in doorway) helps American soldiers from the 199th Infantry Brigade search a hamlet in Gia Dinh province. (NATIONAL ARCHIVES)

CORDS adviser Col. Henry Dagenais, USA (right), with his GVN counterpart (center) and a GVN hamlet chief (left), An Xuyen province, 1967. (COURTESY HENRY F. DAGENAIS)

An American medic (right) gives basic medical treatment to villagers. (COURTESY PETER SCOTT)

Members of the Special Police and the PRUs, along with their CIA advisers, during a joint operation in Kien Phong province. At right is CIA adviser Robert Boyke. (COURTESY ROBERT BOYKE)

Command Sgt. Maj. Michael N. Martin, USA, PRU adviser (second from left), and Chau Doc PRU members prepare to mount an operation against the VCI. (COURTESY MICHAEL N. MARTIN)

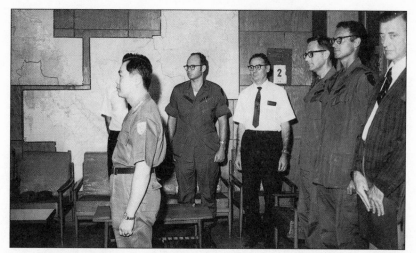

Phung Hoang presentation ceremony in Saigon. Col. Ly Trong Song, chief of Phung Hoang, is at left; CIA officer John S. Tilton, director of Phung Hoang, is at far right. (COURTESY CHESTER B. MCCOID)

Lt. Col. Dao Quan Hien, GVN National Police chief in III Corps (second from right), talks with Daren Flitcroft, CIA region officer in charge, III Corps (second from left), and U.S. Army Col. Norman Furth, III Corps Phoenix coordinator (far right). (COURTESY DAO QUAN HIEN)

A PRU team in the Mekong Delta prepares for a mission near the Cambodian border.
(COURTESY MICHAEL N. MARTIN)

PRU adviser Richard Welcome (left) with PRU members in Binh Thuan province. (COURTESY RICHARD WELCOME)

A large contingent of PRUs in the Mekong Delta awaits orders to begin an operation. U.S. advisers are at the left. (COURTESY DOUGLAS DILLARD)

PRUs get ready to move out against the enemy. (COURTESY DOUGLAS DILLARD)

Soldiers of the U.S. Army's 1st Cavalry Division provide first aid to civilians injured by a VC mine. The explosion killed a woman and a child. (NATIONAL ARCHIVES)

The head of a VC platoon leader who was killed by GVN forces shortly after he and his unit executed GVN officials in Tan Hung Tai village.
(COURTESY HENRY F. DAGENAIS)

A VC defector (left), now serving with a GVN unit, interrogates a VC prisoner in Vinh Long province. (NATIONAL ARCHIVES)

Members of the GVN territorial forces cross a canal during an operation in 1969. (NATIONAL ARCHIVES)

A group of ralliers, people who defected from the Communists to the GVN under the terms of the Chieu Hoi program. (NATIONAL ARCHIVES)

Former GVN officers in a Communist "reeducation" camp after the war. Col. Bui Hop, a former officer of the South Vietnamese National Police, is at upper left, and Col. Nguyen Van Cua, former province chief of Chau Doc, is at lower right.
(COURTESY BUI HOP)

17   The Americans

tilizing the powers that the U.S. government had bestowed on them, certain American advisers in South Vietnam could induce South Vietnamese forces to operate against the VCI and their armed guardians. The U.S. high command used monthly quotas and more subtle forms of pressure to motivate its advisers to push the attack on the VCI. The measures had a greater effect on the American advisers than they had on the Vietnamese, because those who instituted them had direct authority over the advisers.

In the minds of many Americans, numbers of VC cadres captured and killed served as the only indicator of an action unit's success in attacking the shadow government. Like the "body count" of Communist soldiers killed by American forces, "VCI neutralizations" became a crucial measuring stick for American bureaucrats; they expended countless reams of paper recording and processing the monthly VCI neutralization figures for the various units throughout the provinces of South Vietnam. Some Americans high on the bureaucratic ladder attached great importance to these statistics because they believed that they provided the best indicator of performance, which was true in some cases. Others were less convinced of the accuracy and relevance of the statistics, but they felt compelled to emphasize them in their reports to people farther up in the hierarchy who did have confidence in the numbers.

Because of this preoccupation with statistics, some PRU and Special Police advisers and other Americans with substantial influence over action units received praise and promotion from their superiors mainly for the numbers of VC cadres or other VC whom their units neutralized, or for the ability of their units to meet VCI quotas. Even if no one specifically ordered them to neutralize more VCI or VC, they frequently could tell that they needed to produce numbers to get ahead. Sometimes, for instance, their superiors informed them of the numbers achieved by other units in their province or region and commented that the best units had the most neutralizations. Even many advisers without any real power over their counterparts felt pressured to present high VCI neutralization numbers because unreasonable bosses held them accountable for the performance of their counterparts. Advisers also knew that their bosses did not like ineffective subordinates; bosses whose subordinates were not performing well might look bad in the eyes of their own bosses.

Because of these pressures, some American advisers with substantial influence prodded South Vietnamese leaders to perform better or they replaced the leaders. In other instances, however, the end results were not so positive. In response to the pressures, a significant number of advisers in some chains of command arbitrarily inflated the neutralization statistics for units that did not perform well or did not object when the Vietnamese submitted inflated figures. Seldom did anyone from higher headquarters come to verify the advisers' claims, so the advisers usually got away with inflating the figures. Some did so merely to claim that they had attained the objectives that their superiors had assigned to them, but most of them had other reasons as well. A large number of advisers doubted their ability to detect falsification of the statistics by the South Vietnamese and therefore did not try to sort through their inflated figures. Many believed that statistical measurements alone provided a poor gauge of a unit's skill and drive or of the damage inflicted on the enemy, which was true in some instances. In addition, numerous advisers believed that they had more productive things to do than trying to determine whether certain prisoners, ralliers, and corpses matched names on the lists of wanted VCI or in neutralization reports. Some, indeed, found the obsession of headquarters people with statistics absurd, particularly because these people generally accepted the statistical reports without question.

"Almost nobody from headquarters came out to check out what we were doing," Rob Simmons remembered. "Some would come out to the field, but most would not come out except to party. They'd sit in their little offices in Nha Trang and Saigon and read the reports, and that's how they judged the war. 'This number's up, this number's down.' A lot of people complained about the numbers game, especially those of us in the field. We all knew it was a bum system."[1] Col. Carl Bernard commented, "The ability of guys in Saigon to determine whether a report was accurate was zip. Nor were they particularly curious. No one from Saigon could tell who was doing what in the two hundred hamlets in our province at night. They simply had to take the word of the people in the province."[2]

A considerable number of advisers gave inflated statistics because their commanding officers actively discouraged accurate reporting of meager results. They threatened to replace or to damage the careers of subordinates who did not comply with their wishes, although they seldom made the threats overtly. Past removals of insistent advisers and subtle hints from superiors indicated what would happen to advisers who made reports that were not sufficiently positive. When advisers were removed because of problems with their superiors, they were usually transferred to paper-shuffling jobs or other undesirable, career-inhibiting positions in unimportant places where they would have no impact on the Allied war effort. Aggressive advisers wanted to avoid that fate at almost any cost. "Like most of us," Peter Scott said, "I had a great fear of being in the countryside because of the physical danger, but I had a greater fear of being sent back to an office in Saigon or someplace like that because of the boredom and the uselessness of it."[3] Angering a commanding officer also could result in a poor efficiency report, which seriously reduced any chances of promotion.

The discouragement of negative reporting occurred at all levels in both the CIA and CORDS, and it became increasingly prevalent during the war's later years. "Neither the American nor the Vietnamese government encouraged anything but optimistic, success-related reporting," Tom Polgar remarked. "If you were critical about the progress of any authorized activity, you became unpopular with your superiors, who controlled your career advancement. Careerism and conformity were bad enough in the CIA in Vietnam, but reached their heights in the US military, with few exceptions."[4]

Most CIA and CORDS veterans who witnessed U.S. leaders encouraging false reporting laid most of the blame for this problem on subordination of the national cause to the quest for career advancement. This malady is likely to affect any governmental organization, particularly a nonmilitary organization, but it struck the Americans in Vietnam in an unusually acute form. "Up or out" promotion policies that forced officers to leave government service if they did not advance by a certain date increased the importance of career advancement for CIA officers and the military officers in CORDS. Because the military also rotated its officers rapidly through most CORDS positions, these officers did not have time to become deeply engrossed in their work, and they constantly had to worry about the next job assignment. For both CIA and CORDS personnel, competition with officers who exaggerated their achievements encouraged people even more to put career considerations before performance. Morale sank in some cases as people became resentful of dishonest coworkers. Jack Harrell said, "Most guys only had a year or two to make their mark. If they wanted to get good fitness reports, they had to produce numbers.

There were a lot of people who were playing the numbers game and not getting down to the nitty-gritty of trying to win the war."[5]

Some of the restraints that had curbed careerism at other times in U.S. history and during the early years of the Vietnam War began to disappear as the war moved toward its later years. Top civilian and military leaders throughout the war, in contrast to U.S. leaders during some other wars, seldom made much effort to discourage excessively upbeat reporting and sometimes even encouraged it. They wanted positive assessments from their officers because they felt compelled to report evidence of "progress" in the war consistently in order to maintain public support. They also knew that the media would gain access to some negative reports and publicize them, thereby weakening support for the war. The growing perception that the war ultimately was not serving the national interest or any other useful purpose set free the careerist impulses of CIA and CORDS officers alike. After the Tet offensive, they saw that U.S. political leaders were losing their desire to fight the war hard enough to achieve a conclusive victory, as evidenced by U.S. troop reductions and the imposition of other limits on the uses of U.S. military power, and were turning the war over to a South Vietnamese army that, on its own, would not stack up well against the NVA. Most of them also sensed that their nation no longer considered the preservation of South Vietnam as vital to American security. Bruce Lawlor said:

> I believe at some point the Americans in Vietnam—both in the military and the Agency—understood that we were not there to win the war, that the political restrictions placed on the war were such that victory was not this country's objective. At that point, self-interest took over. The attitude seemed to be, "If I can't do the mission I was sent here for, then at least I can get something out of it for myself, for my own career." We abandoned the mission and became careerist. There were some guys over there who were so unproductive that it was ludicrous we were even paying them the money to be there, but they did their time, wrote a few reports, and moved on.[6]

Quite a few advisers from all organizations, on the other hand, told me that their superiors never pressured them in any way to get higher VCI neutralization statistics or to make excessively positive reports. Many of the PRUs and several other units often enjoyed enough real success that the numbers were sufficiently high anyway. In other cases, superiors might have tried to identify lazy or incompetent leaders and advisers, with the help perhaps of operational statistics, and might have forced them to improve their performance or to leave. These Americans doubted, nevertheless, the usefulness of quotas and purely numerical measures of achievement. Those most successful in improving their subordinates had a deeper knowledge of the local situation than statistics could convey. CORDS adviser Lloyd Pomeroy asserted, "Advisers in Kien Hoa province were expected to be honest and objective. If anybody ever needed a role model, he could look to Albert Kotzebue, our province senior adviser, for those qualities."[7]

Some Americans remembered having bosses who looked down on advisers for whitewashing problems. For example, Brig. Gen. James Herbert said, "Reports which said something was working properly, and advisers who made such reports, were usually considered suspect. In the cases I encountered, the way to get additional resources and additional respect as someone who told the truth was to depict the situation as worse than it was. So when things were terrible, we tried to tell the truth."[8] A smaller number of Americans said that they made critical or pessimistic reports despite pressures from above. Many CORDS reports from the provinces, which are now available to the public, do indeed contain gloomy or critical comments about the attack on the shadow government and other aspects of the war. Some of the Americans who wrote these reports risked their careers to further the nation's war effort, for above them somewhere in the chain of command lurked officers and officials who wanted big numbers and upbeat reports. Among the most important reasons for this high level of honesty and commitment were love of one's American compatriots, patriotism, personal integrity, hatred of the enemy, and the belief that the war was important and winnable. Others included professional pride and anti-Communism. Some advisers also developed a strong affection for their South Vietnamese counterparts and the people of South Vietnam.

To assist and encourage the South Vietnamese in their activities against the shadow government, some of the advisers also offered advice. Their South Vietnamese counterparts were more likely to heed the advisers who made suggestions in private and then allowed their counterparts to take credit publicly for the ideas. This method prevented the South Vietnamese from seeming reliant on the Americans and thereby losing face. Maj. Gen. Nguyen Duy Hinh, commander of ARVN's 3d Division, notes: "The best approach for any adviser was to mention a problem, let his counterpart think about it, and in the process, inject suggestive ideas as to how he thought the problem could best be solved. After this process was completed the adviser should then let the Vietnamese voluntarily initiate actions as if they were his own ideas."[9]

The South Vietnamese listened to advisers who accompanied them on operations more often than they listened to other advisers. Advisers who participated in operations developed camaraderie with their counterparts by sharing their risks, pain, and triumphs. In putting their own lives on the line, they also tacitly expressed confidence that the operations were not foolhardy. "Very frequently the lieutenants assigned to Phoenix at the district level became involved in operations themselves," Evan Parker, Jr., said. "They weren't supposed to be combat soldiers, but when you get out there at that level it's very hard to maintain your relationship if you tell the Vietnamese to target some people, and then just say, 'Go get 'em, boys.' The Vietnamese would think, 'It's easy to tell us to go and fight while he sits on his ass back here.' So some of these young fellows just went out and did it. All we said was, 'Don't get hurt.'"[10] Many advisers who could not go on operations because of various prohibitions imposed by the U.S. leadership toward the end of the war told me that this limitation seriously undermined their efforts to gain the respect of their counterparts.

Many of the stronger South Vietnamese chiefs and other GVN commanders normally disregarded the advice of American advisers, although they smiled and pretended to like the advice in order to keep the American money flowing. They viewed many of the advisers, often rightly, as novices who understood little about the war or Vietnam. CORDS Phoenix advisers were particularly young and inexperienced. Vietnamese disdain for foreigners made these advisers' situations even worse. Col. John Bringham, the province senior adviser in Tuyen Duc during the early 1970s, recalled:

> I used to tell my officers, "Put yourself in the place of your counterparts. Wouldn't you think it was some sort of affront if you had been bogged down in the U.S. fighting a war against other Americans for years, and the Germans sent people to advise you? Your reaction would be, 'What do they know about it?'" You just couldn't tell your counterpart how to run the war.[11]

Some American advisers urged their counterparts to work faster or harder, which only irritated them in most cases. The South Vietnamese usually disliked American attempts to make them rush or do more work and often responded to them by working even more slowly or doing even less work. In many instances, the slow pace of GVN activity resulted not from laziness, corruption, or fear of combat or Communist retribution, but from a basic cultural difference: Americans tend to hurry more than the South Vietnamese. In addition, whereas U.S. advisers typically came for a year or two and then left, most GVN leaders had been at war for many years, and they sensed that the war would continue indefinitely. This seeming endlessness encouraged the view that acting quickly rather than slowly was not going to make much difference. "Even though the American effort had been going on for a long time," said Col. Walter Clark, "we were still in a hurry to get the war over with. The Vietnamese, who had been fighting longer than any of us had, didn't see things the same way. They figured, 'Why hustle out on this patrol tonight? There's always tomorrow night, what's the difference? I'm going to get it one of these days anyway, so what's the hurry?'"[12] The South Vietnamese also wanted to take time off from the war to care for their families. Col. Hoang Ngoc Lung noted that "the Vietnamese usually argued that US advisers served only one year, enjoyed a good life and were not immediately concerned about family affairs or anything other than their jobs."[13]

Advisers whose counterparts knew a great deal or paid no heed to advisers often concluded that their advice was useless and thus did not try to give advice. Others who might have helped their counterparts run operations in a meaningful way did not bother giving advice because they did not care enough about their jobs. A substantial number of advisers had little interaction with their counterparts aside from giving them money and supplies; most of them chose to spend their time drinking or enjoying other pleasures. Don Gregg noted, "A lot of the CORDS people and some of the Agency's contract employees had been there a long time, and many were just bureaucrats who were corrupt and having the time of their lives. Their old wives were in Bangkok, and they were shacked up with lovely young Vietnamese girls."[14]

A sizable number of advisers, on the other hand, persistently tried to convince intractable South Vietnamese leaders to follow their advice. Because of self-motivation or pressure to show results in a short amount of time, these Americans had a strong desire to change the behavior of their counterparts. Advisers who had the ability to force their counterparts to act in certain ways—primarily CIA advisers—generally convinced the South Vietnamese to follow some of their suggestions by talking with them. CORDS advisers, who lacked such powers, did not enjoy much success when they pleaded with their counterparts. When an impatient CORDS adviser repeatedly and fervently tried to prod a chief into action without success, a senior American usually had to replace the adviser because, by then, the South Vietnamese had decided to ignore him completely.

CORDS advisers frustrated by GVN intransigence usually fared better by appealing to their superiors, who could pressure senior GVN officials to get more satisfactory results from the people in question or replace them.

Americans at the top echelons of CORDS usually had to tolerate district and province chiefs and their subordinate action unit leaders who ignored the attack on the VCI, for the GVN deemed the program unimportant and the highest U.S. political and military leaders in South Vietnam did not exert sufficient pressure on the GVN to force a change in priorities. The upper-level CORDS officials did try to intervene, however, when these South Vietnamese chiefs did not mount sufficient operations of any sort against the Communist armed forces. They had enough influence to produce changes in GVN behavior in some cases, but they did not always want to use that influence.

CORDS advisers at the district and provincial levels who wanted help from superiors faced some risks that, in addition to the limitations on the powers of their superiors, discouraged some of them from appealing for help. If an adviser fruitlessly complained about something to his South Vietnamese counterpart and the counterpart later heard the same complaint from his own boss, the counterpart most likely would know that the adviser had made his complaint known to the GVN boss in some way. Like most people, the counterpart did not want his superior to hear negative comments about him from other people, so his relationship with the adviser usually soured. Either the adviser or his counterpart would have to be replaced, or the adviser would be worthless. Robert Komer described this state of affairs:

> My province teams and district teams were there, among other things, to report to me how the Vietnamese were doing. I told them, "If there's a chief in this province who's not performing, I want you to tell me. I want you to develop a dossier on this, cite evidence, and I'm going to show that dossier to Ky or Thieu, and get action." I could tell Thieu or Ky, "This guy is just not doing the job. He's spending more time with his mistresses than with his work."
>
> That might register with Thieu if he didn't like the guy already, or it might not. That was dangerous, because it could get back down to the province chief, and he'd know it had come from the province senior adviser. All of a sudden, the two of them would separate, and the province chief would always be too busy to see the senior adviser. I'd probably have to relieve the senior adviser at that point because he wasn't doing me any good, but we had to take risks like that to convince the GVN leadership.[15]

This type of protest sometimes hurt the CORDS adviser by damaging his own commanding officer's image of him. When advisers criticized their counterparts, observers might wonder whether the advisers bore some of the responsibility for the counterparts' shortcomings. Indeed, a counterpart often countered an adviser's accusations by criticizing the adviser. If the adviser had been involved in any questionable activities, the counterpart might have learned about them through the adviser's interpreter—the GVN often recruited interpreters as agents—or other informants. By contrast, advisers who only praised their counterparts found that their counterparts said the best things about them and gave them medals, thus making them look good in the eyes of senior Americans. Brig. Gen. James Lawton Collins, Jr., author of a U.S. Army study on American assistance to the South Vietnamese armed forces, concludes: "Too often advisers did not take firm stands with their counterparts on key issues nor recommend the relief of unsatisfactory commanders for fear that such recommendations would reflect badly on their own abilities."[16] Some senior American advisers directly pressured subordinates to avoid criticizing their counterparts or simply quashed critical reports. If their subordinates were not making the South Vietnamese perform well, these senior advisers reasoned, their own commanding officers might think that they had failed to supervise the subordinates properly.

Despite the multitude of dangers involved in reporting on poor GVN performance to higher levels, many CORDS advisers still did so. In some cases, CORDS succeeded in making the South Vietnamese change their behavior or forced them out of their jobs. During the years after the Tet offensive, in what was undoubtedly the finest achievement of the entire U.S. advisory effort, CORDS helped the GVN in its endeavor to replace numerous inept district and province chiefs. Komer and William Colby, using reports from advisers, persuaded Thieu to remove a large fraction of the many chiefs that he sacked. Of the 20 province chiefs replaced in 1968, 1969, and 1971 for corruption, dishonesty, or incompetence, CORDS had asked for the dismissal of 14. Similarly, during that time, CORDS had requested the replacement of 84 district chiefs out of a total of 124 removed for the same reasons.[17] The Americans also convinced Thieu to replace some of the powerful corps commanders.

Thieu and other senior GVN leaders refused to make a few changes that the Americans recommended because of family ties or other connections. In addition, a fair number of the chiefs removed went on to positions of equal importance and some even received promotions, but most of them were no longer under the jurisdiction of CORDS. They moved, instead, to the regular branches of the South Vietnamese military, which did not purge their ranks to the same extent. Robert Komer said, "Maybe a third of the province chiefs were put into jobs which were just as important as the ones they'd left, but they weren't in the pacification business anymore. I'm sorry about that, but that was the way the system worked."[18]

In theory, advisers who did not serve in the CIA were not allowed to give the South Vietnamese orders, and most of the time they did not. The top U.S. leaders generally wanted to leave command responsibilities and leadership selection to the South Vietnamese in order to foster their self-sufficiency. The South Vietnamese would develop into strong leaders, they reasoned, only when they were allowed to make important decisions. Many policymakers also hoped that leaving the GVN largely independent of direct American control would encourage the South Vietnamese leaders to believe that they were fighting as nationalists, not as colonial puppets, and inspire the masses to embrace this non-Communist nationalism. Some of the American leaders also believed in the principle of self-determination and abhorred the thought of the United States assuming the role of a colonial power. A few U.S. policymakers thought, in addition, that the South Vietnamese understood the war better than the Americans, so the Americans ought not to tell them what to do. The U.S. government, furthermore, wanted to convince the American public and the rest of the world that the GVN was an independent government. Finally, U.S. military leaders avoided forming a joint command with the ARVN because they thought that the lack of a common language and the disclosure of classified U.S. information through ARVN officers who spied for the VC would cause too many problems.

A limited number of CORDS advisers and a larger number of advisers to the ARVN, however, issued orders to their counterparts or commanded South Vietnamese units directly because their counterparts were weak and let them do so. Most advisers, including those who made command decisions for their counterparts, acknowledged that heavy American involvement in operations inhibited the development of South Vietnamese autonomy. As the Americans gradually withdrew their advisers during the early 1970s, they knew that many South Vietnamese commanders who had ceded authority to the Americans were ill equipped to handle their jobs alone. Some, nevertheless, believed they had to lead in place of counterparts who were not getting important jobs done. In many cases, their actions were justified, for their leadership averted imminent disaster. In other cases, the impatience and aggressiveness of some U.S. military officers—which make them better at leading than advising—led them to take control when the situation was not so desperate. Col. Horace Hunter commented, "At the fighting edge of a war, one looks for immediate results. Long-range concerns about the impact on nation building some-times look less important than getting something done right away. The pressure from above for results, and the generally activist philosophy of Americans, encouraged taking over."[19]

Opponents of the official U.S. policy at the time, among them John Paul Vann, Robert Komer, and even some of the South Vietnamese, advocated greater U.S. control over the GVN's leadership. Most of those who had first-hand knowledge of South Vietnamese politics argued that the Americans, in assuming greater authority over the GVN, should restrict their powers to the appointment and firing of the most important military and admin-istrative officials and to the distribution of funds and supplies. Had the United States heeded their advice, in my opinion, it most probably would have improved the GVN leadership considerably. The Americans knew enough able and honest officers whom they could have installed in key positions in place of Thieu's political hacks. They also could have stimu-lated more aggressive behavior among South Vietnamese leaders with the threat of removal. South Vietnamese officers still would have commanded all GVN units, rather than the Americans, who knew less about the war and could not motivate the Vietnamese as easily. American control of funds would have eliminated much of the corruption that depleted the GVN's war supplies, distracted GVN leaders, and robbed the rank and file of the money that they needed to support their families.

Under such a system, South Vietnam probably would have been strong enough that the United States would not have needed to commit large num-bers of troops to the country, thus avoiding the high number of American casualties that gradually weakened the American public's support of the war. The Americans could have kept a fairly low profile and probably would not have suffered any more from charges of colonialism than they actually did, although the charges would have been more accurate. Had the United States needed to deploy many of its ground forces in South Vietnam, it could have kept the South Vietnamese and American armies separate or integrated only low-ranking South Vietnamese soldiers into U.S. units, thereby keep-ing U.S. secrets away from Vietnamese eyes.

South Vietnamese nationalism and autonomy would not have developed as quickly under this arrangement as otherwise. The United States proba-bly could have appeased the South Vietnamese nationalists to some extent by promising to turn over full control of the country to the South Vietnam-ese after the Communist onslaught subsided, but such promises would not have had the same effect as giving them full control. The development of

South Vietnamese autonomy and nationalism, however, should not have been a top priority because the effort to attain this objective, by its very nature, reduced South Vietnam's chances for short-term survival too much. By permitting GVN autonomy, the Americans also permitted the cronyism that so greatly weakened the GVN by putting many ineffective leaders into important positions, and autonomy never fostered a nationalism strong enough to overcome this problem. From 1969 to 1972, it is true, Thieu did replace some of the GVN's worst leaders, especially among the district and province chiefs. During this time, nevertheless, Thieu left many bad generals in power, and he began appointing his political allies in greater numbers after the U.S. disengagement of early 1973. Had the United States controlled the leadership selection, South Vietnam, in all probability, would have had better leaders and therefore would have survived much longer than it did, thus allowing for subsequent development of a more autonomous state. The little-understood PRU program shows that the South Vietnamese could perform extremely well when Americans selected their leaders.

Some commanders of American main force units also contributed to the attack on the shadow government. As soon as Evan Parker, Jr., arrived to head the new program for attacking the shadow government, Gen. William C. Westmoreland told his generals to assist the program. They usually complied, despite their preference for the more glamorous main force operations. "When I attended my first MACV staff meeting," Parker said, "Westmoreland came down the hallway, put his arm around me, and introduced me to the generals. 'General so-and-so, this is Mr. Parker who's going to be on our staff in charge of this new program.' In effect, I was given the seal of approval. When the Army is given an order by its commanding officer, they do it. They may not agree, but they do it. I had also served with some of these officers in an earlier war or I had worked with them in the U.S., so I knew them, and they cooperated fully."[20] Americans who had served at all levels during 1967 and 1968 told me that some but not all American units regularly provided cordon forces or helicopter support to the PRUs, the National Police Field Forces, and other pacification units.

After Gen. Creighton Abrams succeeded Westmoreland in June 1968, he put greater emphasis on pacification and support of the attack on the VCI. He ordered many American military commanders to devote their forces more often to wresting control of populated areas from small VC units and less often to chasing enemy main forces. Joint operations with South Vietnamese pacification personnel also increased in frequency. Abrams put even more emphasis on the use of U.S. troops in pacification roles during the Accelerated Pacification Campaign that ran from November 1968 to January 1969, and this emphasis persisted afterward. Abrams might have chosen this course in part because his views about how to fight the war differed from Westmoreland's. The main reason, however, was that the Communist main forces, after enduring devastating losses during the Tet offensive, were operating primarily in small units. Allied forces could disperse into smaller, stealthier units and move around the village areas without encountering large VC or NVA units. Some American military units, however, continued to concentrate on seeking and annihilating North Vietnamese forces in areas remote from the population. The Allies still had to prevent the NVA from making large incursions into the inhabited areas.

18   Neutralization of Non-Communist Civilians

dherents of the antiwar movement and other critics of the Allies have asserted that GVN officials regularly eliminated enemies of all types as part of the Phoenix program, and that some arrested or killed many people indiscriminately. Political scientist Samuel Popkin, after a visit to Vietnam, contended that the program "has no more precision than a search-and-destroy operation" and that, because of it, "police agents have arrested many peasants who were guilty of only trivial offenses."[1] Professor Marilyn Young, in a recent history of the war, charges the GVN with using Phoenix to blackmail people and settle old scores; she concludes that Phoenix was "frequently mistaken in its targets."[2] Popkin, Young, and most others who share these beliefs do not appear to understand that Phoenix was only a coordination program, albeit one with a catchy name, and that a number of groups with such prosaic names as Provincial Reconnaissance Units, Regional Forces, Popular Forces, and National Police Field Forces carried out the attack on the VCI. This distinction, however, is not important as it relates to the issue at hand; the crucial question is whether the various pacification forces committed the acts ascribed to Phoenix.

Some people wanted to use anti-VCI programs against enemies other than the Communists by identifying them as VCI. Chapter 10 shows that the attack on the VCI had built-in deterrents that prevented most of these people from misusing the programs in this fashion. Allied emphasis on the attack on the VCI did not encourage the GVN to arrest many people, as chapter 16 explains. Certain people and groups who wanted to target their non-Communist enemies nevertheless could try to arrest or kill them without going through the intelligence process. The absence of intelligence or operations paperwork made the subterfuge more difficult to detect, but features built into anti-VCI programs provided obstacles to this sort of misapplication as well. On the whole, a large number of effective safeguards kept the Allies from imprisoning or killing massive numbers of non-Communist civilians, as the antiwar critics alleged that they did, although these safe-guards did not prevent all abuses of the system.

A GVN unit, under the guise of patrolling an area, could easily arrest or kill a non-Communist enemy. GVN leaders who did not participate in such operations almost invariably knew, through subordinates or infor-mants, when units under their command took part in them. Col. Walter Clark spoke of his well-motivated counterpart: "The province chief would find out if any troops were misbehaving. He had his sources in the villages, and he knew everything that was going on."[3] Responsible South Vietnam-ese chiefs, and there were many of them, knew that allowing subordinates to tyrannize personal adversaries was likely to arouse the resentment of the village populations; in most cases, therefore, they punished the perpe-trators and released their captives. Units that went out specifically to neu-tralize non-Communists, therefore, usually did so only at the request of one or more GVN leaders.

Some Americans monitored the South Vietnamese closely enough to know whether they were targeting non-Communists. CORDS could have district and province chiefs and other GVN leaders removed for failing to prosecute the war adequately because it could convince Thieu that their presence seriously weakened his nation's war effort. It could not, however, get these chiefs sacked so readily for neutralizing non-Communist ene-mies. The GVN high command in Saigon did not care much if chiefs arrested or killed a few people whom they disliked, and the chiefs rarely found it necessary to deal with more than a few personal enemies. Nor did top GVN leaders generally oppose the neutralizion of members of opposi-tion political parties and racial minorities. These leaders, indeed, often encouraged the chiefs to neutralize the members of non-Communist groups suspected of anti-GVN activity. Even the senior CORDS leaders were not overly concerned with these problems; if they knew much about them, they generally resigned themselves to the reality that every chief would be able to make a few dubious arrests here and there. They pre-ferred to use what leverage they had to oust Vietnamese officials who did not perform well against the Communists. After all, if the Americans con-vinced the GVN to remove an effective chief for throwing a few ethnic Cambodian politicians into jail, the GVN might replace him with a less effective chief who had also put a few of his enemies behind bars.

Even the Special Police and PRU advisers did not try to discipline coun-terparts who imprisoned or killed their non-Communist adversaries except in rare cases where their counterparts improperly targeted large numbers of people. Jack Harrell said, "You didn't try to find problems with PRU chiefs. You had enough to deal with anyway, without having to look for problems. As long as someone was doing something more sophisticated than skimming or fabricating and the abuses didn't become blatantly widespread, they did what they wanted to do."[4]

A considerable number of additional safeguards, to some extent independent of the intelligence process and of GVN and American control over operations, ensured that the pacification forces would not imprison or kill many non-Communists. When targeting civilians suspected of working for the VC, the Allies normally arrested them in broad daylight in their villages or at a marketplace. They put these individuals in jail and sometimes tortured them, but they seldom killed them unless they knew for certain that they were hard-core VC. Allied units of all types arrested and then imprisoned or released so many people, including some who certainly were VC cadres, that one cannot plausibly argue that they killed all or most civilians accused of collaborating with the VC. According to official statistics, the Allies arrested at least one hundred suspected VCI or VCI supporters for every supposed VC cadre that they targeted and killed deliberately.[5] Although these statistics, undoubtedly, are somewhat imprecise, my interviews with advisers and CORDS documents both indicate that the arrests did indeed greatly outnumber the deliberate kills, so the argument, in general, is still valid. Some PRU teams did not arrest many more VCI or suspected VCI than they targeted and killed, but the PRUs were more aggressive in attacking cadres escorted by armed VC than most other forces were and some almost always functioned as tactical military units.

The GVN put unarmed detainees through a processing system, separate from the military's system for processing prisoners bearing arms, in order to determine their status. Screening committees consisting of GVN officials at the hamlet, village, and district levels reviewed evidence from a wide variety of sources pertaining to the activities of the detainees. When a screening committee determined that it had evidence incriminating an individual as a cadre, it sent the case to the Province Security Committee for further review. The screening committee transferred detainees presumed to be Communist soldiers to the military's prisoner processing system. The other detainees were released.

Province Security Committees, composed of the province chief and a few other senior province officials, met weekly, in principle, to hear the cases of the suspected VCI. They met less often in many provinces, however, because the responsible officials were too busy. The committee members weighed the evidence in each case. Under the provisions of the *an tri* emergency detention procedure, they sentenced those found guilty to prison terms of up to two years and released the detainees found not guilty. The committees reviewed the prison sentences at their completion and could extend them. No guidelines stipulated what sorts of evidence were admissible in the trials or how much evidence was needed to convict. The presiding officials simply looked at all available information and made their own assessments of its credibility. A suspect did not have a lawyer and seldom had the opportunity to say anything in his or her own defense. In addition, the need to process many individuals in a short amount of time sometimes led committees to reach decisions hastily.

American critics of the GVN's legal system emphasize these features because they indicate that the system did not protect defendants' interests, at least not to the extent that they are protected in U.S. courts. These critics wanted the GVN to introduce methods of protecting defendants akin to those in the United States, as well as other elements of American law and the American judiciary, virtually overnight. Such proposals were unrealistic. A third-world country, such as South Vietnam, could not duplicate a Western legal system quickly or easily. Only a tiny minority of the South Vietnamese had any training in legal matters; adopting a judicial system similar to that of the United States would have required educating some people as lawyers and judges over a period of many years. More important, it would have demanded that the South Vietnamese people change their fundamental beliefs about justice and the rights of defendants. Such transformations usually occur only slowly over a long period of time. Moreover, they seldom occur when they are forced upon a people.

Obviously, the detention system permitted senior GVN officials at the provincial level to imprison people without sufficient reason. Undoubtedly, they did so in some cases. The large majority of observers, nevertheless, thought that the Province Security Committees, during most of the war, generally based their verdicts on responsible consideration of all evidence. The only types of prisoners who did not normally receive fair trials were members of certain political or racial groups. Province chiefs and other committee members seldom had old scores to settle with the peasants in their provinces and usually had little desire to imprison them without justification. The comments of an American official concerning the Province Security Committees typify those of most advisers exposed to the committees' work: "Generally these guys are pretty good and if the district people haven't turned up enough evidence, the suspect will be released."[6]

Critics of the GVN frequently contend that it imprisoned tens of thousands of non-Communists for long periods of time, especially after the Phoenix program started. This allegation has no basis in fact. During the late 1960s, GVN officials released the large majority of civilian detainees almost immediately or held them in prison only a short time because, according to the officials, they lacked dossiers or other forms of evidence sufficient to prove that the suspects belonged to the shadow government. Some American advisers knew what the evidence was and what happened to the prisoners, and, indeed, they concluded that the GVN lacked sufficient evidence in numerous cases. Advisers also observed that many other prisoners went free because relatives bribed the GVN, the VC bribed or threatened the GVN, the GVN lacked adequate prison space, or the prisoners gave the Allies useful information.

Most *an tri* sentences were short. The GVN also set many of the sentenced prisoners free by declaring amnesties periodically. Some prisoners had to await trial for several weeks or months, though seldom longer, because of slow processing by the security committees. Sentences meted out to convicted VCI, however, began on the date of arrest, not on the date of conviction. Much or all of a sentence, therefore, might have expired by the time a prisoner received it. During the period 1967–69, even important VCI often spent no more than half a year in jail. Phoenix Director John Mason reported on the state of affairs in October 1969: "75% to 90% of all captured VCI reported neutralized have continued to be released within six months. . . . One major reason for outright or premature release of VCI has been the insufficiency of evidence, intelligence, or any other 'proof' of guilt. Dossiers have been inadequate to support meaningful sentences."[7]

The captured VCI reported neutralized, to whom Mason's report referred, numbered about 11,300 in 1968 and 8,500 in 1969.[8] Most American observers who did not serve in Vietnam did not realize that the Allies arrested far more civilians during this time than those whom they labeled VCI, most of whom were set free by the screening committees and other GVN authorities. The authors of a 1969 Pentagon study estimate that the Allies arrested anywhere from 60,000 to 125,000 people per year.[9] A 1972 U.S. government report indicates that the Allies typically made 180,000 arrests per year.[10] According to Mason's estimate, the number of persons arrested each year who would have served more than six months in prison was no more than 3,000 and possibly as low as 850. The chief complaint of American advisers about the justice system, in fact, was that it let most people go free within a short period of time.

The total number of inmates in GVN prisons also contradicts allegations of a massive increase in civilian imprisonment under Phoenix. From the beginning of 1967 to the end of 1970, the number of civilian prisoners, which included both *an tri* detainees and ordinary criminals, actually declined from 45,000 to 41,000.[11] The GVN undoubtedly did not keep the Americans informed of every single prisoner, but CORDS advisers monitored most prisons and had at least a rough idea of their holdings. Under such circumstances, it would have been difficult for anyone except a senior GVN official to have a non-Communist enemy imprisoned for any appreciable length of time.

As 1970 approached, the Americans attempted to plug some of the holes in the GVN's detention system. They tried to convince the Province Security Committees to sentence more of the VCI suspects who came before them and to sentence them for longer periods of time. Their pleas had a considerable effect in some provinces. In 1970, according to CORDS, the Province Security Committees sentenced 67 percent of VCI suspects given hearings.[12] At the request of the Americans, Saigon dictated that the Province Security Committees had to give important cadres prison terms of at least two years and less important cadres terms of at least one year. The security committees did not always comply with these guidelines, but they did increase the length of many sentences. During 1970, most convicted prisoners received sentences of one year or more and many of them received the full two years.[13] During the early 1970s, the GVN also sent more VCI than before to Con Son Island, where prisoners stood almost no chance of escaping or obtaining premature release. Some American observers found it nonetheless disheartening that many low- and mid-level cadres still spent only two years or less in jail.

Among the American advisers whom I interviewed, some noticed that the GVN sentenced more people without sufficient evidence during 1970 and the first half of 1971 than before in response to American insistence about sentencing. Many advisers nevertheless observed a continued reluctance among GVN officials to mete out sentences when little compelling evidence existed. A June 1971 report from Binh Dinh province states: "A continuing indication of the lack of proper dossier preparation has been the repeated failure of the Province Security Committee to sentence detainees to appropriate [terms of] imprisonment. This has been attributed, time and again, to the failure of Phung Hoang Centers to furnish sufficient evidence to convict those detainees forwarded to the Province Security Committee for trial."[14] The large majority of arrested civilians, in addition, still never had to appear before the Province Security Committees. During 1970, for instance, the GVN labeled only 10,400 of the people it arrested as VCI suspects, roughly the same number as in previous years.[15]

In August 1971, the GVN drastically revised the procedures for Province Security Committee hearings. It allowed defendants to appear in person and to have legal counsel, removed some security officials from the committees in favor of province council members, and restricted sentence extensions. Few villagers were able to obtain legal counsel since lawyers were so scarce, but the other provisions led to a considerable reduction in the percentage of suspects convicted. The province senior adviser of Kien Giang province, for instance, reported shortly thereafter: "October . . . was marked by a sharp decline in the conviction rate of the province security committee. This can be attributed to the implementation of Circular 1042 which has altered *an tri* Procedures to give fuller protection to defendants."[16]

After the start of the Communist Easter offensive at the end of March 1972, the GVN arrested many more people than usual. In the Mekong Delta, it launched a program, called F-6, to imprison people whom it suspected might aid the Communists during the offensive. The province chiefs ordered the arrest of any person identified as a VCI by one credible source. After the GVN put these suspects in jail, where they could not help the Communists in their effort to overrun the country, the Province Security Committees examined their cases closely, as they normally did with VCI suspects. They released most of those found not guilty once the Communist offensive began to falter. The GVN established similar programs in the other three military regions. By late July 1972, the National Police reportedly had detained more than fifteen thousand people as a result of these initiatives, although they had already released more than five thousand of them.[17]

President Thieu declared martial law in July 1972, which allowed him to take further measures against suspected Communists and Communist sympathizers, as well as the non-Communist opposition. The GVN continued to arrest unusually high numbers of people until early 1973. The Americans thought that most of the people detained in IV Corps during this period of more than nine months were VCI or VC supporters but that a significant number in the other areas belonged to non-Communist political opposition groups. Some prominent critics of the Thieu regime found themselves among those arrested.[18] On the whole, however, the advent of martial law did not result in long prison terms for a substantially higher number of indi-

viduals than before, and the prison population did not increase appreciably during these months.

The U.S. antiwar movement attacked not only the GVN's legal system
but also the policy of arresting civilian members of the shadow government. For example, U.S. Congressman Ogden Reid of New York, who
claimed that "nearly all" VCI were "unarmed, noncombatant civilians," condemned Phoenix with these words during congressional hearings on the
program: "By analogy, if the Union had had a Phoenix program during our
Civil War, its targets would have been civilians like Jefferson Davis or the
mayor of Macon, Ga."[19]

Reid's analogy was not quite accurate. The true equivalents of Jefferson
Davis and the mayor of Macon were Ho Chi Minh and the highest-ranking
Communist Party official in a North Vietnamese town. During the Civil War,
the Union's leaders most probably would have arrested Davis and the mayor
of Macon had they been able. They regularly expressed the desire to do so
and, in fact, did arrest some civilian leaders, including Davis, at the end of
the war. The Americans of the Vietnam era would have put the North Vietnamese leaders behind bars had they had access to them; they would have
been foolish to have done otherwise. The VC civilian cadres more closely
resembled the pro-Confederacy agitators in the Union states. Although
the pro-Confederates and the neutralists in the Northern states were
much weaker than the Viet Cong, President Lincoln chose to round up and
imprison—without any trials at all—roughly thirty-eight thousand enemies or suspected enemies of the Union as an emergency measure. Indeed,
the Civil War was not the only one during which the United States imprisoned people without trying them in normal courts. It detained seventy
thousand American citizens of Japanese ethnicity during World War II,
an action approved by the U.S. judiciary. The U.S. Internal Security Act of
1950, which was not even put into effect during a war that threatened the
nation's existence, gave the president authority "to apprehend and by
order detain . . . each person as to whom there is reasonable ground to
believe that such a person probably will engage in, or probably will con-
spire with others to engage in, acts of espionage or sabotage."[20] Almost
any nation facing the imminent possibility of extinction finds it necessary
to detain suspected subversives.

The framers of the Geneva Convention of 1949 sanctioned the arrest of
subversive civilians during times of war. They stated that when a civilian
living in a belligerent power's territory "is definitely suspected of, or engaged
in, activities hostile to the security of the state," the state is allowed "a free

hand in its defense measures without imposing any obligations under the Convention other than the duty to ensure humane and legal treatment."[21] The detention of South Vietnamese civilians by American soldiers also conformed to the provisions of the Geneva Convention.[22] Further, as discussed in chapter 19, a great many VCI did not qualify as civilians and thus had not even the slightest reason to deserve immunity from arrest.

Many opponents of the Allied war effort refer to imprisoned VCI as "political prisoners" in order to cast doubt on the legitimacy of their imprisonment. By 1973, many Americans embraced a rumor, spread by Hanoi, that the GVN held two hundred thousand political prisoners. This total apparently included both Communist cadres and non-Communist civilians. In actuality, the GVN did not have anywhere close to two hundred thousand nonmilitary prisoners in all of its jails. Thorough U.S. Embassy investigations, conducted in response to this allegation toward the end of 1973, determined that South Vietnam's civilian prison population actually had declined since the beginning of the decade to about thirty-five thousand.[23] In addition, "political prisoner" is a rather dubious title to assign to a VC cadre. It suggests that the GVN arrested the person merely for voicing objections to the political system or refusing to cooperate with it, rather than for trying to overthrow it via espionage, assassination, terrorism, or conventional military means.

When Allied forces in the populated areas tried to neutralize individuals other than unarmed, passive civilians, some other factors and realities of the situation usually ensured that they would not neutralize non-Communists. Numerous veterans of GVN operational forces and their American advisers told me that their units tried to kill only people whom they knew to be armed and that if they were armed, they had to be Communist soldiers or illegal cadres. In some cases, the Allies saw the enemy carrying weapons or heard them shooting. If the Allies were operating against a secret VC base, they could safely assume, most of the time, that anyone whom they encountered in the base area was armed.

The Allies also knew that, in all probability, any person moving around at night was an armed Communist or had armed Communist companions. Curfews prohibited villagers from leaving their homes after dark, and most non-Communist villagers were wise enough to obey. A large number of Americans and South Vietnamese told me that their units normally killed people only at night and only when they were not inside hooches (huts), thereby guaranteeing that they did not harm non-Communists. Said Le Van Thai, "Most of the PRU activity was at night. The villagers did not walk around at night in the war area, because they were afraid. Besides the people on our side, only the Viet Cong were out at night. So when we killed people, they were Viet Cong, not innocent people."[24]

Americans and South Vietnamese alike noted that in most situations where bodies were located or prisoners taken after a fight, at least some were found to have weapons or other evidence of affiliation with the Communists, a further indication that armed Allied activity did not target the civilian population. After weapons, Communist documents generally provided evidence the most often. "During my tour in Hau Nghia," Brig. Gen. Stuart Herrington recalls, "I saw many Vietcong politicians either killed or captured. In virtually every single case, those who were killed in ambushes or in their secret bunkers were armed with Russian, Chinese, or captured American weapons. And in most cases, they were carrying a pouch of incriminating documents as well."[25] Photographs also revealed that many worked for, or had worked for, the Communists. "We picked up a lot of VC pictures on bodies, as well as documents," Bruce Lawlor noted. "When we searched a dead VC, we'd often find a picture of three or four or five people standing in front of a Viet Cong flag with AK-47s. In many cases, the guy carrying it or some of the other enemy dead were in the picture. If you had a picture of a guy with an AK and a Viet Cong flag, it was a pretty clear indication as to which side he was on."[26]

Allied personnel whom I interviewed also said that most firefights between pacification forces and small Communist units did not occur in the middle of a hamlet, so they were not likely to hurt civilian bystanders. Pacification forces usually ambushed and otherwise engaged the VC cadres and other Communists only on the outskirts of hamlets and areas farther away from the hamlets. Some pacification forces spent almost all of their operational time running ambushes in places where they stood little chance of harming civilians. Rick Welcome described the PRUs that he advised: "We were basically a small tactical combat outfit. There was always a number of military targets available in the area. Most of our operations were platoon size, about thirty to forty men, and we would set up ambushes against local Viet Cong outfits."[27] When pacification forces did enter a hamlet in large numbers to find cadres, any VC present usually tried to flee, because they feared being outnumbered or surrounded. Allied cordon forces only shot at those who fled, and ordinary citizens knew this fact well enough. If people fired back at the Allies from inside the hamlet, the pacification forces usually did not call in air or artillery strikes, even if they were available. Many wanted to avoid the use of highly destructive weapons because they had relatives in the hamlets or because the hamlet residents supported the GVN and might leave if harmed by GVN weaponry. The pacification forces often met the enemy at short distances, and enemy forces frequently numbered only a few soldiers, which also discouraged the use of heavy firepower. Francis West, in reference to the CAP platoon in Binh Nghia village, writes: "[T]he Americans had to patrol with the PFs, whose own families were scattered throughout the hamlets and who were naturally concerned about the use of any weapon which might injure their relatives. The rifle—not the cannon or the jet—was to be the primary weapon of the Americans in Binh Nghia."[28] Allied units, including the PRUs, did not often sneak into hamlets in small groups to neutralize someone; the intelligence generally was difficult to obtain, and the risks were exceedingly high. John Mullins said, "All the stuff you hear about going in during the middle of the night to snatch somebody out of bed or kill somebody very seldom happened. You ran such a risk of getting the wrong person, and of running into guards."[29]

The Communists sometimes forced non-Communist civilians to accompany them and carry loads or perform other work. Allied pacification forces injured and killed many civilians under these circumstances. The Allies could not avoid firing on groups consisting of both Communist soldiers and non-Communist villagers. Had they adopted such a policy, the Communists always would have taken civilians with them as human shields so that the Allies never could attack them.

Individual members of GVN organizations who went out alone and killed their adversaries stood a somewhat better chance of avoiding punishment. Villagers might not see a murder or, if they did, not recognize the perpetrator. If villagers witnessed the killing and identified the murderer, however, GVN leaders were likely to find out about it and take disciplinary action. No one knows how many people were murdered by individual GVN personnel, but most veterans of the war with whom I spoke said they doubted that the number was very high. For the most part, the murders that took place were of a personal nature and had nothing to do with the Allied attack on the Viet Cong shadow government.

A very small number of American advisers murdered civilians, most often out of meanness or hate, rather than the desire to claim that they had killed VCI. Their superiors usually learned of the killings directly or indirectly from witnesses in the villages or from Allied personnel, according to people whom I interviewed, because most Americans did not know enough about the villages to stand a good chance of sneaking in and murdering someone undetected. In most cases, American leaders removed advisers suspected of murder immediately. Some went to trial for murder, although the evidence was often insufficient to produce a conviction. Others did not, for lack of concrete evidence or for the sake of a person's or an organization's reputation. Rob Simmons said:

> From time to time a PRU adviser, generally one of the military guys, went out target-shooting. Target-shooting meant going out to shoot people, usually from an aircraft. At my level, we'd find out about it really quickly. You couldn't do these things without word getting out. The Vietnamese at every level had advisers, so at every level there was an opportunity for some American to receive a report. The CIA was not the most popular organization in Vietnam—the State Department, USIA [U.S. Information Agency], and USAID hadn't liked the CIA since the time it was established. If the province chief told his province senior adviser, if the district chief told his district senior adviser, if any of a number of Vietnamese told their counterparts about this guy doing something in a chopper, the Agency would hear about it. Or the chopper pilots would report it. Anyone in the CIA could be polygraphed in Saigon at any time if he had a problem with one of his officers. The Agency, for its part, might be tempted to cover up this type of activity or paper it over, but they would get the guy out of there.[30]

The belief that Phoenix indiscriminately imprisoned and killed tens of thousands of villagers owes much of its popularity to the proliferation of inaccurate information. Yoshia K. Chee and Kenneth Barton Osborn are two of the most famous examples of dubious sources on the issue of indiscriminate detention and killing, but there are many others. Although evidence discrediting some of these sources is publicly available, it is usually overlooked. The first public allegations of Phoenix misdeeds involved Francis Reitemeyer and Michael Cohn, two U.S. Army lieutenants who were trained as Phoenix advisers at Fort Holabird in late 1968. Shortly thereafter, both requested honorable discharges, claiming that they were conscientious objectors. A federal judge ultimately granted the discharges. In connection with the request for conscientious objector status, Reitemeyer's lawyer issued a statement describing the training for the Phoenix program that the two men allegedly received. According to the statement, Army instructors told Reitemeyer that his job as a Phoenix adviser "was to supervise and to pay with funds from an undisclosed source 18 mercenaries (probably Chinese, none of whom would be officers or enlisted men of the U.S. military) who would be explicitly directed by him and other advisers to find, capture, and/or kill as many Viet Cong and Viet Cong sympathizers within a given number of small villages as was possible under the circumstances. Viet Cong sympathizers were meant to include any male or female civilians of any age in a position of authority or influence in the village who were politically loyal or simply in agreement with the Viet Cong or their objectives. The Petitioner [Reitemeyer] was officially advised by the lecturing United States Army Officers, who actually recounted from their own experiences in the field, that the Petitioner as an American Adviser, might actually be required to maintain a 'kill quota' of 50 bodies a month." [31] Journalists Judith Coburn and Geoffrey Cowan discovered the Reitemeyer story and wrote about it in *The Village Voice* in December 1969. Coburn and Cowan also claimed to have found other sources that confirmed the allegations. "As documented in the Reitemeyer paper," they asserted, "it is widely accepted by most Americans who have traveled extensively in Vietnam that there are monthly kill quotas for each area team." [32]

After the *Village Voice* article appeared, information casting doubt on the validity of this story came to light. Reitemeyer and Cohn, it turned out, had been dismissed from intelligence school for academic failure. More important, during Reitemeyer's training time, U.S. Army officials had learned that he told a girlfriend he was receiving training in assassination techniques. They had asked Reitemeyer to make a sworn statement that he was not receiving such training, and he had complied. [33] There are other obvious problems with the accusations. Phoenix advisers from the military, with few exceptions, did not supervise or pay people of any nationality. During my interviews for this book, I could find no adviser from any organization who had ever heard of any pacification unit receiving orders to kill a certain number of people per month. None ever knew of any pacification unit that systematically captured or killed civilians who did not belong to the VC but were simply loyal to them or agreed with their objectives. When I asked Phoenix advisers if their instructors ever said they would have to operate under such conditions, all answered in the negative.

In his best-selling book *Soldier,* Lt. Col. Anthony Herbert claims that the Special Forces unsuccessfully tried to put him in command of "execution-teams that wiped out entire families and tried to make it appear as though the VC themselves had done the killing." [34] According to Herbert, these teams were an integral part of the Phoenix program. Yet, Herbert states that the Special Forces tried to put him in charge of the teams in November 1965, which was a year and a half before ICEX and two years before the Phoenix program, respectively, came into being. Herbert asserted that he had witnessed many other atrocities, as well, and that his superior officers had ignored him when he told them about the events. After he made his charges public, newspapers and television shows told his version of the story and presented him as a hero who refused to tolerate the Army's evils.

CBS News producer Barry Lando, who believed Herbert when he first heard the story, investigated the accusations thoroughly because he wanted to do an "admiring profile" of Herbert. After looking into matters further, however, Lando concluded that Herbert had deceived the public. Armed with a wealth of evidence, Lando demolished Herbert's credibility in a *60 Minutes* program on 4 February 1973 and in an article in the *Atlantic Monthly*. Some of the events that Herbert described actually had occurred, Lando said, but many of the more lurid ones clearly had not. Lando talked to a large number of Herbert's former comrades, including many who praised his abilities in the highest terms, and they—as Osborn's fellows had done—described Herbert as a person frequently given to exaggeration and fabrication. For instance, Capt. Bill Hill, whom Herbert tried to use as a witness to support his case, told Lando, "Herbert is the best battalion commander I ever had. But for some reason he's become a liar, it's all so much garbage. . . . I used to rave about him to my wife. It kills my soul about him because I admired him so much."[35] Investigators from the U.S. Army's Criminal Investigations Division interviewed more than three hundred people who might have known about the events Herbert described in his book. The investigators likewise discovered that knowledgeable interviewees refuted many of the atrocity allegations, and they found no evidence that Herbert's superiors had ignored or covered up any wrongdoings that came to their attention.[36]

Jeff Stein, who said that he served in a military intelligence unit in Da Nang, told author Michael Maclear that, in the environment of the Vietnam War, "atrocities become normal; atrocities are taught to us as being normal." Stein gave an example: "I would send in a report which would say, one person who was suspected of being Viet Cong, unconfirmed, uncorroborated, should be at this point, coordinate, at this time, on this day, and I would find out later that a B-52 strike had hit that spot at that time and wiped out the whole village. That I think is an extreme example of how involved the military machine got in the cutting edge of Phoenix."[37]

Every participant with whom I talked denied that such an event, as described by Stein, could have occurred, except in the extremely unlikely event that a B-52 was supposed to bomb another target at that time and hit the village by mistake. B-52s would not purposefully have bombed a village even if an NVA battalion occupied it, let alone an unconfirmed VC suspect. Strict orders prohibited B-52 strikes near populated areas, and, in fact, B-52s mistakenly hit populated areas only a very few times during the entire course of the war. If the Allies had wanted to do something about an unconfirmed VC suspect, they would have sent a group of armed men to the village with orders to apprehend the suspect.

Mike Beamon, who asserted that he had served as a PRU adviser and a SEAL, described to author Al Santoli a string of atrocities that he and his comrades supposedly had committed. They included regularly going into hooches to grab people and then booby-trapping the hooches in order to kill family members when they came out, attacking a VC cadre in a marketplace full of people and apparently killing many of the bystanders, and executing ordinary villagers found in their homes simply for the sake of killing. The program in which he participated, Beamon concluded, was "an advanced boot camp to train operatives for other kinds of terrorist activities that the United States runs all over the world."[38] B. G. Burkett reviewed SEAL records and determined that no one named Mike Beamon ever served in the SEALs.[39] Bruce Lawlor, whom Santoli interviewed as well, also told me that Beamon is an imposter.[40]

One of the most interesting cases that I encountered involved Professor Larry E. Cable, a prominent academic who has written a few books about the Vietnam War and has lectured at many of the nation's finest military institutions. I met Cable at a conference on the Vietnam War in the spring of 1996. While giving a presentation at one of the conference sessions, he stated that he had served in Vietnam during the war and had spent part of that time as a PRU adviser. I asked him, therefore, if I could interview him for my book, and he agreed. During the interview, he stated that he had advised the Quang Ngai Special Platoon, which he described as a highly effective paramilitary force under the auspices of the CIA, during 1965 and 1966. He subsequently advised the Quang Ngai PRUs, he said, from 1967 to 1969. He told me that the units with which he worked never engaged in any abuses of the population because he led them directly and prevented the abuses. He noted, however, that other PRUs and other pacification forces did so, primarily because many American advisers were too ineffective to stop them. Cable said that some U.S. pacification advisers also mistreated, tortured, and killed civilians. He added that province chiefs frequently put innocent civilians in jail and tortured them for monetary reasons.[41]

Much of Cable's testimony conflicted with the accounts of PRU advisers whom I had interviewed previously. In addition, I had already interviewed a CIA officer, Bob Wall, who had been the CIA's officer in charge of paramilitary programs in Quang Ngai during 1966, and he had made no mention of a special platoon or any similar paramilitary force in the province. I subsequently contacted Wall and Rudy Enders, who had been the CIA's senior adviser in I Corps for the same programs that Wall had advised—PRU, RD Cadre, and Census Grievance—from 1966 to 1969. Both Wall and Enders stated that no such unit as the "Quang Ngai Special Platoon" ever existed. Both asserted that Cable could not possibly have been an adviser to the Quang Ngai PRUs or any similar CIA-advised organization in Quang Ngai at any time between 1965 and 1969. Only one person at a time advised the CIA's paramilitary programs in Quang Ngai during 1965 and 1966, and for a time that person was Bob Wall. Wall and Enders gave me the names of the other people who advised these programs during the period 1965–69, none of which resembled the name Larry Cable. All of these people, in addition, were considerably older than Cable, and at least one of them is deceased. Wall and Enders both pointed out other inaccuracies in Cable's statements as well, such as his claim that he and his PRUs were engaged in reconnaissance activities northwest of Khe Sanh during the Tet offensive of 1968.[42]

Wall and Enders gave me a list of questions to ask Cable that anyone could have answered had he worked for four or five years with the PRUs or any other CIA program in Quang Ngai. I called Cable again, told him that CIA veterans had disputed his claims, and asked him if he could give me proof of his service in Quang Ngai. He refused to provide documents or photographs. When I asked him basic questions from the Wall/Enders list—such as, "What were the names of the districts in Quang Ngai?" and "What were the names of your direct superiors?"—he refused to give answers. He asserted that he did not need to prove his credentials to me or anyone. He also claimed that after serving in the Marines as an enlisted man and officer before his work for the CIA, he never received a DD-214 form. The military issued this form, which lists information about a soldier's service, to almost all Vietnam veterans, including those who advised the PRUs. Cable asserted that none of the CIA's employees in Vietnam knew each other's real names. All of the numerous CIA veterans whom I interviewed, however, said the opposite. Many of them, moreover, gave me the names of fellow CIA advisers that I know are real names because either I had already interviewed the individuals or I subsequently found the names in telephone books and contacted the individuals.

B. G. Burkett checked the personnel records of all the U.S. armed services and did not find any record bearing the name Larry E. Cable—Cable's legal name. This fact, by itself, strongly suggests that Cable never served in Vietnam.[43]

A recent instance of fraud involves author Joel M. Hutchins. On the cover of his 1996 book, *Swimmers among the Trees,* Hutchins is described as a "highly decorated SEAL veteran" who served in the U.S. Navy SEALs for five years. Hutchins asserts in the book that "excesses were not the norm" for Phoenix, but he also writes:

> Those actively opposed to U.S. involvement in the war have alleged that [neutralization] statistics were manipulated intentionally to conceal that three to five times as many suspects had actually been killed during Phoenix operations. They also alleged that torture was a main interrogation tool. In general, they painted a picture of the Phoenix Program as nothing more than a sadistic killing machine, without adequate leadership, totally out of control. Some of these allegations are, unfortunately, true. In some areas of South Vietnam, indefensible excesses did occur, with certain district and province officials using the cover of the operation to eradicate present or future political or personal foes. In such cases the victim's fate was sealed if the power of the unscrupulous perpetrators was sufficient for them to manipulate the local PRUs or ARVN officials. In many ways the atmosphere of Phoenix operations in isolated areas was similar to that of Salem, Massachusetts, during the despicable period of its witch hunts.[44]

Investigations by independent researchers, as well as a belated investigation by the book's publisher, revealed that the Navy has no records of a SEAL named Joel Hutchins. The publisher subsequently divulged that Hutchins said that he had graduated from a "modified" SEAL training course in Maryland and that he considered himself to be a SEAL because he had accompanied SEAL teams during combat tactical patrols in Vietnam.[45] According to Capt. Larry Bailey, a highly respected SEAL who served in Vietnam and subsequently became commanding officer of the SEAL training school in Coronado, California, no SEAL training has ever taken place in Maryland. B. G. Burkett obtained Hutchins's military records and discovered that he had served in Vietnam for only eleven months, not as a SEAL but as a Navy hospital corpsman. In addition, according to his records, Hutchins did not even receive the Combat Action Ribbon, which was awarded to any member of the U.S. Navy or Marine Corps who came under hostile fire.[46]

Some people have sought to discredit the Phoenix program by blaming it, incorrectly, for causing the infamous My Lai massacre of March 1968, during which U.S. soldiers, under the guidance of Lt. William Calley, slaughtered several hundred defenseless villagers in a hamlet called My Lai 4. Author Douglas Valentine tries hard to substantiate this accusation. He points out that Task Force Barker, the battalion to which the American forces involved in the My Lai killings belonged, received a Phoenix blacklist for My Lai 4. Valentine also notes that, after the massacre, province Phoenix coordinator Robert Ramsdell of the CIA said that he had thought only VC guerrillas and VC sympathizers lived in the village and only the guerrillas would be there that morning.[47] This information is accurate. Taken alone, it suggests that Calley and the other American soldiers killed all of the people in My Lai 4 because of information received from the Phoenix coordinator.

To determine the actual role of Phoenix and the CIA, however, it is necessary to look at details that Valentine omits. All of the people who were killed in My Lai 4 could not have been on a Phoenix blacklist, as Valentine implies. Certainly, the infants who died at My Lai were not on the blacklist. The Allies also did not include "VC sympathizers" on their blacklists. None of the Americans who participated in the massacre, moreover, ever said that they used a blacklist, from Phoenix or anyone else, to identify people before killing them. Whatever intelligence Calley and his men had received, it was obvious to them after they entered My Lai 4 that the villagers were not Communist soldiers but unarmed, overtly passive civilians. Once they recognized this fact, Phoenix guidelines, as well as U.S. Army regulations, required that they treat the villagers as the civilians they were, not as the armed combatants they had been reported to be. They could have arrested all but the young children as VCI suspects, but they were strictly forbidden to kill anyone. Finally, Task Force Barker was a military unit under the command of Lt. Col. Frank Barker, USA, and not under the control of CORDS or CIA personnel; the military, therefore, had full responsibility for its treatment of unarmed villagers who clearly posed no immediate threat.

Valentine also incorrectly charges that the Special Police, who indeed were responsible for the Phoenix mission of identifying and neutralizing VCI, participated in the massacre at My Lai 4. Valentine states: "As in any large-scale Phoenix operation, two of Task Force Barker's companies cordoned off the hamlet while a third one—Calley's—moved in, clearing the way for [Capt. Eugene] Kotouc and Special Branch officers who were 'brought to the field to identify VC from among the detained inhabitants.'"[48] For this quotation, Valentine cites the Peers Report.[49] The quote did not, in fact, come directly from the Peers Report; it is an inaccurate paraphrase. According to the Peers Report itself, the police actually went to work between 1530 and 1700, after the Americans had left My Lai 4. None of the detainees whom they handled came from My Lai 4.[50]

Some of the critics of Allied policy who say that the attack on the VCI killed and imprisoned huge numbers of Communists also try to prove their point with statistics. They observe that the decline over time in the total number of VCI, as estimated by the Americans, was far smaller than the number of neutralizations reported. This discrepancy existed, they argue, because the Allies captured or killed many thousands of ordinary citizens and called them VCI, thereby inflating neutralization numbers without affecting estimated strength.[51]

This analytical method is so thoroughly flawed that it cannot prove anything. First, the shadow government replaced some lost cadres with new people, so the Allies could neutralize these cadres without causing a decline in overall VCI strength. Second, a limited number of VCI ralliers and captured VCI spent little or no time in prison and returned to the shadow government after capture. According to the statistics, they were neutralized, but they remained part of the VCI. Third, those who look at the change in estimated VCI strength over time assume that the neutralization statistics included only two categories of people as VCI—true VC cadres and non-Communist civilians targeted by the GVN. As chapter 16 discusses, however, the Allies reported many people as "neutralized VCI" who did not fit into either of these categories. Thousands of supposed neutralized cadres were civilians and VC soldiers who were apprehended or killed in the course of other activities, many of which had nothing to do with the attack on the VCI.

Fourth and finally, Allied estimates of VCI strength were extremely unreliable. The people who prepared the estimates based their figures primarily on dubious information in captured VC documents; the VC often exaggerated their strengths in their reports to Hanoi to make themselves appear stronger than they were, just as they exaggerated the number of spies they had in the GVN. In addition, many cadres occupied more than one position in the shadow government, a fact obscured by confusing aliases. As a result, analysts frequently counted such individuals more than once. Further, the GVN and the VC used different province boundaries, which greatly complicated the work of the Allied personnel in each GVN province who had to estimate the VCI strength in their province. When they looked at captured documents listing VCI strength in a VC province, they could not know for sure how many of those VCI operated in their GVN province. The Allied estimators for the various GVN provinces did not work together closely enough to overcome this problem. A recurring lack of agreement over VCI totals among American organizations also indicates that strength estimation was far from an exact science. In 1968, for instance, the U.S. military put the number of VCI at 85,000, the Phoenix Directorate estimated it to be 99,000, and the CIA's figure was 111,000.[52]

Most of the knowledgeable Americans, as well as the South Vietnamese, whom I interviewed said that some pacification units captured or killed non-Communist civilians but that most of them victimized only opposition political groups and racial minorities. The war against the VCI contained mechanisms powerful enough to prevent units from targeting other non-Communist civilians in most cases. Based on information that he obtained from the National Police, Evan Parker, Jr., concluded, "In some areas, particularly in the North, there were other political parties that were more interesting to a lot of Vietnamese than the Communists. Some of these people were not in hiding, so you could arrest them and push them around without getting hurt. The Communists, on the other hand, were hard to identify and hard to find, and if you went out and messed around with them they'd fight back."[53] It should be noted that most of the political organizers whom the Government treated in this manner resided in towns and cities, as opposed to the rural areas where the war against the VCI took place. In addition, the layers of secrecy surrounding the operations of South Vietnam's political forces and the involvement of the VC in allegedly non-Communist political groups prevented most people, especially the Americans, from knowing how many members of the supposed non-Communist opposition in the GVN's prisons actually had served the Communists in some capacity.

With regard to racial minorities, South Vietnamese policemen and soldiers did not spend much time targeting specific individuals. Rather, they tended to arrest and otherwise harass the people in these groups when they did not cooperate during searches of their villages or when a fit of bad temper struck a policeman or soldier. Harrell, for example, told me, "If the Vietnamese were working in a Montagnard area, they would certainly be more harsh and brutal with the Montagnards than they would be with their own people."[54] This phenomenon was not a result of the attack on the VCI. It occurred, rather, because the GVN allowed its armed ethnic Vietnamese forces to operate in villages populated by unarmed members of racial minorities whom they disliked.

Some senior GVN officials arrested ordinary citizens and held them until they paid a bribe, or threatened arrest unless they were paid. Such practices, however, were not as widespread as critics often allege. A few officials did not engage in any corrupt activities. Most GVN officials were corrupt to some degree, but most of them relied on more lucrative and less problematic forms of corruption than blackmailing the peasantry to satisfy their financial desires. "GVN leaders didn't need to put villagers in jail in order to demand bribes for their release." Ed Brady explained. "They had so many more profitable means of corruption available to them."[55] Those who did extort the villagers usually demanded money as a form of punishment after a person had been arrested for suspicious activities or VC sympathies. They seldom arrested large numbers of people simply to get money. Said Jim Ward, "Most of the GVN officials couldn't support their families with their salaries, so they had to find other ways to obtain money. If someone took money here and there for a favor or took something small from a VC family, that would be considered normal. On the other hand, if someone harassed or arrested innocent civilians and forced them to pay large bribes, that would be considered corrupt, and people would get upset about it. As a result, the latter occurred much less often."[56]

Many American advisers vehemently denounce the theory that the attack on the VCI caused the imprisonment or killing of large numbers of non-Communists. Considering that many of these same advisers candidly acknowledge the prevalence of other GVN misdeeds, such as corruption and the torture and execution of prisoners, and that valid evidence to the contrary has not come to light, it is inconceivable that many of them are trying to hide the behavior of the South Vietnamese in this regard. "The overwhelming majority of those captured on Phoenix operations," Herrington asserts, "were picked up based upon tangible and credible evidence, rather than on the mere say-so of one person motivated by some sort of personal grudge."[57] When I interviewed Rob Simmons, he said:

> The fact of the matter is, there was a North Vietnamese initiative to recruit civilians in the South who became the VCI. There was a North Vietnamese initiative to arm and equip these people. There was a North Vietnamese initiative to infiltrate military weapons, personnel, and equipment into the South to defeat the government of South Vietnam. That was the Vietnam War. In the Vietnam War, the two sides fought, and killed each other, and got killed. Did somebody have a vendetta against someone else somewhere along the line? Well, probably. But the fact is that there was a war going on. It's simple. I wasn't in Vietnam so I could pursue some vendetta against somebody. The police chief and the Special Police chief weren't living up in Phu Yen to pursue a vendetta. If they'd had a vendetta against anybody, it would

have been back home where they came from, not up in Phu Yen. They didn't know anybody up there—that's why the Government had put them there.[58]

Intentional killings of non-Communists, according to every adviser whom I interviewed, were particularly uncommon. American advisers and good South Vietnamese leaders exercised considerable control over the target choices of the PRUs, the forces most likely to kill civilians. Most GVN leaders told their units to avoid killing villagers without warrant, and some severely disciplined those who disobeyed. "The idea that we were out there just killing everybody that we came across willy nilly is ridiculous," John Mullins said. "People died, but they were killed during legitimate combat operations."[59]

19 Assassinations

The word most closely associated with the attack on the Viet Cong shadow government in popular lore is "assassination." Many American commentators repeatedly call the attack on the VCI an "assassination program," usually in an effort to demonstrate the involvement of the United States in immoral activity. Pulitzer Prize–winning journalist Seymour Hersh, for instance, states, "The PRUs, under the control of the Central Intelligence Agency, had by 1969 been responsible for thousands of assassinations in South Vietnam."[1] Some American opponents of the war even call the attack on the VCI a "murder program." Longtime *New York Times* reporter Tad Szulc, referring to 20,000 people listed as "VCI killed" in official CORDS statistics, states: "During the years 1969–72, as many as 20,000 Viet Cong or suspected Viet Cong are believed to have been murdered under the aegis of Operation Phoenix. . . . Along with the My Lai massacre of Vietnamese civilians by American troops, Operation Phoenix unquestionably looms as one of the most degrading enterprises carried out by Americans in Vietnam."[2]

Few commentators explain exactly what they mean when they say that Phoenix was a program of assassination or murder. Some of them, however, at least indicate or imply who the targets were. One segment of this group charges that many civilians who supported the VC, but who were not cadres, were assassinated or murdered. A second segment says that many civilians who were killed did not help the Communists voluntarily at all. The term *murder,* moreover, connotes the killing of an unarmed person who is not working directly for a political entity, so those who made the murder accusations imply that the murder victims were non-Communist civilians. Chapters 10, 16, and 18 address the issue of neutralization of non-Communists. A third segment claims that the Allied assassins or murderers victimized numerous civilians who served in the Viet Cong as political officials. Journalist Michael Drosnin calls the attack on the VCI "a secret war aimed not at the enemy's soldiers but at its civilian leaders."[3] Douglas Valentine contends, "Central to Phoenix is the fact that it targeted civilians, not soldiers."[4] The killing of civilian political officials is indeed the most appropriate definition of the term *assassination*. This chapter discusses the extent to which this type of killing occurred.

The sources used to support the charge of widespread assassination are inaccurate. They include many of the questionable people mentioned in chapters 8 and 18. One person whose testimony is used to support allegations of assassination is Elton Manzione. Manzione told Valentine that he served in Vietnam as a SEAL in 1964 and worked with the Counter-Terror Teams. He subsequently went AWOL (absent without leave) and joined the Vietnam Veterans against the War, he said, because "many of us realized we were no longer the good guys in the white hats defending freedom—that we were assassins, pure and simple."[5] Valentine says of Manzione, "His military records show that he was never even in South Vietnam."[6] This fact should have given Valentine reason to question Manzione's honesty, but he uncritically accepts Manzione's contention that the U.S. Navy had falsified the records.

B. G. Burkett, historian Dale Andradé, and Comdr. Frank Brown investigated Manzione's allegations. SEAL records do indeed indicate clearly that Manzione never served as a SEAL in Vietnam and that the other people he identified as the members of his SEAL team never did either. Burkett, Andradé, and Brown all asserted that the U.S. Navy never would have tampered with records in the way that Manzione contended. The three knowledgeable investigators also talked to many former SEALs who would have known Manzione had his testimony been true—the SEAL community is quite small—and none had ever heard of him.[7] When I wrote to Manzione in early 1992 and asked to interview him, he wrote back, "I was not actually part of Phoenix, but of ICEX. I wouldn't be interested in doing an interview as I have plans for a book of my own."[8] Manzione said that he left Vietnam in 1964; ICEX did not begin until 1967. His book has not yet appeared, and he recently refused another interview request.

That Allied pacification forces killed large numbers of Communist political cadres while fighting the shadow government and the small Communist armed units in rural South Vietnam is clear. Whether or not these killings were assassinations depended on the circumstances under which the cadres lived and died. In a great many cases, the cadres lived under circumstances that differed greatly from those depicted or suggested by the assassination theorists. By the late 1960s, almost all of the overt, illegal political cadres—the people who mobilized the population and ran the entire VC apparatus—carried arms or operated alongside armed Communists, and most did both. Particularly important people in the shadow government usually traveled with ten or more armed men. Armed VC also stood guard around hamlets during the times when the overt cadres visited them and around clandestine VCI meetings, and they protected the hiding places of the VCI.

Illegal cadres bearing arms, as well as the Communist soldiers who escorted illegal cadres, posed a direct military threat to Allied forces, as did all armed Communists. They were at least as unlikely to surrender without attempting to defend themselves as regular Communist soldiers. As a result, the Allies usually had no choice but to attack groups of Communists that contained illegal cadres in the same manner as they would attack any group of Communist soldiers. Depending on the disposition and material assets of Communist and Allied forces and the intelligence available to each, the Allies might ambush the cadres and their comrades while they were traveling, mount a raid or assault against a fixed position they occupied, call in air or artillery strikes on them, or engage them with small-arms fire. The Allies could not arrest them any more easily than soldiers in most wars can arrest each other. Herrington explains, "Since the 'illegals' always traveled with an armed military escort, the chances of capturing them without a fight were slim."[9]

The VC's decision to operate primarily at night, in fact, made them even more difficult and risky to capture than soldiers operating during the day. Allied forces were less likely to locate wounded, isolated, or demoralized Communists, who were the people most likely to surrender, in the dark. The greater uncertainty of the enemy's whereabouts and activities at night also discouraged Allied forces from trying to capture enemy personnel whom they had trapped or come upon by surprise, whereas they might have captured them fairly easily by day. "At night, you could hardly see your hand in front of your face," John Wilbur said. "Some guy's running around with a gun and you're not going to shoot him? You don't just sneak up and tap the guy on the shoulder and say, 'Stop. We're the police, and we just want to capture you, Mr. VC.'"[10]

The behavior of the illegal cadres made them, in essence, soldiers. According to most interpretations of the rules of war, the act of carrying weapons or serving alongside military forces conferred combatant status on them and deprived them of any of the theoretical rights to immunity from military attack normally granted to civilians. After all, it would be as silly to ask soldiers on one side of a conflict to refrain from killing a group of people scattered among the enemy forces as it would be to tell someone fishing with a net to avoid snaring particular members of a school of fish.

Because the illegal cadres qualified as soldiers, the killing of these cadres constituted the killing of soldiers, rather than the assassination of civilian political leaders.

Only in a few cases did the Allies have a realistic chance of neutralizing illegal cadres by methods not involving combat. Attempting to convince them to spy or defect was difficult because the Allies could not easily contact them, and many were not inclined to abandon the VC anyway. The Allies could spread false information about cadres in order to discredit them among other Communists, but this technique did not often succeed. Arresting cadres without a fight generally was feasible only if the Allies achieved complete surprise and the cadres had relatively few escorts and insufficient means of escape. Allied forces encountered such conditions primarily in areas long controlled by the VC. Rear Adm. Irve LeMoyne explained that lax security in these areas permitted the PRUs to surprise and capture many VCI unopposed during his tour: "Sometimes, we'd arrive at three in the morning, and there might be a scuffle, but no one was killed. We were in what was considered VC territory, and the VC weren't expecting us. We had overwhelming force on the scene at the time, though we couldn't have hung around for long, and didn't. The VC weren't suicidal—they would surrender." [11] After a few such victories, however, the VC caught on and operated more cautiously. By the end of the 1960s, moreover, almost no areas remained under this type of VC domination. The only other situations in which the Allies were likely to capture illegal cadres without a struggle involved cadres trying to sneak into villages by themselves. "Sometimes the guy made a mistake, like visiting a girlfriend or visiting his family," Col. Viet Lang said. "That was the only way to capture him easily." [12]

Both the CIA and CORDS ordered their personnel to attempt to arrest or capture all targeted VCI if possible. They were to use force only when arrest proved impossible. The two organizations emphasized that such a policy yielded valuable intelligence through prisoner interrogation, though they also put the policy on record to deflate assassination charges. In the relatively small number of cases where the situation did not clearly demand a purely military operation, most Americans and many South Vietnamese did try to capture illegal cadres alive when the risks involved were not too serious. They did not do so because their superiors forced them to—they could have evaded the orders—but because they thought it would yield better results in the long run. "When operating against a VCI," Col. Doug Dillard noted, "our first priority was always to capture. If you killed a Viet Cong leader, he or she could be replaced with maybe a dozen people within hours or days. Maybe you had cut off a few years of experience, but you had not solved the problem. If you captured and debriefed him or her, then there was a possibility of rolling up the entire net."[13]

Some Allied forces were not so concerned about taking prisoners and seldom took any risks to capture the enemy. Others hated the VC enough that they preferred to kill them. Some also feared that captured VC would not remain in jail long; only by killing them could they put their enemies out of action permanently. Most interviewees told me that a considerable fraction of the South Vietnamese involved in pacification attached little importance to capturing the enemy. A much smaller percentage of U.S. advisers, they said, held this view, primarily those with military backgrounds rather than civilians in the CIA who did not have such backgrounds. Because the military training and experience of the former had focused on killing the enemy in combat, some of them found it difficult to concentrate on other goals. In addition, some had joined the armed forces in the first place because they wanted to fight, whereas CIA officers without military experience generally cared more about developing and exploiting intelligence.

PRU advisers detailed from the military usually were the least concerned of any advisers about taking the enemy alive, as even others in the U.S. military acknowledged. While preparing for Vietnam duty at the Foreign Service Institute, Col. Horace Hunter met some military personnel training to be PRU advisers whose attitudes he found disturbing. "Their response to most theoretical problems was to kill someone," Hunter said. He believed that some were psychologically unstable. CIA officers at the institute told Hunter that they were well aware that certain trainees held such attitudes and that they would keep control of those people when they became advisers. "In Vietnam," Hunter continued, "I found some of the same types associated with Agency programs. One fellow who leaps to mind was a rather mindless and obnoxious captain who was a PRU adviser. He lacked a social conscience, and was a liar and a blowhard. Some of the professional CIA types in the provinces were first rate. I doubt they would have condoned misconduct, but others would have. There were too many opportunities for misusing the system for it to have functioned perfectly."[14] Many other U.S. Army and CIA officers lauded the dedication and integrity of some PRU advisers, but a number of them also made complaints similar to Hunter's about particular people. The CIA generally did keep the worst of this bunch out of advisory roles and usually—but not always—prevented the PRU advisers from becoming too unruly.

The Americans created incentives to encourage pacification forces to take the VC alive and keep them alive. The CIA sometimes gave higher rewards for capturing cadres than for killing them. CORDS tried to encourage more captures and fewer killings by giving the GVN a goal of achieving 50 percent of all VCI neutralizations through the sentencing of captured VCI to prison terms. This initiative had little effect on GVN behavior; it did not cause an increase in the arrest and sentencing of VC cadres and a decrease in VCI deaths, as supporters had wanted, nor did it produce an upsurge in the unjust arrest or sentencing of people who were not cadres, as opponents had feared. The GVN did not even bother to use tricks to meet the goal, as sentenced VCI remained at roughly 30 percent of total neutralizations.[15] When incentives did work, they usually prevented only the execution of Communist prisoners, because in relatively few instances did operational planners have much choice ahead of time as to whether they would attempt to capture or kill.

The legal cadres lived as civilians and relied on secrecy, rather than arms, for protection. According to the people whom I interviewed and other sources, almost all of the Americans and many South Vietnamese avoided killing legal cadres except for the few who carried arms. They preferred to convince them to remain in the VC and spy for the Allies or to rally to the GVN. If unarmed and unprotected cadres did not respond to the Allied entreaties, or if the Allies decided not to make such appeals because they predicted that the cadres would flee and help the VC elsewhere, the Allies usually arrested and interrogated them. As indicated in chapter 18, the PRUs and other forces did not kill large numbers of unarmed civilians whom they suspected of working for the VC, but they did kill some, primarily those who were dedicated legal cadres.

The execution of legal cadres did not constitute assassination, as I have defined it, because the legal cadres were spies and terrorists, not political officials. They engaged mainly in intelligence gathering, infiltration of GVN organizations, and covert killing of civilians and GVN personnel, but not in overt political activities. Many Americans condemned the GVN for executing such prisoners instead of imprisoning them. International law, interestingly, does not lend support to their position. According to the Geneva Convention of 1949, the GVN was allowed to try these cadres for treason and sentence them to death. In fact, it was allowed to execute even those VCI who truly were civilian political officials, such as the tiny minority of illegal cadres who did not rely on armed protection.[16] The GVN, like many other nations that have put subversives to death under similar circumstances, frequently did not hold fair trials for the accused, but this reality concerns only the GVN's implementation of the killings, not the policy of execution itself.

The argument against execution, therefore, must be made on the basis of morality, not legality. A number of Americans claim that the GVN was a bad government and thus did not have the "right" to use such strong means to defend itself. This type of theorizing, however, is useless. One might make a more persuasive case to a government by arguing that the act of executing the prisoners instead of imprisoning them was itself immoral. Some advisers, indeed, said as much to their counterparts, but they did not convince the South Vietnamese to spare prisoners on grounds of morality very often. Even if one believes that this type of execution is immoral, indignant condemnation of the GVN on this point would appear to be unwarranted, considering that the Communists also executed numerous people and committed many other savage deeds.

Some analysts use statistics to refute those who refer to all of the VCI killed by the Allies as the victims of assassination. They cite CORDS statistics, which indicate that fewer than 10 percent of all VCI reported killed had been targeted specifically by the forces most closely associated with the attack on the VCI,[17] and they note that the other cadres died in the course of regular military engagements and were identified only after the fact. Most of the thousands of VCI reportedly killed, they conclude, could not possibly have been assassinated because they died like soldiers. Although many VCI certainly were killed in regular military battles, statistical analysis cannot reveal what proportion of the killed cadres actually suffered this fate because the statistics are grossly inaccurate. Numerous problems inherent in neutralization reporting resulted in either inflation or deflation of the total numbers of VCI reported killed in different types of operations. Nor do the VCI killed figures indicate whether or not the cadres were defenseless.

The best evidence available on the infrequency of assassination is the testimony of American advisers. Almost all of the American advisers with whom I talked denied that their pacification units regularly killed defenseless Communist political leaders or members of the civilian population. Many of them denounced the theory that the GVN assassinated large numbers of people, and added that the killing that did occur was not immoral. Dean Almy said:

> I don't think the PRUs or Phoenix were immoral. We were in a war, and this is one of the instruments you use to win a war. It wasn't an assassination program. The VCI were a part of the enemy. Americans were being killed in

Vietnam, including some of my friends, and some of the VCI were responsible for it. We did the same things in World War II. You have to go back to
the question of whether we should have been in Vietnam; if we were going
to be there, it was a necessary program.[18]

Lloyd Pomeroy, who was more pacifistic than most advisers whom I interviewed, told me:

If you accept the need to have a war, then I think an effort like Phoenix is
necessary. You go after the political underpinnings of the other side. I think
war is an absolutely brutalizing, inhuman act. It's a misuse of the life force.
If I were to get involved in another one, I would want to do so in a capacity
that was some helping profession—a social worker, a psychologist, a medic,
a clergyman, something like that. Because war sucks, period. But within
the context of a war, something like Phoenix is worthwhile.[19]

Critics of American policy in Vietnam often blame the American military and the CIA for assassinations, torture, mistreatment of non-
Communist civilians, and other misdeeds of the South Vietnamese. Some
say that these Americans told the South Vietnamese to commit such acts,
whereas others fault them for tolerating abuses while providing the training and funding that allowed most of the South Vietnamese forces to commit them. This criticism is largely misplaced. Many American advisers
tried to prevent GVN personnel from abusing their powers, either by influencing their behavior or having them removed from positions of authority. The majority of them did not interfere to a greater extent because they
lacked the authority or because they wanted to encourage South Vietnamese independence. A minority of them irresponsibly neglected their
supervisory duties, but such people exist in any large organization. Americans from the CIA and CORDS designed and carried out the attack on the
VCI because their political leaders had commanded them to help the rest of
the Allied forces win the war, and they generally tried to accomplish that
goal without inflicting unnecessary suffering on the civilian population.

If any Americans deserve blame for the excesses of the attack on the
VCI, they would be those at the top level of the U.S. government who made
or influenced the decision to intervene in Vietnam. They chose to enter the
type of war in which unjustified arrests and killings are unavoidable and
to give most advisers relatively little authority over their counterparts.
These officials did not send the United States into war to further American
economic interests, to protect South Vietnam's wealthy elite and suppress

its peasants, or to kill people of a foreign race. They thought that the United States had to stop the Communists in South Vietnam to prevent further Communist expansion in Asia and the rest of the world and to maintain the credibility of the United States among its allies threatened by Communism. Preventing the spread of Communism was a noble goal. Considering the relatively small amount of immoral activity on the part of Allied personnel, a topic covered in further detail in chapter 24, I think it reasonable to conclude unequivocally that the participation of the United States in the war, as a whole, was not immoral.

In hindsight, however, one can see that the war in Vietnam was a poor means of pursuing that goal, given the refusal of the U.S. government to take control of the GVN or to invade or obliterate North Vietnam. It cost the United States too much in lives and money and divided its society too greatly. The United States, it is true, would have suffered additional tactical setbacks, such as the Communist takeover of neighboring non-Communist nations that built up their strength during the U.S. intervention, had South Vietnam fallen earlier. Nevertheless, the negative repercussions of lost U.S. credibility and of Communist expansion in Asia in the event of South Vietnam's collapse could not have undermined U.S. interests critically, as American politicians of the Vietnam War era had believed they would. Most foreign policy experts, moreover, now believe that the United States would have fought under considerably more favorable circumstances had it made a stand against Communism in Thailand instead of in Vietnam. Strategic errors, such as putting too many restrictions on the bombing of North Vietnam and refusing to send troops into Cambodia and Laos until late in the war, also raised the costs. Some people would call immoral the failure of American leaders to foresee the results of U.S. intervention, but I prefer to call it foolish.

The United States was not the only country that caused the Vietnam War to continue for so long. North Vietnam easily could have withdrawn its troops from South Vietnam and concerned itself with other matters, such as economic development. The morality of Hanoi's decision to keep fighting would depend on the way in which Hanoi conducted the war and on the postwar fate of the people over whom the war was fought, the South Vietnamese. Chapters 24 and 25 discuss aspects of the Communist war effort that might have been immoral, and the final chapter describes what happened to the South Vietnamese after the war.

PART FIVE: Damage Inflicted on the Shadow Government

20 Neutralization Statistics

tatistics seem to fascinate Americans more than they fascinate most of the world's other peoples. Perhaps this obsession stems from an American preference for absolutes, or from a faith in science, or from the conviction that the use of statistics has helped American business succeed. With regard to the war against the VC shadow government, many senior American officials and outside observers viewed numbers of neutralizations as the best or only measure of success. Many Americans, unfortunately, also tend to accept statistics without questioning their source and to misinterpret what statistics actually mean. Those Americans who trusted the neutralization numbers committed both errors.

The war against the VCI neutralized cadres in four main ways: defections, arrests, captures, and killings. Statisticians usually lump arrests (the apprehension of cadres posing as ordinary civilians) together with captures (the apprehension of cadres operating with military units). The war against the VCI, as I define it, included not only actions taken deliberately against the VCI as part of the attack on the VCI but also the many other Allied actions taken primarily to achieve different objectives that happened to cause problems for the shadow government. Phoenix tried to include all neutralizations caused by the war against the shadow government in its statistics, not just those produced by the attack on the VCI. This policy permitted much of the statistical falsification described in chapters 16 and 17. It inadvertently allowed the Allies to use seemingly impressive statistics to make misleading claims of success in the attack on the VCI. Phoenix adopted this policy so that it could measure the total losses suffered by the shadow government and use that information to gauge the remaining strength of the VCI. The nationwide totals, which captured so much attention in the United States, are given in Table 20–1.

In reality, neutralization statistics were so inaccurate that any attempt to estimate total neutralizations numerically is fruitless. Some of the major reasons for this inaccuracy are explained in previous chapters, most of them involving capturing or killing. Chapter 15 shows that the PRUs did not report all of their neutralizations to Phoenix or to anyone else, and that most of their statistical reports

235

Table 20–1 Phoenix/Phung Hoang Neutralizations, 1968–1972

YEAR	RALLIED	CAPTURED	KILLED	TOTAL
1968	2,229	11,288	2,259	15,776
1969	4,832	8,515	6,187	19,534
1970	7,745	6,405*	8,191	22,341
1971	5,621	5,012	7,057	17,690
1972 (as of 31 July)	1,586	2,138	2,675	6,399
Total	**22,013**	**33,358**	**26,369**	**81,740**

*Beginning in 1970, only VCI receiving prison sentences of one year or more were counted.

Note: The original table gave 1969 as the starting date of the revised guidelines concerning VCI captured statistics. The guidelines did not change until 1970. See MACCORDS-PHD, "Phung Hoang End-of-Year Report for 1970," 11 May 1971, U.S. Army Center of Military History, Washington, D.C., p. 11.

Source: Adapted from "Vietnamization of the Phung Hoang (Phoenix) Program," discussion paper, 18 September 1972, U.S. Army Center of Military History, Washington, D.C. p. 1

remain hidden. Chapters 16 and 17 demonstrate that the South Vietnamese, for a variety of reasons, often identified non-VCI as VCI in their reports and that GVN leaders and American advisers failed to detect and reject many of the bogus reports. Chapter 18 notes that the Allies captured many VCI and reported them as neutralized but then released them from captivity after a short period of time. Some rejoined the shadow government, but the Allies had no way of knowing exactly how many.

Many other difficulties confounded the attempts of Phoenix and other organizations to count the total numbers of VCI captured or killed. One was the inability of American Phoenix advisers and their Vietnamese counterparts to check every battle site for dead VC cadres. Some Phoenix and Phung Hoang personnel did not visit the sites because the operational forces at the sites did not inform the Phoenix centers of their operations. When informed of the locations, some personnel did not go because they did not care or lacked the necessary time. In certain cases, Phoenix and Phung Hoang personnel did not look for bodies because they knew or suspected that Communist military forces remained in the battle area. "Sometimes we didn't go to battlefields because the enemy was still active in the area," Peter Scott recalled. "We didn't want to take a Jeep through that kind of an area."[1]

When Phoenix personnel did search the battlefield, they frequently did not find the enemy's dead. The Communists excelled at removing their fallen comrades from the scene of battle before the fighting ceased. "Most of the time," recalled Command Sgt. Maj. Mike Martin, "the VC either took their bodies with them, hid them, or buried them on the spot. That's why it was so hard to get an accurate body count."[2] Many wounded VCI left the battlefield with their comrades but died later of their injuries. Certain types of terrain, such as jungles and swamps, concealed corpses so well that searchers often could not find them, and heavy weaponry disfigured or dismembered bodies beyond recognition.

When the Phoenix centers did not send anyone to the sites, they had to rely on the operational forces involved to identify the bodies, photograph them, or transport them to the centers. The operational forces sometimes had to leave the battlefield to avoid a superior enemy force or to fight elsewhere and thus could not search for enemy dead and wounded or transport them. They had little desire to perform the tasks when it meant putting their lives in danger. "The PRUs weren't going to waste their time bringing bodies back after a mission," Dan Mudrinich said. "They were told, 'You go in, do your mission, and get the hell out of there. We don't care about having bodies brought back.'"[3] In some cases, the Allied forces merely made a guess, based on what they had seen during the operation, as to the number of enemy dead. If they came back later, chances were good that the Communists had removed the bodies. When Allied forces attacked the Communists with artillery or airpower, they often were reluctant to risk sending men onto the ground afterward because an ambush or mines might be waiting for them. Rudy Enders explained his attitude after successful air attacks on Communist bases: "Just by counting the enemy losses, we'd probably sustain a number of casualties to mines and booby traps. We didn't want to do that, so we didn't try to make a count. It was irrelevant, because the damage was already done. What you were really up against was enemy capability, not numbers. We'd usually find out later what happened anyway. We were putting pressure on them, and one of them would defect who was there during the attack. He'd tell us what happened."[4]

Like Phoenix advisers, operational forces that searched a battlefield frequently did not find the VCI who had died. In many instances when they did locate the bodies, they did not take the bodies with them or photograph them, and they often failed to identify them as VCI, particularly if the forces were composed of foreign or nonindigenous troops. Numerous units reported all of the enemy dead as Communist soldiers because they did not know enough about the local VCI to identify any specific cadres. A 1969 report on the overall status of the National Police Field Forces states, "Most

[NPFF] company reports do not separate VCI from VC, since the NPFF company seldom knows the classification placed on those they have killed and captured."[5] The CORDS report from Khanh Hoa province for the month of October 1968, in reference to South Korean Army operations conducted during the previous six months, states, "Total reported body count in these operations approaches 1000, but not one single VCI elimination can be credited to any of them because none of the KIA were identified."[6] Some units that identified dead VCI did not report their results directly to the Phoenix centers. Referring to Allied main force units of all nationalities, the Phung Hoang 1970 annual report states: "VCI killed by tactical forces during normal small unit operations/ambushes, etc., frequently are not identified as VCI due to inadequate liaison between the tactical unit and the Phung Hoang centers."[7] In addition, military units frequently sent captured VCI into military prisoner of war channels and no one from Phoenix ever discovered that they were political cadres.

The numbers of reported VCI rallied probably were more accurate than those of VCI captured or killed. Former VC who worked for the Chieu Hoi organization and other GVN organizations knew the faces of many VC in their respective provinces and could verify identities in many cases. Various GVN personnel and Americans questioned ralliers to check their stories. Many U.S. advisers in the Chieu Hoi centers and other advisers would notice if their counterparts greatly exaggerated the numbers of incoming ralliers and would adjust the figures accordingly. The statistics on ralliers, however, also had major shortcomings. As mentioned in chapter 9, a limited number of VC cadres rallied but then returned to the Communist side after enjoying food and rest in the Chieu Hoi centers at the expense of American taxpayers. Other cadres who remained loyal to the VC rallied in order to infiltrate GVN programs, such as the PRUs and Armed Propaganda Teams, or to become legal cadres, but the number of cadres who did so was not high. In addition, the GVN occasionally forced non-Communists to become VCI ralliers. When the GVN accused them of Communist involvement or wanted to punish them for aiding the VC, it sometimes allowed them to choose between imprisonment as VCI or defection. They invariably chose to defect and enjoy the comforts offered by the Chieu Hoi program.

The GVN's Third Party Inducement program proved much more detrimental to statistical accuracy than these other factors. Under the terms of this program, which lasted from 1967 to 1969, the GVN offered rewards to anyone who induced a Communist to rally. The program caused the number of ralliers to mushroom. Some South Vietnamese convinced friends or relatives in the VC to rally, but others presented non-Communist friends or relatives as VC or VCI ralliers. A fraudulent rallier typically received part of the reward from the third party. GVN officials often took their cuts, as well, in return for tolerating the deceit and even encouraged people to rally fraudulently so as to increase the flow of American money into their pockets. In some places, the Americans estimated that as many as half of the people who rallied through this program did not belong to the VC.[8] Some Communists and non-Communists also rallied in more than one province in order to collect multiple rewards, thus inflating the statistics even further. Brig. Gen. James Herbert commented:

> The Vietnamese are very flexible, and they know how to beat the system. If you had a reward for becoming a Hoi Chanh [rallier], some VC would rally and collect the reward. After a period of time, they'd be fed back into the society. They might wander somewhere else and give up there. They'd give a different alias each time, and communication among the various provinces was not very good, so they could do it easily. I think a VC could almost make a living giving himself up across the country.[9]

Considerable disagreement among the Americans over the VCI rallier numbers provides further evidence that the statistics were far from precise. A Rand Corporation study gives figures for VCI ralliers that differ sharply from those of Phoenix (Table 20–2).

A few analysts use an alternative method to calculate total VCI neutralizations. They subtract the estimated nationwide VCI strength on a given date from its estimated strength on an earlier date and conclude that the difference equals the number of VCI neutralized during that period. If, for example, the shadow government had 80,000 cadres on 1 January 1969 and 60,000 cadres on 1 January 1971, they reason that the Allies had neutralized 20,000 cadres between those two dates. This method does not have some of the shortcomings that the method of adding together official neutralization reports has. It does not credit the Allies for neutralizing non-Communists and Communists who did not serve in the shadow government. Nor does it count as neutralized the cadres who rallied or were captured but later rejoined the shadow government. Because the declines in estimated VCI strength from 1967 to 1972 were much smaller in magnitude than the reported neutralizations, advocates of this subtraction method assert that actual neutralizations were much smaller in number than the Allies claimed. This analysis is the same as the subtraction analysis discussed in

Table 20–2 VCI Rallier Statistics, 1968–1971

	RALLIERS (IN THOUSANDS)			
SOURCE	1968	1969	1970	1971
Rand[1]	3.8	12.6	11.4	6.6
Phoenix/Phung Hoang[2]	2.2	4.8	7.7	5.6

[1]Cited in Thomas Thayer, *War without Fronts: The American Experience in Vietnam*, Boulder, Colo.: Westview Press, 1985, p. 200.
[2]"Vietnamization of the Phung Hoang (Phoenix) Program," discussion paper, 18 September 1972, U.S. Army Center of Military History, Washington, D.C., p. 1.

chapter 18, which commentators use to demonstrate that most neutralized people were not VCI, except that it does not try to explain why the reported neutralization numbers were so much higher than the declines in overall VCI strength. Again, replacement of cadres and the difficulties inherent in estimating VCI strength render this methodology useless.

Some analysts employ additional types of statistics to judge the war against the VCI. On the basis of the ranks attributed to neutralized VCI in the Phoenix statistics, they claim that the war against the shadow government neutralized almost exclusively low-level VCI. They contend that even if the Allies neutralized large numbers of VCI, the failure to neutralize higher-level cadres prevented the war against the VCI from causing much damage because the Communists would have had little difficulty in replacing low-level cadres. Defense Department analyst Thomas Thayer, a leading proponent of this theory, argues that the attack on the VCI was not very effective because of the "inability of the Phung Hoang effort to go to the heart of the communist control organization."[10] Thayer explains:

> The real problems of Phung Hoang effectiveness began to appear when the quality of the communists taken out of action was examined. The purpose of the program was to dismantle the driving force behind the communist forces, namely, the party leaders operating at the top of the structure. However, in 1970 and 1971 (through March) less than three percent of the VCI Members killed, captured or rallied were full or probationary party members above the district level. . . . Well over half of all communists neutralized were nonparty members (the party was very small so this was no surprise), and three-quarters operated at the village level or lower.[11]

These statistics, again, are the product of faulty data collection methods. Not only did the Allies report many non-VCI as VCI, they also assigned false ranks to many of the VCI whom they did neutralize. The South Vietnamese often assigned high ranks to corpses and, to a lesser extent, to prisoners and ralliers, who actually were low-ranking Communists or not Communists at all. In so doing, of course, they wanted to make their reports look better. Jack Harrell commented, "I would say that in many cases, few of the people we captured or killed were as important or as highly placed in the VCI as they were classified."[12] The ranks of the cadres actually neutralized and the relevance of this issue to the war against the VCI as a whole are examined in chapter 21.

21 Actual Viet Cong Cadre Losses

Although statistics reveal almost nothing about the neutralization of VC cadres, a substantial amount of useful evidence exists concerning the overall losses suffered by the VCI through neutralizations. This evidence does not suffice to permit any sort of legitimate numerical estimates of neutralizations. It does, however, allow for general assessments of the damage that the various types of neutralization inflicted and of the shadow government's overall losses.

A great amount of evidence indicates that the Allies arrested, captured, and killed large numbers of VC cadres from 1967 to 1972. A large portion of these neutralizations occurred during the Tet offensive of 1968. At the time, many American journalists portrayed the offensive as a VC victory, and much of the American public believed them. U.S. public support for the war deteriorated to some extent as a result. In actuality, however, the Allies dealt the Communist forces a terrible defeat. The Communists launched most of their Tet attacks on the night of 30–31 January 1968 during the Tet holiday celebrations. Communist armed forces and cadres, the large majority of them South Vietnamese rather than North Vietnamese, assaulted most of South Vietnam's towns and cities during the offensive. By violating a holiday truce to which they had agreed, the Communists caught the Allies off guard in many places. A large percentage of GVN personnel were away from their bases to celebrate Vietnam's most sacred holiday with relatives when the offensive started. Fewer Americans were off duty, and many U.S. units had been put on alert before the offensive started, but the Communists caught some American forces unprepared as well.

Although surprise allowed the Communists to move freely among the town and city residents and attack Allied forces unexpectedly in most areas during the first hours of the offensive, the Communists did not generate popular uprisings or inflict devastating casualties on enemy forces during this crucial period. Within a few hours, Allied forces in all of the targeted towns and cities recovered from their initial shock and counterattacked the Communists, in many cases with heavy weaponry. Surrounded by hostile civilians who betrayed their location to the Allies, and concentrated in unfamiliar areas vulnerable to conventional military attack, the Communist soldiers and cadres felt the weight of many heavy blows before giving up the offensive and retreating to the countryside. The Allies drove the Communists out of most of the towns and cities within a few days, although Communist forces remained in Saigon for a couple of weeks and in Hue for about a month. After the failed attacks, a significant number of the legal cadres who had participated openly in the offensive tried to mix in with the civilian population again. The Allies subsequently identified and arrested many, if not most, of them.

No one knows how many Communists perished or fell into Allied hands, but all parties later asserted that the VC lost an extraordinarily large portion of its strength during the offensive. Political cadres who had come from the countryside suffered heavy losses, as did the legal cadres from the town and city committees of the Communist Party. In some villages, towns, and cities, the VCI virtually ceased to exist. A former cadre and Party member who rallied during the offensive testified:

> The VC had thrown all their armed forces, all their political cadres into the battlefield. All the Party's agent networks and the village infrastructures had been forced to stop all their routine activities two months before the offensive so as to concentrate their efforts in preparation [by] providing support to the attacking troops, such as motivating and concentrating the civilian laborers and collecting money for the finance sections. Further, other special branches and Party Chapters had to supply at least 30 percent of their man power to the Army, taking up the job of motivating and leading the people movements once the capital was occupied. ... The offensive ended with a tragic defeat. The loss in men was tremendous, and the number of weapons captured was too great (the transportation of weapons and ammunition to the capital had required a minimum time limit of 7 months and had been extremely difficult), too many political cadres were killed in action.[1]

Gen. Tran Van Tra, one of the top Communist generals, wrote after the war that during the offensive, "we suffered large sacrifices and losses with regard to manpower and material, especially cadres at the various echelons, which clearly weakened us."[2] Having already lost many cadres from 1965 to 1967, the shadow government staggered out of the Tet offensive in tatters. It suffered additional losses during the so-called mini-Tet offensive, another unsuccessful offensive against the cities in May 1968.

During the 1972 Easter offensive, the shadow government also sustained unusually high casualties, though much fewer than during Tet-68. Jack Harrell recalled, "In the spring offensive of '72, we got some VCI when they came in, primarily from across the Cambodian border. Quite a number of them exposed themselves at that time. The most significant decrease in VCI strength, aside from the Tet offensive, was during the '72 offensive."[3]

Although most historians today agree that the VC and the VCI incurred very heavy losses during the Tet offensive of 1968, they differ about the Allies' success in capturing and killing the shadow government's members in the ensuing years. Some skeptics dismiss reports of success as propaganda used by the U.S. government and the GVN to exaggerate their achievements or to mask the detention and killing of non-Communist civilians. This view was particularly popular during the war and in the years immediately following it. A few years after the war, however, many Communists and former Communists started to state openly that the Viet Cong infrastructure lost many thousands of cadres after Tet to Phoenix or pacification. Most of them testified to this fact either in public or to foreign journalists who did not support the Allied cause in Vietnam, so it is safe to assume that their statements were not distorted. That most Vietnamese Communist leaders tended to understate, not overstate, their side's failures added to the credibility of the statements. These Communist accounts have convinced many, though not all, historians that the Allies eliminated large numbers of VCI after the Tet offensive.

Some observers speculate that the Communists lied when commenting on the effectiveness of Phoenix. Perhaps, the observers reason, the Communists wanted to blame Phoenix for their deteriorating performance so that they would not have to admit that the whole pacification program was overpowering them, or that the Southern Communists no longer had the will to continue the fight, or that the rural population no longer wanted to help them, or that huge numbers of cadres were abandoning the party. A highly destructive Phoenix could allow the Southern or Northern Communists to save face to some extent with the high command in Hanoi or with other onlookers. The Communist sources themselves, however, contradict this scapegoat theory. In their secret wartime communications, the Southern Communists acknowledged that all of these factors, as well as Phoenix, caused them great difficulty. COSVN Resolution 14, for instance, states that "the expansion of the guerrilla warfare has been slow and limited, and thus failed to meet the requirements dictated by the General Offensive and Uprising Campaign. It is not yet widespread and strong enough to successfully play its strategic role. . . . Popular forces and revolutionary bases, though achieving some typical successes, are not fully developed. We have not yet promoted a widespread armed struggle movement among the masses."[4]

So many Allied personnel and other Allied sources, moreover, tell the same story of numerous VC cadre losses after Tet that there can be no doubt that the Communists are telling the truth about the extent of the losses. A sample of Allied sources concerning the general effectiveness of Allied operational forces in neutralizing VCI appears in chapter 15. Other information available to Allied intelligence agencies further suggests that the shadow government sustained heavy losses of illegal and legal cadres, particularly at the hamlet and village levels. Higher-level VCI, according to many sources, regularly had to step into village-level positions to replace lost cadres in much of South Vietnam. Where the shadow government lacked many upper-level cadres, moreover, it did not reassign district-level cadres to the village level but appointed single cadres as the chief executives of several village Party committees. Allied intelligence agencies also repeatedly reported during the war that "double hatting"—the assignment of two or more cadre jobs to a single individual—became increasingly widespread and that the Party frequently had to transfer military cadres to political cadre positions because of political cadre losses.[5]

Among historians who believe that the Communists did endure heavy cadre losses, there remains little agreement about how the Allies captured and killed so many cadres. Their disagreement has not heretofore led to many new insights on the issue because their interpretations generally have lacked sufficient corroborating evidence. The majority of Communist leaders who mentioned the enormous losses of cadres said that Phoenix or Phung Hoang had neutralized the cadres. Former VC Minister of Justice Truong Nhu Tang, for instance, writes in his memoir, "In some locations . . . Phoenix was dangerously effective. In Hau Nghia Province, for example, not far from our old base area, the Front infrastructure was virtually eliminated."[6] Col. Bui Tin told Pulitzer Prize–winning journalist Stanley Karnow that Phoenix cost "the loss of thousands of our cadres," and Gen. Tran Do, the Communists' deputy commander in South Vietnam at that time, described Phoenix to Karnow as "extremely destructive."[7] When I visited Hanoi in 1995, I found that most Communist leaders had not changed their interpretation. Maj. Gen. Le Van Duong, for example, deputy director of the National Defense Academy, said, "In some regions, the people on our side suffered heavy losses because of Phoenix."[8]

After the war, some Communist leaders even claimed that the Phoenix statistics—often derided as grossly inflated—understated the actual neutralizations. Seymour Hersh recounts that Nguyen Co Thach, a senior North Vietnamese diplomat during the war who later became North Vietnam's foreign minister, told him that Phoenix "had slaughtered far more than the 21,000 officially listed by the United States. 'We had many weaknesses in the South,' Thach said, 'because of Phoenix.' In some provinces, 95 percent of the Communist cadre had been assassinated or compromised by the Phoenix operation."[9] Le Duc Tho, who directed the Southern Communists throughout the war, also offered a grim assessment of the losses, although he did not mention Phoenix by name. In 1976, he told the fourth party congress at Hanoi that, during the latter part of the war: "The grassroots party organization suffered heavy losses—hundreds of thousands of cadres and party members sacrificed their lives or were sent to prison."[10]

Many observers accept the Communists at their word and thus ascribe the cadre losses to the Phoenix program or the Phung Hoang program. As chapters 11–13 explain, Phoenix and Phung Hoang merely attempted to coordinate intelligence sharing and encourage existing entities to neutralize the Viet Cong cadres. At best, these programs made minor improvements to the performance of the operational forces before mid-1969, and they contributed to performance to an even smaller extent thereafter. Phoenix and Phung Hoang could not possibly have damaged the shadow government to any great extent.

The Communists, then, used the term *Phoenix* to refer to some other element or elements of the war against the VCI. The Communists often used terms rather loosely, so this imprecision is not surprising; the important question is how loosely they used this term. Some historians conclude that the Communists who talked about the effectiveness of Phoenix used the term to refer to pacification or to all Allied military activities. These historians rely on faulty evidence. Many draw heavily on the testimony of CORDS advisers, who knew little about the CIA's attack on the VCI and said that the attack on the VCI—as they knew it—was ineffective, whereas pacification or regular military activities were effective. As evidence, many of these historians cite flawed statistics indicating that most captured and killed cadres fell victim to the military operations of the Allied main forces and territorial forces. Because these historians believe that only the regular military activities of the pacification forces—primarily the territorial forces—and the main forces damaged the Communists significantly, they conclude that any Communist talk of heavy losses had to refer to these forces.[11]

I did not discern the Communists' interpretation of the term *Phoenix* until I came to some conclusions about other aspects of the war against the VCI that differ sharply from those of other historians. Among the most important of these conclusions, discussed in chapter 16, is that the PRUs neutralized more cadres and other Communists in the villages than most CORDS advisers and other Americans thought. Another conclusion is that organizations that usually kept fairly quiet besides the PRUs, most notably the Special Police, unconventional ARVN and U.S. military units, and the Kit Carson Scouts, made smaller but significant contributions to the village war, as did the more well-known National Police Field Forces. After arriving at these conclusions, I tried to find out whether the Communists included any or all of these forces in their definition of Phoenix, for these forces bore a closer resemblance to the Phoenix program than did pacification in general or all Allied military operations. I also tried to determine what other forces, if any, fit the Communists' definition of Phoenix.

After tracking down a large amount of evidence, much of it previously undiscovered, and studying it for a long time, I concluded that the PRUs, Special Police, unconventional ARVN and U.S. military units, Kit Carson Scouts, National Police Field Forces, and other small paramilitary forces constituted Phoenix in the minds of the Communists. I also found that the Communists considered neither the territorial forces, the backbone of pacification, nor the main forces, the instigators of other military activity, to be components of Phoenix. Some historians speculate that the Communists tended to lump all sorts of Allied forces together and call them by a single name because they did not recognize all of the different types of Allied forces. A wealth of evidence, however, indicates that the Communists were able to distinguish between individual Allied forces quite well and that they chose to include only a select group of all of the Allied forces in their definition of Phoenix.

The Communists had sources in enough units of every major GVN operational organization to keep them apprised of the organization's modes of activity and its general effectiveness. Even the PRUs, the South Vietnamese forces most capable of keeping Communists out of their ranks, did not remain free of Communist spies. Among the people interviewed for this book, Col. Viet Lang (quoted on the subject in chapter 7) was not the only one who knew firsthand of Communist infiltrators amid both the rank and file and the leadership of the PRUs. Rudy Enders recalled, "In 1971, we discovered that the Hau Nghia PRU chief was a VC. We arrested him and turned him over to the MSS."[12] Bruce Lawlor said the CIA learned during the Easter offensive that the Quang Tri deputy PRU chief was working for the VC.[13] With such access to information, the Communists could not possibly have been ignorant of the distinctions between any of the Allied forces that operated nationwide.

Substantial numbers of Communist documents and other Communist sources, some of which the U.S. government declassified only recently, indicate the types of forces that the Communists generally included in their definition of Phoenix and verify that they viewed Phoenix as something separate from the GVN territorial forces and the Allied main forces. One captured Communist document, based on briefings by Gen. Vo Nguyen Giap and other top Communist officials from late 1969 and early 1970, states:

> The [Allied] main force units operate from the disputed area to the border area. The Regional Force[s] try to eliminate our local force troops and agents operating in the safety areas. The Popular Forces try to annihilate our guerrilla troops in the safety areas. Special Forces operate in the border area and along our supply routes. Pacification and Phung Hoang (Phoenix) forces are being activated and developed. Phung Hoang (Phoenix) forces in the villages . . . consist of police, security, reconnaissance, and rural development personnel and agents of intelligence organizations.[14]

A captured Communist directive dated 10 March 1971 asserts that the Allies "consider rural pacification an important strategic factor in winning the people in our liberated areas. In recent attacks, the enemy has applied the 'triangular warfare' tactic which consists of intelligence, psychological, and guerrilla warfare. The enemy has made the best use of psywar, Chieu Hoi, and, especially, espionage activities used in the Phuong Hoang Campaign. He thinks that if the Phuong Hoang Campaign is successful, his rural pacification program will succeed and political problems will be settled satisfactorily."[15] A few Communist documents went farther, providing the true definition of Phoenix as well as identifying the other organizations involved in attacking the VCI. A 1971 document captured in VC Military Region 7 states, "(Phuong Hoang intelligence committees) are actually intelligence information research, analysis, and exploitation units. They provide plans for police force operations and attacks on our infrastructures. This organization is composed of police, military security, province reconnaissance agents, pacification personnel, and local Puppet administrative officials."[16] The authors of these documents, like American CORDS and CIA advisers, failed to teach most of their compatriots that Phoenix and Phung Hoang technically were separate from the operational forces.

Communist sources also gave descriptions of Phoenix that matched the typical activities of the PRUs and similar forces. A Communist radio station, for instance, announced in October 1969: "U.S. imperialists have poured dozens of million dollars for CIA to carry out the Phoenix plan: Sending spies and rangers to carry out espionage, assassination, and abduction operations, conducting long-term raids against small areas to investigate and terrorize every citizen, and massacring our compatriots en masse."[17] A report from the Communist Party's Central Committee concerning Binh Dinh province in 1969, where Phoenix and Phung Hoang were feeble as usual, credits Allied "reconnaissance, intelligence, and Special Forces" with successes that closely resemble the work of the PRUs. The report states that the enemy "has placed 300 well-trained personnel into liberated and newly controlled areas." Because of the enemy's use of spies, prisoners, and defectors and the investigation of VC families, the document continues, "The revolutionary movement of the masses has been wickedly oppressed and appeased." It also notes, "Due to the overt activities and lack of vigilance of our cadre in some places, the enemy has recently discovered our underground hideouts and arrested our covert agents. This fact has caused us many difficulties and losses."[18] In fact, according to Dean Almy, Binh Dinh had some of the best PRUs in Vietnam.[19]

Postwar Communist testimony also indicates that the Communists have continued to define Phoenix as they did during the war. Nguyen Thi Binh, the VC's famous foreign minister during the war and now the vice president of Vietnam, described the Phoenix program to me as follows: "The Phoenix program was a cunning ploy by the Americans because it employed many tricks to infiltrate our ranks and eliminate our patriotic elements. The most truculent part of the Saigon regime forces was that which was trained and brainwashed by the Americans."[20] The PRUs resembled the effective, American-trained forces that she associated with Phoenix much more closely than any other Allied forces. In a recent article, Gen. Tran Van Tra differentiates between pacification and Phoenix when he notes that, after Tet, the Communist cadres "were faced with the enemy's intense counterattacks and its pacification operations and Phoenix program."[21] The organizations that fell under the Communist definition of Phoenix performed particularly well in areas where postwar Communist sources credit Phoenix for hurting the VCI. Truong Nhu Tang, as mentioned above, claims that Phoenix wiped out most of the shadow government in Hau Nghia province. PRUs from Hau Nghia and from several other

III Corps provinces, with the help of CIA interrogation officer Orrin DeForest and his III Corps interrogation center, neutralized large numbers of VCI in Hau Nghia during the late 1960s and early 1970s.[22]

Although GVN territorial forces and Allied main forces did not neutralize most of the political cadres whom the Communists reported as lost to Phoenix, they did neutralize many thousands during the period 1968–72. The territorial forces and main forces captured and killed numerous VCI in normal military operations, particularly those that took place in the village areas, and a much smaller number of VCI during their search operations in the hamlets. Communist documents testify to the successes of the territorial forces and main forces in eliminating Communist personnel in and around the villages. For example, a 1971 COSVN directive states:

> Pacification and counterpacification struggles by enemy and friendly forces were and are being conducted under highly violent forms. During the past two years, the U.S. and puppet [regime] focussed their efforts on pacifying and encroaching upon rural areas, using the most barbarous schemes. They strengthened puppet forces, consolidated the puppet government, and established an outpost network and espionage and People's Self-Defense Force organizations in many hamlets and villages. They provided more technical equipment for, and increased the mobility of, puppet forces, established blocking lines, and created a new defensive and oppressive system in densely populated rural areas. As a result, they caused many difficulties to and inflicted losses on friendly forces.[23]

The Chieu Hoi program cost the shadow government an enormous number of cadres. Many of the Americans and South Vietnamese whom I interviewed for this book had firsthand knowledge of the Chieu Hoi program, and almost all of them said that a great many true VCI and other Communists rallied in the areas where they worked. Only those who served in sparsely populated provinces, where VCI activity was minimal, did not witness large-scale rallying.

The Communists counted defection as one of their greatest problems. Deputy Secretary of COSVN Hai Van, according to Hackle, stated in September 1969 that "the Party viewed the Chieu Hoi program as being more dangerous than the Phung Hoang [and Accelerated Pacification Programs] and conceded that there would always be a problem of cadres' rallying, even during a cease-fire." In addition, Hackle said, "Hai Van conceded that the Party had been seriously hurt by the Chieu Hoi Program, especially since Tet 1968, but he reiterated that one must anticipate such GVN measures, difficult as they may be, and devise appropriate countermeasures. He mentioned no specific numerical figures of Party members who had rallied, but he did reveal that they ranged from village Party chapter secretaries to regimental level cadres."[24] Although Hai Van said that the party considered the Chieu Hoi program to be more dangerous than Phoenix and pacification, he did not necessarily mean that Chieu Hoi caused more VCI losses. Captured and killed cadres, in all probability, outnumbered the cadre ralliers. Ralliers, however, provided the Allies more information about the Communists and put more Communists in jeopardy than did captured or killed cadres, thus making one VCI rallier more dangerous than one captured or killed VCI.

The shadow government lost other cadres in ways that the American neutralization categories generally ignored and that the Allies could not have measured. One of these, the decision of disaffected cadres to desert instead of rally, resulted in large numbers of cadre losses. The fear that the VC or the GVN beat or killed ralliers more often than deserters inclined some VCI to attempt desertion rather than defection. When compared with rallying, however, desertion had disadvantages that encouraged the majority of those wishing to leave the VCI to rally rather than to desert. Most deserters could not live in areas under GVN control for long without facing imprisonment because they did not have legal GVN identification, as did ralliers. Usually, they could not live in the few areas under VC domination because the VC cadres would try to punish them or force them to help the cause. Deserters, unlike cadres who defected through the Chieu Hoi program, did not receive food and shelter. Most potential deserters could avoid these problems only if they succeeded in obtaining refugee status, which usually was difficult for young and middle-aged men.

Most of the neutralized cadres did not serve at positions above the village level. Neutralization statistics, for once, provide some useful evidence. As mentioned in chapter 20, statistics show that most neutralized VCI served at the village level or below, and many observers noticed a tendency among Allied forces to inflate the ranks of people whom they reported neutralized. It would seem highly probable, therefore, that the percentage of cadres above the village level is even smaller than the relatively small percentage in the statistics. Even if many of the reports were completely false, the ones most likely to have been false are the reports of higher-level neutralizations. All veterans of the war whom I interviewed and other relevant sources of information confirm that the overwhelming majority of neutralized cadres served at the hamlet or village levels.

The nature of the war in Vietnam during the late 1960s and early 1970s, indeed, guaranteed that the VC cadres would suffer most of their losses at the lowest echelons. The Allies could not possibly have captured or killed cadres at the district level and above in any significant numbers. Like most hierarchies, the shadow government had far more people at the lower levels than at the higher levels. Even if all cadres had been equally vulnerable, the bulk of neutralized cadres would have been at the lower levels. Political cadres above the village level seldom traveled to the villages or elsewhere; when they did leave their hiding places, large numbers of armed VC traveled with them. The hamlet- and village-level illegal cadres, by contrast, attempted to visit the villages and carry out the overt functions of the shadow government in the villages when feasible, and they usually could not take exceedingly large numbers of armed men with them because of personnel shortages or the need for stealth. Under these circumstances, they were quite vulnerable to Allied operations. Most of the legal cadres, many of whom the Allies arrested, also served at the hamlet or village levels of the shadow government. In addition, cadres from the lowest administrative levels were most likely to rally. They faced more hardships and danger than the upper-level cadres, and tended to be less dedicated.

Contrary to the contentions of commentators, the scarcity of higher-level cadres among the total VC cadre losses did not prevent the Allies from inflicting serious damage on the VCI. The Southern Communists, it is true, could not have survived without the leadership of the high-level cadres, but they could accomplish little when they lost as many cadres at the hamlet and village levels as they did during the late 1960s and early 1970s. These cadres had the responsibility of executing almost all of the policies that allowed the VC to control and make use of the village populations. As indicated in chapter 3, the Party believed that it could not mobilize the masses for war without the *chi bo,* the Party organization at the village level. District-level cadres routinely stepped into vacated village-level leadership positions because these positions were so important. Shorn of hamlet and village cadres, the cadres above the village level were like the colonels and generals of an army deprived of enlisted personnel and junior officers. Thomas Roberts, a Phoenix adviser in Binh Dinh province, observed:

> When you remove the village-level cadres, you are effectively killing the organization. The hamlet not so much, but when you remove the control-

ling elements at [the] village level, you are killing the VC infrastructure. You can either do this by killing the guys, by capturing them, [by] making them rally, or you can do it by forcing them into the hills.[25]

In addition, some hamlet and village cadres were more important than the term *low level* suggests. Hamlet and village cadres who occupied leadership positions, in contrast to the lesser hamlet and village cadres, had to perform well in order for the shadow government to stand any chance of functioning in a village. Some of the top village cadres, such as party secretaries and security section chiefs, visited their villages regularly. Others decided to stop going to the village areas in order to avoid being captured or killed, but they had to delegate much of their leadership responsibility to subordinate leaders and send them to the villages in order to keep the shadow government operating in those areas. Whatever the case, hamlet and village VCI who held leadership positions of some type had to visit the villages if they wanted to carry out the shadow government's functions; in so doing, they made themselves vulnerable to Allied operations. As an inevitable result, the Allies captured or killed many of them. When the VC lost significant numbers of hamlet- and village-level leaders and subordinate leaders after the Tet offensive, the performance of the VCI almost always deteriorated. The shadow government obtained new cadres slowly because it trained cadres in small numbers over a long period of time, and because it chose cadres selectively and had few people from which to choose as a result of general recruiting difficulties. The shadow government could replace hamlet and village leaders by downgrading higher-level cadres, but then it exposed its better people to neutralization, and it did not have large numbers of them.

To help prop up its ailing Southern infrastructure and to increase Northern control, Hanoi began to send more and more Northern cadres to the South. Whereas cadres born in North Vietnam had occupied only a few shadow government posts in the early and mid-1960s, they held a preponderant share of them, including a large majority of the higher-level positions, by 1972. Hanoi tried to continue sending Southern cadres, rather than Northern cadres, to visit the hamlets and ask the population for support, but personnel shortages became so severe that it sometimes had to employ the Northerners even in this role. Dr. Duong Quynh Hoa, a high-ranking VC leader who has remained in Vietnam since the war ended, told Karnow how the Party handled the heavy losses of Southern political cadres to the Tet debacle and Phoenix: "Growing numbers of North Vietnamese agents were sent south to fill the vacuum. They rebuilt the southern Communist apparatus, and they remained after the war to manage it—often antagonizing their southern comrades, who, despite an abstract commitment to national cohesion, clung to their regional identity."[26] Some observers have speculated that Hanoi knew all along that the Tet offensive would fail and launched it simply to cripple the Southern Communists and thereby remove the threat of a Southern Communist rebellion against the Northern Communists. Some of the facts surrounding the offensive support this hypothesis, whereas others argue against it. No conclusive evidence has emerged, and it might never emerge.

The Communists tried to compensate for their horrendous cadre losses during the period 1967–72 by recruiting Southern villagers in addition to infusing Northerners. The replacements, however, failed to keep pace with the losses. Because of the deficiencies of VCI strength estimates, it is impossible to estimate numerically how much the total cadre strength of the shadow government shrank during these years, but numerous Communist and Allied sources indicate that it experienced an enormous decline. Contraction of hamlet and village infrastructures accounted for most of the decrease. In 1970, a rallier from VC Soc Trang province told the Allies a story of the shadow government's declining fortunes that was repeated in similar form in almost all of the provinces. The rallier disclosed that the VCI "had been able to recruit only about 100 new members for [the People's Revolutionary Party] in the past two years. The seriousness of this problem becomes apparent when this recruitment is viewed along with their losses—over 1500 PRP members killed, rallied or deserted during the two-year period."[27]

22 Additional Setbacks for the Shadow Government

lmost all commentators, regardless of their opinions of the neutralization statistics, gauge the success of the war against the VCI solely by the numbers of neutralized cadres. Yet, cadre losses and the decline in overall VCI strength do not explain fully the impact of the war against the VCI. Nor, indeed, do they reveal entirely why the VCI did not enlist enough people to replace their losses and why VCI performance in general deteriorated.

The war against the VCI caused the shadow government to change its activities in ways that reduced its effectiveness. In some villages, the Allies did not eliminate all of the VC cadres but they neutralized enough cadres and other VC or made life so dangerous for the Communists that the remaining overt village VC chose to hide away from the population and discontinue their activities. Near the end of the war, researcher James Trullinger spent five months in My Thuy Phong, a village in Thua Thien province. While interviewing villagers and GVN and VC personnel, he discovered that the village's shadow government had suffered this fate in 1968. During that year, the U.S. military decided to build a camp in an unoccupied section of the village, and American soldiers began combing the surrounding area for VC. The local people informed Trullinger of subsequent developments. He writes:

> A peasant recalled what happened. "The Liberation Army had to take its guerrillas and its cadres out of the village," he said, "because they would have been killed if they had remained behind. Many people who supported the revolution were sad at that, and the Liberation cells became weak." Several confirmed this contention about the cells, and noted that between 1968 and 1972, the People's Revolutionary Party had no influence in the village, and the Front functional groups no activities.[1]

Prisoners and ralliers from Long An province, who were questioned in early 1970, similarly said that this phenomenon began to occur on a large scale in 1969 as the Allied pacification effort grew stronger.

"In many areas," according to their testimony, "cadres went into hiding and were unable to conduct District and Village-level meetings or operations."[2] The Allies thus rendered VCI useless even though, technically, they did not neutralize cadres.

In many cases, the danger of Allied operations did not force the shadow government to stop functioning altogether but did inhibit its activities. The illegal cadres, almost all of whom did not live in the hamlets by the late 1960s, often curtailed their visits to their areas of responsibility or took fewer helpers during their visits to decrease the likelihood of encountering Allied forces. Because of the cadres' reduced access to the population and their use of fewer assistants, they could not obtain personnel, taxes, or intelligence from the hamlets as effectively as they had previously nor could they give as much assistance to Communist soldiers.

Reduced access not only decreased opportunities for taking the villagers' assets, it also decreased the effectiveness of other methods that the VC cadres used to obtain villager support and build their power in the villages. The elaborate set of National Liberation Front associations and committees, through which the shadow government had organized the village masses so efficiently, ceased to function in most villages because of the cadres' prolonged absences. The cadres could not perform as much of the propaganda work that had helped to make the villagers cooperative in the past. Without strict regimentation of daily life, villagers could hide their children or their property from the cadres. The cadres no longer could prevent the movement of villagers into areas where they could communicate with Allied personnel, nor could they keep Allied intelligence gatherers out of the hamlets, both of which weakened VC counterintelligence. The VCI's capability to abduct and kill civilians and GVN personnel deteriorated the least, but the perpetrators' chances of running into trouble on their way to and from their targets had increased because of the stronger presence of Allied forces. A report from Hackle describes some of the difficulties that the Allied forces caused for the shadow government in Tay Ninh province during 1970:

> The pacification program in Tay Ninh province has succeeded in restricting the access of the Viet Cong to the people and this is creating serious difficulties. The disruption was so great during the first half of 1970 that the VC were unable to fulfill 90 percent of their operational plans. . . . Because of the almost constant Allied presence in the area, guerrillas are no longer able to move around freely in the province and many of the local populace have been restricting their movements to times when Allied units are in the area to protect them.[3]

In many areas, as mentioned in chapter 6, the shadow government began employing large numbers of legal cadres during this period in order to reduce its vulnerability to Allied operations. Because their identities generally remained hidden, these cadres still were able to collect intelligence; attempt to infiltrate GVN organizations; and, on occasion, perpetrate isolated acts of violence. Their inability to propagandize, recruit, conscript, and tax villagers and perform other overt shadow government duties, however, severely limited their effectiveness. Allied operations also diminished their ability to perform some duties. The legal cadres could not snoop around in the villages or recruit useful spies in the hamlets or GVN organizations as easily as they once had because the GVN's leadership—and thus its counterintelligence efforts—had improved. Both the legal cadres and their agents and informants in the GVN experienced much more difficulty in relaying time-sensitive tactical intelligence to the appropriate people fast enough because contacting them in the countryside was now less safe. The legal cadres, moreover, frequently were low in number or poor in quality, and their reliability was always questionable because of their frequent exposure to Allied propagandists and intelligence personnel.

The rising dangers involved in traveling and conducting meetings also inhibited communication among the VC cadres in many cases. When they were unable to communicate, higher-level cadres could not provide policy guidance to their subordinates or motivate them during difficult times. Those at the upper echelons also could not receive regular status and intelligence reports or check up on their subordinates, thereby reducing their ability to appraise local conditions and issue appropriate orders. A Communist document explains the predicament: "District Party committee members failed to successfully help cadre in villages. They did not know the enemy schemes and properly assess the enemy schemes and properly assess the enemy, friendly, and the people's situation in hamlets and villages. The cutting off of the communication lines from hamlets to villages and districts caused bad influence to leadership."[4]

The ability of the Allies to drive the Communist armed forces out of a populated rural area and keep it free of those forces largely determined the extent to which the Allies inhibited the VCI's overt activities. Some observers refer to this ability as the ability to provide security to the area. I use the term *security* in this way. Others use VC and GVN political capabilities, as well as the relationship between the armed forces, as indicators of security. The CIA and CORDS did so during the war, and they used an elaborate and highly controversial system called the Hamlet Evaluation System (HES) to rate the level of security—according to this definition—in all of South Vietnam's hamlets. Although my definition of security does not take political factors into account, HES ratings corresponded fairly closely to hamlet ratings that did not do so. Both the GVN and the VC generally conducted political activities more effectively in areas that they dominated militarily. As a result, in order to determine trends in the level of security according to my definition, the HES ratings should be informative, if they accurately measured what they were supposed to measure.

For most of the HES program's duration, U.S. advisers completed detailed forms each month for every hamlet. During the later stages of Vietnamization, the advisers gave the South Vietnamese responsibility for the reports. The HES forms required entry of a wide variety of information about the military and political activities of the two adversaries in each hamlet, such as the number of Communist military actions and the presence of the GVN hamlet chief. The Americans processed the HES data and rated hamlets in which the Allies maintained some presence from "A" to "E," with "A" being the most secure. Hamlets completely controlled by the VC received a "V" rating. According to HES statistics, 8.2 million more South Vietnamese lived in secure areas during 1972 than during 1967. The percentage of the total population living in secure areas increased from 42 percent to 80 percent during that period. In addition, according to the HES, the percentage of the population living where the VCI could not move freely rose from 56 percent in December 1969 to 80 percent in December 1971. The HES also indicated that, in contrast to the early years of the war, many of these people experienced better security because Allied personnel improved security in their home areas, not because they migrated to more secure areas.[5]

Numerous CIA and CORDS advisers, including most of those whom I interviewed, have made known their opinions about the HES. Most said that imprecision plagued the system. Some of the Americans and the South Vietnamese, they asserted, did not have enough time or desire to check the hamlets themselves, so they relied on the opinions of others or simply created data that seemed reasonable. Some, especially the South Vietnamese, provided false information to give the hamlets better security ratings than they deserved. In addition, both Americans and South Vietnamese used a host of tricks to boost the HES reports without improving the GVN's position in the countryside. Col. Walter Clark gave an example. "The Vietnamese knew how to play the HES game," Clark said. "If you had a dispensary in a certain village, you could check a good block on the HES report. The Vietnamese put a concrete box together, painted a red cross on it, and walked away.

There was no medicine, no doctor, no nurse, but they counted it as a dispensary, and we couldn't check it all. They played games like that constantly."[6]

Pressure from both GVN and U.S. commands to report "progress" promoted these practices. Leaders in Saigon and Washington wanted to demonstrate that the GVN firmly controlled most of the countryside to their own people and to the Communist negotiators, with whom, for most of this period, they were trying to reach a peace settlement. Bruno Kosheleff of USAID and Stan Jorgensen of the U.S. State Department wrote of the HES after a thorough assessment of Quang Nam province in 1969:

> 1969 Pacification goals were set unreasonably high in many areas. Both Americans and Vietnamese at the district level where the reports are originated were inclined and often pressured to submit reports showing progress. This led to unduly high HES ratings being registered and a widespread corruption of the C category. In I CTZ, command emphasis in the direction of showing progress regardless of the facts was strong in the American command channel. It was even stronger in Vietnamese channels, where General [Hoang Xuan] Lam emphatically declared in an open meeting that there would be no regression in I CTZ and that 1969 goals would be met. President Thieu decided to reduce the number of GVN hamlets by some 15% throughout the countryside. This order resulted in the writing off or gerrymandering out of existence a number of D, E, and VC hamlets with 257 hamlets dropped in 1969 alone.[7]

In the final analysis, HES figures undoubtedly were inflated in many cases, but they revealed an accurate trend, a sharp improvement in security for most rural areas between the middle of 1968 and the Easter offensive of 1972. Part of the gain occurred because segments of the rural population in insecure hamlets, for a variety of reasons, moved into more secure areas. The most important reason why villagers moved was to escape Allied military operations in and around the hamlets, particularly those involving heavy firepower. These operations killed and injured numerous villagers; destroyed the villagers' homes and livestock; and, along with defoliation, destroyed their crops. VC exploitation and mistreatment of the population also caused many people to flee their hamlets. Allied troops intentionally moved some civilians out of their homes in insecure areas in order to keep them from assisting the Communists and to prevent the Communist military units from taking cover behind them. The Allies employed this practice particularly often during the first years of direct American military involvement. At the end of 1967, the U.S. high command forbade further compulsory relocations in order to reduce the negative publicity generated by the refugee problem, but relocations continued on a fairly large scale in some areas, particularly in I Corps, into the 1970s.

From the mid-1960s to the early 1970s, several million villagers became refugees at one time or another. Countless hamlets were abandoned entirely. The rate of flight from the villages skyrocketed after American forces arrived in 1965. It declined sharply after 1968, primarily because the Allies ran highly destructive military operations near the villages less often and because the VC lost control of many hamlets. The displaced often spent some time in dirty, cramped refugee centers before finding a place to start anew. A large percentage of them eventually resettled in the swollen towns and cities; the Allies estimated that the percentage of South Vietnamese citizens residing in urban areas jumped from 15 percent in 1960 to 40 percent in 1970.[8] Another large fraction of refugees, however, returned to their original hamlets once they became relatively safe or moved to more secure rural areas.

Some Americans argue that the evacuation of the hamlets from 1965 to 1968 had serious negative consequences for the Allied effort to control the countryside. Many of the refugees who had been neutral previously, they contend, became angry at the Allies for compelling them to move through the use of heavy Allied firepower or for relocating them forcibly. Incited by Communist proselytizers in the refugee camps, the argument continues, these refugees chose to join the VC. George C. Herring asserts, "A large portion of South Vietnam's population was left rootless and hostile, and the refugee camps became fertile breeding grounds for Vietcong fifth columns."[9] Chapter 25 examines in detail the attitudes of the refugees. For the purposes of this chapter, it is necessary only to point out that most refugees, in reality, did not try to join the VC. VC sources acknowledge that the emigrations denied them access to the resources of most of the departed villagers and also prevented them from taking cover behind the villagers. The VC distrusted the few refugees who wanted to join them because they suspected them of being Allied spies. The Communists consistently lamented that the abandonment of the hamlets hindered them far more than it helped them. A former village cadre remarked:

> The more that people migrated to the Government areas, the less production workers, corveé laborers, and informers the Front had. The Front would no longer have the people to support them and with whom they could min-

gle to hide. Many young men from the village went to the Nationalist areas, enlisted in the Nationalist army and returned to the village to fight against the Front. This fact demoralized and confused the Front cadres the most.[10]

Cao Van Luong of the History Institute in Hanoi told me, "Millions of people left the countryside for the cities because of the American bombing, which weakened the Communist Party."[11] In the years after the Tet offensive, the departure of villagers generally hurt the GVN's cause more than Hanoi's cause because the Allies controlled the resources in most hamlets and lost some of these resources, principally agricultural products and intelligence, when villagers departed. By then, however, far fewer villagers were fleeing their hamlets.

The Party's responses to the exodus of the mid- to late 1960s also indicate that it viewed the net effect as harmful to the Communist cause. The VCI warned villagers not to leave, threatened or harassed those who attempted to leave or their relatives, and called on refugees to return, but their protests seldom succeeded. Villagers sneaked out at night, if necessary, or left with Allied troops when they came to their hamlets, and they seldom returned to VC areas. A rallier from Kien Giang province, for instance, recalled, "Most of the villagers had left, so those who remained wanted to leave. Therefore, the cadres were troubled, [and] they tried to stop the villagers from leaving. . . . There were no people in the hamlet to work for them. I felt that the cadres were also afraid that those who were disappointed with them might bring the GVN soldiers to the hamlet to capture them."[12]

The Communists attacked refugee camps and other GVN areas, usually in vain, in order to abduct refugees or to convince them that living in VC areas was no less safe than in GVN areas so that they would return. Louis Wiesner, who served in Vietnam with the CORDS refugee division from 1968 to 1970, writes of the Communists:

> Their attacks on civilians were deliberate and frequently indiscriminate, intended to terrorize the survivors and bend them to the Communist will. In the period 1968 through 1971, many of the VC/NVA attacks were on refugee sites, with the objective of forcing the inhabitants to return to Communist-controlled territory. Thus, for example, in the four months from May through August 1968, there were 45 such attacks in I and II CTZ alone. In the last two of those months over 1,725 houses were destroyed, over 53 refugees were killed, more than 112 were wounded, and over 36 were abducted.[13]

Had many refugees wanted to join the VC, the Communists would not have resorted to such attempts at intimidation because they would have only alienated potential recruits. Kosheleff and Jorgensen reported:

> The VC have in the past directed numerous attacks against the refugee camps. Captured documents regarding the 1970 Tet offensive, which never materialized, state that refugee camps were to be a primary target. Harassment and abductions were planned toward the end [of] intimidating refugees and forcing them to desert the camps and return to VC controlled areas. This, of course, tends to corroborate the argument that relocating people and clearing areas has hurt the VC/NVA.[14]

Bringing security to the people in the hamlets, as opposed to having the people move to secure areas, required considerable time and effort. During 1967, the Allies did not improve the average security in the inhabited hamlets, and, at the end of 1967 and the beginning of 1968, security deteriorated as the Communists stepped up their attacks on Allied pacification personnel and programs. Security plummeted during the Tet offensive of 1968 because the Allied pacification forces left the hamlets to defend the towns and cities. The period from mid-1968 to the Easter offensive of 1972 witnessed a great improvement in security, which even affected most of the villages where the Communists previously had been quite powerful. Allied counterattacks in the village areas began in the middle of 1968 and rose sharply in intensity when the three-month Accelerated Pacification Campaign kicked off in November. By early 1969, the Allies returned security in the countryside to roughly its pre-Tet levels.

By the end of 1969, the Allied main forces had eliminated the shield of the larger Communist main and local forces in and around most villages that had protected smaller Communist units, and the Communists did not attempt to use large forces again in most of the village areas until 1972. The Communists could have deployed larger military units and run more operations during this period, but they decided, in most instances, that these practices would cost them too many men without causing sufficient damage to the enemy. The Allies had become quite adept at destroying large Communist formations, and the Communists were trying to recuperate from their losses of 1968 and the first half of 1969. Col. Jack Weissinger, province senior adviser in Hau Nghia from 1969 to 1971, said, "When we left, after all of those damned years, we couldn't find a squad, we couldn't find four or five people to come up against in a military way. We had all kinds of units and all kinds of conventional power, but it just couldn't be applied in any meaningful way because we had already accomplished our military mission. We had rid the country of overt, organized military opposition."[15] Nguyen Van Thanh, a high-ranking VC commander until he defected, described to Jeffrey Race the Communists' position in Long An by 1970: "[I]t became impossible for concentrated forces to conduct military operations or even to move in groups larger than half a dozen individuals."[16]

With the Communist shield shattered, the territorial forces, PRUs, and other South Vietnamese pacification forces, as well as some main force units, broke into smaller units, which allowed them to operate with greater stealth and to cover more territory. Driven by stronger leaders, in many cases, than previously, they mounted many successful attacks against the smaller groups of Communists with which the illegal cadres now traveled. The report of Kosheleff and Jorgensen states: "The continued acceleration of VCI and Cheiu Hoi rates, even after the discontinuance of large scale US Marine Cordon and Search Operations which strongly supported these programs, verifies to some extent that the enemy main force impotence has exposed the local force and infrastructure to heavy GVN pressure."[17] Before the Tet offensive of 1968, Allied pacification forces that had cleared an area of large Communist forces usually moved on to a different area within a short time, thus allowing the Communists to return in large numbers and reassert control over the hamlets after they had gone. During the subsequent period, the territorial forces often remained in an area long after the Allies had cleared it initially of big Communist units. The territorial forces first established control in a few hamlets, often in those surrounding a town or city or an Allied base, and gradually moved into adjacent hamlets. They spread Allied security like an "oil spot," as Americans often called it. At times, most notably during the Accelerated Pacification Campaign, they disregarded the oil spot concept and moved rapidly into large numbers of disconnected areas. By subjecting the small Communist forces to unrelenting pressure when they tried to visit the hamlets, the territorial forces slowly eroded the Communist presence in most of the populated rural areas.

In early 1970, while serving as the top CORDS officer in IV Corps, John Paul Vann explained the crucial role of the territorial forces to Sen. J. William Fulbright at a congressional hearing:

> [I]n the Delta in 1969 we pacified 1,000 additional hamlets in a 12-month period. Coincidentally, we recruited and trained 1,000 additional RF and PF platoons and put them in those hamlets. They are still there. That also,

> sir, is why, unlike any other pacification program, this one cannot be rolled
> back by sudden political reversal. This is one in which the enemy, if and when
> he begins to react to it—I don't really think he can, but if and when he does—
> can't come in and overrun two or three hamlets and then have the whole
> province or whole series of provinces collapse. He is going to have to eat those
> hamlets up platoon by platoon and this is going to be awfully costly to him.
> This is the great difference now. We occupy those hamlets; the government
> has control there. We are there 24 hours a day. We are staying there and we
> intend to stay there.[18]

The GVN's hamlet and village administrations and the People's Self-
Defense Forces also contributed, to a lesser extent, to the spread of permanent control over the villages. A document concerning the Cao Su district in the VC Ba Ria–Long Khanh province, dated 20 May 1970, recounts
that the enemy "succeeded in reconsolidating his village and hamlet oppressive administrative machineries and exercising a closer control over the people. This impeded and weakened our struggle movement in comparison
with those in other districts."[19]

The Allied main forces destroyed many of the Communists' secret bases
during this period and, in the process, eliminated Communist armed forces
that participated in the village war. The destruction also forced political
cadres and their escorts to commute longer distances between their sanctuaries and operational areas, thus increasing their vulnerability to Allied
operations. The most dramatic success in base destruction occurred in 1970
when Allied forces moved into Cambodia. Until then, the Communists had
been using the Cambodian sanctuary more frequently as Allied pressure
made their existence within South Vietnam increasingly difficult. Whereas
critics in the United States denounced the incursion as an immoral widen-
ing of the war—they ignored the fact that Hanoi had widened the war into
Cambodia long before by using it as a base area—most people in South Vietnam at the time, on both the Communist and the Allied sides, viewed it as
prudent and effective. The Communists, who had been surprised at the
Americans' refusal to enter Cambodia earlier, could not understand the
uproar in the United States; they did not view the action as immoral and
undoubtedly would have done the same had they been in their enemy's
position. Brig. Gen. Stuart Herrington discussed the incursion with former Communist Party village secretary Hai Chua. VCI from Chua's village, which was located in Hau Nghia province, had used Cambodia as a
sanctuary until the Allies moved in. Herrington recalls:

I had always associated the 1970 cross-border operations into Cambodia by American and South Vietnamese troops with the controversy over Cambodian neutrality—or with the tragedy of Kent State. But to Hai Chua and his Vietcong friends, these operations had meant something quite different. The destruction of their Cambodian sanctuary had been disastrous for the Hiep Hoa Vietcong. Overnight, Chua and his comrades had been denied the convenience of their medical facilities, schools, ammunition dumps, and food storage sites. Cambodia (Chua called it *phia sau*, "the rear") had been a place to go to escape the pressures of "the front" *(phia truoc)*. The denial of these facilities had brought home to Chua and his fellow cadre that there was literally "no place to hide" from the increasingly lethal war.[20]

Truong Nhu Tang later acknowledged, "The American bombing and invasion of Cambodia largely accomplished its immediate goals," of which the most important was gaining a year of time for the Allies to strengthen their defenses with minimal Communist interference.[21]

Almost all Allied observers in Vietnam noticed a dramatic security improvement between the Tet and Easter offensives. Even those who were skeptical of Allied security claims because of exaggerated reporting before Tet-68 or HES inaccuracy concluded that Allied control over the countryside had increased tremendously. Allied personnel in a single unescorted Jeep traveled roads that they would have traveled only in a large, heavily armed convoy during the mid-1960s. GVN officials no longer needed entire platoons as armed escorts when they visited the hamlets. Allied forces entered hamlets unopposed that they could have entered previously only at a considerable cost in lives.

The Communists repeatedly acknowledged that the Allies dominated most of the hamlets militarily. "Presently," states a Communist assessment of VC Region 5 in November 1969, "the enemy is oppressing and controlling the people and gathering them along communication lines, around provinces, districts, and bases. He uses large armed forces to hold them, uses spies and local administrative personnel, and sets up more fences, etc. These activities have caused us many difficulties." The assessment also poses the question: "Why could we not control the people although we had made so many efforts and conducted so many fierce attacks against the enemy? Should we continue this way? Certainly not."[22] The captured Communist document outlining the opinions of Gen. Vo Nguyen Giap and other top Communist officials in late 1969 and early 1970 admits, "[The enemy's] urgent pacification plan had good results: From 5,920 hamlets, the number of pacified hamlets has increased to 7,920 hamlets."[23] Given the Communist tendency to understate their difficulties in their documents, the number of "pacified" hamlets probably was even greater. At this time, South Vietnam had roughly 10,600 hamlets.[24]

In a few areas of South Vietnam, the security situation did not show substantial improvement. In most of these areas, the Allies did not make a serious attempt to fight the village war, normally because the area was sparsely populated or because its location made it strategically insignificant. One such area was An Xuyen, the southernmost province. Others included some of the highland provinces and many hinterland areas within the northern coastal provinces. In a few of the more populous districts and provinces, security improved considerably during this period but the Communists retained a stronger military presence than elsewhere. The GVN leaders in some of these areas were mediocre and did not fight as aggressively as they could have; in others, mostly in northern South Vietnam, the Communists kept up their troop strength despite heavy losses by replenishing it with steady streams of North Vietnamese personnel. In a small number of areas, the Allies faced both of these problems. One such area was the densely populated region of South Vietnam that proved most difficult to pacify, the northern section of Binh Dinh province. During 1969 and 1970, the U.S. 173d Airborne Brigade broke down into squads and platoons and attacked the Communists in this area much as the territorial forces normally did. The Americans inflicted considerable casualties on the Communists and seriously weakened Communist control of the countryside. The security situation deteriorated soon after the Americans left, however, because North Vietnamese infiltrators continued to pour in and the GVN leadership in the province became passive. In mid-1971, the province senior adviser reported:

> The enemy has the ability and capability to do almost anything he chooses at any time. Conversely, friendly forces also have the ability and capability to do anything they want at any time they choose, but they do not appear to want to do anything at any time. At the present time there are adequate Vietnamese forces in the Province to handle the situation, but until they receive the necessary command guidance, direction and leadership, the enemy will continue to gain support from the people.[25]

During the initial phase of the Easter offensive, security declined somewhat in many provinces, especially those in I Corps, the highland provinces of II Corps, and Binh Long province. North Vietnamese main force units moved into some of the populated areas, and the GVN had to use pacification forces, as well as the ARVN, to halt the NVA advance. A few provinces fell almost entirely under NVA control, but otherwise the Communists did not capture much populous land, for the South Vietnamese contained most of the NVA thrusts. The fighting continued for several months, during which the GVN's forces, backed by U.S. air power, drove the NVA out of most of the village areas that they had occupied. The level of security returned, more or less, to what it had been before the offensive in many areas but remained slightly lower in others.

During the last months of 1972 and January 1973, the possession of land and hamlets became a crucial issue because the Americans and the North Vietnamese were negotiating a cease-fire, as well as an end to direct U.S. military involvement in the war. Both the Communists and the GVN mounted campaigns to take populous territory from the other, and each enjoyed some marginal successes. The negotiations eventually led to an agreement known as the Paris Peace Accords, and the cease-fire went into effect on 27 January 1973. Before long, both the GVN and the North Vietnamese were violating the cease-fire regularly in order to damage the enemy and to snatch more land and hamlets. During the first year of the cease-fire, the South Vietnamese improved their military position in many of the populated areas where the Communists had possessed some influence. The North Vietnamese often preferred to avoid fighting because they did not wish to anger the United States, and they needed to recover from their failed offensive of the previous year. The Communists tried in vain to revive the VCI and revolutionary warfare in the villages during this period. Gen. Hoang Van Thai, commander of all NVA forces in the South, states in his history of the war's final years: "In just over a month following the signing of the Paris Agreement the enemy made deep inroads into many areas under our control, especially in the vicinity of towns and villages along major routes. All told, they reoccupied almost all the 394 hamlets which had been liberated by us before the signing took place." Thai also notes that at the beginning of 1974, the GVN possessed "a fairly complex defensive system in the countryside which enabled them to control many densely populated areas and mobilize resources and manpower for the war effort."[26] COSVN Resolution 12 of February 1974 states that the enemy "is still in control of densely populated areas and a number of strategic lines of communication," and adds, "Although our liberated areas are large, they are not populous."[27]

In 1974, as the North Vietnamese Army grew stronger, the Communists became increasingly powerful in some villages of the Mekong Delta, but the GVN remained the dominant power in the large majority of the villages in the Delta and elsewhere. A COSVN directive of August 1974 states: "The enemy still has strong points such as a numerically large army and control over populous and rich areas. This thus permits him to continue sweeping off resources and pressing people into his army."[28] Col. William Le Gro, who remained in South Vietnam until the end of the war as the U.S. Army's chief intelligence officer, provides an account of events similar to that given by the Communists: "During the last two years of the war, the South adopted an aggressive defense that strengthened its influence and improved security in the populated regions of the country."[29] From the beginning of 1975 until the GVN's swift collapse in April, the Communists assumed control of some strategically placed villages as they moved toward the towns and cities, but many populous rural areas did not fall until the very end.

Other problems besides cadre losses and Allied security efforts impaired the functioning of the shadow government. Changes in the composition of the VC cadres caused a drop-off in performance. Although the shadow government remained somewhat selective in its choice of cadres and its promotion process, the radical decline in overall cadre strength necessitated that it lower its standards somewhat. The thousands of North Vietnamese who had become shadow government cadres generally functioned less effectively than the Southern cadres. Many South Vietnamese villagers retained their traditional dislike of the North Vietnamese. They were less likely to cooperate with North Vietnamese cadres than with South Vietnamese cadres and more likely to report the former to GVN authorities. The many Northerners who were relatively new to their operational areas lacked the familiarity with their areas and the local residents that had helped the Southern cadres to defend themselves and attack GVN forces. North Vietnamese soldiers in both the NVA and the VC—VC units contained North Vietnamese replacements by the late 1960s—milked the hamlets directly or alongside the cadres and, likewise, did not interact well with the people. John Paul Vann wrote to a friend that the North Vietnamese forces "are nearly as alien in this country as are our U.S. forces and receive only that support and assistance from the population that they are able to coerce through fear."[30]

The shadow government also experienced many problems in obtaining villager assistance because of a general decline in the willingness of villagers to help the VC (see chapter 25). A former district-level cadre, for example, described how the villagers' reluctance affected the shadow government's counterintelligence activities: "During the years of 1962 and 1963, the villagers often called on the [VC] Security cadres and spontaneously reported strangers moving back and forth to them. . . . Now, the people have ceased giving this kind of support to the Front, and become indifferent. This state of things is causing great difficulties for the Security Section."[31] The GVN political apparatus, in addition, recruited, drafted, taxed, obtained intelligence information, and performed counterintelligence tasks more effectively during these years than in previous years, thereby reducing the resources that the Communists could try to take. Chapter 25 discusses the reasons behind this change as well. Villager behavior and the GVN's political successes, to some extent, were the result of the shadow government's predicament. Fewer South Vietnamese wanted to support the VC, in part, because the shadow government was weak and no longer came to their hamlets often enough to enlist their support. The GVN performed its political tasks more efficiently, in part, because it no longer faced as much competition and interference from Communist cadres and armed forces.

Many of the Southern VCI disliked the Northerners as much as the ordinary villagers did. That the Northerners were taking over more and more of the leadership positions within the Southern Communist movement spawned the most resentment. Friction between Northern and Southern cadres damaged not only morale within the shadow government but also inhibited cooperation among its members. A COSVN-level communications officer, who defected shortly after the January 1973 cease-fire because his wife had died under VC care during childbirth, told Frank Snepp of the animosity between the North and South Vietnamese. "This guy said that politically the VC were defunct," Snepp recalled. "More and more Northerners were showing up, and as a result there was tremendous dissension in the ranks." Snepp added that the Allies sought to take advantage of the discord by luring the Southern Party organs themselves away from the North, but with little success, probably because the cadres sent down from the North had a tight grip over them. The Allies tried in vain, for instance, to proselytize the Saigon Party Committee.[32]

The spread of distrust within the Communist ranks constituted another by-product of the war against the VCI. This little-known phenomenon weakened the shadow government significantly. Because the Allies often received information from sources in or close to the VC as the pacification effort improved, cadres feared that their colleagues might betray them. As mentioned in chapter 14, the Allies sometimes planted seeds of suspicion about the loyalties of individuals through tricks or rumors. In addition, as thousands of cadres and other VC rallied, each rallier's former VC comrades and his or her relatives still within the VC came under suspicion. According to Donald Colin, the most damaging aspect of a rallier's defection was that "everyone with whom he has come into contact will be tarred with the suspicious brush of association with a traitor."[33] Because the members of the shadow government so often suspected one another of collusion with the enemy, they could not cooperate with each other as easily as they once had.

Suspicion also forced the shadow government to alter its behavior directly. When someone rallied or was arrested, the illegal VCI often relocated their bases, rotated their personnel, or operated less frequently in their villages out of fear that the rallier had divulged their hiding places and routes of travel to the Allies. Legal cadres often had to flee their operational areas when Communists who knew them rallied, thus blowing their covers. Mistrust of released prisoners and ralliers deterred the shadow government from reintegrating these individuals into the VC. Suspecting all released prisoners of collaboration with the enemy, the VCI either refused to allow them reentry into the VC or assigned them jobs of minimal significance for a long probationary period, during which they had minimal access to important information. According to a MACV report, a cadre who defected in 1970 asserted that "Hoi Chanhs [ralliers] and released GVN detainees were kept under close observation for several years before being entrusted with any but low-level VC support tasks."[34] Communist Party members, unlike many American critics of GVN prisons, believed that the GVN prison system caused inmates to side with the GVN more often than the Communists.

The VC's numerous defeats and problems during the late 1960s and early 1970s caused a decline in morale within the shadow government that further reduced its effectiveness. A typical Communist report, written in the northern part of the country during 1969, reads, "A number of personnel showed a tendency to respond to the enemy pacification program (especially in Area K). They were not eager to do their tasks, attend meetings regularly, or participate in Party activities. They also spoke at random, lacked a sense of responsibility and organization, did not strictly execute orders, had little will to fight, and feared hardship."[35]

23 The Shadow Government in Decline

Because of the shadow government's permanent personnel losses and its other problems from 1968 to the end of the Vietnam War, it failed to maintain its previous levels of activity. Many sources indicate that, nationwide, the shadow government did not perform its key tasks nearly as frequently or effectively as it had in the past, with the exception of the kidnapping and killing of civilians and GVN officials. As a result of the shadow government's decline, the nature of the war in South Vietnam underwent a dramatic transformation.

During 1967 and early 1968, the shadow government recruited and conscripted slightly fewer people in South Vietnam than the VC lost. From mid-1968 to the end of 1969, the shadow government's personnel acquisition decreased drastically. From 1969 to the war's end in 1975, the VCI recruited and conscripted at rates far lower than previous rates. COSVN Resolution 9 acknowledges that "the replenishment of forces, especially for units at region level and even for many provincial units, is still beset with prolonged difficulties."[1] A COSVN directive dated August 1974, not long before the war's end, affirmed that one of a "number of shortcomings and weaknesses adversely affecting our gains" is "the slow building-up of our forces that failed to meet the requirements."[2]

Recruitment problems combined with heavy losses shrank the Southern Communists so much that, by the early 1970s, they became a small and weak adjunct to the mass of Northerners who ran the war for Hanoi in South Vietnam. In addition to maintaining a large NVA presence in the South and installing Northern cadres into the shadow government, Hanoi was filling many vacant positions in VC military units with Northerners. In so doing, it helped to sustain the popular belief in the West that the Southern Communists were strong and largely autonomous. By the Easter offensive, most political and military elements of the VC contained few Southerners. Mai Thi Trang was one of several COSVN-level cadres who defected in early 1972 after COSVN issued Resolution 20, which acknowledged that the Communists were recruiting and conscripting few people in South

Vietnam by that time. She gave her debriefers additional information that confirmed the resolution's conclusions. Orrin DeForest, who talked with her at length, recounts:

> As a high-ranking political officer, Mai Thi Trang knew the truth behind COSVN 20 firsthand, province by province. Recruitment problems had grown to disastrous proportions. Those who understood what was happening believed that the relentless pressure from the Americans and the South Vietnamese had finally crushed the Vietcong. There were only about a dozen or two main-force battalions wandering around out there, where there used to be 150. Units that hadn't received substantial reinforcement from the North were so far down they were barely functional. . . . The NVA was taking over everything. The Vietcong—the Southern revolutionary forces that had borne the brunt of this war since the beginning—was history.[3]

The shadow government experienced similar difficulties in collecting agricultural and monetary taxes from the villagers. During 1967 and the first half of 1968, Communist taxation fell well short of the desired results, which caused serious food shortages in some areas. From the middle of 1968 onward, taxation declined sharply and food shortages became far more acute for the Communists in many places. The deputy chief of a village finance and economy section in Hau Nghia province, for example, described the decline after Tet-68:

> The taxation situation had deteriorated tremendously. . . . We had promised to topple the puppet government with the General Offensive and had collected extremely heavy taxes on the basis of this pledge. In 1969, when I attempted to tax again, the people were angry about this. This attitude, combined with the decimation of our cadre and the enemy build-up, resulted in a great drop in taxes collected. From January to October 1969, we were only able to collect 300,000$ in all of Hiep Hoa as compared to 1,700,000$ in 1968.[4]

Assessing the overall Communist achievements in intelligence gathering is more difficult. Hanoi employed highly secretive intelligence networks that operated independently of, and spied on, the Southern Party structure, which makes it harder to find concrete evidence concerning these networks. Their acquisition of intelligence did not diminish during the late 1960s and early 1970s as much as did their acquisition of other resources because the war against the VCI did not obstruct intelligence collection to the same extent; intelligence collection did not require overt group activities that Allied pacification forces could thwart by military means. The Communists continued to receive some accurate intelligence reports from their legal cadres, as well as from informants and agents in much of South Vietnam.

Captured documents and other sources, nevertheless, indicate that the Communists did not collect intelligence information in the villages or in GVN organizations as effectively on the whole as they had before. The loss of cadres, the reluctance of the people to help the VC, improved Allied counterintelligence, and the increased difficulty of contacting informants and agents all weakened intelligence gathering. A Communist document from northern South Vietnam, for example, lays out in considerable detail VC failures in intelligence collection during the first part of 1969. "In brief, our investigation task is incomplete and improperly prepared," it reads. "We lack a systematic organization and are only feeling our way through the situation. We failed to meet the requirements of the situation and could not effectively cope with the enemy's cunning schemes and stratagems."[5] It lists many weaknesses:

> Cadre specialized in investigating the enemy situation were too few in nearly all local areas.... The number of agents who are operating in different enemy organizations was either too small or nonexistent in some areas.... The recruitment of agents in some areas was made by means of the relationship between friends and families or among the hired laborers (in the 2nd Precinct). For this reason, most agents could not perform their tasks well.... Higher echelon agents and agents who have frequently contacted the enemy and operate in controlled areas, though existing, are few in number. Our activities were thus affected, and we failed to collect much information on the enemy's situation.... The maintenance of secrecy with regard to agents was poor. We have not yet corrected this situation. Cadres were interested in discussing the tasks assigned to other agents (especially liaison agents). For this reason, whenever an agent was detected or captured, we were forced to withdraw a number of agents who were operating (in the same area).... Most [agents] stayed in the outer perimeter of the enemy's position. They dared not make a deep penetration into the enemy's area to collect intelligence information and seize documents. For that reason, we failed to deal the enemy deadly blows to create a repercussion in cities and towns.[6]

A 1971 VC document from a district in the Mekong Delta states, "Development of our forces in weak and enemy controlled areas was poor. Our agents operating in these areas were numerous. We could not contact them and stay close to the people in order to initiate struggle movements. Almost all of the people living in base areas were illegal agents. However, their activities were still sporadic and sluggish. This was a main weak point of our Party headquarters.... At present time, agents operating in weak and enemy controlled areas are very few."[7]

On the whole, the decline of the Viet Cong shadow government during the late 1960s caused serious problems for the Communist war effort. The great reduction in Communist recruitment and conscription in South Vietnam and the consequent shrinkage of the Southern Communists decreased Hanoi's military capabilities in South Vietnam. After Tet-68, the Hanoi regime could not infiltrate the South with enough North Vietnamese for the Communist forces to maintain previous strength levels. The disappearance of Southerners from the Communist forces also promoted a certain amount of unity among the Southerners now serving in or supporting the GVN, which by this time meant most of the South Vietnamese population. Given the importance of personnel, especially indigenous personnel, to the Communist military effort, the shadow government's inability to bring more South Vietnamese into the VC's ranks represented the most serious blow that pacification dealt to the Communist Party.

The VCI's recruiting difficulties, as mentioned briefly in chapter 22, also helped the GVN to bring most of South Vietnam's young men into its main forces, territorial forces, and other organizations. The ARVN's expansion and improvement permitted the withdrawal of American and other foreign Allied troops. This development, in turn, diminished Hanoi's ability to motivate its troops by demonizing their Caucasian and other non-Vietnamese adversaries and bolstered the GVN's ability to convince the ethnocentric South Vietnamese that it was not dependent on foreigners.

The VCI's decreased taxation and weakened logistical system limited the number and scale of Communist military operations. In some cases, these deficiencies forced Communist military personnel to perform the shadow government's duties instead of participating in military operations. Certain Communist units devoted all of their time to obtaining food or transporting supplies; in some areas all of the Communist main force units at various times focused solely on these tasks. In order to perform these duties, the diverted troops had to move into populated areas, where the Allies had more forces and intelligence sources than elsewhere and thus could find and attack them more easily. The Communist main forces, in addition, had to rely more heavily on supplies transported from North Vietnam and Cambodia by porters who otherwise would have been fighting. U.S. aircraft destroyed many of the porters and their loads on their way to the war zone.

The decrease in the shadow government's ability to provide intelligence and guides to the Communist units and to eliminate Allied spies also caused considerable difficulties. Without these aids, the North Vietnamese soldiers walked into ambushes and came under air and artillery attack much more frequently, and found hiding places less easily. John Mullins said, "At one point we had enough of the VC infrastructure in Thua Thien policed up that a fresh North Vietnamese battalion came down through the Ho Chi Minh Trail and into the province and was lost for eighteen days, wandering. They had no idea where the hell they were, until they finally ran into the 101st Airborne Division. All the trail watchers were gone."[8] Although the Communists maintained an impressive number of spies throughout the war, the VC's intelligence was not valuable enough to play a major role in the GVN's downfall. GVN forces regularly inflicted heavy losses on their foes from 1968 to 1974 in spite of the Communist Party's intelligence system.

The weakness of the shadow government and Allied success in pacification, by themselves, could not prevent Hanoi from winning the war. During the last years of the conflict, the North Vietnamese pursued a strategy that would allow them to defeat the GVN regardless of the shadow government's performance. The failure of the 1968 Tet offensive and another general offensive during 1969 had led to considerable disagreement among North Vietnamese leaders over future strategy. By 1971, if not earlier, however, the deciding authorities in Hanoi had put an end to the dispute and chosen to employ NVA main force warfare in an effort to take the towns and cities—and thus defeat the GVN—as soon as possible. They would not deviate from this strategy for the rest of the war.

Since mid-1965, when U.S. military units had foiled the attempt of Communist main force units to finish off the GVN, the presence of U.S. units had prevented the Communist main forces from seizing and holding the towns and cities. U.S. ground forces were downsizing during 1969 and the early 1970s, and almost all of them had left Vietnam by 1972, although American airpower remained until 1973. Once the North Vietnamese military planners saw that the U.S. forces were leaving for good, they knew that their prospects for main force victory had improved tremendously; the ability of South Vietnam to defend itself from the NVA main force units after the U.S. withdrawal would depend on the performance of the ARVN, which had progressed from a poor army only to a mediocre one. The North Vietnamese leaders illustrated their linkage of U.S. withdrawal to ultimate victory when they discussed the matter among themselves in late 1969: "[The enemy's] failures are due to the political situation in the United States, and not to our strong attacks. . . . We can say that the enemy has been defeated. He has begun to withdraw his troops. . . . Will the Puppet Government be able to replace the Americans? Reality shows they cannot."[9]

Hanoi's strategy emphasized reliance on the NVA because the North Vietnamese ruling clique had concluded that efforts to mobilize South Vietnam's villagers via the shadow government could not, in the near future, provide Communist main force units with enough recruits and conscripts to conquer South Vietnam's coveted towns and cities. They wanted to win quickly because they feared that circumstances would change and decrease their chances for a main force victory. The decline of the VCI, therefore, played an important role in the decision to focus on large main force offensives.

The inferior capabilities of the VCI and the other VC involved in the village war had little effect on the outcome of the NVA's main force offensives once an offensive began. NVA units could race through the countryside to reach the towns and cities with little interference from most of the GVN pacification forces, who had grown strong in the villages as the VC had grown weak. The small, lightly armed pacification troops, no matter how competent they were, never stood a chance of stopping the large main force units. The only aspects of the VCI's deterioration that had a significant, immediate impact on the advancing NVA were the decreases in the shadow government's intelligence and counterintelligence capabilities, factors of considerable importance only when GVN main force units were operating in the area and could exploit the intelligence. The war against the VCI, nevertheless, had a strong impact on the conditions under which the Communists launched their offensives. The Communists' shortage of rural South Vietnamese personnel, the GVN's large-scale use of the South Vietnamese villagers, and Communist logistical weaknesses that resulted from the war against the VCI all gave the GVN's main forces important advantages that put them in a better position when the time came for main force warfare.

Some NVA and VC units, in conjunction with the remaining shadow government cadres, continued to operate as guerrillas in the village areas during the last years of the war. They did so, however, only because such tactics kept their casualties low and forced the GVN to disperse its forces, thus rendering the GVN more vulnerable to large main force attacks. The pacification forces could not weaken the Communist forces seriously by attacking these guerrillas and cadres. Some commentators fault the GVN for paying too much attention to the Communist guerrillas and cadres during this period. The GVN's efforts to dominate the village areas by maintaining large numbers of Regional Forces and Popular Forces, they contend, actually diminished its chances to win the main force battles and thus the war as a whole. The territorial forces officially numbered 520,000 in 1972, whereas the personnel of the South Vietnamese Army and Marines together numbered 425,000.[10] Because Hanoi's main forces posed a much more serious threat to South Vietnam than the small Communist forces in the villages, the critics assert, Saigon should have transferred some members of its territorial forces to main force units. This criticism, in reality, is unjustified. The GVN formed many of the Regional Forces into regiment-sized units to serve as main force units when necessary. These units frequently fought the Communist main forces as effectively as some ARVN units, if not more so, because many province chiefs surpassed ARVN commanders in leadership ability and the territorial forces knew their operational areas better than ARVN units did. They did not always have the necessary firepower and mobility, but poor logistics caused that problem, not the fact that they were Regional Forces. They could have faced similar logistical difficulties had they been ARVN units. Nor, as chapter 26 explains, were personnel shortages among the most serious problems of the GVN's main forces.

A number of historians have asserted that the war against the VCI hurt the Allied chances for defeating the Communist main force offensives in a different way. They claim that it helped turn American public opinion against the war, which led to U.S. troop withdrawals and reduced U.S. aid to the South Vietnamese main forces. John Prados, for example, contends, "The fact that Phoenix *was* politically controversial in the United States further reduced U.S. freedom of action in pursuing the war."[11] This allegation is also inaccurate. The outcry against "Phoenix atrocities" did not surface until after congressional hearings on pacification in August 1971. By 1971, most Americans already had decided what they thought about the war in Vietnam and did not change their opinions substantially. Many have not altered their views to this day. The only factors, by this time, that continued to change public opinion to any significant extent were despair over the growing U.S. casualty lists in light of Hanoi's persistence in fighting and doubts about the importance of the Vietnam War to American national interests. By this time, too, the United States had already withdrawn most of its troops and was preparing to remove the rest as part of the Vietnamization program.

The Communist drive for large main force triumphs began on 30 March 1972 with the Easter offensive. The Communists did not expect to conquer all of South Vietnam's towns and cities with their first large offensive. Rather, they hoped to achieve more limited objectives, such as capturing territory or provincial capitals, embarrassing President Nixon and thereby hurting his chances for reelection, and improving their bargaining position at future negotiations with the United States. Hanoi mustered 125,000 troops, almost all of them Northerners, for the ill-fated offensive. Thanks to the generosity of the Soviets and the intricate logistical network linking North Vietnam to South Vietnam, the North Vietnamese also employed hundreds of tanks and an impressive array of artillery pieces and missiles. The Communist units invaded South Vietnam in each of the corps areas, although their attack in IV Corps was considerably smaller than those in the other areas.

The Easter offensive featured large assaults by Communist infantry and armor, the sort of attacks that the Americans had envisioned when they set up the ARVN in the 1950s. Within the offensive's first month, Hanoi's forces in I Corps captured Quang Tri City, the capital of Quang Tri province. In II Corps, they seized much of Binh Dinh province and threatened Kontum City, the capital of Kontum. In III Corps, they laid siege to An Loc, the capital of Binh Long province. The majority of ARVN units did not fight as tenaciously as their North Vietnamese opponents during the first month, and some performed quite poorly. American airpower, however, gave them a large advantage, which allowed them to prevent further NVA encroachment. Thieu subsequently replaced some of his less effective generals, thereby improving the performance of some ARVN units considerably. These units and elite South Vietnamese units, with the assistance of U.S. airpower, eventually drove the invaders out of Quang Tri City, turned back the Communists at Binh Dinh and Kontum, and broke the siege at An Loc. The Allies pummelled the NVA units badly until they abandoned hope for any sort of victory and retreated into the wilderness.

Because the Easter offensive was closely contested, the advantages that the war against the VC shadow government conferred on the GVN's main forces did contribute meaningfully, perhaps decisively, to the GVN's victory. These advantages, however, were not powerful enough to play a role in determining the victor of the Communists' 1975 offensive, although they did make victory more difficult for the Communists. They could not prevent the ARVN, weakened for reasons unrelated to the village war, from succumbing to this massive and well-equipped North Vietnamese onslaught. The North Vietnamese tore through the countryside and took the towns and cities, where the GVN had concentrated most of its main forces and its leaders, and then quite easily mopped up the remaining resistance in most parts of the countryside. Had the ARVN been stronger in 1975, the war against the shadow government would have deserved some of the credit for giving the South Vietnamese at least a chance to fight on decent terms. Fortune, however, did not grant the South Vietnamese Army such strength.

PART SIX: Villager Attitudes

24   Abuse of the Population

prominent Vietnamese professor once suggested to me that I investigate the extent to which the attack on the VCI alienated the villagers of South Vietnam. Quite possibly, the professor said, the abuses of the attack on the VCI made the rural population unwilling to cooperate with the GVN and thus prevented the Saigon regime from building the support it needed to fight the North Vietnamese. After I began looking into the matter, I realized that little evidence exists concerning the attitudes of the villagers toward the attack on the shadow government. Although the large majority of villagers did not understand what Phoenix or Phung Hoang were, their ignorance makes little difference because the people who might have alienated the villagers served in other organizations involved in the attack on the VCI. Most villagers certainly knew the difference between various types of police and military forces. Yet, the hamlet residents whose complaints about the behavior of Allied forces were recorded during this time frequently did not single out particular organizations. Information concerning the villagers' opinions of certain parts of the attack on the VCI, therefore, does not suffice to permit generalization.[1]

Because villager testimony that directly addresses the attack on the VCI or all of its components cannot reveal the general thoughts of the populace, answering the question as accurately as possible calls for two indirect modes of inquiry. The first, discussed in this chapter, involves an analysis of the extent to which the components of the attack on the VCI and other Allied military activities treated villagers in ways that might have alienated them. It covers all types of abuse in order to put those of the attack on the VCI into perspective. A considerable amount of information relevant to this analysis is available. The second investigation, described in chapter 25, involves an examination of the villagers' attitudes toward the total abuse they received from the Allies and toward the war in general. I then use the results of these inquiries to determine the villagers' opinions about the attack on the VCI.

Previous chapters discuss many of the Allied activities that might have caused villagers to dislike the GVN. The Allies arrested tens of thousands, if not hundreds of thousands, of villagers each year. Some of the detainees did not support the VC in any way or supported them only when the VC coerced them. Of those undeservedly detained, a fair number suffered beatings or other forms of physical abuse. The large majority of these prisoners, however, did not remain in custody for more than a couple of days, and most of the others against whom little incriminating evidence existed spent only a few weeks or months in prison. The frequency of these abuses and errors varied considerably from province to province and depended on the GVN leaders and the status of the war in each province.

Government forces also abused the villagers in ways not directly related to their official duties. They often took food and other objects of value from villagers, primarily from pro-VC families. "Our soldiers only got enough money to feed their families," Brig. Gen. Tran Van Nhut told me. "When they went fighting they needed more food, so sometimes soldiers took food from a village. You could not control it all the time, but sometimes we put the people who did that in jail."[2] Hungry soldiers were not the only culprits; even members of well-fed units, such as the PRUs, stole chickens and other items from villagers. "The PRUs weren't angels," Col. Viet Lang said, "but the Americans paid them well, so they weren't as bad as the ARVN troops."[3]

Less often, the GVN's armed men beat or raped villagers. HES data from the late 1960s, for instance, show that the ARVN and territorial forces committed major and minor acts—most of them minor—that harmed the population in approximately 42 percent of all hamlets each year.[4] Some units consistently committed serious offenses, whereas others seldom did. South Vietnamese units not drawn from a local area were more likely than indigenous units to perpetrate crimes in that area. Racial minorities received particularly poor treatment at the hands of ethnic South Vietnamese units. The most important determinant of a unit's behavior toward the populace, however, was the quality of its leadership. American advisers normally did not prevent the abuse of villagers, for most of the same reasons that they did not keep their counterparts from torturing prisoners.

Generally, American soldiers displayed more restraint than the South Vietnamese in dealing with unarmed villagers under nonthreatening circumstances. Many adherents of the American antiwar movement, as well as most of Hanoi's own propagandists, claimed that U.S. troops regularly raped and killed ordinary villagers, but the evidence does not bear out this conclusion. Numerous U.S. infantry veterans who had served in other wars or who advised South Vietnamese units have told me, as well as other historians, that U.S. soldiers sexually abused village women no more frequently than soldiers generally do in such a war and less often than South Vietnamese soldiers did. Most of these former infantrymen have asserted that murder and torture of villagers seldom occurred. Eric Bergerud, in a history of the 25th Division that ranks as one of the most thorough and accurate studies of American soldiers in the war, concludes, "Although the atmosphere in rural Vietnam was tense, dangerous, and ugly, there is no evidence of willful murder of civilians by 25th Division soldiers. It is very possible, even likely, that murders took place. Yet, they were almost certainly rare. Many veterans are outraged by the image that still exists in some quarters today of the American soldier as an indiscriminate killer."[5]

American troops, however, mistreated the South Vietnamese peasants fairly often in less harsh ways. The most frequent offenses included shooting farm animals, pushing around villagers, and running villagers off the road with large vehicles. The frustration of losing buddies near the hamlets caused many American soldiers to use the villagers as scapegoats. Another crucial reason for the abuses was the presence of many enlisted men and officers poorly suited to participation in such a war. Many enlisted personnel in Vietnam had scored lower on intelligence tests than had American soldiers of previous eras; a program called "Project 100,000," instituted during the mid-1960s to help the poor, had lowered the test scores needed to enter the military. The enlisted ranks also contained substantial numbers of young men who came from broken families and had weak educational backgrounds. Many individuals with such abilities and backgrounds, it should be noted, behaved properly toward the populace, whereas many other Americans did not. According to U.S. government reports, nevertheless, these people were less likely, on average, than others to obey basic rules of warfare or to interact tactfully with the South Vietnamese villagers.[6] A significant fraction of America's bright, well-educated young males avoided serving in Vietnam, and many of them, at the time, condemned U.S. soldiers in Vietnam for mistreating civilians. Their refusal to join the armed services forced the military to send to Vietnam not only enlisted men more likely to misbehave, but also—by limiting the number of officer candidates—officers more likely to tolerate misbehavior.

Far worse than the American troops in their handling of civilians, and worse even than most ARVN troops, were the members of the South Korean armed forces. They were less numerous than the American and South Vietnamese troops and operated primarily in selected parts of I Corps and II Corps, but tales of their penchant for wanton violence and destruction reached all corners of the country. A 1968 CORDS report on the ROK (Republic of Korea) 2d Marine Brigade describes some of their typical exploits:

> [A]ctions harmful to pacification include ROK atrocities earlier this year against over 80 women and children (many belonging to families of PF soldiers) in a hamlet in Dien Ban District from which they had taken sniper fire; ROK capture, multiple-raping, beating, and severing of the arm of a woman caught carrying VC letters; the ROK reputation among people working in their fields of shooting first and asking questions later; and, the general attitude of the ROK Marines toward the Vietnamese people.[7]

GVN personnel engaged in a wide range of activities that Americans would call corrupt involving aspects of their jobs besides the attack on the VCI. For example, they imposed their own "taxes" on local businesses, formed their own businesses and shut down any potential competition, sold materials that the Americans had given to the GVN for free distribution to villagers, took kickbacks from contractors, and skimmed off some of the pay of their subordinates. The hamlet populations usually accepted such activities, when practiced in moderation, as a normal part of life. They did not view them as corrupt. Many servants of the GVN, however, did not always keep their self-gratification at a moderate level. U.S. advisers did little to correct the endemic corruption because American leaders prevented them from doing so, on the grounds that fighting this problem would seriously damage relations with the GVN.

Rob Simmons was not as quick to condemn GVN officials for corruption as some Americans were, but he too believed that certain GVN officials exceeded the accepted limits. Simmons recalled,

> I submitted a couple of reports out of my province on GVN corruption that got as far as our regional headquarters in Nha Trang. I was given the word through message traffic that this was all very nice but it wasn't being sent on to Saigon— it was being filed at Nha Trang—and that I didn't need to go out of my way to get this stuff because there wasn't a big requirement for it. Basically, the U.S. policy was, "We are not going to address the issue of corruption in this government, because we have other problems that we have to deal with, and we have to maintain some sort of relationship with our counterparts. To write about corruption would disrupt those relationships, so it's not an issue to report on."[8]

Corruption, it should be noted, was less widespread after the Tet offensive than before because of the general improvements of the GVN leadership. Although many strong leaders did engage in corruption, they tended to do it on a smaller scale than did weak leaders. Either their efforts to fight the Communists left them little time for corruption, or their sense of dedication to the cause restrained them.

A relatively small number of civilian bystanders suffered injury or death during combat between Allied pacification forces and small Communist forces. The combatants normally used only small arms, which limited the amount of extraneous violence that these engagements could produce. The territorial forces, serving as they did in their native areas, could and did discriminate carefully when choosing their targets. The PRUs and other able pacification forces, in addition, usually had their most violent encounters with the Communists at night on the outskirts of hamlets or between hamlets, areas that curfew-conscious civilians generally avoided. A much larger number of villagers fell victim to Allied small-arms fire because the Communists forced villagers to accompany Communist armed forces as laborers. Most of the damage and killing that the Allies brought down on the rural population, however, resulted from the use of heavy weapons in and around the hamlets. Artillery, helicopters, airplanes, and heavy ground weapons inevitably wounded or killed bystanders and destroyed their property during engagements in the populated rural areas. In a few cases, most of them involving South Vietnamese or South Korean forces, the Allies used heavy firepower without having evidence of a Communist presence, in order to avoid conducting reconnaissance or to harass the villagers. Most of the time, however, a village area endured the use of such weapons only when the Allies knew that Communist forces occupied it. Because much misinformation has clouded the American public's perception of high-intensity combat in the villages, it deserves clarification.

To restrict the use of firepower in the interest of minimizing civilian casualties, the U.S. Army issued a famous set of rules of engagement (ROE). These conformed to most standard interpretations of the "rules of war," but the realities and necessities of the Vietnam War ensured that the Allies could not avoid destroying a great many hamlets even if they followed the ROE. The ROE required that soldiers warn the residents of a hamlet before they opened fire on it when they had not received fire from the hamlet but suspected an enemy presence there. Commanders could fire without warning, however, if a warning might jeopardize a mission. Because warnings typically gave Communist forces additional time to prepare defenses or to flee, commanders sometimes took advantage of this exception and did not issue warnings. Officers calling for air or artillery strikes in populated areas had to obtain clearances from higher-ranking Americans and South Vietnamese, except in special zones from which civilians had been cleared. Other rules included a prohibition against helicopters and airplanes firing at targets that the crews had not identified visually. Some officers did not obey these rules because of the risks inherent in obeying them, or because they did not know all of the rules and relied mainly on common sense. Sometimes, too, officers failed to control trigger-happy subordinates.

Countless critics of the U.S. military involvement in Vietnam accuse U.S. forces of employing heavy firepower near the villages without restraint. In reality, American forces often displayed a considerable amount of restraint when firing into village areas, especially when the chances of harming bystanders exceeded the chances of harming the enemy. In some cases, U.S. military field commanders demanded and enforced strict adherence to the ROE or put other restrictions on the use of firepower. Higher authorities often denied requests for air and artillery strikes. The common sense of the soldier behind the trigger also inhibited wanton use of massive firepower. The Communists, after all, would not have moved into the hamlets so often had they not benefited from such restraint. Donald Pearce, a CORDS adviser in the Cu Chi district of Hau Nghia, explained, "The VC were very smart. They moved in and around inhabited areas as shown on the map and used them as staging areas because they knew that U.S. artillery would not fire on them. I let more VC go free and observed them moving across country than I ever killed with artillery fire."9 South Vietnamese and Korean commanders, by contrast, generally did not care as much about hurting civilians and therefore limited their fire for the sake of civilian bystanders less often. The American advisers to some South Vietnamese units, however, restricted their use of heavy weaponry.

The decision of whether to fire on enemy forces in a GVN-held or a contested hamlet called for a careful assessment of the consequences for pacification and military objectives. If the enemy consisted of a significant number of main force troops, a commander who wanted to achieve the best military ends normally had to employ heavy firepower to kill them. The Allied main forces that fired into hamlets from the mid-1960s on usually operated in areas where the Communists possessed substantial main force strength, not just a few guerrillas, a fact that critics of American firepower usage generally ignore. The main forces normally left areas where Communist forces were not so strong to troops of the pacification forces or to main force soldiers operating in a pacification role, both of whom employed heavy firepower much less often. Without heavy firepower, the Allied infantry faced a good chance of suffering horrendous casualties at the hands of heavily armed Communist forces in these areas. As indicated in chapter 14, even the extraordinarily competent PRUs avoided operating where the Communists had sizable military forces because they lacked the necessary air and artillery support. The Communists inside the hamlets often enjoyed key military advantages. They frequently fought from bunkers, trenches, or tunnels, which gave them particularly good chances of inflicting heavy losses on infantrymen who assaulted their positions. Where open fields surrounded a hamlet, attacking ground forces lacked the necessary cover. If water or mud surrounded a hamlet, they could not move quickly enough for an effective assault. In addition, the concealment of Communist positions made estimating enemy strength a difficult task. In areas of heavy main force activity, it was usually safest to assume that the enemy forces in a hamlet were large and well armed and to use heavy weapons against them. Given the American commanders' concern for their soldiers and their desire to minimize casualties in order to maintain U.S. public support, along with the relative indifference of many South Vietnamese and South Korean commanders toward civilian casualties, few were willing to mount costly ground assaults on occupied hamlets.

Additional military considerations called for the use of heavy weapons in the village areas. Had the Allies avoided firing on the Communists whenever they occupied hamlets or moved through villages, the Communists could have milked the peasants' resources and maneuvered in those villages without having to worry about enemy interference. When traveling through the countryside, they could have dodged most Allied attacks by retreating into hamlets as soon as they came under fire. Communist forces located in hamlets could have attacked Allied forces passing by without fear of major counterattacks. From hamlets along major roads, they could have fired on Allied vehicles at will. Allied reluctance to use firepower in populated areas also would have invited the Communists to attempt the occupation of towns and cities.

Some critics of Allied reliance on heavy firepower contend that Allied forces should have surrounded Communist-occupied hamlets and waited for the Communist main forces to emerge. Allied forces could not have afforded to implement such a policy. The Communist forces would have escaped through tunnels or, if the cordon was too tight, simply waited out the Allies indefinitely. The Communists would have tied down an inordinate number of Allied troops by putting soldiers in hamlets all over the country, and the Allies would have needed additional troops to supply those surrounding the hamlets. The Communist forces not sitting in hamlets would have launched concentrated attacks on the waiting Allied troops and ambushed their supply troops.

Many U.S. and South Vietnamese officers and most South Korean officers used, or sought authorization to use, heavy firepower against any Communist main forces found in the village areas. These officers wanted to maximize Communist casualties and, in some cases, to drive civilians out of the hamlets. They tended to believe that the ROE unnecessarily restricted the use of force, although they did not advocate immensely destructive actions, such as the use of B-52 bombers near the hamlets. Other Allied commanders, by contrast, opposed most uses of heavy firepower in the villages. They thought that the destruction would turn the villagers against the Allies and also harm the Allied publicity effort. Still others favored a strict adherence to the ROE, which put them in a position somewhere between these two extremes.

The most perceptive commanders, however, generally were those who believed that determining the most appropriate course of action required a more thorough examination of the situation at hand. In contrast to some of their colleagues, they realized that firing into contested or pro-GVN villages could, on the whole, hurt the Allied cause, but that firing into pro-VC villages could not. These commanders knew that use of heavy firepower in GVN or contested villages might compel villagers to flee, thereby preventing the GVN from obtaining food, intelligence information, and other resources from them. They also knew that the use of heavy weapons in VC villages usually induced villagers to help the VC less or to flee to GVN areas and stop helping them altogether. A wise commander, therefore, would try to weigh the resources in the countryside that he likely would sacrifice against the military advantages that he likely would gain before firing on enemy main forces in friendly or contested villages, but he would not hesitate to fire on them in VC-controlled villages.

Many members of the American antiwar movement view the Allied use of heavy firepower in the populated rural areas as the most immoral of all Allied actions during the war. The Allies, according to most of the critics, deserve the blame for the damage that their weapons inflicted on South Vietnamese civilians and their property simply because the Allies chose to use those weapons. Some antiwar spokesmen go on to argue that the Allies made the situation worse by failing to provide adequate care for all of the refugees generated by the destruction. Yet this logic is hardly compelling. Stronger is the argument that most of the responsibility for the destruction caused by Allied firepower and any related indictments of immorality belong to the Communists.

Armed Communists chose to launch military attacks from hamlets and take refuge in them when the Allies attacked, thereby drawing fire on the hamlets. Many of them chose to dress in civilian clothing so that Allied troops had difficulty in telling soldier from civilian. On many occasions, they deliberately tried to draw fire on hamlets, especially GVN hamlets, by firing at the Allies and then fleeing before the destruction began. International rules of warfare, as established by the Geneva conventions and similar bodies, forbid all of these practices because of the obvious risks that they create for civilians. The 1949 Geneva Convention states that fighters must carry arms openly and have "a fixed distinctive sign recognizable at a distance," and that "the presence of a protected person may not be used to render certain points or areas immune from military operations."[10] By contrast, the Allies' heavy bombardment of enemy soldiers in populated areas did not violate standard international law, as established by the Geneva conventions, regardless of whether the civilians supported those soldiers. The framers of this legal code apparently understood that restricting a belligerent's use of weapons when its enemy used civilians as cover handicapped that belligerent too severely and encouraged the use of civilians for this purpose. In addition, the Communists did not try to give medical care to villagers displaced by the fighting, feed them, or help them to establish a new life elsewhere, whereas the Allies devoted considerable, if not always sufficient, resources to such efforts.

Other adherents of the antiwar movement contend that the Viet Cong enjoyed much more popularity than the GVN, and thus had the right to use whatever methods they needed to win regardless of any rules of warfare, but that the GVN did not have the right to break the rules. Some even assert that the GVN did not have the right to try to win, not only because the VC were so popular but also because this popularity forced the GVN to fight in a way that killed large numbers of civilians and offered no hope of victory unless it reached the point of genocide. Michael Walzer, an influential moral theorist, claims that once "the [VC] guerrillas consolidated their political base in the villages," the GVN faced a situation in which "[t]he war cannot be won, and it should not be won. It cannot be won, because the only available strategy involves a war against civilians; and it should not be won, because the degree of civilian support that rules out alternative strategies also makes the guerrillas the legitimate rulers of the country."[11]

The two preceding arguments contain five serious flaws. First, as chapter 25 indicates, the relative popularity of the two sides in the hamlets was hardly as clear as the proponents of these arguments suggest, and it changed over time for a variety of reasons. Second, when assessing the opinions of the South Vietnamese about the VC and the GVN, the proponents ignore the attitudes of South Vietnam's town and city populations, which were solidly pro-GVN. Third, popularity does not guarantee the moral legitimacy of a political movement; a considerable number of brutal tyrants have enjoyed great popularity. Fourth, the large-scale killing of villagers by Allied firepower resulted not from the Communists' popularity but from choices made by the Communists. During the period when the Communists enjoyed the population's favor, they chose to take cover from Allied attacks in the hamlets, attack Allied forces from within hamlets, and build fortifications in the hamlets almost invulnerable to light weapons. In most cases, they could have avoided doing so and spared the hamlets from destruction. The Communists also chose to take cover in and attack from the hamlets, and they continued to bring destruction upon the hamlets, long after they had ceased to enjoy the sympathies of the residents. Even if local pacification forces and the villagers wanted to keep the Communists out of their hamlets, they usually could do little to prevent a large Communist main force unit from coming in. Fifth, the Communists did not need to violate rules against dressing as civilians and taking cover in the hamlets in order to win the war. These ruses did not give them military advantages sufficient to affect the course of the war decisively, and they often had negative political consequences.

These arguments fall flat on practical grounds as well. Arguing that a nation engaged in war should select its methods based on its popularity is a useless enterprise. No belligerent power will ever believe that its cause is wrong and accept restrictions on its military actions as a result. Regardless of how many books are written about the "rights" of belligerents, politicians and generals will continue to place moral constraints on military operations only when their own conscience or political sense tells them that the restraints are advisable under the current circumstances.

Many opponents of the Allied war effort argue that the civilian population suffered much more damage in the Vietnam War than in any other war because of the repeated and extravagant employment of Allied firepower in the village areas. Political scientist Guenter Lewy, in his excellent book on the war, concludes that the history of recent wars disproves this assertion. According to Lewy's estimates, North and South Vietnamese civilians probably accounted at most for 45 percent of all persons killed in North and South Vietnam from 1965 to 1974. By comparison, civilians accounted for approximately 40 percent of all deaths during World War II and 70 percent during the Korean War.[12] Lewy's calculations contain a fault, but this fault actually makes the percentage of civilians killed in Vietnam larger than it should be.[13] All of the statistics concerning the Vietnam War and the other wars are somewhat suspect, as Lewy readily acknowledges, but the basic conclusion, in my opinion, is accurate. American veterans of multiple wars often scoff at the idea that the Americans' use of firepower in Vietnam was immoral and unprecedented in the history of warfare. Among them is Col. Lewis L. Millett, who fought in World War II, received the Medal of Honor in the Korean War for battlefield bravery, and served as the II Corps Phoenix coordinator during the early 1970s. "I fought in Italy during World War II," Millett said. "If we wanted to take a town, we'd blast it all to pieces first. We weren't going to risk American lives by not doing that and letting the enemy shoot first. If there happened to be civilians there, tough. But Vietnam was different. There was agitation about it back in the U.S., and they were telling us, 'You can't fire unless you're fired upon.' That was absolutely ridiculous."[14]

Inaccurate comparisons with past events also have been used in attempts to put the attack on the VCI into historical perspective. Numerous commentators claim that the advent of the Phoenix program ushered in an era of unjustified arrests, torture, and indiscriminate killing that far exceeded in magnitude the misdeeds of the Diem regime. Never before in the history of the GVN, they proclaim, had villagers received such poor treatment at the hands of the government and the Americans. Frances FitzGerald states:

> With the Phoenix program the United States succeeded in fashioning much the same instrument of civilian terror that the Diemist laws for the suppression of Communism had created in 1957–1958. The only difference was that given the numbers of American and GVN troops and the participation of statistics-hungry U.S. intelligence services, the terror was a great deal more widespread than it had been before. The program in effect eliminated the cumbersome category of "civilian"; it gave the GVN, and initially the American troops as well, license and justification for the arrest, torture, or killing of anyone in the country, whether or not the person was carrying a gun. And many officials took advantage of that license.[15]

The history of pacification in South Vietnam from the Diem era to the Phoenix era contradicts this description of events. Diem's campaign against the VC and former Viet Minh during the mid- and late 1950s resulted in the imprisonment and killing of many thousands of people. Many, if not most, of those killed were Communists, but some of the prisoners were only Communist sympathizers or were not Communists at all. P. J. Honey, a British expert on North Vietnamese politics, received an invitation from Diem to tour the "reeducation centers" Diem had built to imprison suspected subversives. After interviewing villagers, Honey concluded that "the consensus of the opinion expressed by these peoples is that . . . the majority of the detainees are neither communists nor pro-communists." [16]

GVN pacification forces of the Phoenix era targeted, imprisoned, and killed civilians much more discriminately than Diem's police had done because of several vital differences between the Diem and Thieu administrations. The United States did not directly control any of the programs in the Diem period, whereas the CIA later controlled the crucial PRUs and, to a lesser extent, the less effective Special Police. When the CIA did have control, it installed good leaders and inhibited the improper targeting of individuals. U.S. advisers often accompanied GVN units, which they did not do during the 1950s, and discouraged the torture or killing of some prisoners. Under Diem, policemen regularly imprisoned and killed civilians with little or no incriminating evidence. Thieu's judicial system, though far from perfect, tried most VCI suspects and set the large majority of them free within a short period of time. Further, during the 1950s, most Communists were men of military age who lived as legal citizens in hamlets full of military-age men. During the Phoenix era, men of military age still held the most important cadre positions, but they now lived away from the hamlets as illegal cadres, and the hamlets rarely contained military-age males. As a result, GVN personnel had much greater cause during the 1950s than later to suspect civilians of occupying important positions in the local VCI.

FitzGerald and others who draw the comparison with Diem contend that the GVN treated civilians much more benevolently from 1960 to 1967 than after Phoenix began. This claim is also inaccurate. During the period 1960–67, all of the major organizations that functioned during the late 1960s existed or came into existence, and all had been arresting, torturing, and killing VCI for some time before Phoenix began. South Vietnamese personnel of all sorts arrested, tortured, blackmailed, and killed non-Communist civilians on many occasions during this period. That Allied propaganda started to attribute their actions to Phoenix and Phung Hoang in 1967 did not change the nature of their behavior. A CIA intelligence estimate of January 1969, referring to the attack on the VCI, states: "Until mid-1968 the GVN gave no more than lukewarm support to the effort. In part this has been the legacy of a long era of political insecurity, during which intelligence, security, and police activities were often directed against non-Communist groups rather than against the VC."[17] Many villagers and ralliers interviewed during this period recounted experiences similar to those of a Communist Party member from Dinh Tuong province who defected in March 1966: "At the beginning of 1961, the Front became more active [in my hamlet], and the GVN control became tighter. In tightening their control, the GVN local officials overdid a few things. For example, they suspected the villagers and arrested innocent people. The SDC beat up and arrested innocent people and extorted money from them."[18] Some villagers and other witnesses knew of people who, during the period 1960–67, convinced the GVN that their personal enemies belonged to the VC. "One guy who was a source of information about the VC relieved his family of three generations of debt," recalled Patrick McGarvey, who worked with the Counter-Terror Teams in 1964. "He turned in phony reports fingering as Viet Cong people his family owed money to."[19]

The Phoenix and Phung Hoang programs did little to change the behavior of the pacification forces. The Phoenix quotas seldom had much impact because the GVN high command did not force its subordinate commanders to adhere to them. Rewards offered as part of the revamped attack on the VCI were too small to cause a major increase in activity against VCI or supposed VCI. The intelligence sharing spurred by Phoenix and Phung Hoang generated only a small number of operations against civilians, most of whom actually were VCI. FitzGerald's claim that Phoenix authorized U.S. soldiers to torture or kill anyone, according to the Americans whom I interviewed and many other U.S. veterans, is inaccurate.

Some reasonably reliable statistics also support the conclusion that the GVN did not display much more restraint in handling civilians during 1960–67 than during the Phoenix era that began in mid-1967. Had the GVN embarked on a campaign of indiscriminate arrests and killings, the civilian prison population in South Vietnam presumably would have swollen tremendously, starting in mid-1967, as the Allies rounded up many more people than usual and kept them in jail. Yet, as mentioned in chapter 18, the total number of civilian prisoners actually declined from forty-five thousand in 1967 to forty-one thousand in 1970.[20]

The shrinkage of the prison population and additional evidence suggest that Allied pacification forces arrested and killed fewer non-Communists per year during the existence of Phoenix than during the preceding years. The leadership of GVN pacification forces during the Phoenix period either remained at previous levels, as with the PRUs, or improved, as with most others. Strong leaders, discussed in chapters 10 and 18, generally prevented their units from targeting the wrong people, aside from those in certain political and racial groups. More cadres lived in hamlets full time as civilians, more villagers assisted the VC, and fewer villagers cooperated with the GVN during the early and mid-1960s than later, so GVN forces were more likely to suspect and harass villagers without evidence during the earlier period. The Allies had better intelligence during the later period because of pacification successes and leadership improvements, so they could distinguish better between Communists and non-Communists. When the Americans searched villages from mid-1967 onward, they brought along GVN policemen or other South Vietnamese more often than before, in part because of Phoenix. As a result, far fewer villagers had to endure American searches and screenings, which usually lasted longer and achieved less than those conducted by the more knowledgeable Vietnamese.

From 1967 onward, the attack on the VCI and pacification in general actually reduced other types of misery that the Allies inflicted on villagers. They weakened the VC shadow government significantly, which, by reducing the VC's recruiting capabilities, contributed to the virtual disappearance of large Communist main force units from most villages during the years after the Tet offensive. The smaller size of the remaining Communist forces made them less vulnerable to the shotgun effect of heavy weaponry and more often prevented the Allied main forces—now smaller as well—from attacking them until they were too close to hit with air or artillery strikes. Allied use of firepower near the hamlets consequently declined. Allied military commanders also wanted to fire heavy weapons into hamlets less often, as GVN control over the hamlets expanded, in order to preserve the GVN's pacification gains. In addition, the weakness of the Communist main forces, along with better GVN leadership, allowed the territorial forces to take over pacification gradually in most of the country, and the territorial forces preferred to use heavy firepower quite sparingly. When the attack on the VCI and other elements of pacification wiped out all of the VC and VCI in a village or forced them to stop operating, it removed all need for the use of heavy weapons in the village as long as NVA troops stayed away. "A lot of people in the U.S. complained that attacking the VC infrastructure was inhumane," Peter Scott said, "but in reality, the opposite was true. If you eliminated the local VC, you could eliminate the need to use bombs and gunships around the villages, which hurt the villagers far more than the pacification troops ever could."[21]

Some statistics show that Allied usage of heavy firepower in populous areas declined during the years after the Tet offensive. The figures pertain to phenomena that the Allies could measure easily, so they are quite accurate by the standards of Vietnam War statistics. From January 1969 to January 1971, the percentage of air sorties against targets within one kilometer of inhabited hamlets fell from 15.2 percent to 4.1 percent, and within two kilometers from 25.4 percent to 10.8 percent. At the same time, the total number of Allied sorties in South Vietnam declined dramatically, from 188,308 in 1969 to 46,909 in 1971. The percentage of villagers who said that no artillery or air strikes had landed in their hamlets or the vicinity during the past month rose from 69.8 percent in December 1969 to 89.0 percent in December 1971.[22]

The growing presence of the pacification forces boded well for the villagers in other ways. Soldiers of the territorial forces and other indigenous GVN personnel did not abuse the villagers as much or as arbitrarily as other soldiers and policemen. They had a better idea of who supported the VC, and they had relatives and neighbors there whom they did not want to offend. Trullinger notes that in My Thuy Phuong village, the ARVN 1st Division mistreated the villagers to a greater extent than the territorial forces. Village residents told him that this phenomenon "was due to the local ties of [territorial] forces soldiers. Local soldiers were generally more considerate in performance of military tasks than nonlocals. This was due to local soldiers' fear of censure in their home areas for improper behavior. Nonlocal soldiers, in contrast, had little fear of censure in communities not their own."[23] The territorial forces and other indigenous forces also prevented ARVN soldiers and non-Vietnamese soldiers, sometimes by force, from harassing the villagers in their areas. Stronger and more honest hamlet and village officials, brought to power by the pacification program and the superior district and province chiefs, discouraged the main force soldiers, as well as the pacification forces, from acting improperly.

Nonindigenous pacification forces also tended to treat the people better than the main forces because they served under province or district chiefs who usually cared more about the villagers—the chiefs depended more heavily on their assistance—than did ARVN commanders. Numerous U.S. advisers noted that GVN pacification forces treated the villagers with excessive harshness only on occasion. Rob Simmons told me, "By American standards, you might say the GVN people often mistreated the population, but by Asian standards I thought they were incredibly restrained most of the time."[24]

The misbehavior of ARVN troops also declined during the Phoenix era. From 1960 to 1967, ARVN soldiers beat, robbed, and otherwise abused the villagers with great frequency. An ex-cadre from Phu Yen province provided a description of the ARVN troops in his village during the middle of 1965 that could have applied to the ARVN soldiers in many hundreds of villages across the country:

> The people didn't dare say anything, but they were dissatisfied because there were innocent people who were arrested and killed. They denounced the ARVN's doings—destructions, seizing of poultry and harsh words with the people who hadn't given information about the VC. . . . The people were afraid. They hadn't done anything wrong. They had only done their duty as people in a Revolutionary, Communist area. The GVN came and considered anyone as a Communist. So the people were worried. In fact, there were people arrested, beaten and tortured.[25]

ARVN soldiers had the same lust for theft and physical abuse of the villagers throughout the war, but they had fewer opportunities to indulge it after 1967. Better ARVN leaders averted some crimes against the people during the ensuing period, but a change in the ARVN's military activities was the most important hindrance. During the early 1960s, when the Communists did not have many main force units, most ARVN units were stationed in the populated areas to put down VC uprisings and attack the guerillas. In 1964 and during the first half of 1965, they turned much of their attention to fighting the ascendant VC main forces, both in the village areas and in areas remote from the population. After the U.S. troops arrived in 1965 to assume the burden of fighting the main force war, the ARVN again focused its activities on pacification. Throughout the period 1960–67, therefore, numerous ARVN units occupied, or operated regularly in, the populous sections of the countryside. Although they normally shied away from aggressive military undertakings, these units found plenty of opportunities to oppress the villagers. Following the Tet offensive, as the United States began removing its troops, the ARVN no longer could afford to let the Americans do all of the main force fighting. By that time, too, the Allies had shattered the Communist main force shield in the inhabited areas and strengthened the territorial forces, so the territorial forces began to assume primary responsibility for security in most villages. As a result of these developments, ARVN troops went on more operations, frequently in regions remote from the population, which gave them less time and opportunity to cause mischief in the hamlets.

The various programs associated with the attack on the shadow government undoubtedly angered and frustrated many villagers from 1967 to the end of the war. Responsibility for most of the problems, however, belongs to the basic components of pacification, all of which had existed for years before the advent of the new attack on the VCI in 1967. The pacification organizations' mistreatment of the population tended to decrease, rather than increase, from 1967 onward. Conventional Allied military operations, where they occurred, disrupted the villagers' lives to a far greater extent. They, too, caused more injury to the populace during the first years of American ground force involvement than later in the war. Allied actions as a whole, nonetheless, led to enough misery during the latter period that, conceivably, they could have caused the alienation of many peasants from the GVN. Chapter 25 explores the question of whether the Allied actions actually had such an effect.

25   Changing Attitudes

lthough the political situation differed significantly among provinces, popular attitudes toward the war followed the same general trends over time throughout most of South Vietnam. As chapter 3 explains, the VC revolution received the approval of a large share of villagers as it spread during the early 1960s. Many of the people in a large number of South Vietnam's hamlets joined the VC or supported them actively. In each of the hamlets where the VC flourished, the shadow government drove out the dedicated GVN supporters, who were usually few in number, or cowed them into submission. Although most American observers understood little about why the hamlet residents adopted the positions they did, they generally recognized that the large majority of villagers in many hamlets favored the VC and opposed the GVN.

In 1965, these attitudes began to change. Yet, many Americans did not perceive this change—then or since—and thought that the attitudes of the villagers remained more or less the same. Frances FitzGerald addressed this issue when, in 1974, she called on the U.S. government to stop aiding the GVN on the grounds that this move would lead to the peaceful formation of a coalition government in the South, and not to a violent Communist takeover. The GVN at that time, FitzGerald claimed, "has no popular support."[1] In a postwar work, historian James Gibson contends that the shadow government continued to gain the assistance of many villagers in the later phases of the war because of "NLF organizational strength and the persistence of social conditions in the countryside that made revolutionary war appear to peasants as the only possible path to major social change."[2]

Many Americans, including a substantial number of advisers, argue that the Allied use of heavy firepower in the populated areas and the destruction that resulted from it caused villagers to remain more sympathetic to the VC throughout the war. Some also contend that the Allies did not implement effective political programs to complement their military initiatives, so the GVN's popularity could only deteriorate as the violence mounted. Historian Loren Baritz, for instance, claims, "All the technology and all the technocrats could not solve the equation between the guerrillas and their village support. The fundamental issue was always political, and neither detention nor killing was germane."[3] Some Americans assert that Phoenix made the people indifferent or hostile toward the GVN in the war's later years. Author Cecil B. Currey, who wrote under the pen name of Cincinnatus and claimed that he was a senior field officer in the U.S. military,[4] advances this theory in his book *Self-Destruction.* He contends that "Vietnamese nationals felt more estranged from their government because of their fears that at any moment, someone might target them as an enemy of the state, with consequent arrest, torture, imprisonment, or death."[5]

Other American commentators argue that the VC did become less popular after the Tet offensive, but that apathy, at best, characterized the prevailing mood toward the GVN. Historian Ronald Spector writes, "Although support for the NLF had become far more difficult and dangerous for the rural Vietnamese, he still felt no strong incentive to cast his lot with the Saigon government." Pacification had improved the GVN's position, Spector argues, but only because the Allies had put more armed men into the countryside, not because of changes in the people's attitudes or behavior. "In the end," he writes, "despite a promising land reform program, despite continued U.S. development efforts, despite attempts to restore 'traditional' village government, the success of pacification rested only on superior military forces."[6]

Only a few American commentators have sought to examine this issue in any serious fashion. Many who express opinions on it look only at evidence from the war's earlier years, which is more plentiful and more accessible, and simply assume that this evidence pertains to all periods of the war. Others base their judgments primarily on the testimony of American soldiers, who regularly sensed an air of hostility in the hamlets; they fail to recognize that the Americans usually operated in the hamlets most likely to support the VC and that unfriendliness toward the Americans did not necessarily mean sympathy for the VC. Many who talk of the VC's continued popularity, moreover, belonged to the American antiwar movement and thus have ulterior motives for downplaying or ignoring evidence indicating shifts in the villagers' moods. They want to prove to themselves or to others that the attitudes of the earlier period persisted because one of their main objections to the war is that America's enemy supposedly enjoyed far greater popularity than its ally.

One of the few historians who did look into the matter in greater depth, Gabriel Kolko, argues that "the hostility toward the RVN and the United

States increased" during the late 1960s and early 1970s. The villagers became increasingly reluctant to assist the Communists during this period, according to Kolko, only because collaboration entailed greater dangers for them than before. The bulk of villagers had not changed their political convictions, Kolko asserts, for the Party had "planted a deep radical culture, at least among the poorer peasantry." During the last few years of the war, Kolko adds, the shadow government regained the support of much of the rural population.[7]

The conditions of village life changed radically in much of South Vietnam between 1965 and 1972, and this altered the villagers' outlook on the war immensely. The introduction of U.S. troops in 1965 led to the most obvious change in village life, a much higher level of violence. Many more villagers than before watched the Allies use machine guns, rockets, napalm, and other weapons to attack Communist forces in their hamlets, and many more suffered the loss of relatives and property. The suffering that the war, as a whole, inflicted on the villagers changed not just in magnitude, however, but in purpose as well. Much, if not most, of the earlier damage to the populace had consisted of such actions as the beating or arrest of a local boy, the theft of a chicken, or the indiscriminate firing of a few artillery rounds into a hamlet. These acts showed villagers that the GVN deliberately targeted them and not the VC. Allied uses of violence in the subsequent era were aimed primarily at Communist soldiers inside the hamlets, rather than at the hamlet residents. The villagers appreciated this factor and attached considerable importance to it.

Contrary to the expectations of many Americans, the escalating violence of the village war did not turn villagers against the GVN or endear the VC to them. When powerful Allied attacks commenced in villages whose residents supported the VC, the populace's willingness to cooperate with the VC usually dropped off rapidly. A former district-level cadre, for example, recalled how he and the other cadres appraised the situation after high-intensity warfare had arrived in their area: "All of us agreed that the people were then very tired of the war and that they were also very afraid of it. That is why all the policies of the Front have run into difficulties. The amount of tax collected and the number of the conscripted youths diminished noticeably, although the cadres did their best to cope with the situation. The increasing intensity of the war, the intensive and frequent shellings and strafings were considered the real causes of the deterioration of the people's enthusiasm."[8] He said that the Party used the destruction for propaganda purposes both inside and outside Vietnam, but he believed its overall effects devastated the Party's war effort. "From experience, I realized that the Front is most strong in villages which haven't been shelled and that on the contrary, it weakens there where shellings frequently happened. To wage Front propaganda, to sow hatred against the GVN, Front cadres need quietude. In Long Dinh [district] where shellings have greatly affected the people's welfare, it is very difficult for the cadres to win the villagers' support. It is also very difficult to make the villagers carry out activities which are necessary to the Front to launch its phases of offensive activities. These observations of mine made me think that the Front is very active and harmful in quiet areas, while it is weakening there where the GVN is active. So, if humanitarian considerations are to be discarded, I will say, as a pure military statement, that shellings really serve the final victory of the GVN."9

Because the VC forces repeatedly failed to win tangible victories over Allied forces in areas of heavy military activity and because Allied activities made life as a member of the VC harder and more dangerous, service with the VC seemed less attractive to young villagers and the parents who heavily influenced their decisions. The failure of the VC to live up to earlier promises of quick victory made the villagers particularly suspicious of VC recruiters. One rallier remarked, "The people said that if national reunification was close at hand they would gladly let their children fight for the Front, but since the war was going to last for a long time they didn't want to let their children join the Front. They said that their children would run the risk of getting killed, and that with their children gone no one would help them in their farm work."10

The improved ability of Allied forces to identify VC supporters also eroded the people's willingness to assist the VC in some cases. With better intelligence, some Allied forces intimidated, arrested, and tortured fewer nonaligned civilians but performed the same acts more often on VC supporters. For example, the growth in the number of VC defectors after the Americans intervened in 1965 and the consequent improvement of Allied intelligence made many villagers reluctant to support the VC. A 1967 Communist report from a village in Bien Hoa province notes:

> A great majority of the defectors are young people, thus, they have caused our people to lose confidence in the young guerrillas and cadres. People now have the opinion that the young men are active but are also subject to fear of bombings and firing and thus would rally to the enemy and denounce many of our activities. . . . Such thoughts have greatly lessened the people's support for the Revolution as well as the people's contribution to the com-

mon task of the Revolution. This is because our people are afraid that by dint of contributing to the Revolution they will sooner or later be noticed by the defectors.[11]

Most villagers, as events would have it, blamed the VC for the destructive battles in and around the hamlets and resented them for it. Some of the villagers criticized the Allies, as well, for the attacks. A cadre who rallied at the end of 1966 described the public's mood in his village after a destructive Allied helicopter attack:

> Seeing that their homes had been burned down, their possessions destroyed and their family members killed, the people cried and cursed loudly both the Nationalists and the Communists. . . . The Nationalists brought planes there to attack them, killing people and destroying people's homes. Why didn't the Nationalists let their troops fight? As for the Front, the people ridiculed the VC by saying that they called themselves revolutionaries but they only hid among the people and caused them many sufferings. People got killed because of bombs and bullets which were meant primarily for the VC. If the liberation fighters were so brave why didn't they live outside of the village and save people from having to bear the strafings?[12]

Generally speaking, though, the villagers put the largest share of the blame on the VC. Numerous Communist prisoners and ralliers, many of them quite objective in their appraisals of the war, made this observation. If the Communists continued to come under Allied attack in the hamlets and flee each time, the villagers reasoned, they were not accomplishing anything but adding to the people's woes. A former VC guerrilla platoon leader from Quang Tin province said, "In 1963 and 1964 the VC held [the] upper hand in my village, but since October 1965, the ARVN troops have been winning. . . . If the VC had been able to win some battles the people would support them, but they'd not only failed to fight against the ARVN, they'd also dragged the people into the troubles. Therefore, the people became fed up."[13]

The villagers did not assign much blame to the Allies for the attacks because they respected the power of the Allies and believed that Allied forces had no realistic choice but to use powerful weapons against the Communists wherever they could find them. They faulted the Allies only when they mistakenly unleashed heavy weapons on hamlets not containing Communist soldiers. A former district-level cadre from Binh Dinh province said of Allied shelling, strafing, and bombing, "I thought that the attacks were mostly caused by the presence of Front forces in the hamlets, but from time to time they weren't justified. This was perhaps due to wrong information having been given to GVN forces or to the carelessness of some GVN or American leaders. The villagers only blamed the GVN when the attacks weren't justified. With regard to all the attacks resulting from VC activities, they blamed the Front, sometimes openly."[14]

Contrary to some opinions, people who fled their hamlets liked the VC less after they became refugees. Chapter 22 presents Communist testimony and actions indicating that the Party believed the refugee flow decreased its ability to obtain the villagers' support. One might infer that the exodus of refugees hurt the VC only because it put the refugees in places where they could not come into contact with the VC. In reality, however, almost all refugees had enough freedom of movement that they could try to help or join the VC. They did not try to assist the VC mainly because they did not like the VC. Villagers who chose to leave because of Allied attacks usually blamed the VC more than the GVN for their troubles, as did the many who left because the VC demanded too much of them. A rallier from Quang Nam province said in 1967, "The villagers began to hate the VC after so many of them were innocently killed and their standard of living became increasingly difficult. In addition, the VC promised to liberate the villagers, but all the villagers saw around them was killing and starvation. They had to go find freedom for themselves and for their families. They started to move out of their native villages in the beginning of 1967."[15]

The villagers forced by Allied troops to leave their hamlets and those who left because defoliants had destroyed their crops attributed their misfortunes, more often than not, to both the VC and the GVN. Many of the refugees, in addition, disliked their new living conditions and would have preferred a return to farming. Most, nevertheless, had no desire to go back to hamlets under VC control—where conditions usually were even worse— or to support the VC, who no longer could offer them a good life. The GVN could fan their discontent with the Communists and build their allegiance to the GVN because GVN officials could propagandize them, whereas the shadow government could not. A former VC cadre explained why most villagers had left his village and few wanted to return as long as the VC controlled it:

There are two reasons for the villagers leaving the village for GVN areas. The first and basic reason is the people's fear of the bombing and shooting. The people are afraid for their own lives. The second reason is those who left to go to GVN areas met GVN cadres who educated and explained to them what the opportunities of life in both areas are. The villagers could see for themselves that life in GVN areas brings them freedom and comfort, and so, they passed the word on to others. Thus, a movement started, and the families began to leave, one after another.[16]

The large-scale fighting in the villages also began to increase the standing of the GVN in the villagers' eyes. From 1965 onward, Allied forces usually defeated or drove away the Communists during engagements in or around the hamlets. The Americans and Koreans fought more aggressively than the South Vietnamese had before, and, when in the early 1970s the South Vietnamese took back control of the main force war, their performance showed notable improvement over that of the early 1960s. The Americans also had bigger and more accurate weapons and used them more carefully, so they hit the Communists much more often than had the ARVN blunderers who had handled heavy weapons previously. These military encounters usually convinced the villagers that the Allies were strong and the Communists weak. Allied military triumphs, the Allies' wondrous high-tech weapons, and the strong Allied military presence in the countryside impressed the people enormously. As always, the large majority of villagers favored the side that was most likely to win, and thus the Allies became more attractive to them. The villagers' growing desire for peace and security gave them further reason to support the strong, for their support meant that the strong would win and end the violence more quickly. Sheer military force did help the Allies to gain the sympathies of the rural population.

James Trullinger, at the time, was more sympathetic to the VC than to the GVN, a position that he has since reversed. He found, however, the tendency to support the likely winner even in a village with a history of exceptionally strong VC sympathies, a fact that argued against the contentions of most VC supporters in the United States. Trullinger states that many people tried to placate the Allies and the Communists by helping each side "during the extended periods of political uncertainty about local balance of power, but when that balance clearly shifted in favor of one side, there were corresponding shifts among the uncommitted—and sometimes among the committed, too. Many began to support the side which appeared stronger, sometimes abandoning support for the seemingly weaker side."[17] The following captured VC document acknowledges the loss of popularity that the Communists suffered because of military defeats: "The enemy conducted intensive attacks against stepping-stone and fringe areas and sometimes concentrated his attacks on urban and base areas. Such activities have caused many difficulties for us, since many of our cadre and agents have been either captured, killed, or detected. This has adversely affected the implementation of our strategic plan. As a result of enemy activities, a number of people have become confused and have lost their confidence in our cadre and troops."[18]

The Tet offensive seriously damaged the VC's popularity among villagers. The VC's humiliating defeat and their consequent loss of prestige accounts for much, but not all, of the villagers' disillusionment. Many villagers resented that the VC cadres demanded major sacrifices of them and made them bold promises of victory, then squandered their sacrifices and failed to deliver on the promises. A district-level defector explained:

> Before the Tet events, the VC said that they only needed seven days to achieve the revolution. They needed the support of the population; they collected very heavy contributions arguing that they needed the contributions to bring about peace and prosperity; but after the anticipated seven days they said that this was only a first stage, the first wave. When the second stage came on the 7th of May (1968) they said there was then an almost complete destruction of the enemy, to step up to the third stage which would be in August, 1968, and which was also to be the final stage; but, as a matter of fact, there has been no final stage at all. . . . These facts have accounted for the cadres' and the general population's losing confidence in the success of the revolution by the Front.[19]

The Communists also offended numerous peasants by launching the assaults during the sacred Tet holiday. "After this offensive," said a North Vietnamese sergeant, who rallied during February 1968, "the GVN has won more and more friends, thus reducing the number of former enemies. That was due to the VC breach of trust during the Tet truce and also to the effectiveness of the Chieu Hoi program."[20]

In his monthly report for February 1968, the province senior adviser of Tay Ninh province states:

> The change in the attitude of the people during the past month has been dramatic. Many segments that earlier could be described as neutralist or, at best, lacking in full support to the government have now moved into the government camp. The basic cause of this change has been the viciousness of the Viet Cong attack throughout the nation combined with the unsuccessful Viet Cong actions within the province. The fact that the Viet Cong violated the Tet holidays, violated the "sanctuary" of the area around the Cao Dai temple, and suffered defeats every time they met the GVN/FWMF

[Free World Military Forces] forces within the province have all contributed to this change in attitude.[21]

Huge numbers of villagers lost their enthusiasm for the VC because the
level of prosperity in hamlets where the VC had substantial influence began
to fall in 1965. Allied heavy weapons and defoliants destroyed crops, and
Allied forces confiscated or destroyed rice and farm animals. Loss of family
members to the VC and GVN drafts and to Allied firepower reduced the labor
supply. Some farmers stopped working when military operations in their area
began or appeared imminent, and farmers often had to perform work for the
VC without compensation. The VCI decreased the villagers' income further
by raising taxes. A VC soldier captured in Quang Ngai province during 1967,
when asked the most important reason that the villagers had turned against
the VC, gave a typical response: "The fact that they had to work for the VC and
neglect their work. Because the people could no longer work for themselves,
they didn't have the means of subsistence and had to starve and suffer."[22]

Communist coercion itself also injured and angered many villagers. As
the villagers became less cooperative and the VC's possession of hamlet
resources fell, the Communists increased their use of threats and force
against the villagers. The shadow government more often conscripted villagers for military or other purposes and took money and goods without
asking. Attempts to threaten, abduct, torture, or kill villagers and GVN
officials who did not cooperate with the Communists rose in frequency. A
CIA report from July 1967, for example, reads, "The VC are suffering from
a shortage of tax income all over the country. Raising tax levels has served
to make collection all the more difficult, and local units are increasingly
resorting to terrorism to enforce payment. In several different parts of the
country individuals have been 'executed' for non-payment of taxes."[23]

Less discriminate forms of force turned many people against the VC as
well. Killings of GVN sympathizers and people who worked for the GVN in
jobs not directly related to the war increased considerably. In rural areas
where most of the population supported the GVN, the Communists frequently tried to overrun and slaughter the territorial forces, the hamlet
and village officials, and their families. They wanted to deter stout anti-
Communism, discourage people from living in GVN areas, and eliminate
hamlets that provided the GVN with personnel, food, and intelligence. "I
couldn't count the number of cases where the little triangular forts of the
Popular Forces were wiped out by Communist main force units," Brig. Gen.

James Herbert told me. "The Communists killed all the soldiers and their families. It happened all over the country."[24]

In many areas where the Communists had relatively little influence over the population, they resorted to indiscriminate acts of violence against civilians. The Communists routinely fired mortars into GVN areas, set off bombs in the markets, mined the roads that civilians traversed, and committed other terrorist acts that served no direct military purpose. Statistics indicate that, from 1968 to 1972, roughly 30,000 civilians per year went to GVN hospitals with injuries from mines and mortars, weapons with which only the Communists could have harmed civilians, and these weapons killed many others. The number of civilians with mine and mortar wounds, in fact, greatly exceeded the number of civilians wounded by Allied shelling and bombing.[25] The statistics are somewhat imprecise because hospital personnel often found it difficult to determine the origins of wounds. In addition, numerous residents of towns and cities fell victim to mines and mortars, so the statistics do not indicate how many villagers received injuries. Many of the war's participants whom I interviewed, nonetheless, confirmed that mines and mortars produced high numbers of casualties among the villagers. Some said that, from what they saw, these casualties exceeded the number from Allied heavy weaponry.

The Communists tried to draw Allied heavy-weapon fire on GVN-controlled hamlets, with some success, by shooting at Allied troops from within the hamlets and then bolting. From time to time, according to Americans and South Vietnamese who worked or lived in the countryside, the Communists razed entire hamlets and killed all of the inhabitants. John Peterkin, for example, a district senior adviser in Phong Dinh province, witnessed such barbarity in his district. The Communists, Peterkin said, "would attack small hamlets at night. They'd just kill, wantonly kill." He described arriving at one hamlet the morning after the NVA came in. "A hand here, a leg there. Mothers shot up. It was like a massacre. They killed everyone in the hamlet, except a few who escaped. They did it because there was an outpost there."[26]

Violence against GVN supporters and inhabitants of GVN areas did not occur every day in most provinces and seldom occurred at all in some. The number of incidents, nevertheless, was still fairly large. Some commentators assert that even small doses of Communist terrorism paralyzed the village populations. The Allies, they say, had to "protect the people" from terrorism in order to obtain their support. The history of both the VC and the

GVN during their times of strength, however, contradict this argument. The villagers deeply resented the Communist atrocities of the late 1960s and the 1970s. Many of the former U.S. and GVN personnel whom I interviewed recalled that numerous villagers who lost relatives to Communist terror during this time became devout anti-Communist crusaders.

The easiest way to explain the reasons behind the villagers' hostile response to Communist terrorism is to compare this terrorism with two other types of violence against the South Vietnamese people. The first is the inadvertent wounding and killing of civilians by Allied heavy firepower from 1965 onward. The circumstances that caused the villagers to tolerate the destructiveness of the firepower (described above) were absent in the case of Communist terrorism after the Tet offensive. The Communist killing did not target enemy personnel, nor did it inflict damage on enemy forces and thereby decrease the enemy's chances of victory. The villagers, therefore, viewed it as senseless. In addition, it disrupted the lives of the civilian population to a much smaller extent than did heavy Allied firepower, so it could not, by its mere destructiveness, engender widespread apathy in GVN areas as Allied firepower had done in many VC areas during the mid-1960s. The second item of comparison is the GVN's violent mistreatment of villagers during the pre-1965 period. Like Communist terrorism of the post-Tet period, this mistreatment was not aimed at enemy personnel, it did not decrease the enemy's prospects for victory, and it was too small in scale to render the people apathetic. As a consequence, it had the same effect on the people as Communist terrorism after Tet; as indicated in chapter 3, this violence contributed significantly to the unpopularity of its perpetrators. The Communists undoubtedly appreciated to some extent the negative consequences of indiscriminate violence, which—along with the risks involved in conducting terrorist operations—explains why they did not use terrorism more often than they did.

The expulsion of the VC political cadres from their areas of operation during the mid- and late 1960s and their declining ability to visit the hamlets contributed directly to the growing reluctance of villagers to assist the VC. These realities greatly reduced the cadres' opportunities to endear themselves to the populace by the methods used during the early 1960s. They did not have time to help the villagers with their work, they no longer had the power to keep abusive GVN personnel out of the hamlets, and they could not propagandize the people as often as their enemies could. The authors of a Party Resolution written in the Mekong Delta during mid-1971, for instance, lament, "Party members failed to stay close to the people to promote their life and interests and provide effective leadership for their struggles, thus limiting our activities and the development of the Party. . . . A number of people displayed a pacifistic attitude, were bribed, and served among the enemy as henchmen because we failed to stay close to and indoctrinate them in time."[27]

Because the number of South Vietnamese Communists dwindled to a small fraction of previous strength by 1970, the VC no longer could rely so much on fostering local support through cadres and soldiers native to a locality. The Southern villagers, moreover, disliked the North Vietnamese who were taking a much more prominent role in the Communist war effort. "In Tan My village," Brig. Gen. Stuart Herrington recalls, "the Vietcong appointed a new village secretary and charged him with responsibility for rebuilding the village organization. The new man was given a squad of North Vietnamese soldiers to perform the security tasks normally done by village guerrillas—a measure that underscored the depth of the revolution's problem in Tan My. The new village secretary was not a Tan My native, and the use of northern troops in the village was bound to alienate the people."[28]

For the South Vietnamese peasant, life was much better in hamlets where the GVN had all or most of the power than it was in VC-dominated hamlets. In GVN hamlets, villagers generally enjoyed greater safety and most of them obtained a substantially larger amount of wealth than villagers in VC or hotly contested hamlets. U.S. aid programs brought money, technologically advanced equipment, superior agricultural supplies such as "miracle rice" seeds, and other useful commodities to these areas. In addition, many of the men who worked for the GVN could spend some of their time helping their families with farming or business activities. Rice production was booming; it increased from 4.3 metric tons in the 1966–67 crop year to 6.1 million metric tons in 1971–72.[29] During the last year of the war, the South Vietnamese economy experienced a sharp downturn, but most of the negative consequences affected city residents, not villagers.

American aid improved public facilities, utilities, and roads. Enhanced Allied security reduced the Communists' ability to destroy development projects and allowed the villagers greater freedom of travel, thus increasing their opportunities to take their products to markets. Le Thi Anh, a writer who opposed both the Thieu regime and the Communists, described the Mekong Delta of the early 1970s: "In the countryside . . . everybody had a motorized sampan [rivercraft]. Everybody was well-dressed and had radios and sewing machines. Everybody was well fed, happy and prosperous. . . . The rural areas especially enjoyed great benefits from the American presence. Telephones, new roads and bridges—we never had those kinds of things before."[30] Some areas of South Vietnam, particularly in the northern provinces, did not match this description, but a great many did.

An important reason for the health of the rural economy, and itself a very important political development, was an aggressive GVN land reform campaign. During the early 1960s, Diem's ineffectual efforts at land reform had come to a halt, and the redistribution of land remained a nonissue during the years immediately after his fall because both the Americans and the South Vietnamese feared that land reform would further destabilize a ruling class already in turmoil. By the late 1960s, despite the efforts of the VC to reorder rural South Vietnamese society, a large number of hectares remained in the hands of landlords who rented the land to tenants or hired laborers to till it, and they did not wish to part with their holdings. Although the tempest of war gave villagers much else to worry about, many landless villagers still considered land ownership a crucial issue.[31] In 1968, Thieu finally revived GVN land reform efforts. Early that year, he began distributing government-owned land to thousands of families. In February 1969, he enacted a law allowing farmers to maintain their rents or land holdings for one year, so that landlords could not repossess land or raise rents when Allied forces supplanted the VC in a hamlet. Villagers in these hamlets, the theory went, no longer would have to fear immediate economic losses when Allied forces took over and thus would have less cause to resist the Allies. During 1969, as it turned out, GVN officials usually allowed VC-installed farmers to keep their land, but they failed to prevent a considerable number of landlords from raising rents.

President Thieu signed into effect the momentous "Land to the Tiller" law in March 1970. To all tenants and to all villagers farming on land distributed by the VC, this law gave legal title to the land that each of them cultivated. Saigon paid the original owners a certain amount of money, and the amount of compensation satisfied most landowners. Land to the Tiller reduced the maximum allowable land holdings of an individual to 15 hectares, and anyone holding that much land could do so only if that person's own family members farmed the land. By the end of 1973, the GVN had issued approximately 1.2 million hectares to roughly 950,000 titleholders, which exceeded its redistribution goal of 1 million hectares.[32] In the Mekong Delta and the provinces around Saigon, the program worked extremely well. It redistributed about one half of all land used for rice cultivation in the Delta. In most of I Corps and II Corps, however, the GVN distributed relatively few parcels of land. It made no serious attempt to institute these reforms in the highlands, and stiff opposition from village officials and landlords prevented redistribution in the lowlands. The populations of the I Corps and II Corps provinces, however, were considerably smaller than those in III Corps and IV Corps, so land reform did affect the large majority of peasants. It reduced the percentage of South Vietnam's total cropland cultivated by tenants from 60 percent to 10 percent in three years.[33]

Some villagers complained that Land to the Tiller committed injustices against them. Those landlords still residing in the hamlets often had to wait a year or longer to receive compensation for their land. Some soldiers who served away from their villages and rented their land temporarily to others had to surrender their land. On occasion, landlords and village officials in III Corps and IV Corps used tricks to prevent the distribution of land. Most American and South Vietnamese observers, nevertheless, including many of those skeptical about the program's overall significance, concluded that Land to the Tiller improved the material well-being of millions of peasants. Land to the Tiller title recipients watched their incomes rise sharply now that they no longer had to pay rents or work for others. Researchers from the Control Data Corporation conducted a thorough study of Land to the Tiller in forty-four secure and contested villages in the Mekong Delta during the first half of 1972. They found that 89 percent of new landowners surveyed said that life in their hamlets had improved since the program began, and only 2 percent said it had become worse.[34]

A few critics of Land to the Tiller contend that the GVN and wealthy South Vietnamese citizens restricted the popular benefits of Land to the Tiller by creating cartels for the purchase of agricultural produce and the issuance of credit that gouged the new landowners. Insufficient evidence exists to determine the bargaining power of the produce buyers, but it is clear that their behavior did not seriously hurt the farmers. Farmers generally had no complaints about what they received for their toils.[35] Cartels definitely did not dominate the credit system in the villages. The availability of credit at reasonable interest rates, in fact, increased considerably during the late 1960s and early 1970s. Many villagers received loans for agricultural purposes at relatively low rates from the GVN. Most others could obtain the loans they needed from relatives, friends, or neighbors. Villagers who had received land through the Land to the Tiller program often obtained credit more easily than they had as tenants because lenders considered landowners less risky customers.

Landlords who had treated tenants and wage laborers poorly no longer troubled those who received Land to the Tiller titles. No more could they overwork peasants or drive them off of ancestral lands. "The landlords once had an awful lot of power," one farmer said. "Tenants were merely their slaves and had to work from dawn to dusk. . . . For every ceremonial feast the tenants had to come work and to bring rice or poultry to put on the altar. . . . They were afraid if they did not do so the landlord would be angry and might take back his land. . . . Now they are no longer afraid."[36] The status of title recipients did not increase so much that they could move into the ranks of GVN officialdom above the village level, but social mobility of that magnitude never became a major concern of the masses. Prosperity, safety, and freedom from oppressive authorities remained much more important issues for them. Most also preferred living in their native villages, surrounded by family and friends and ancestral spirits, to living in district or provincial capitals.

Although most analysts of Land to the Tiller agree that the program benefited many villagers economically, they differ over its impact on village political opinion. A few of the VC's American supporters doubt that it affected attitudes in the countryside at all. More moderate critics state that Land to the Tiller probably caused villagers to look more favorably on the GVN but that the program had only marginal influence on the villagers because it was merely a response to the VC's pressure and it essentially sanctioned revolutionary changes implemented by the VC. This complaint, however, actually embodies the sentiments of Westerners still bitter at the GVN for its earlier policies, not those of the South Vietnamese peasants. Here again is an example of Westerners projecting their own beliefs onto the South Vietnamese. Most South Vietnamese villagers cared much more about their current well-being than about what the GVN and the VC had done in the past. They tended to lean toward the group that could best serve their interests in the present, which at that time was the GVN. Field researcher Charles Callison, who studied four fairly secure Delta villages in great detail, notes, "As far as the [Land to the Tiller] Program was concerned, very few farmers in our sample seemed inclined to give the NLF much credit for 'forcing' the Thieu government into it, as a more sophisticated view might well do. . . . That the government was trying to 'buy the hearts of the farmers' and win greater rural support was unquestioned, but this was perceived as a good thing for the government to do and an excellent way to do it."[37] Many observers also noticed that the general prosperity in GVN areas made the GVN more popular. "Areas that became more firmly under GVN control over time became more prosperous," Ed Brady said. "On the average, people realized they were better off under the GVN, and certainly they realized they became more prosperous. Prosperity meant the world to them. They tended, therefore, to favor the GVN over the VC."[38]

The GVN built up its political and military organizations in the countryside during this period and improved its political position as a consequence. From 1969 to the end of the war, it recruited far more villagers than before for the territorial forces and other organizations that operated in the countryside. President Thieu's belated decision to implement universal conscription after the Tet offensive bolstered the GVN recruitment drive. The People's Self-Defense Forces also engaged many villagers, though they participated in fewer activities than full-time GVN personnel. By bringing so many villagers into the GVN ranks and keeping them in their native areas, the GVN dramatically improved its popularity among the villagers, just as the VC had gained popularity earlier in the war by using cadres and soldiers in their native areas. The ARVN and other national organizations grabbed most of the other eligible males. Virtually all villagers, therefore, now had relatives in the GVN, whereas much fewer had VC relatives, and they tended to endorse the side for whom their relatives served. Those who had relatives in both the GVN and VC either remained neutral or preferred the side that employed more of their relatives, which, for most, was the GVN.

Some Americans contend that the GVN coerced many people into joining its organizations during this period and therefore offended the villagers and produced unwilling soldiers and officials. The GVN often did use coercive methods, but that fact did not usually alienate the villagers or undermine the morale of GVN personnel in the countryside. Coercion often aided both sides in obtaining and maintaining the villagers' cooperation during the Vietnam War, particularly when charismatic or powerful leaders did the coercing, as was generally the case for the VC in the early and mid-1960s and for the GVN after Tet-68. Traditional South Vietnamese obedience guaranteed that compulsion would succeed more often than not.

Elections for hamlet and village councils formed another part of the GVN's rural political program. Diem had abolished elections of hamlet and village officials, and his henchmen had appointed them thereafter. After Diem, the elections returned in some areas, but district and province chiefs frequently manipulated them. In the years following the Tet offensive, the GVN—with prodding from CORDS—extended the elections to almost all hamlets and villages. The elected councils appointed hamlet and village chiefs and other executive officials, thousands of whom took month-long training courses from CIA and South Vietnamese instructors at Vung Tau and in the provinces. Many U.S. officials and other Americans who did not appreciate the cultural gulf separating the South Vietnamese from the Americans believed that the democratic character of the election process by itself would make villagers more sympathetic toward the GVN. It did not. The villagers lacked the Americans' admiration of democracy and clung to their authoritarian traditions.

During the early and mid-1960s, GVN village council members typically were wealthy landlords, political appointees foreign to the village, and others who were not necessarily concerned about the welfare of many villagers. Numerous GVN officials and U.S. advisers have said, to me and to others, that many district chiefs continued to rig most hamlet and village elections in their districts during the years following the Tet offensive. Some of them also said that the higher GVN authorities frequently let ineffectual political hacks or outsiders win the elections.[39] Such charges were accurate in many instances. The interference of the district chiefs during these years, however, did not always put ineffective people into hamlet and village leadership positions. Because better district chiefs came to power after the Tet offensive, they often appointed able and well-motivated individuals to these positions and inspired them to perform well. Col. Walter Clark noted, "The district chiefs exercised pretty strong control over the village chiefs. If the district chief was a good leader, he would motivate his village chiefs to perform well."[40]

Some district chiefs, in addition, did not meddle with the hamlet and village elections. A fair number of these elections resulted in significant improvement in the quality of hamlet and village council members and other leaders. All of the reasons for the GVN's growing popularity mentioned above encouraged more villagers to seek GVN leadership positions or to vote for leaders who would resolutely defend the villages from Communist intrusion. Although the villagers were not particularly enthusiastic about democracy, some realized that they might best serve their own interests by taking part in the elections because they perhaps could choose leaders better than could the district chiefs. The people in some hamlets and villages, on the other hand, elected weak leaders out of ignorance or out of the fear that strong leaders would invite Communist attacks on their hamlet or village. In August 1971, Donald Colin asserted that the election of low-level administrations "is the area that [has] shown the greatest improvement during the time I have been in Vietnam, and also the area in which the most work remains to be done. The second go-around of real village elections in the spring of 1970 saw many examples of people 'throwing the rascals out' and bringing in new Village Councils and Village Chairmen. Out of 52 elected village governments in Vinh-Binh, there are about a dozen really outstanding village chiefs and a dozen really poor village chiefs with the bulk of them being merely adequate. While this indicates a long way to go, it is also a lot better than the totally grim picture of village administration two years ago."[41] Good hamlet and village leaders, together with other GVN pacification leaders, strengthened the popular image of the GVN by helping and propagandizing the villagers, much as strong village leaders had done for the VC in the past.

Thieu abolished the hamlet elections in September 1972. The district and province chiefs subsequently selected all hamlet officials and many of the village officials. In 1973, Thieu introduced what he called the "Administrative Revolution." At Thieu's request, district and province chiefs assigned more GVN officials and soldiers to hamlet and village administrations. Despite the contraction of democracy during this period, the grassroots administrations did not become less effective. If anything, according to a variety of sources, they became more effective. District and province chiefs proved their ability to appoint adequate leaders on their own. Trullinger describes how the local administration in My Thuy Phuong village improved in leadership, strength, and discipline—and thus became more popular— from 1973 onward:

> An Army captain came to the village to coordinate all local security activities. Many Government soldiers and villagers noted that the arrival of the captain brought improvements to the provincial forces patrols, operations, and static guarding assignments. Government soldiers became more alert on duty and improved marksmanship. Discipline tightened. Soldiers engaged in little looting. And desertion became infrequent.[42]

Some Americans thought that democratic elections for politicians above the village level would improve the GVN's image in the countryside and help the Saigon leadership to develop a "political base" there. Thieu, therefore, held such elections. That Thieu manipulated these elections to help gain victory for his allies, that he gave little power to the winners, and that he arrested or silenced some segments of the national non-Communist opposition parties is largely irrelevant. These elections simply did not stimulate the villagers, who knew or cared as little about higher levels of government as they did about democracy. Even when higher authorities interfered excessively with village life, few villagers viewed elections as a means to improve the situation. They sought, instead, to join forces with opposing higher authorities. In most of East Asia, in fact, where political and cultural traditions are authoritarian and not democratic, the suppression of political opposition above the level of the village occurs regularly during peacetime as well as during wartime. The practice does not arouse much indignation among the population. The people view the destruction of one's opposition by any means as a sign of a leader's strength, not of weakness or depravity as Westerners might view it. A good example is North Vietnam during the Vietnam War. The North Vietnamese leaders routinely locked up or executed dissenters, yet almost all North Vietnamese citizens obeyed their leaders and carried out their orders in a highly efficient manner.

By the end of 1968, most of the villagers who had once supported the VC without hesitation no longer looked favorably on the Communists, and their opinions of the Allies were marginally better than they had been during the early 1960s. From 1965 to 1968, countless VC prisoners and ralliers echoed the comments of this former cadre and Party member from Phong Dinh province: "Most people became resentful of the VC. Before, the VC promised victory and peace. The people believed them because they were living under VC control. As time went on, the people didn't see the peace they were wishing for and they realized that the VC had lied. I think that the people liked to live with the GVN because they could specifically enjoy some freedom and some tranquility."[43]

The popularity of the VC did not decline so rapidly after 1965 in parts of a few South Vietnamese provinces, primarily villages of marginal significance in the central coastal provinces and villages in relatively unimportant provinces, such as An Xuyen. The VC retained a certain amount of popularity in some areas even into the 1970s. As chapter 22 indicates, the Communist military forces were often much stronger, relative to Allied forces, in these areas than elsewhere, which inhibited many of the developments that made the Allies more popular in most of South Vietnam. The population remained fairly poor in some of these areas, despite GVN economic programs, because of the scarcity of land or the absence of land redistribution, thus hindering the GVN's efforts to win over the people with enticements of wealth. The families in many of the areas where the VC retained popularity had been committed to the VC for a longer time and in greater numbers than families elsewhere, and the GVN did not recruit as heavily in those areas. Brig. Gen. Tran Van Nhut told me that, during the early and mid-1960s, "there was more sympathy for the Communists than for us, because of family relationships, in the central area, mainly Quang Nam, Quang Tin, Quang Ngai, and Binh Dinh. Later in the war, the Communists were less popular, but when I was commander of the 2d ARVN division at Chu Lai, I knew that in some places even the RF and PF were sympathetic to the VC."[44]

From 1969 onward, VC popularity in the rural areas continued to decline, and the popularity of the GVN increased considerably.[45] By 1972, in all but a few places, the large majority of hamlet dwellers had decided that they preferred GVN rule to Communist rule. Only a small minority, composed almost exclusively of the relatives of the remaining VC, still hoped for a Communist victory. Many Americans noticed the new attitudes. Col. Walter Clark, for example, said, "In 1971 and 1972, as the GVN presence became stronger and the Viet Cong became weaker in my province, there was considerable evidence that the villagers believed the mandate of heaven indicated they should support the GVN. There were many instances when people provided information voluntarily. Some cooperation still came as a result of pressure from local GVN commanders on the peasants, but by that time I think harsh coercion was not as prevalent as it once was."[46]

The Communists themselves, in their secret wartime correspondence, acknowledged that the GVN enjoyed considerably greater popularity from 1969 to 1975 than they did. A captured directive written during February 1970 in the VC's Quang Nam province (akin to the GVN's Quang Tin province), an area with a tradition of strong support for the VC and one in which GVN land reform did not occur, states:

> [The enemy] has tricked and bribed the youths in our liberated areas to side with him and has poisoned the minds of the students and teenagers in his areas and debauched them in an attempt to enroll them in his anti-revolutionary forces. Recently, in our province which is one of the enemy's accelerated pacification priority areas, the enemy has implemented these plans, met with some success, and caused us a number of difficulties. . . . The people, especially parents of youths, have not paid particular attention to the indoctrination of their children. On the contrary, some of them have even forbidden their children to perform revolutionary tasks. They have spread passive, feudalistic, and backward thoughts to their children, thus undermining their revolutionary enthusiasm and badly affecting their lives. Furthermore, some people were deceived by enemy psywar activities and told their children to surrender to the enemy, or persuaded them to stop working for us and side with the enemy. This is a great shortcoming in our leadership, organization, and motivation of the people to participate in the anti-American Resistance for National Salvation.[47]

An April 1974 Communist document pertaining to all of South Vietnam states: "Our Party Chapters are not yet close to the masses and have so far failed to become the nucleus to guide the in-place movement. Our in-place forces are still weak and undermanned; the guerilla warfare movement is not yet strong."[48] In reference to the GVN, the document reads: "Police, local administrative, psychological warfare, and espionage apparati, and the reactionary and depraved culture will continue to oppress, dupe and poison many people in the areas under their control."[49]

In the end, the injustices associated with the attack on the VCI had little effect on villager attitudes. Unjustified arrests and torture were more likely to arouse the villagers' wrath than some of the more damaging Allied activities, most notably the use of heavy firepower in the village areas, because they often appeared to be the result of malice or carelessness. Several factors, however, usually put limits on the extent of the people's anger. As people with great respect for strength and authority, the villagers often accepted the arrests somewhat fatalistically, especially when detainees were not tortured, kept in prison for more than a day or two, or forced to pay a bribe. Arrests had become almost customary in some hamlets, which also helped an attitude of resignation to develop. In addition, the VC had kidnapped numerous innocent villagers and hurt many in other ways, which made the GVN detentions seem more forgivable. Whatever resentment—it normally ranged from minimal to moderate—that the arrests generated in an area did not affect popular attitudes significantly in most cases, let alone alienate villagers from the GVN. As the general attitudes of the villagers indicated, the factors that made the GVN more popular had far more influence over the villagers than the suffering caused by unjustified arrests and torture and other Allied activities.

26   The Impact of the
              New Attitudes

ommon misjudgments about the attitudes of the South Vietnamese villagers during the Vietnam War have been accompanied by misinterpretations of their significance. Of the commentators who portray the peasants as hostile or apathetic toward the GVN from 1968 to 1975, many conclude that the villagers' attitudes consequently stymied pacification or prevented the GVN from maintaining effective opposition to the Communist main force units once the Americans left. Thus, it doomed the GVN. Michael Walzer states that "victory depended above all upon the pacification of the countryside. . . . Pacification required a political base, and such a base seems to have been lost even before the arrival of the American army. 'Our' Vietnamese, the various Saigon regimes and their officials and soldiers, had painfully little local support."[1]

Chapter 25 shows that the villagers looked more favorably on the GVN than on the VC during the late 1960s and the 1970s, and that few had any desire to cooperate with the VC. Chapters 22 and 23 explain how the uncooperativeness of the villagers, in conjunction with the weakness of the Viet Cong shadow government, harmed the Communist war effort. These chapters, however, do not indicate how the GVN's popularity affected the villagers' behavior toward the GVN, or how this behavior affected the course of the war. Many observers in Vietnam during the late 1960s and the 1970s commented that the popularity of the GVN helped it to mobilize the masses on its behalf. A large number of them noted that the popular economic benefits offered by the GVN, such as Land to the Tiller and the overall rise in income, increased the villagers' willingness to join the GVN, give it intelligence, and support it actively in other ways. The Control Data Corporation study concludes that the Land to the Tiller program was "helping turn a once-disaffected, politically neutral mass of potential and sometimes actual revolutionaries (formerly providing rice, information, labor and military manpower to the enemy) into middle-class farmers in support of the regime."[2] Col. Edward Metzner, during tours as a province senior adviser in Vinh Binh from 1970 to 1971 and in Kien Giang from 1972 to 1973, noticed: "People everywhere were risking getting off the political fence and committing themselves to the government's side. However, they did so only because it was in their best interest economically to do so and the other side had no better alternative to offer."[3]

Witnesses also say that building up the territorial forces and the hamlet and village administrations with indigenous personnel helped to stimulate the civilian population, as well as the new GVN employees. Land reform and the spread of prosperity strengthened the bonds of community because more people believed that they had a stake in the affairs of the village, thereby increasing the villagers' willingness to help the GVN. Charles Callison reports that most village leaders told him, "Since the distribution of wealth is more equal, village society is more egalitarian; the new [land] owners are more enthusiastic about things and take a more active part in community affairs."[4]

The Communist leadership also stated that the GVN's programs at the hamlet and village levels were increasing support for the GVN. COSVN Resolution 9, written before most of the land reform occurred, notes that GVN political initiatives were hurting the VC seriously: "The enemy constantly uses economic measures, psychological warfare, decadent culture, etc., to influence and dominate all political, economic and cultural aspects in the rural areas. Therefore, the key problem now in the liberated zone is that we must motivate and unify the peasant bloc."[5]

High-ranking defector Nguyen Van Thanh told Jeffrey Race that a "decisive new element" had begun to hurt the VC in Long An province during the middle of 1969. This element consisted of several GVN initiatives: "One of these changes had been a partial reconstitution of the government's village apparatus. A second had been the psychological impact of the government's land-reform proposals, widely propagandized at the time. A third important change had been the considerable expansion of the Popular Force and People's Self-Defense Force organizations."[6]

Popularity, however, did not cause the rural populace to assist the GVN, contrary to what is commonly imagined. It did not provide the driving force for the GVN's pacification or military efforts. Nor did a lack of popularity in certain areas necessarily thwart these efforts, although it could slow them down. Most villagers had good cause to remain apathetic even if they looked favorably on the GVN. In contested areas and many of the allegedly secure areas, the Communists retained some power, so villagers had to be wary of helping the GVN too much lest the VC or the NVA harm them. Villagers also were not overly enthusiastic about giving up their children or their possessions to the GVN or anyone else. Most of them, undoubtedly, wished that both sides would simply leave them alone.

Villagers who were inclined toward inertia, however, usually supported one or both sides to some extent because they seldom were left alone. In contested areas, where the desire to be left alone was strongest, the GVN and the Communists tried to make peasants help them through a combination of compulsion and persuasion. Both sides normally enjoyed some success, for the villagers would still act if prodded. An insightful CIA report from June 1968, when much of the countryside was considered contested, states:

> The predominant sentiment . . . is probably one of increasing concern to avoid the hazards of war. . . . Left to themselves [the South Vietnamese] are likely to remain uncommitted and disengaged until a decisive break in the struggle becomes obvious. . . . Most of the people respond to power and authority, whether that of the Viet Cong or the GVN.[7]

The most important factor in obtaining villager support was leadership. Throughout this book, I attribute tremendous power to leadership, as if it were some magical force with which the GVN or the Communists could overcome almost any form of human apathy or reluctance. It was, in fact, such a force, from the beginning of the village war until its end. As the rise of the Viet Cong demonstrated, only a competent and devoted elite of leaders could organize large numbers of villagers to act. The second most useful tool in getting the villagers to cooperate was strength, which often was the product of good leadership. Strength and the success that demonstrated strength had a magnetic effect on the opportunistic villagers. Thus, the GVN's fine leadership and its strength advantages during the post-1968 period induced many villagers to cooperate willingly with the GVN. Although good leaders and strength contributed to the GVN's popularity, these factors did not influence the villagers' behavior simply because they were popular. They acted on villagers in ways that the other determinants of popularity did not.

The main contributors to GVN popularity besides leadership and strength were the personal benefits the GVN offered to villagers, aside from the benefits naturally accorded those who serve the strong. Offers of personal benefits alone never roused the peasants to action. The effectiveness of these offers, rather, depended on the actions of leaders. Popular policies gave leaders valuable ammunition for propaganda battles when they competed with leaders of another powerful political movement for active villager support. By promising new and obtainable benefits or pointing out existing benefits to the villagers, leaders could gain the cooperation of some villagers who otherwise would have ignored their pleas. Herein lay the means of turning the movement's popular political undertakings into active support. At times, one side had much more to give than the other. The VC had better advantages to offer during the early 1960s, principally the possession of land and the removal of abusive GVN officials. In the latter stages of the war, the GVN had a great deal more to offer, including economic prosperity, Land to the Tiller titles, relative freedom from destructive military encounters, and the possibility of serving in the territorial forces near one's family.

Offers of benefits exerted considerable influence on villagers if neither of the competing powers definitely seemed superior to the other on the basis of leadership and strength. If, on the other hand, one power's leadership and strength undeniably made it appear the better of the two, villagers were likely to base their choice of allegiance primarily on leadership quality and strength, and thus to support the clearly superior power. In areas where GVN leaders failed to bring economic prosperity, land reform, and other benefits to the villagers, they often obtained villager support strictly because of good leadership and demonstrations of strength. The GVN already enjoyed considerable strength advantages in most places by this time, so success hinged primarily on leadership. When the GVN installed good leaders, it succeeded in forming village governments and effective territorial forces from the hamlet populations in every single province, including the coastal provinces from Phu Yen to Quang Nam where many villagers still were poor and landless and had relatives in the VC.[8] In the many areas where the Viet Cong shadow government had lost most or all of its influence over the villagers, the GVN could mobilize the villagers by assigning leaders of a lesser caliber as well. On the other hand, where the VC still had good leaders or strength and the GVN lacked able leadership or strength, the VC stood a good chance of enlisting the aid of villagers.

Americans may find it difficult to comprehend the preeminence of leadership and strength in South Vietnamese village politics, for these forces do not play the same role in their own country. Americans scrutinize the ideas and proposed policies of political candidates before selecting them. Charisma is an important attribute for an American leader but usually not the most important, and strength is not an issue because political opponents do not compete by force. South Vietnamese villagers of the 1960s and 1970s, when faced with a choice of political leaders, did not examine the political platform of each candidate so carefully when deciding whom to support because their traditions and the circumstances of war usually compelled them to attach greater importance to leadership and power. These differences reflect profound differences between the two countries in the nature of political power. Whereas "public opinion," the sum of the population's views on political ideas and issues, in large part determines who becomes America's political leaders, the selection of leaders in rural South Vietnam depended more than anything else on the skills and accomplishments of the elites to whom the supreme commanders in Hanoi and Saigon had assigned leadership roles.

Some analysts argue that the GVN's popularity did not engender much support among the population because the GVN did not try to trade popularity for support. They emphasize that the beneficiaries of Land to the Tiller and other GVN programs that improved village life did not have to support the GVN to receive those benefits. The GVN, they contend, at least should have made the distribution of Land to the Tiller titles contingent on support for the GVN, as the VC presumably had with their land reform program, so that the villagers had a tangible incentive to assist the GVN. This criticism, however, is based on a misinterpretation of villager behavior. The proposed policy would not have increased popular support significantly in areas under GVN control because the villagers there did not need such an incentive; it even might have caused some pro-VC families in VC-dominated hamlets to strengthen their commitment to the Communists out of fear that GVN officials who took control of their hamlets would confiscate their land because family members served in the VC.

Throughout the war, when the GVN and the Communists actively demanded the villagers' support, the villagers gave it to one or both of them. When faced with only one political force that had any power, they supported it to some extent. Under no circumstances, however, did they avoid supporting anyone when at least one powerful authority called for their assistance, contrary to the claims of Land to the Tiller critics. The charisma, power, and propaganda of the leaders drove the villagers to act. A good leader could obtain supporters simply by giving land or other benefits to everyone or promising to do so. He did not need to give it only to those who helped him or announce such a policy, for the people did not drive such a hard bargain. In the early 1960s, VC cadres had often bought support simply by doling out land to most villagers, discussing the land reform in their propaganda, and requesting the people's support. Previous Vietnamese rulers had done the same with land and other benefits. The words of an elderly peasant show that the GVN used the same traditional technique and achieved the same result: "Many years ago, Emperor Khai Dinh taxed the people, and took people from the village to work for him. Emperor Minh Mang did the same. But always they gave us something first, like land, or money, or maybe a new market. It's the same now. Emperor Thieu and his group give us some things, and we have to be his servants. It's always the same for people in this village."[9]

The words of a village chief from Phong Dinh province also are instructive: "About 50 percent of the tenants in this village were Viet Cong or VC sympathizers before the [Land to the Tiller] Program; but now, due in large part to this program, they are beginning to believe the government is trying to help them and they are much more cooperative and responsive than before."[10] The chief emphasized that the villagers' beliefs about what the GVN was doing for them made them more "cooperative and responsive," in other words, more willing to serve leaders when asked to do so.

Some critics of the GVN advance a more sophisticated version of the thesis that the Allies failed to gain the allegiance of the villagers and thus could not make pacification work. The villagers had become so apathetic toward the Allies, they assert, that the GVN could not find people suitable for service in hamlet and village administrative roles. Aside from the fact that many villagers were more sympathetic to the GVN cause and that pacification worked much better than this argument suggests, success in the village war did not depend on the willingness of villagers to organize opposition to the enemy by themselves. In the VC's case, the high-quality leadership of the top Communist Party officials in Hanoi produced excellent leadership among the VC all the way down to the hamlet and village levels. Leadership qualities in the GVN system had a similar trickle-down effect. Thieu picked and motivated the GVN's district and province chiefs, whose leadership largely determined how well the pacification effort would function. The district and province chiefs controlled the territorial forces, the forces most crucial to pacification. They also could appoint hamlet and village officials of at least adequate ability or help them to gain election, and then motivate them. A good district or province chief, therefore, could get all of these people to work effectively and thus ensure good GVN performance in the village war. The GVN did not need to put villagers into district and province chief positions. The numerous effective district and province chiefs who assumed power after Tet came from the ARVN officer corps, which did not accept ordinary peasants.

All in all, despite the weakness of some GVN leaders, the combination of leadership, strength, and offers of benefits allowed the GVN to obtain the services of most military-age village males and to induce a large fraction of them and other villagers to prosecute the village war effectively during the period 1969–75. Thus, contrary to what many of the GVN's critics claim, the behavior of the villagers aided pacification considerably. Numerous veterans of the war recounted events similar to those described by Stephen Dukkony: "When I arrived [in January 1972] there was almost no threat to the security of the people in Go Cong, however, the NVA efforts and those of the VCI to enter the province after July required the people to choose between the two sides in their own defense. Except for a few small areas where an enemy force was present for a few hours at a time, the people visibly supported the GVN by providing information and by defending their hamlets against the VC. This stand-up and be counted situation proved that the people clearly sided with the GVN."[11]

By 1972, as chapter 23 indicates, the survival of South Vietnam depended mainly on the ability of the ARVN to defend South Vietnam's towns and cities from the North Vietnamese main force units, not on the village war. Popular attitudes, therefore, could have affected the war's outcome only by influencing ARVN performance. As it turned out, the attitudes of the peasants before they entered the Army had little effect on their military performance. Leadership, far more than anything else, determined how well ARVN soldiers would fight, provided that they had sufficient supplies and did not have to worry about the safety of their families. Good ARVN junior and noncommissioned officers generally motivated the enlisted men to fight aggressively and not desert. As with the territorial forces, strong high-level leadership produced the same kind of leadership at the lower levels. Defense Department analyst Thomas Thayer, for example, explains the transformation of the ARVN 7th Division in 1969–70 after U.S. units left its area and the division proved incapable of taking over the Americans' work:

> Recognizing the problem, President Thieu relieved the division's commander and appointed an aggressive brigade commander from the ARVN airborne division to the job. No other measures were taken nor was additional support

furnished. The new commander quickly turned the division into an effective fighting unit, furnishing strong evidence that replacing a poor commander with a good one was the best way to improve a poor ARVN Division.[12]

Lt. Gen. Vinh Loc, II Corps commander from 1965 to 1968, asserted, "As a rule, if the division commander was good, the division was good. If he was bad, the division was bad."[13]

Some commentators contend that the ARVN should have allowed peasants to serve in important leadership positions. Such a move, they say, would have allowed peasants with the ability to lead well to replace some ARVN leaders who lacked that ability and would have kept charismatic peasants who longed for upward social mobility away from the VC. This argument not only exaggerates the peasants' desire for social mobility but also underestimates the difficulty inherent in extending the privileges of the poorer villagers while shrinking those of the upper classes. Had Thieu undertaken such a drastic reform, some of the senior ARVN officers who were his most important supporters might have turned against him. The ARVN officer corps had enough capable and motivated men from the wealthier segments of the South Vietnamese population that it did not need to draw men from the reservoir of peasants. The wealthier people, most of whom now lived in towns or cities, and most other South Vietnamese in the towns and cities strongly preferred the GVN to the VC throughout the war, and some of them possessed good leadership skills and a strong desire to succeed.

The overall quality of the ARVN officer corps, it is true, did not match that of the Communists because political scheming and obsession with corruption weakened the ARVN corps to a greater extent. The ARVN, nevertheless, had enough good officers to fill the small number of high-level leadership positions that largely determined the ARVN's fighting capabilities. Contrary to what most American critics of the GVN believed, pervasive apathy among the GVN elite was not the main cause of the ARVN's leadership difficulties. "The required leadership was certainly available in the South Vietnamese armed forces," Col. William Le Gro remarks, "but it was not allowed to surface and take charge in enough situations."[14]

The problem, then, lay in the quality of the leaders who held the important posts within the ARVN. Nguyen Van Thieu was a moderately capable commander in chief who could install competent and aggressive subordinate commanders when he wanted to, as his overhaul of the district and province chiefs during the years following the Tet offensive demonstrated.

Unfortunately for the GVN, Thieu too often appointed men to key ARVN positions for their political loyalty, rather than their abilities, because he feared that his subordinates might try to overthrow him. Thieu, indeed, frequently made a conscious effort to choose generals who were ineffective because the stronger and more charismatic generals stood a better chance of marshaling the support of other ARVN leaders and mounting a successful coup against him. Although American pacification advisers succeeded in getting Thieu to replace many poor district and province chiefs with better people, the U.S. military command seldom convinced Thieu to sack the generals who controlled the main force units.

The inability of the commander in chief to gain the firm allegiance of much of the officer corps was perhaps an immutable characteristic of the Saigon political system. Thieu's predecessors all had encountered the same problem. The urban elites of the South tended to be individualistic and conspiratorial, and they did not submit easily to the will of a supreme leader. By contrast, the North Vietnamese belonged to a culture that put more emphasis on subordination of the individual to the group and thus had less difficulty in uniting against the enemy. In addition, GVN presidents could not eliminate their rivals easily because of American pressure to tolerate dissent, whereas Hanoi's leaders systematically crushed their opponents without restraint.

The ARVN's high-level leadership deficiencies grew worse after most of the Americans left in early 1973. Thieu became increasingly worried that ARVN officers were scheming to overthrow him, and the Americans gave up what influence they had possessed over ARVN leadership selection. Some excellent commanders remained in important positions, and the ARVN's leadership was good by the standards of a third-world country, but, on the whole, it did not stack up well against the NVA's leadership. After the war, Robert Komer recalled:

> I started out looking at Vietnam as a problem in resource allocation, and ended up looking at Vietnam more as a problem in getting the right Vietnamese in the right jobs. . . . It was much less a question of the size of the ARVN or the size of the Vietnamese Civil Service than of the qualities of leadership. . . . The problem we never solved was how to get the right people in the right jobs doing the right thing at the right time.[15]

The weakness of the top ARVN leaders, including Commander-in-Chief Thieu, was one of the most important reasons why the ARVN failed to halt the 1975 North Vietnamese offensive. Their mismanagement and corruption throughout the preceding years had depleted ARVN's military supplies and equipment, which contributed to shortages of vital items among many units during the war's last months. Poor leaders had allowed high desertion rates to erode many units. The deployment of ARVN forces also put the South Vietnamese at a serious disadvantage. Thieu spread his forces over a large area in order to thwart Communist attempts to retake the populated areas through political activity and low-intensity guerrilla warfare. He strengthened the population control system in the countryside to an extent that few of his American critics appreciated. It did enable the GVN to make use of village resources and largely kept the Communists from doing so, but it weakened the defense of the cities, a fact often ignored by many American advocates of pacification. Thieu also tried to defend remote provincial capitals in the highlands. He presumed that American bombers would help his dispersed forces fight off the NVA because Nixon had promised to help him in the event of a large NVA offensive, but Nixon's political woes would prevent him from making good on that promise.

As the thrusts of the 1975 NVA offensive cut into the South, some South Vietnamese units fought poorly or simply collapsed because of bad leadership. With the North Vietnamese piling up victories, the ARVN running out of supplies, and American help not coming, ARVN leaders grew increasingly demoralized. The GVN high command made some major strategic blunders during the NVA offensive that ensured a rapid ARVN defeat, most notably the unplanned retreats from Kontum and Pleiku and the transfer of the Airborne Division from I Corps to Saigon. In both I Corps and II Corps, the ARVN also suffered tremendous losses to desertion because it had allowed soldiers' families to live in the same areas as the soldiers. When ARVN units retreated or panic-stricken civilians fled, soldiers often left their units to help their families. The roads became clogged with civilians and deserters, which impeded the movement of the remaining ARVN units.

The ARVN faced other difficulties during its last months that made defeat much more likely, none of which had anything to do with the attitudes of the villagers. Heavy fighting between the ARVN and the NVA during the war's last years and reductions in U.S. aid contributed heavily to the shortages of military supplies and equipment. Because of the scarcity of matériel, the ground and air mobility of ARVN units declined drastically, as did their access to air and artillery strikes. As mentioned in chapter 23, the United States no longer supported the ARVN with its airpower as it had during the Easter offensive of 1972. These developments severely curtailed the ARVN's capability for attacking enemy main forces and defending South

Vietnam's towns and cities. This pronounced weakening of the ARVN contributed greatly to the demoralization of many units near the end of the war, including units that had effective leaders. The departure of most of the Americans and the aid reductions led to massive unemployment and high inflation in the South, so numerous ARVN soldiers no longer had enough money to provide their families with the bare essentials. Many soldiers, as a consequence, left duty temporarily or deserted to help their families. Where leadership was poor, economic woes also led to declines in discipline and morale. Meanwhile, the North Vietnamese had built up their logistical lines to the South after the 1973 Paris Peace Accords without interference from the United States. They eventually sent enough troops and Chinese and Soviet matériel to the South to give their main forces decided advantages over the ARVN in firepower and mobility.

The North Vietnamese offensive lasted for most of March and all of April 1975. Although some of the outgunned and outmanned ARVN units repelled the attackers with heavy losses because of good leadership, the NVA had too many strong, well-led, and well-supplied main force units for the weakened and dispersed ARVN to handle. One by one, South Vietnam's towns and cities fell to the North Vietnamese. Powerless to stop the onslaught, bewildered villagers and GVN pacification troops cowered as the large NVA units sped through the countryside on their way to the towns and cities. Although the GVN had won the struggle for control over rural South Vietnam and the allegiance of its inhabitants, it lost the war.

PART SEVEN: Postlude

27

Theories of Revolutionary Warfare

he main body of this book does not attempt to compare its conclusions with prevalent theories on revolutionary warfare or with conclusions about wars of a similar nature. I place discussions of theory at the end for an important reason. Many political scientists and a few historians use history merely as a vehicle for proving theories. Rather than first trying to describe the events in question as accurately as possible, as I attempt to do in this book, they present history and theory together in ways that illustrate the theories as effectively as possible. When history is used in such a manner, unfortunately, the theories tend to overpower the history. Typically, after the theoretician conducts a limited amount of research, he or she becomes convinced that particular theories are accurate. The theoretician thereafter is determined to prove the theories, and, as efforts to prove them move along, he or she becomes less and less likely to throw out theories in light of new evidence because too much has been invested in proving the original theories. The theoretician is likely to downplay or ignore evidence that contradicts the theories and to distort or incorrectly interpret history in order to validate them, which not only damages historical interpretation but also renders the accuracy of the theories suspect.

The highly theoretical works on the Vietnam War offer flawed historical and theoretical conclusions because they suffer from such weaknesses. Two of the most highly acclaimed, *The Army and Vietnam* by Andrew Krepinevich, Jr., and *Deadly Paradigms* by D. Michael Shafer, exemplify the problem. In *The Army and Vietnam*, Krepinevich attempts to prove that the effort to preserve South Vietnam failed because the U.S. Army and its South Vietnamese protégé behaved as if they were fighting a conventional opponent, rather than one employing the methods of revolutionary warfare. As I explain repeatedly in this book, most Allied tactical choices were appropriate. The Allies ultimately foiled the Communists' revolutionary warfare and lost the war because the ARVN's main forces could not stop the NVA's conventional attacks in 1975. Shafer, in *Deadly Paradigms*, asserts that all Allied counterinsurgency efforts in Vietnam failed and explains the failure with theories. He ignores the numerous Allied counterinsurgency successes of the post–1965 period, many of which contradict his theories.

For a history of a revolutionary war or for a theoretical work on revolutionary warfare, it is better to examine as much of the available evidence as possible and to interpret it before coming to any conclusions about the validity of particular theories. Knowledge of theoretical concepts or of analogous situations, it should be noted, frequently can aid the examiner by suggesting historical factors that might have played a part in the events under study, which the examiner can then investigate. Once the historical exploration is complete, useful discussion of theories or the analogies from which they are drawn requires a diligent search for important differences between wars as well as similarities, a task that theorists often neglect. Each revolutionary war differs from all others in many crucial respects, and the differences—although they often appear smaller than the similarities—can be crucial. The inability to perceive these differences has produced many incorrect theories and analogies, and consequently many disastrous wartime decisions.

Some revolutionary wars, including the Vietnam War, vary so greatly over time and space that they essentially consist of a variety of small wars that differ significantly from one another. The Vietnam War, indeed, featured a large number of the elements normally described by revolutionary warfare theorists. One might be tempted, therefore, to try to present a comprehensive description of revolutionary warfare theory on the basis of a single war. No war of which I am aware, however, and certainly not the Vietnam War, contained enough variation to include all of the basic scenarios possible in a revolutionary war. For this reason, and because of considerations of space, I do not attempt to set forth a comprehensive set of theories on revolutionary war in this chapter. I do not even discuss the theoretical implications of every detail in this book, for that task also would require a quite lengthy treatment. Instead, I use the findings of the book's main body to discern the most important areas where existing theory is inaccurate or inadequate.

Theorists normally define revolutionary warfare as warfare waged by insurgents attempting to overthrow a regime on behalf of a cause. The insurgents usually come from and operate in the rural areas within the regime's borders and usually have a considerable number of civilian supporters in those areas. The counterinsurgent regime typically controls most or all of the towns and cities and possesses significant main force strength. Some theorists acknowledge that the insurgents eventually will form main force units to defeat the counterinsurgents completely, but most focus primarily on the previous phases of the insurgency, when the insurgents fight as guerrillas against the counterinsurgents' forces. Because counterinsurgent forces and insurgent forces often try to achieve the same goals, such as gaining the population's support and inhibiting the enemy's intelligence collection efforts, some theories actually apply to both sides. For simplicity's sake, however, I follow the convention used by many theorists of describing most situations as though the insurgents always occupy one position and the counterinsurgents another, with each occupying the position that it is more likely to occupy.

One of the most basic and widely accepted theories about revolutionary warfare, which often provides a starting point for discussion, is that large segments of the rural population are willing to help the insurgents overthrow the existing government. The large majority of theorists also argue that many of the villagers believe in the insurgents' cause. Coercion or the threat of it alone can convince certain individuals to go along, they contend, but the insurgents cannot win over large numbers of people unless they have some sort of positive political agenda. Because a large fraction of the villagers want to support the insurgents, the theory continues, insurgent forces can obtain personnel, food, intelligence information, and other useful items from the villagers. The South Vietnamese villagers of the 1960s and 1970s fit this description to some extent. VC coercion would not have co-opted much of the populace without offers of land reform and elimination of unpopular GVN personnel. Yet, the theory fails to take into account other essential reasons for the Viet Cong's rise. The VC gained much popularity in the villages through forces beyond the appeal of their political cause and intimidation, namely good leadership and displays of superiority over the GVN. Later in the war, the GVN also gained some popularity because of its effective leaders and its success in defeating the VC. Satisfying the grievances of the peasants or giving them things they enjoyed was likely to increase popularity, but these other factors, at times, overrode the importance of the benefits offered by one side or the other.

Some theorists contend that the counterinsurgents should try hard to destroy the insurgent political infrastructure. A number of them even argue that the counterinsurgents ought to make it their top priority. A different group of revolutionary warfare theorists, on the other hand, downplays the leadership's importance. They claim that the insurgent political program and the masses to which it appeals, not the infrastructure, are the source of insurgent power. If the counterinsurgents neutralize some of the insurgent leaders, they claim, new leaders will arise from the masses. The counterinsurgents, therefore, can defeat the insurgency only by instituting political reforms that placate the peasantry.

In the case of the Vietnam War, the preceding interpretation is incorrect. The decline of the VCI after the Tet offensive certainly helped to ruin the South Vietnamese Communists, and such a decline most likely would have the same effect on any similar movement. The performance of almost all civilian and military governmental organization's throughout the world depends heavily on leadership, and the dependence is strongest in countries with authoritarian traditions. When leaders are arrested or killed, the primary impetus for action weakens; if enough leaders are eliminated within a short period of time, this impetus disappears, and followers are likely to revert to passivity. The neutralization of numerous VC leaders who served at the village level and the consequent weakening of the VCI provide good examples of the problems that leadership losses can cause. If the organization that runs the insurgency is authoritarian, as are most insurgent organizations, the leadership is likely to consist of a relatively small elite that cannot quickly replace large losses with adequate people because the leaders take time to develop. The apprehension or killing of insurgent leaders does not necessarily make the people angry and increase their desire to fight the counterinsurgents unless a strong racial, religious, or ethnic conflict, such as did not exist in South Vietnam in most cases, divides the insurgents from the counterinsurgents. Indeed, the elimination of leaders makes villagers less sympathetic to the insurgency if they prefer siding with those who are strong and successful, as they did in South Vietnam. Destroying the insurgents' infrastructure also helps the counterinsurgents to carry out their own political program by eliminating competition for the villagers' resources. Implementing a political program before destroying the enemy's infrastructure, in fact, is quite difficult because the enemy cadres can obstruct it through intimidation, violence, and propaganda. Both the VC and GVN land reform programs did not achieve their maximum political effect until the enemy infrastructure had been rendered ineffective.

The differences among wars are large enough that the counterinsurgents can determine the best means of battling the insurgency only by examining their own war in detail. To accomplish this task in the most effective way, counterinsurgent policymakers first have to determine the strengths and weaknesses of each side in the conflict. Armchair strategists often recommend that a counterinsurgent power adopt a method of warfare that another government has used successfully against an insurgency. All too often, however, the counterinsurgent power lacks the capability to pursue the recommended policy because it does not have the strengths of the other government, or it faces an enemy immune to the policy because the enemy does not have the weaknesses of the other insurgency.

Theorists who advocate dismantling the infrastructure often make inappropriate recommendations of this nature. Many propose that the counterinsurgents adopt particular methods of neutralizing the insurgent infrastructure without investigating the obstacles that the counterinsurgents might encounter if they do so. The insurgents know how important their infrastructure is and they try to protect it, especially its more important members. The covert, or legal, cadres are protected by secrecy. The counterinsurgents can identify them only through village informants who happen to discover their identities or through sources within the insurgent organization; these assets are not always available. The overt political cadres, who are responsible for the central task of mobilizing the villagers, realize that the populace knows who they are and might betray them to the enemy, so they try to stay away from counterinsurgent military and police forces. These cadres might enjoy a variety of advantages or employ a number of schemes that help them to avoid the enemy. Sometimes, the counterinsurgents cannot reach the cadres because they lack the armed strength needed to penetrate the insurgent-controlled areas. When they can enter areas under insurgent domination or when insurgent cadres venture into contested areas, insurgent intelligence systems might warn the cadres of an approaching enemy and allow them to escape. The GVN faced both of these obstacles during the early 1960s and consequently stood no chance of eliminating a sizable portion of the overt insurgent infrastructure.

In other cases, the insurgents might put their political cadres together with armed men who do not live among the population, as the Vietnamese Communists did in most places by the late 1960s. The counterinsurgents can eliminate these members of the infrastructure only with their armed forces in a military engagement. If the counterinsurgents have excellent intelligence, which they usually do not have, they can identify and target the units with which the cadres operate. If strong and aggressive enough, the counterinsurgents can eliminate some of them haphazardly by operating in the village areas. In addition, counterinsurgent operations in and around the villages can force the insurgent infrastructure to curtail or cease its visits to the villages, so the cadres cannot perform their duties as effectively, if at all. When counterinsurgent operations reduce the infrastructure's visits to the villages, the cadres still might be able to kill people in the villages rather easily. Such killings, however, do not necessarily demoralize the villagers, and they can rouse them to action against the perpetrator, a problem that both the GVN and the VC confronted at times.

Revolutionary warfare theory asserts, correctly, that counterinsurgent forces need accurate intelligence in order to locate and eliminate many of the stealthful insurgents. It says little, however, about how to obtain such intelligence. Part II of this book describes the numerous ways in which the Allied forces collected intelligence for use against the VCI and the other VC involved in the village war. Some of these methods will work in other wars; some will not. Again, in every case, one must first look at the characteristics of the war. Space considerations preclude examination of the applicability of each intelligence method to other situations, but a few examples serve to illustrate the point.

Each side's mode of operations greatly affects the intelligence needs of the counterinsurgents. If the insurgents' overt political cadres live more or less permanently with the population, as the VCI did during the early 1960s, the counterinsurgents need different types of intelligence than if the cadres cling to armed guerrilla forces, as the VCI did later in the war. In the former case, discovering the identities of the cadres will lead to their neutralization, unless insurgent protection systems prevent counterinsurgent forces from reaching the villages while the overt cadres are still there. In the latter case, the counterinsurgents need tactical military intelligence to locate the forces with whom the cadres travel, except when lone cadres sneak into populated areas, as they sometimes do. If covert insurgent cadres reside in the villages, the counterinsurgents can easily round up the cadres whom they can identify.

The value of particular sources of intelligence varies tremendously from one war to another. If the insurgent forces come from a culture, such as that of South Vietnam, in which family members influence them heavily, the counterinsurgents might be able to persuade the insurgents to defect or to provide information if the counterinsurgents can identify their relatives and persuade those relatives to help in converting the insurgents. The counterinsurgents themselves might have relatives in the insurgency or in the villages whom they can easily persuade to provide information. Some theorists claim that the counterinsurgent government cannot get intelligence from the rural population if it does not enjoy its sympathies or if the insurgents dominate the population and are in a position to kill any of its members at will. In Vietnam, however, the GVN regularly received intelligence from villagers, even in hamlets where most people actively supported the VC and the VC had much more power than the GVN. Coercion and money caused some villagers in the VC-dominated areas to supply information, but most of the information came from relatives of GVN personnel. The VC discovered relatively few of the informants because villagers and GVN personnel normally managed to meet where no Communists or Communist spies would see them, and intelligence collectors generally kept their informants' identities secret, especially if they were relatives. In other countries, counterinsurgents might not enjoy such ties with the population, or the villagers might not be as vulnerable to coercion and offers of money as those in South Vietnam. In addition, insurgents might have better means of identifying and neutralizing the informants of the counterinsurgents.

The level of violence and danger in the war also affects the amount of intelligence available. During the Vietnam War, Communists serving in areas of heavy Allied military activity defected in large numbers and brought with them great amounts of information. Where military activity was less intense, fewer Communists defected and thus the Allies, on the whole, obtained less information from defectors. The Vietnam War featured much more main force warfare than most insurgency conflicts, largely because of the presence of North Vietnamese and U.S. troops. Most counterinsurgents, therefore, are unlikely to receive as many insurgent defectors as did the GVN.

Some theorists note the importance of intelligence for the insurgent forces and mention the primary sources of insurgent information, which are informants within the rural population and spies within the counterinsurgent organizations. They say little, however, about what the counterinsurgents can do to stymie the insurgents' intelligence efforts. The counterinsurgents can reduce the flow of information to the insurgents from the villagers in several ways. When they can identify the insurgents' informants, they can punish or imprison them. For this task, counterinsurgent forces need good access to village residents and effective ways of eliciting the truth from them, or they need sources of information originating within the insurgency. The counterinsurgents do not always have such resources available. The counterinsurgents can also diminish the information flow by inhibiting or preventing contact between villagers and the insurgent infrastructure. Counterinsurgent forces must either weaken the infrastructure or establish an armed presence that makes entry into the village areas risky for the insurgents.

To stop spies within counterinsurgent organizations, counterinsurgent leaders can neutralize some of the insurgent spies through careful investigations. This process requires good leadership, and, because it is so difficult, it is unlikely by itself to discover many of the guilty even if the leadership is excellent. The counterinsurgents can obtain information on spies from defectors, captured documents, agents, prisoners, and other insurgent-based sources, but these types of sources might be scarce, and the insurgents might have effective means of hiding their spies' identities from most of their own people to prevent leaks, as the VC often had. The easiest and most consistently effective method to frustrate traitorous spies is to minimize the exposure of information to people within counterinsurgent organizations by using the methods described in chapter 14.

Few theorists have paid much attention to intelligence sharing in revolutionary wars. The Phoenix and Phung Hoang programs, because they were so large and well documented, provide one of the best cases in history for examining this issue. Allied intelligence-collection organizations generally gave little information to Phoenix or Phung Hoang, or to any other organization, because of the fear that others would compromise their sources or get credit for the work they had done. Phoenix and Phung Hoang caused intelligence agencies to share intelligence only when someone with authority over a variety of agencies, such as a GVN district or province chief or a CIA province officer in charge, forced them to share in one way or another. The more organizations there were in a district or province and the larger the number of people with authority over them, the more difficult it was to induce intelligence sharing. In other revolutionary wars, the sharing of intelligence on the insurgent infrastructure is likely to involve the same problems and solutions.

The Vietnam War shows that certain types of operational forces can combat insurgent forces much better than others. The PRUs and the best units of the Regional Forces demonstrated that mobile forces with good intelligence can wreak havoc on an opponent waging revolutionary warfare, even in areas dominated by the enemy, unless the enemy has large and effective main forces. This type of force, however, requires superior leadership and obedient rank-and-file soldiers, assets not always available to counterinsurgents. The achievements of the territorial forces and some other pacification forces indicate that indigenous units enjoy significant advantages over other units. Members of indigenous units obtain a greater degree of cooperation from the population because it contains their friends and relatives. Knowledge of local society, enemy personnel and sympathizers, and terrain affords them a better chance of defeating the enemy. When sufficiently effective and large in number, they can remain in a village permanently and thus deny access to the enemy. If they remain in the same place each night, however, they are vulnerable to concentrated insurgent attacks. Conventional military forces can be broken into small units that employ tactics similar to those of the territorial forces or the PRUs. If drawn from other areas of the country or from a foreign nation, as usually occurred in South Vietnam, these forces lack the crucial rapport with the population and knowledge of operational area. They can alleviate this problem by staying in one place for a long time or by working together with local counterinsurgent personnel.

Many revolutionary warfare theorists assert that police forces can and should play a major role in defeating any insurgency, as they have done in many revolutionary wars, but the case of South Vietnam indicates otherwise. The GVN's police enjoyed some success throughout the war in rounding up covert VC cadres, both in urban and rural areas. Typically, they learned the identities of these cadres and then, alone or with other forces, arrested them in their homes or in market areas. In the 1950s, Diem's police succeeded in taking into custody or killing some overt cadres. From 1960 onward, however, once the overt cadres instigated the full-blown insurgency, the police apprehended few overt cadres. During the early and mid-1960s, the police did not dare come close to many VC-dominated hamlets because the local VC were much more heavily armed than the police. The dangers of traveling in the countryside also limited the ability of the police forces to make contact with informants and agents. When the police did attempt to reach a hamlet containing illegal cadres, the VC often had intelligence capabilities that gave the cadres advance warning of the approaching enemy, thus allowing them to flee. Later in the war, most of the overt cadres operated almost exclusively alongside Communist military forces, who again possessed too much firepower for the police to handle. During the period 1960–75, therefore, the police usually could help to neutralize overt VCI only by giving the intelligence to military or paramilitary forces, which they did not do very often, or by going on operations with such forces, which they did fairly often in some places but usually not with dramatic success.

Examination of other Allied operational forces offers further evidence that the police played a relatively minor role in defeating the VC. The territorial forces and the PRUs, both paramilitary forces, in many cases identified as many of the covert cadres as the police did, in large part because they had better access to the villagers than did the police. Because the overt VCI decided to operate alongside military forces, Allied paramilitary and military forces found and eliminated many more overt cadres by employing normal military intelligence and operations procedures than the police were able to find through investigative work.

The tremendous differences in capabilities among the various Allied forces discredits the theory that force ratios can predict who will win a revolutionary war. Many theorists assert that counterinsurgents need a certain ratio of counterinsurgent troops to insurgent troops, generally between ten to one and twenty to one, in order to defeat the insurgency. These individuals usually ignore the quality of the opposing forces and the advantages that their environment affords them, two factors so important that they render abstract ratio calculations meaningless. Anyone assessing the interaction between forces must first find the answers to many questions about the forces involved. How useful is the intelligence available to each side? How mobile are the troops? What effects does the terrain have on military operations? Do one or both sides regularly employ main forces in a conventional manner? How good is the leadership on each side? How many replacements can each side obtain? In South Vietnam, ten Regional Forces soldiers led by an excellent officer often accomplished more in a month than one hundred members of a Regional Forces unit whose leader was passive or incompetent. A battalion of ARVN soldiers provided with good intelligence and helicopters was able to inflict many more casualties than a battalion of similar quality that had few intelligence assets and no helicopters. While the theorists claim that counterinsurgents must outnumber insurgents by a wide margin to defeat them, Allied forces on many occasions dealt the enemy crushing defeats in areas where they did not outnumber the Communists by such margins. One could try to estimate the ratio needed to win within a certain period of time by considering all of the factors specific to the situation, and a small group of theorists has tried to do so. The changes in the factors over time, however, are so unpredictable and the interactions between them so complex and difficult to quantify that such estimates are not likely to be accurate.

A major shortcoming of most of the literature on revolutionary warfare theory is that it understates or ignores the problems that the counterinsurgent power faces when the insurgents develop main force strength and enter the final phase of revolutionary warfare. When aided by excellent intelligence capabilities, as they most often are if they have reached the final phase, strong insurgent main forces usually can destroy the enemy's smaller forces when they attempt to enter areas under insurgent control. The Communist main forces possessed this capability during the mid-1960s. Only when counterinsurgents have highly effective forces that can operate with stealth and obtain help from the population—which the Allies did not have in substantial numbers during the mid-1960s—can they hope to achieve anything militarily or politically with small forces in insurgent-held areas. Even such forces as these generally must avoid getting close to large insurgent main force units, as the history of the PRUs indicates. When counterinsurgents must operate in large units, their forces cannot maintain an armed presence over a large amount of territory. As a result, they cannot deny the insurgents access to many villages or establish pacification forces and programs in many villages.

Counterinsurgents faced with this unenviable scenario have no sensible choice but to fight the insurgents primarily with main force units. Many theorists criticize such reliance on main force units, but the alternatives they advocate, such as the use of pacification forces or of mobile, insurgent-style cadres and guerrillas, in most instances are no longer viable at this point. The counterinsurgents are likely to find the road they now must take a difficult one, as the Allies did during the mid-1960s. The insurgents often do not have cities, overt bases, or fixed lines of communication that they must defend, in which case they do not need to assign large numbers of their soldiers to static defense duties. The counterinsurgents, by contrast, must use large numbers of troops to guard their own dispersed cities and bases against large insurgent main force attacks, and they might have to use an additional number to protect lines of communication. Because insurgents likely have superior intelligence capabilities, mobile insurgent forces probably can choose to evade or attack counterinsurgent forces that operate in the countryside. Only counterinsurgent forces that have great technological advantages, such as the U.S. main forces in South Vietnam, or a tremendous superiority in troop strength or fighting skills stand much of a chance of defeating large insurgent units in the village areas.

If insurgent main forces suffer exceedingly heavy losses, they lose their hold over the village areas and allow smaller counterinsurgent forces to operate. No matter how powerful the counterinsurgent main forces are, however, they might have little or no chance of eliminating the insurgent main forces completely. If losses become severe, the insurgents might be able to disperse and hide their forces or move them into sanctuaries, as the Vietnamese Communists often did from 1965 onward. If the insurgents have an external source of soldiers and supplies that the counterinsurgents do not destroy, as the Communists had in North Vietnam, they can maintain main force activity at some level indefinitely if they choose to do so.

Theorists often criticize counterinsurgents for attacking insurgent forces that occupy uninhabited areas, even if the areas are not far removed from the villages. The counterinsurgents, they argue, ought to keep their forces in and around the populous rural areas and fight the insurgents when they come to these areas to obtain the villagers' resources. Yet, if insurgent main forces have numerous soldiers in an uninhabited area and counterinsurgent pacification forces occupy villages in the vicinity, the counterinsurgents, in most cases, would be wise to disregard such advice. If counterinsurgent main forces do not wear down such insurgent main forces or stop them while they travel toward the villages, the insurgents most probably can form large units, overwhelm the pacification forces in the villages, and take whatever they want from the villagers, as the Communists did at times to the Allies. Counterinsurgent main forces that attack large insurgent main forces in unpopulated areas, moreover, can inhibit or prevent these forces from striking directly at the cities and other vital centers; counterinsurgent pacification forces cannot do the same, because they lack the military power to halt the insurgents' advances or to keep them from feeding off the population. The main forces of the counterinsurgents have the option of waiting until the main forces of the insurgents come to the village areas before attacking them, but then they risk damaging the villages and driving away their supporters in the countryside. Counterinsurgents who hold the upper hand in the village areas but face an enemy possessing powerful main forces, therefore, normally should assign large numbers of people to each of three different types of forces: pacification forces in the rural areas, static guard forces in the urban areas and perhaps also along lines of communication, and mobile main forces that attack the insurgents whenever they can.

Main force warfare between insurgents and counterinsurgents in populous rural areas can inflict great damage on the civilian population, especially when it involves heavy firepower. The insurgent forces might take cover behind the civilians, regardless of what the civilians think of them. This tactic allows the insurgents to disguise themselves, makes the enemy reluctant to fire, and convinces certain onlookers that the counterinsurgents, when they do fire, have no concern for the welfare of the people. Counterinsurgent leaders are inclined to fire into the villages for reasons of military necessity, though they may be forced to restrain their fire for a variety of other reasons. Many theorists believe that the user of firepower estranges those villagers who suffer injury or loss of property. Limited and, at times, indiscriminate use of firepower by the South Vietnamese government up to 1965 did push some villagers toward the Viet Cong. Large-scale damage caused by heavy firepower, however, especially if the firepower is directed at enemy forces and helps to defeat the enemy, can have a different impact. In South Vietnam, it constituted a setback for the side that was more successful at using the resources of the villagers. If the VC had controlled a village before a destructive attack, the villagers cooperated less with the VC and blamed the VC for their troubles, even though the VC did not inflict the damage with their weapons. Because the VC did not control areas untouched by the war, many survival-driven villagers moved to areas under Allied control, thus denying the VC access to them. When the Allies had held the village before the damage occurred, they lost important assets in the countryside if the residents moved to towns or cities.

When attempting to defeat insurgents, a nation that seeks to maintain a good image at home or abroad can take action to limit negative publicity. One option is to keep controversial programs secret, as the United States did fairly effectively with the PRUs. When word of the program's existence leaks out, however, the public imagination, encouraged by bogus sources, often conjures up fantasies of wrongdoing. This fate eventually befell the attack on the VCI, parts of which were secret. Another option is to keep journalists out of the war zone. Such a prohibition can prevent a hostile media from feeding the public a diet of misleading tidbits of information, as often occurred during the Vietnam War. For a democratic state, of course, there exists the danger that military or political leaders will use such a prohibition to conceal actions that most citizens would strongly oppose. A third and quite safe option is to give counterinsurgency programs bland names. Opponents of the Allied war effort criticized Phoenix more vehemently than the far more active Provincial Reconnaissance Units, in part, because the name *Phoenix* sounded more dastardly.

28   Reflections

The Vietnamese

T he end of the war brought little comfort to the people of South Vietnam. The many Americans who opposed the Allied cause during the war and who now dominate America's media and universities seem to have paid little attention to postwar South Vietnamese history. These people have made no significant films about postwar Vietnam and written almost no books about it. This silence is astonishing, not only because Vietnam played such an important role in their lives, but also because so many of them said during the war that they opposed U.S. involvement out of concern for the South Vietnamese people. Had this concern been genuine, the fate of South Vietnam since 1975 would have compelled them to employ their strident voices on behalf of the South Vietnamese. Left-wing historian David Hunt recently expressed his regret over the decision of the American Left to ignore post-GVN Vietnam: "The real failure came after 1975, when events demonstrated the limits of our analysis, and, instead of persisting with efforts to understand and to help the Vietnamese, we stopped thinking about them. Our silence on a front where the Left once held forth with a brash self-confidence amounts to an abdication."[1]

The few veterans of the antiwar movement who have spoken out about the current situation in Vietnam are, for the most part, those who have turned against the antiwar movement. Many former antiwar activists, however, remain outspoken about what happened in Vietnam before the war's end. They continue to describe the Vietnam War as if it lasted only from 1965 to 1968 and involved only foolish or sadistic Americans flailing blindly through a hostile Vietnamese countryside. They complain about the errors of American anti-Communists that led to the Vietnam War but ignore their own errors in judgment, such as their faith in the benevolence of the Vietnamese Communists.

It seems likely that American opponents of the war keep quiet about postwar Vietnam because the South did not become a better place after the Communist takeover, as they had claimed it would. By all accounts, it became much worse in the years following the North Vietnamese victory and has remained worse. As soon as the Communists took power, they crushed their potential opposition. They largely refrained from violence in Saigon and the other major cities because foreign journalists were watching. In the countryside, out of foreign view, however, they killed a great many GVN leaders, rank-and-file personnel, spies, and Communist ralliers, along with some non-Communist political and religious leaders and other educated people. Two instructors from the University of California at Berkeley interviewed more than eight hundred refugees in the United States and France and concluded that the Communists executed at least sixty-five thousand people for political reasons between 1975 and 1983, the bulk of them in 1975 and 1976.[2] The refugees whom I interviewed also spoke of widespread killing after the war. Although the exact number of victims may never be known, it was undoubtedly quite large, far larger than the Western media presumed.

The Communists also imprisoned many hundreds of thousands of people from these groups in squalid "reeducation camps"—prisons bearing the same name as Diem's prisons of the late 1950s. The prisoners performed manual labor every day; in the evening, they had to listen to or read Communist propaganda and discuss it. Some remained in these camps for a decade or longer, although the Party released most of the prisoners by the late 1980s because of the expenses involved and pressure from foreign countries. Each year, ten percent or more of the inmates perished, mainly because of starvation, lack of medical care, torture, and execution. During the years following the war, furthermore, Communist mistreatment and expulsions forced many hundreds of thousands of people, including a large portion of the despised Chinese minority, to flee. Most of these "boat people" had to pay large bribes to Communist officials as they left, and a substantial number died as they sailed for other lands.

Whereas the Thieu regime had tolerated a certain amount of dissent, if only because of American pressure, the Communists forbade all public criticism of the regime and locked up anyone who violated the prohibition. Although the Hanoi government recently has made some token gestures toward improving human rights in response to Western protests, it continues to imprison most serious dissenters. When I visited Hanoi in 1995, Nguyen Ngoc Dien, deputy director general of the Institute for International Relations, complained to me that Westerners were always pestering him about Vietnam's human rights practices. He did not hesitate to defend his nation's policies. "We have human rights for the majority," the smiling Dien said. "Only for the minority, who want to do ugly things, we do not have human rights. When I go to America, there are some dishes I like, and some I don't like. When you are here in Vietnam, there are some dishes you like, and some you don't like. I can't make you eat what you don't like, and you can't make me eat what I don't like. So you cannot make us do things with human rights that are normal in your country."[3]

The Communist rulers have not behaved more virtuously than their GVN predecessors. Most who took control in 1975 came from North Vietnam and treated the South Vietnamese with as much contempt as had any GVN rulers. Party officials, confronted by the wealth of the South and no longer constrained by the urgencies of fighting, started to enrich themselves soon after the war in all the ways familiar to Thieu's officials. The revolutionary selflessness that the Party had introduced did not last. Party leaders now own many lucrative businesses, and they take kickbacks from those they do not own. They tolerate large-scale drug use and prostitution, which they had vowed to eliminate during the war, because of the profits they earn from them. They enjoy expensive luxuries, while most of their fellow citizens remain poor. In 1995, after I interviewed one general in Hanoi, I watched him drive away in a new Japanese sport-utility vehicle that would have cost $30,000 in the United States and far more in Vietnam because of taxes and corruption. He sped past ordinary, bicycle-riding citizens, whose average wage was $25 per month.

A few senior Party officials now acknowledge these problems openly, but they have done little to eliminate them. Nguyen Van Linh, for instance, admitted in 1993, "Not a small number of people, including leading cadres in charge of high-level leadership and management apparatuses, have taken advantage of loopholes in mechanisms and policies to misappropriate public funds, accept bribes and seek personal gains in an illegal manner. . . . Corruption, smuggling, and bribery have reached such a widespread and alarming proportion that many people regard them as a national disaster."[4]

The economy in the South, though freed of the burdens and damages of war and aided by the Soviets, degenerated rapidly after the Communists took over. The Communists removed profit incentives by dictating what crops farmers could plant and limiting the prices that they could charge. The Party persuaded or coerced many thousands of people to live and farm in areas abandoned during the war or in remote areas that had never been cultivated. Agricultural efforts at these settlements often failed miserably. In 1978, the Communists brought into reality the peasants' worst nightmare by collectivizing agriculture in the South, as they had planned to do all along. Rice production plummeted. The regime also took control of all major private businesses and tried but failed to develop heavy industries. The invasion of Cambodia in late 1978 further weakened the economy. In recent years, the Party has abandoned its socialist practices and built a market economy, which has improved the economic situation considerably, but unemployment and poverty remain large problems.

Many members of the U.S. antiwar movement contended at the time that all American involvement in the affairs of South Vietnam was harmful. Yet, South Vietnam has suffered greatly from the absence of the United States, and not only because U.S. military assistance had allowed the GVN to remain in power. Gone are the American aid that helped the GVN prosper and American pressure on behalf of human rights. Communist Party leaders, in fact, now concede that South Vietnam would enjoy a better economy were the United States involved in its affairs. They say that they want to resemble more closely the economic powerhouses of Asia, such as Thailand, South Korea, and Taiwan, nations that developed their strength under the American aegis. Some even assert bluntly that they would like the United States to help them improve their economy. "Our country is poor, but we want to be rich like America," commented Nguyen Trong Phuc, dean of the Party Historical Faculty at Ho Chi Minh National Political Academy. "We want to learn from the Americans how to get rich." [5]

Many of the South Vietnamese who had remained faithful to the Party until the war's end subsequently realized that the "liberators" from Hanoi were worse for South Vietnam than the GVN's leaders had been, and some of them fled the country. Truong Nhu Tang, one of the most prominent members of the group that left Vietnam, writes in his memoir:

> [The North Vietnamese Communists] made it understood that the Vietnam of the future would be a single monolithic bloc, collectivist and totalitarian, in which all the traditions and culture of the South would be ground and molded by the political machine of the conquerors. . . . The PRG [Provisional Revolutionary Government] and the National Liberation Front, whose programs had embodied the desire of so many South Vietnamese to achieve a political solution to their troubles and reconciliation among a people devastated by three decades of civil war—this movement the Northern Party had considered all along as simply the last linkup it needed to achieve

its own imperialistic revolution. After the 1975 victory, the Front and the PRG not only had no further role to play; they became a positive obstacle to the rapid consolidation of power.[6]

Having endured great hardships and forsaken the family bonds that are the traditional source of comfort and happiness for the South Vietnamese, many former VC could only regret that they had ever joined the Communists. One Southerner, who had served in a high-ranking position with the Communists before fleeing to France, said, "I wasted twenty-five years of my life with them. My wife still won't forgive me."[7]

Since the war ended, people who served in the GVN have received less attention than the Americans and the Communists involved in the war. Only their internment in the reeducation camps has attracted much interest, and then only in certain quarters. Most of the GVN veterans themselves have chosen to say little. Some who do talk display a complete lack of objectivity. Like most of the Communist leaders whom I met in Hanoi and certain radical American antiwar activists, many claim that their side never made any mistakes and never mistreated South Vietnamese civilians. This lack of objectivity forced me to seek confirmation from U.S. advisers about almost everything that the South Vietnamese interviewees told me. In the course of my research, however, I did meet a number of former GVN personnel who spoke without significant bias. One of these people is Brig. Gen. Tran Van Nhut, who left Vietnam at the end of the war with his wife and four sons. They came to the United States, where Nhut worked as a mechanic and electrical technician. He retired a few years ago. Three of his sons are engineers, and the fourth is a dentist. One of the GVN's most famous leaders because of his performance at An Loc in 1972, Nhut has served as president of both local and national Vietnamese associations in the United States. He still thinks with regret of his nation's demise and, like many ARVN veterans, attributes the final defeat to the reductions of U.S. aid and air support that coincided with Nixon's downfall. Nhut told me, "I trusted President Nixon. He was a very strong man, and he was very smart. When I learned Nixon resigned, I thought Vietnam could no longer hold." When asked what he thinks of life in America, Nhut said, "It's a nice life, and you can have everything you want. But we still miss our country, and I still think one day we will go back to Vietnam—to a free Vietnam, not to the Vietnam that exists right now."[8]

Tran Ngoc Chau spent two years in a reeducation camp after the war.

The Communists then released him but forced him to write a study of the GVN for Moscow's use and to spy on his friends. In 1979, Chau escaped to America. Though poor on arrival, Chau and his family, like many Vietnamese refugees, have achieved the American dream. "Because of my position in Vietnam," Chau said, "I avoided working for Vietnamese when I came to America, so I went to work for Americans." He started working at minimum wage, then went to college, and obtained better jobs. "I love this country," Chau told me. "I'm grateful to this country because my children got a very good education here. Among my seven children, I've got two doctors, a dentist, a lawyer, two engineers, and my other daughter is now working on her doctoral thesis at Carnegie-Mellon. So I'm very happy, very grateful. I'm also happy because in the last fourteen years, all members of my family have been behaving very decently. No one did anything bad."[9]

The Communists arrested Lt. Col. Dao Quan Hien after the fall of Saigon. Although Hien had relinquished his position in 1971 after suffering a combat wound that blinded him, the Communists put him in a reeducation camp for eight years. "The Communist regime accused me of having connections with the CIA," Hien explained. "Because I worked for many years in the police and intelligence services, I was interrogated many times."[10] After his release in 1983, Hien asked if he could leave the country and go to France or the United States. In 1987, he received permission to emigrate to the United States. Hien retains a strong interest in the war. I last talked to him shortly after the appearance of Robert McNamara's book, *In Retrospect.* Hien had heard a good deal about it, but he did not have a Braille copy to read. He eagerly discussed the book with me at considerable length and added that he had also talked about it as a guest on a local radio talk show.

Vo Van Dinh served time in a reeducation camp after the war. He escaped in 1976 and went to Cambodia to organize armed resistance to the Communists. A significant number of former GVN personnel tried to build anti-Communist forces after the war, primarily in Cambodia and the Montagnard areas in the highlands, but they never recruited enough members to pose a serious threat to the Communists. The Communists captured Dinh not long after his escape and imprisoned him again. In 1981, he sneaked out of Vietnam by boat. Like most Vietnamese in America, he strongly dislikes the current regime in Vietnam and, by Vietnamese standards, is exceptionally objective. "The Communists said they would get rid of corruption," Dinh told me, "but now they are more corrupt than the Thieu government was. They take from the people and do not protect the people." Like many perceptive Vietnamese, Dinh contends that even Communist Party leaders who no longer believe in Communism or Socialism must still claim to be socialists so that they do not lose face. "No one believes in Communism, but they use Communism as a cover—they hide behind it, so they can keep control of the country," Dinh said. "I don't think the Communists will last much longer." The children of Party members who, in recent years, have come to the United States to attend universities and start businesses, Dinh believes, will take power eventually and purge the country of Socialism's worst evils. Dinh blames the GVN's defeat on the U.S. aid cutbacks but nonetheless criticizes the GVN's top leaders for leaving South Vietnam as it neared collapse. "I have no respect for President Thieu and the other leaders who fled the country," Dinh said. "They should have stayed in the country to the end. They abandoned us."[11]

Le Van Thai worked for the CIA as an interrogator in Bien Hoa after leaving the PRUs. At the end of the war, he tried to leave Vietnam with his family, but the Communists caught them. "They put me and my family in jail," Thai recalled during an interview. "After sixty days they released my wife and children, but I was kept in a small container for six months. After that, they sent me to a reeducation camp." The Communists suspected that Thai was a CIA agent, but they did not know that he had worked for the PRUs or CIA interrogators during the war. One day, after 2½ years in the camp, he saw a former Viet Cong whom he had debriefed while working for the Americans. This rallier was a prisoner at the camp now. "I was scared he would tell the Communists who I was," said Thai, who knew that the Communists had killed some former PRUs after defeating the GVN. "As a result, I escaped. I went into the jungle by foot for three weeks, and then came to Bien Hoa, where my family was. I got false papers, and I stayed with some friends who were Catholics, like me, for one year. They were very kind and didn't tell the Communists." He and some friends built a boat. They put twenty-seven people on board and set sail during the rainy season in order to avoid Communist detection. A Norwegian tanker picked them up, and they eventually found their way to the United States. After working and going to college for several years, Thai bought a convenience store, which he still owns and operates. "America is a big opportunity for everyone in the world to work and get jobs," Thai added, "but we still miss the old country. In Vietnam, the governments have changed very often in history. I think the Communists will lose power sometime soon. When that happens, I can go back freely."[12]

The Americans

During my sophomore year at Harvard University, as American troops in the Middle East awaited the order to attack Iraq, I came across a startling article in *The Boston Globe*. The newspaper had hired a polling agency to survey Vietnam veterans from across the country about the Iraq crisis, and it was now releasing the survey results. Of the six hundred veterans surveyed, 58 percent said that they believed a U.S. attack on Iraq would be justified if diplomacy failed to remedy the situation. A simultaneous *Globe* survey of one thousand Americans from the general population nationwide, by contrast, found that only 39 percent of respondents thought so. According to these same surveys, only 8 percent of the veterans thought that U.S. forces should leave the region, compared with 18 percent of Americans as a whole.[13]

Despite the size of the veteran survey and the importance of its implications, the article appeared on page 28 of the newspaper. The editors undoubtedly decided to put this survey as far from the public notice as possible because its results contradicted the liberal newspaper's core beliefs about the war; America's liberal intelligentsia has long held that the horrors of the war turned most U.S. veterans against the use of American military power abroad. The author of the article, in fact, acknowledged that the survey "found that Vietnam veterans are more hawkish than the warweary Vietnam veteran portrayed so often in the American news and entertainment media."[14] This article fanned some doubts that I already had about common stereotypes of the Vietnam veteran and caused me to look further into the matter.

Discovering what Americans involved with the attack on the VCI now think about the war was a difficult business. I realized that I was not likely to learn much from the survey course on the Vietnam War that I was taking. Most instructors and students in the course believed that the large majority of Vietnam veterans were guilt-ridden, pacifistic misfits, and that most others were neo-fascists. They saw no need to investigate the veracity of this theory. Books, magazines, movies, and other media often mislead, rather than inform. Oliver Stone's movie *Heaven and Earth* exemplifies the American intelligentsia's portrayal of a postwar veteran who had participated in Phoenix. Tommy Lee Jones plays veteran Steve Butler, husband of protagonist Le Ly Hayslip, whose autobiography inspired the movie. Butler becomes despondent after returning to the United States because, as he explains to his wife: "I'm a killer. I killed so many over there.

I got so good at it that they assigned me to the Project. You know, black ops. We killed sometimes three or four a night. All kinds. Rice farmers. Rich fat cats bankrolling the VC units. It was a complete mind-fuck." Tears roll down Steve's cheek, and Stone shows a brief clip of Steve cutting a Vietnamese man's throat, while Steve continues: "I was in hell. I was in pure hell. Maybe I went *dinky dau* over there. Maybe I am nuts. Who the fuck knows? The more I killed, the more they gave me to kill. Do you know what it's like doing that? It's like being eaten alive from the inside out by a bellyful of sharks."[15] Steve's inner turmoil proves so great that he kills himself.

I decided to look into this story. Hayslip told me that when Oliver Stone wrote the screenplay, he actually based Butler's monologue on the claims of a man named Cliff Parry to whom Hayslip once was engaged and who claimed to have participated in the Phoenix program. Hayslip, it turns out, wrote in one of her books: "It seems Cliff Parry was a professional swindler—a pathological liar and con man—with a long list of aliases." Hayslip, in fact, became one of the victims of his swindling and lying. She concluded that Parry might never have been in Vietnam, as did a clergyman who knew Parry and was a Vietnam veteran.[16] This troubling information did not deter Stone from presenting the statements as fact in his supposedly nonfictional movie.

After talking with many Americans who participated in the attack on the VCI, I discovered that none of them fits the stereotypes in the least. Most, in fact, resent the propagators of these stereotypes. Almost none of them thought the war or the attack on the VCI was immoral, and most saw their service in Vietnam as a positive experience. Most have worked in good jobs since leaving Vietnam and have caring families. They share many common beliefs about the war, although they disagree on certain points. Their perspectives and views differ somewhat from those of the average American soldier because most were officers of the CIA or the U.S. military. On the fundamental issues of the war, however, they generally agree with the enlisted men. An extensive 1980 Veterans Administration survey of Vietnam veterans found that 91 percent of respondents, including 90 percent of those with heavy combat exposure, said that they were glad to have served their country in Vietnam. It also found that 74 percent of respondents and 69 percent of those with heavy combat exposure said that they enjoyed their time in the service.[17] Roughly the same percentage of the people whom I interviewed said the same. A representative sample of their opinions and reflections follows.

Gary Mattocks remained in the CIA after the war. He spent most of his time in Latin America and also did some work there for the Drug Enforcement Administration. Like many who served in Vietnam, he believes that he and the other Americans were fighting for a good cause in that country. Mattocks told me, "Most of the people that I went over there with believed very strongly in what we were doing. We thought we were going to save Indochina from Communism, and that what we were doing was for the good of the U.S. national interest and national security." He blames U.S. congressional reductions of aid to the GVN for the war's inglorious end. "We believe to this day," Mattocks asserted, "that if it had been done properly, and the commitment and the resolve had been there, it would have been different."[18] Many Americans whom I interviewed contended that aid maintained at previous levels or continued U.S. air support probably would have allowed the South Vietnamese to hold off the Communists. They added, correctly, that either would have represented a small amount of money compared with what the United States had already spent on the war, as well as a small price to pay to save a nation in which the Americans had invested so much.

Brig. Gen. James Herbert told me that he is not satisfied with his time in Vietnam because, like many veterans, he believes America's political leaders engaged the United States in the war without having the will to take the measures necessary for victory. "I wish that I had known in 1965 that there was no intent to win," he lamented. "There was only an intent to engage. I wish we'd had a U.S. commitment to win." Rules that prohibited Allied forces from entering Cambodia and Laos, he thinks, ensured failure. "I know people who were severely disciplined for crossing the Cambodian border to chase a VC unit. I thought to myself, 'How stupid can you get?'"[19]

Jim Ward is currently the reigning triathlon world champion in the age seventy-five and over group. He keeps himself busy with preparations for upcoming events, and he still spends a lot of time thinking about the war. "Vietnam affected my life tremendously." Ward told me. "My only son was killed there. He was a first lieutenant assigned as an RF/PF adviser. I lost a lot of friends there, Vietnamese as well as Americans, a lot of guys who worked for me." Ward explained why his son had wanted to go to Vietnam. "He said, 'Dad, I'm just sick and tired of arguing with all the kids in college. They think we're doing the wrong thing out there in Vietnam, and I try to explain that we're doing the right thing.' I told him at the time, 'I'm not so sure we're doing the right thing in Vietnam. I don't think we're doing very well out there,' but I added, 'Yes, I think we ought to stop Communism in the area if we can.' He got out of college after three months and joined the army."[20]

Ward had misgivings about the war effort, not because he found it morally repugnant but because he doubted whether the Allies could prevail, given the ways in which American leaders had decided to fight the war. He thought it unwise to use U.S. units in the populous areas of Vietnam and believed that the American forces ought to go into Laos to obstruct the infiltration from North Vietnam. Opponents of the American war effort often claim that half of American veterans believe that the United States should have stayed out of Vietnam, in order to suggest that many veterans share their belief that the war was immoral.[21] In reality, however, most veterans who thought that the United States should have stayed out of Vietnam disapproved of the intervention not because they believed that it was immoral but because they considered it impractical. They either believed, like Ward, that American political leaders would not let the military take the measures that were needed to win the war, such as entering Cambodia, Laos, or North Vietnam or bombing more targets in North Vietnam, or believed that the war was inherently unwinnable. Of the veterans surveyed for the 1980 Veterans Administration study, in fact, 92 percent agreed with the following statement: "The trouble in Vietnam was that our troops were asked to fight in a war which our political leaders in Washington would not let them win." Only 6 percent disagreed.[22]

Rex Wilson calls his years of service in Vietnam and Laos the most fulfilling years of his life. "I was doing things I thought were really important, and I was proud to be doing them," he said. "For me, the risks were exhilarating." He does, however, find the American evacuation of Vietnam morally reprehensible. "We just left those people who were loyal to us in the lurch. The way we left there still causes me a lot of pain and makes me angry. The whole world saw how we bailed out of there, and how we put whores on the choppers instead of some of the people that had worked for us for twenty years and had risked their lives for us."[23]

Many Americans with whom I talked expressed feelings of shame and anger at the American failure in 1975 to extract some of the South Vietnamese who had worked for the Americans. A few also complained that the United States, at the end of the war, should have destroyed all GVN documents that identified Allied personnel and agents. They consequently blamed U.S. leaders for the Communist capture of these documents, which, they claimed, led the Communists to imprison numerous South Vietnamese people. Most of the inverviewees, however, dismissed this contention. They pointed out that the United States did not have sufficient personnel to destroy all of the documents in the time available and that destroying the documents earlier would have demoralized the GVN. They also did not think that the United States had a moral obligation to do the GVN's work.

The anguishes of the American failure did not leave Ed Brady alone for a long time. "It took me ten years before I was willing to go to the Vietnam Memorial," Brady confided. "The first four times I went there, I only went after midnight, during rainstorms, because it reminded me of monsoons. It took a lot of determined effort for me to go to look up a name. It took me six trips between the wall and the book to even remember a name, which is obviously repression. It was only last year that I ever took my daughter to the memorial and it was only the third time I had been there with anybody else, so it's twenty years later and I'm having all this difficulty coping with it." When he returned from Vietnam, the desire to distance himself from his feelings about the war drove him to work hard. So did the perception that he needed to catch up with people in the United States who had not spent the time away that he had. Brady said, "I felt that I was behind, that nobody cared about what happened in Vietnam, and that my experience there was worthless compared to what other people had done and what people wanted here. I believed that I had to work twice as hard to succeed because I had to catch up."[24] Brady eventually became a successful businessman.

Vietnam profoundly changed Brady's views on foreign policy and politics, as it did for many veterans: "When I went to Vietnam I was a very idealistic, anti-communist, pro-democracy person who thought it was a very simple black-and-white issue, and I came back thinking it was very gray and very difficult to decide what's right and what's wrong." He also said, however, "I thought the activities I was engaged in were good and useful things. Otherwise, I wouldn't have spent all that time in Vietnam." He strongly criticized some U.S. policies in Vietnam but added, "I think the Vietnamese bear a large part of the blame for why we failed. I don't think we're mainly responsible. They were responsible for themselves. That took me fifteen years to figure out." He still thinks that the United States should try to promote democracy in the world, but, like many Vietnam veterans, he does not think that the United States can change the behavior of stubborn people outside of its borders. "If we went into the former Yugoslavia and stayed for twenty or thirty years, over time things might gradually get better. But the idea that we can go there for a year and fix it up and come home is totally ridiculous. I have very little confidence and very little faith that the American public or the government has the stamina and the know-how to carry out that sort of thing."[25]

After the fall of Saigon, Jack Harrell brought a former PRU officer, whom he had known during the war, and several other refugees to his hometown. He found jobs for them and places for them to stay. Nowadays, Harrell uses his spare time to teach religion and provide counseling in prisons. "It's really a fulfilling activity," he said. "What most of them need is somebody to tell it to them straight, who will do it not in anger but to do it in a sincere effort to help. You just look them in the eye and tell it to them straight. Once they leave, they never go back [to prison] because you've changed them in heart and in attitude." Looking back on his experiences in Vietnam, Harrell commented, "I'm satisfied with what I did. I'm not satisfied with the outcome. Not at all. The war did not have to end the way it did."[26]

Rudy Enders faults American political leaders for not taking control of the GVN. The ineffectiveness and corruption of the GVN leadership used to anger him to no end, just as they angered many other advisers. Enders said, "We should have demanded that the lives and the money we were expending were being spent for a worthy cause, not to fatten some guy's nest." Enders also resented the GVN's decision to put off the implementation of universal conscription and to sit back while the Americans did most of the fighting. "There was no reason for us to continue sending hundreds of thousands of people to Vietnam," he asserted, "when their population was perfectly capable of handling the problem on its own. It used to make me really mad to see a South Vietnamese nineteen-year-old riding around on a motorcycle in Saigon who had never been drafted, while our young guys were sent out there to tramp around in the jungle after only six months of training and fight these people who had been fighting for years. It just wasn't right."[27]

George French served with the CIA during the late 1960s as III Corps deputy region officer in charge, chief of Phoenix operations, and province officer in charge in Tay Ninh province. He is the only veteran I met who said he experienced serious psychological problems as a direct result of witnessing and experiencing the war in Vietnam. "When I came back from Vietnam in 1969, I was a physical and mental wreck," French recalled. "I couldn't drive a car, and I was nasty with my family. They had a hard time with me for a while. I had to go to a doctor." French blames his troubles on the high risk of death that he faced while finishing his tour in Tay Ninh province. After a short time, he brought his problems under control and, in 1971, returned to Vietnam for another tour with the CIA. He is quite satisfied with his CIA career, but he remains unhappy about his experience in Vietnam. "I've been bitter about Vietnam," French said, "because it was a war we couldn't win."[28]

Harvey Weiner, a CORDS Phoenix adviser in Chuong Thien province during 1969 and 1970, also expressed dissatisfaction with his experience in Vietnam, but for personal reasons. "No one wanted to go to Vietnam," Weiner said. "I wanted to practice law, but I had to do two years of military service, and spent one of them in Vietnam. I'm sorry I went to Vietnam. I was married at the time, and it was a year away from my wife. It was a year of worry and distress for my family and for myself."[29]

Brig. Gen. Robert Montague is retired and spends his time hunting, fishing, and playing golf and tennis. For several years, he has been suffering from bone marrow cancer, and he is constantly receiving chemotherapy. During the war, he often went into the field to check the results of defoliation operations involving the chemical Agent Orange, in part because he advocated the use of defoliants. His exposure to Agent Orange, now known to be a carcinogen, might have caused the cancer. Montague, nonetheless, said that his service in Vietnam had been "absolutely a positive experience" for him. "It was a big challenge," he told me cheerfully, "and it was really exciting, because you could get things done. You were making the difference."[30]

The only person I interviewed who considers the attack on the VCI or the entire Allied war effort to be morally repugnant is Ralph McGehee. McGehee worked as Gia Dinh's province officer in charge for a couple of months in 1968 and then worked with the Special Police in Saigon from 1968 until 1970. He later wrote an unauthorized book about his career with the CIA in which he leveled a host of harsh criticisms against his former employer, and eventually overcame the CIA's efforts to block the book's publication.[31] McGehee's chief complaint about the Allied effort in Vietnam is that the VC was popular and the GVN was not. "We were there to impose a U.S.-controlled regime over Vietnam," McGehee said. "We refused to admit the real strength of the South Vietnamese Communists. Had we ever done it, then we would have had to come up with totally new justifications for being there or just pulled out. The South Vietnamese Communists organized the villagers probably by the millions. The most we ever recognized in the Agency estimates—this was based on the courageous efforts of Sam Adams—was about six hundred thousand guerrillas. We never did include the Front organizations, although Ho Chi Minh, Giap, and the various Communist leaders said, 'This is a people's war, it's organizing the people in the villages.' The Communists announced that they had seven million Front members in Farmer's Liberation Associations, Women's Liberation, Youth Liberation, and some twenty-seven other liberation associations. All of the time I was there, I was saying, 'We're not reporting on the numbers as they really exist. We're not counting the Front men.' The other thing was that you had thirty thousand penetrations in the Thieu government. The CIA was offering instant promotion for anyone who could get a significant penetration of the VC, and no one qualified. It gives you some idea of where the loyalties lay." [32] By the late 1960s, as mentioned in chapters 22 and 25, the Front organizations became completely inactive in most hamlets and the VC enjoyed little popularity, regardless of what the Communists might have said. Chapter 7 indicates that the estimate of thirty thousand VC penetrations was a gross exaggeration and that the GVN, independent of the CIA, had a substantial number of penetrations of the Viet Cong.

Frank Snepp is often portrayed as a man disillusioned with the American war effort, much as McGehee is. Antiwar writers frequently cite his impassioned criticisms of the U.S. war effort—some of which pertain to the attack on the shadow government, with which he had little to do—as evidence of American incompetence or wickedness. When I talked with him, however, I found that his popular image is inaccurate. Snepp told me that he thinks some of the South Vietnamese involved in attacking the VCI and their U.S. advisers were excessively bloodthirsty, but he does not believe that the American conduct of the war was immoral. The mishandling of the evacuation at the end of the war is the only major U.S. action that he finds reprehensible. He attributes America's failure to its unwillingness to take many casualties and to inflict as many casualties as it could on a foe who cared little about how many people it lost. "There were two different cultures fighting in Vietnam," Snepp remarked. "One of my station chiefs once said during a conversation with a Vietnamese counterpart, 'That's like kicking a guy when he's down.' The counterpart said, 'That's the best time to kick him.' In that remark, flippant though it was, is a key to understanding why the war was lost. One of the studies I had a tangential input into right before I went to Vietnam was a study of whether or not the bombing of the dikes in North Vietnam would stop the Communists. The conclusion was that something like two million North Vietnamese would die, if not in the bombing, then in the aftermath. It would have crippled the North Vietnamese to the extent that they would have been put out of commission, surely, for several years. It would have bought time for the South. Kissinger and the U.S. decided that it was not to be, a point that I like to bring up with a lot of my antiwar friends. The U.S. government decided not to do it, for a moral reason. It couldn't kill that many people. It could not rationalize killing two million people. I don't think the North Vietnamese ever reached that level of morality."[33]

Snepp also thinks that the humanitarianism of the Americans at the tactical level impeded success in the war: "I think we Americans often, in our smug, morally imperialistic way, complain, 'The South Vietnamese were pushing the Phoenix program to the limit and killing people.' But I'm still not sure the South Koreans didn't have it right. What they would do when they found somebody trying to come in over the wire, they'd hang him on the wire as an example. That sure stopped infiltration. Nobody would fight the South Koreans in the highlands, and they were terrible terrorists."[34]

Bob Boyke is proud of his service in Vietnam. In contrast to many of the other Americans who share this pride, he is also extremely tolerant of Americans who opposed the war. "If antiwar protesters honestly had convictions that the war was wrong," he told me, "there's nothing wrong with them. That's their opinion. They had to do what they had to do; I had to do what I had to do." He does have his doubts, however, about their motives. "I suspect a lot of personal interest was involved with many of the protesters. I don't think you'd get that kind of enthusiastic demonstration against the government if the draft and the actuality of going to Vietnam weren't forced upon them." He has not lost his faith in the patriotism and anti-communism that caused him to go to Vietnam, and subsequent history makes him confident that he chose the right path. "You just hope you've made the right decision. I would suspect that there are a lot of people who went to Canada or avoided the draft through chicanery who feel a lot more guilty than I do."[35]

Rick Welcome is more of an isolationist than most veterans. He supported the war when he went to Vietnam, and he still believes that it was a noble effort. By the time he returned from the war, however, he had decided that the United States should not interfere in the affairs of other countries. "Who are we to force our views on other people?" Welcome asked. "I don't like us in the role of the world's policeman. We've got our own problems here. Let's try to solve them before we try to inflict our views on the rest of the world." From a personal standpoint, Welcome said, the war benefited him tremendously. "I volunteered because I thought it would be exciting. My whole reason was, 'Here's a war going on and I'm going to be part of it. I want to see if I've really got the balls to go out there and be shot at.' I went there just to see what kind of an adrenaline high I could get out of it. I came back humbled, contrite, and certainly more introspective and in touch with myself. I came back as a better human being, as a more sensitive and caring individual. I think everyone has to be humbled at points in their lives so they can grow. Nobody likes it, but it makes a better person of you." Welcome believes that all Americans should have to serve in the military. "Everyone needs to learn that we may need to make some sacrifices for our country. There's a price for all the benefits we enjoy in this country. Plus, it's good discipline."[36]

Welcome found that the war also changed him in other ways that set him apart from his American peers who had not gone to war. "My success in the business world has been modest," Welcome explained. "I am not the hard-charging corporate type who's going to work eighty hours a week for a corporation. That's not in me anymore. I'm far more concerned with being a good husband and a good father. I see people who I think are far less qualified than I, but certainly more aggressive, get ahead of me in the business world. That's something I had to come to terms with, because I couldn't provide my family with all the material benefits that perhaps they can provide their families with. But the flipside is that my kids love me. I've got a seventeen-year-old daughter and a fifteen-year-old son who have never caused me a problem and they think I'm the greatest person on the face of the earth. So that's ample compensation for the fact that our house has only eight rooms instead of twelve rooms, and I'm driving a truck instead of a Mercedes."[37]

After serving in Vietnam, Dean Almy became the CIA's deputy chief of the Far East Division and was responsible for Southeast Asia. He now lives in Maine and serves as chairman of the local city council. Almy explained his decision to go to Vietnam: "I wanted to go because I wouldn't have wanted to be in the agency for the rest of my career and not have been one of the guys in Vietnam, just as I was always glad I was one of the guys who served in Korea and in World War II. I thought Vietnam was important to our country. I believed in it. My conviction that we were doing the right thing is not as strong now as it was at the time, though I still think it was the right thing to do. I now think the North Vietnamese probably were going to win in the long run, once we left, because they were tougher and better organized than the South Vietnamese. Now that Communism isn't a threat anymore, it's very easy to say, 'Well, maybe that wasn't all necessary.' But I still believe there was a struggle going on for the world. The Communists were hoping to take over Indonesia, Vietnam, Laos, and Cambodia. They would have gone into Thailand. It's not exactly the domino theory, but I have no doubt that they wanted all of Indochina plus Thailand, and the Communist Party tried to take over Indonesia about three times. We had to fight them in all these places, until Communism collapsed, which happened much sooner than I had expected. We may have saved Thailand by prolonging the war."[38]

Rob Simmons remained in the CIA until the late 1970s. He then became a staffer in the U.S. Senate and rose to the position of staff director of the Senate's Select Committee on Intelligence. At present, he is a state representative in Connecticut and teaches courses on intelligence at Yale University. Simmons has no regrets about going to Vietnam, even though it led him to break a family tradition of work in the newspaper business. "I had to confront the situation of the war and the draft," he said, "and I ultimately decided that I did not want to be a spectator for the most traumatic event of my generation, which was the Vietnam War. As a young college grad, I didn't feel comfortable avoiding the draft, or going to Canada, or staying in graduate school. It just didn't seem right. So I never would have done things differently."[39]

Peter Scott now teaches and writes for a magazine. He is also working on a book about the Khmer Krom, an ethnic Cambodian minority that fought for the Americans against the Vietnamese Communists and joined the side of the Lon Nol government during the war in Cambodia. Like many veterans, he blames the American antiwar movement for most of the psychological problems endured by the Americans who served in Vietnam. Because numerous opponents of the war harshly criticized U.S. soldiers for serving in Vietnam and almost none showed the soldiers any gratitude, Scott and many other veterans felt betrayed and isolated when they returned home. Scott said, "We were loyal to our leaders, to our ideals, to each other, and yet ideologues chose us as scapegoats for failed political programs. That was a very bad mistake, because it diminished the confidence and morale of the military and inflicted much more emotional pain on many veterans than the war did." He also dislikes the way in which his antiwar peers claimed most of the nation's and the world's attention. "In the sixties, when the hippies said, 'The whole world is watching,' they were right. They were right in that the whole world was watching and believing that the hippies represented the entire generation. Those of us who were in the service, who were not sitting and yelling in the streets, did not agree with them one bit. They were by no means the majority, not then and not now."[40]

Scott views his service in Vietnam as a very positive experience. "I think the Army made a man of me, whether you like that expression or not. I learned the Big Lesson, which is that I'm expendable for a larger purpose. That's an important thing for every man and woman to learn, because it breeds humility and makes you a stronger and better person. I think I became more appreciative of this society, and of life itself. The war was the most frightening time of my life, but it was also the most exhilarating time. People wouldn't just say they were your friend. If they were your friend, they'd risk their life for you. Most veterans are better off for their experience, except for the ones who bought into that 'victim' stuff, claiming the soldier of Vietnam is a victim. It's a simple trap. If you claim victim status and exploit it, then you get immediate group gains—you get media attention and people feel sorry for you. Resisting victim status is harder at first, but you gain individually in the end because it toughens you and strengthens you."[41]

Col. Walter Clark believes that the U.S. cause in Vietnam was a noble one. As he learned more about the war while he was in Vietnam and afterward, however, Clark became disenchanted with some of the Americans who controlled the war effort. "I was disgusted at the politics of running the war," Clark told me. "Even very young military officers are taught to identify a mission and to figure out how to accomplish it. The United States didn't seem to have much of a mission or know how to accomplish it. We never lost on the battlefield but we lost the war. I was disillusioned by the arrogance of the Robert McNamaras of the world and that whole damn crew that was around Kennedy and later Johnson. They weren't soldiers. They were politicians and academicians, silver-tongued guys who interfered in military matters and didn't know what the hell they were doing."[42] Clark became so disgusted with some of the higher-ranking officers with whom he served that he later turned down an offer of promotion to brigadier general, choosing retirement instead.

Clark speaks regretfully of the social turmoil and decay that occurred during the war. He took the battalion under his command to Chicago twice during 1968, the first time to protect the city in the aftermath of the assassination of Martin Luther King, Jr., and the second time to guard against disturbances during the Democratic national convention. In 1969, as an officer with the 5th Mechanized Division, he conducted reconnaissance in American inner cities and prepared civil disturbance plans. "That hurt," he said. While a student at Carlisle Barracks during the war, he also had a good view of the antiwar protesters. "You'd see all these college kids tromping around holding up signs," Clark recalled, "and the post commander would always send some very learned officers out to rap with these guys and tell the Army's side. I remember a team being formed of some very good combat commanders, a chaplain, a judge advocate, and a medical officer, all students at the college, to go out by invitation and speak at various colleges. They'd get pelted with eggs and tomatoes and get booed off the stage. Nobody listened to them, and nobody wanted to listen to them." Clark served his last years with the Army as commandant of The Citadel. "I think it was the most meaningful job I've had, because I influenced quite a number of young men who are becoming very successful nowadays as they grow older."[43]

Bruce Lawlor left the CIA in 1974 and became a lawyer. Lawlor, like a large number of other people whom I interviewed, thinks that many Americans greatly exaggerate the prevalence of psychological problems among Vietnam veterans. A few people actually have serious problems, he contends, and many were unhappy on their return because much of society did not accept them or looked down on them. But, he notes, many supposedly troubled veterans did not actually serve in Vietnam, and many true veterans have misused their veteran status. "There are a lot of guys who want to use it as a crutch," Lawlor told me. "Every time they screw up in their life, they try to blame it on the war. That's absolute BS." In 1984, Lawlor ran for state attorney general in Vermont. During the election campaign, his opponents learned of his service in Vietnam and claimed that his work with the PRUs made him a war criminal. One article accused him of killing sixty thousand people. He lost the election. Lawlor said of the mudslinging, "I really resented it at the time. I probably lost the election because I got so angry at it that I couldn't keep my sense of perspective."[44]

Lawlor has had other experiences that have given him a low opinion of some people opposed to American involvement in Vietnam. "You develop a certain cynicism about the antiwar people," he said. "A female lawyer once asked me sincerely whether I had killed any babies. I didn't know how to respond to that. How do you answer an idiot like that? I think the guys who were involved in it have got to talk about it. We've got to tell what really happened. It's an education process. If we talk enough about how it really was, sooner or later the credibility of these idiots is going to be gone, because the PRU program wasn't a conspiracy. It was never an assassination program. People who say it was an assassination program need to go out some night in an area where you know there are enemy forces coming in. It gets pretty damn intense. Sometimes we made mistakes, we went in the wrong direction, we screwed up, but there was no evil intent. There were a lot of very honorable people in that program."[45]

Glossary

ACofS assistant chief of staff

an tri Republic of Vietnam's process for sentencing captured VCI to detention terms

APP Accelerated Pacification Program

APT Armed Propaganda Team, a group of armed men who tried to convince the VC to defect

ARVN Army of the Republic of Vietnam

CAP Combined Action Program, a program that combined U.S. Marines and South Vietnamese Popular Forces into platoons to defend specific villages

CDEC Combined Document Exploitation Center

Chieu Hoi Vietnamese term for "open arms"; Republic of Vietnam's program that encouraged the Viet Cong to defect and helped defectors to return to normal life

CIA Central Intelligence Agency

CIDG Civilian Irregular Defense Group, an armed unit composed of anti-Communist Montagnards

CinCPac Commander in Chief, Pacific

CofS chief of staff

COMUSMACV Commander, U.S. Military Assistance Command, Vietnam

CORDS Civil Operations and Revolutionary Development Support, U.S. organization created in May 1967 to control all American pacification activities except those of the Central Intelligence Agency

Corps see CTZ

COSVN Central Office for South Vietnam, headquarters that directed all Communist activities in South Vietnam

Counter-Terror Team elite paramilitary unit under the control of the Central Intelligence Agency; they evolved into the Provincial Reconnaissance Units

CTZ Corps Tactical Zone, a group of provinces; the Allies divided South

Vietnam into four Corps Tactical Zones; also called Corps or Military Region

DEPCORDS deputy for CORDS

DIOCC District Intelligence and Operations Coordinating Center; see Phoenix center

district a group of several villages; the Allies divided South Vietnam into approximately 250 districts

DRV Democratic Republic of Vietnam, the Communist state in North Vietnam

DSA district senior adviser, the CORDS adviser in a district who was in charge of all other CORDS advisers within the district

EVAL evaluation

FWMAF Free World Military Assistance Forces, the military forces of the Allies; also referred to as FWMF

GVN Government of Vietnam (South Vietnam); also referred to as the Government

hamlet a cluster of homes; several hamlets constituted a village

HES Hamlet Evaluation System, a statistical system that measured security in the hamlets of South Vietnam

hoi chanh a Communist who had defected through the Chieu Hoi program

ICEX Intelligence Coordination and Exploitation, U.S. program, created in mid-1967 to coordinate intelligence and operations against the shadow government; later renamed Phoenix and given responsibility for advising the South Vietnamese Phung Hoang program

ID identification

illegal cadre a Viet Cong cadre who carried out the overt functions of the shadow government

JCSM Joint Chiefs of Staff memorandum

KIA killed in action

legal cadre a Viet Cong cadre who lived amid the civilian population and carried out covert shadow government functions

MACCORDS Military Assistance Command, Civil Operations and Revolutionary Development Support

MACDR Military Assistance Command, Delta Region

MACJOIR acronym for the deputy commanding general for Military Assistance Command, Civil Operations and Revolutionary Development Support

MACV Military Assistance Command, Vietnam, the U.S. military command in South Vietnam

MR Military Region; see CTZ

MSS Military Security Service, the counterintelligence branch of the Army of the Republic of Vietnam

NLF National Liberation Front, the front organization used by the Vietnamese Communist Party to conceal its control of the Viet Cong

NPFF National Police Field Forces, combat policemen of the Republic of Vietnam

NVA North Vietnamese Army

PAVN People's Army of North Vietnam; Communist designation for North Vietnamese Army

PF Popular Forces; see RF/PF

PH Phung Hoang

PHD Phung Hoang Directorate

Phoenix see ICEX

Phoenix center center for implementing Phoenix at a given echelon; representatives of various Allied organizations coordinated intelligence and operations in the center; also known as Intelligence and Operations Coordination Center

PHREEX Study Phung Hoang Reexamination Study, a study of Phung Hoang conducted by CORDS in 1971

Phung Hoang South Vietnamese organization parallel to Phoenix

PIC Province Interrogation Center, site of important civilian interrogations in a province; operated by the Special Police and the Central Intelligence Agency

PICC Province Intelligence Coordination Center/Committee

PIOCC Province Intelligence and Operations Coordination Center; see Phoenix center; in this book, PIOCC also connotes the Phoenix system before the actual creation of the centers

POC Police Operations Center, center for coordinating police activities and planning police operations in an area

POIC province officer in charge, the officer of the Central Intelligence Agency with authority over all CIA activities in a province

PRG Provisional Revolutionary Government, entity established by the Communists in 1969; purported to govern South Vietnam

province a group of several districts; the Allies divided South Vietnam into forty-four provinces

PRP People's Revolutionary Party, Southern Communist Party, controlled by the Communist Party of North Vietnam

PRU Provincial Reconnaissance Unit; see Counter-Terror Team

PS Public Safety

PSA province senior adviser, the CORDS adviser in a province who was in charge of all other CORDS advisers within the province

PSB Police Special Branch; see SP

PSCD Pacification Security Coordination Division

PSDF People's Self-Defense Force, local militia units composed of all able-bodied villagers not otherwise employed by the Republic of Vietnam

PSG Pacification Studies Group

rally (verb) to defect through the Chieu Hoi program

R and R rest and relaxation

RD cadres Revolutionary Development cadres, GVN cadres who sought to counter the presence of the Viet Cong in the villages by using methods similar to those of the Viet Cong cadres

RF Regional Forces; see RF/PF

RF/PF Regional Forces/Popular Forces, local militia units of the Republic of Vietnam; also called territorial forces

ROE rules of engagement

ROIC region officer in charge, the officer of the Central Intelligence Agency with authority over all CIA activities in a Military Region

ROK Republic of Korea

RVN Republic of Vietnam, the non-Communist state in South Vietnam

RVNAF Republic of Vietnam Armed Forces

SDC Self-Defense Corps, militia units of the Republic of Vietnam; a predecessor of the RF/PF

SEAL Sea-Air-Land (Team), elite commando team of the U.S. Navy; members of the team are referred to as SEALs

SP Special Police, the main intelligence arm of the Republic of Vietnam's National Police; sometimes referred to as Police Special Branch or PSB

SVNLA South Vietnam Liberation Army, the Viet Cong armed forces

Tet-68 Communist offensive during the Tet holiday of 1968; also referred to as Tet offensive

TOC tactical operations center, center for coordinating all Allied operations within a specific area

USA U.S. Army

USAID U.S. Agency for International Development

USIA U.S. Information Agency

USN U.S. Navy

VC Viet Cong, the South Vietnamese Communists; the term is also used to refer to an individual member or a group of members of the South Vietnamese Communists

VCI Viet Cong infrastructure, the Viet Cong shadow government; the term is also used to refer to an individual or group of individuals who served in the Viet Cong shadow government

village a group of several hamlets

VNQDD Viet Nam Quoc Dan Dang, a South Vietnamese political faction that opposed the Communists

Notes

T he largest share of the documents used in this study belong to the U.S. Army Center of Military History in Washington, D.C. Because the center normally does not permit outside researchers access to its documents, it does not assign file, box, or folder numbers to most documents. As a result, the notes cannot provide a more precise location of these documents than merely CMH (Center of Military History).

The National Archives Branch at Suitland, Maryland, has a wealth of documents, most of which have not yet been processed, from U.S. government agencies. All documents labeled Suitland are located in Records Group 472, Records of the United States Army Vietnam, MACCORDS, Information Center, Command Information.

The Lyndon B. Johnson Library (denoted here as LBJ), Austin, Texas, has a good collection of documents from the Johnson era; many of these documents are in the National Security File (NSF). The U.S. Military History Institute (MHI), Carlisle Barracks, Pennsylvania, possesses some worthwhile documents. The Douglas Pike Collection (cited as Pike Collection), Texas Tech University, Lubbock, Texas, is available on microfiche under the title, *The History of the Vietnam War*, and contains numerous useful documents, especially captured Communist documents.

The Widener Library Microform collection (cited as Widener) at Harvard University, Cambridge, Massachusetts, also has some pertinent documents. I made extensive use of the Rand Corporation's interviews with Vietnamese during the war. The interview transcripts are available at Widener Library and a number of other large libraries. I found some of the studies written by Rand analysts helpful as well; because there are so many, I list only the most important ones in the Selected Bibliography.

More than one hundred people involved in the war against the Viet Cong shadow government communicated their thoughts to me in person, on the telephone, by mail, by fax, or by tape between 1992 and the summer of 1996. To simplify matters, I use a broad definition of the term "interview" and cite all of these communications as interviews. For a variety of reasons, approximately twenty-five contributors asked that I not mention them, either by name or by pseudonym. Their comments influenced the book, but I did not quote any of them directly. The following is a list of the other contributors. I assign pseudonyms to some of the Vietnamese at their request, as indi-

cated in parentheses following their names. Note: A Vietnamese personal name is
given in the order of family name, middle name, and first name.

Dean Almy
Capt. Larry Bailey, USN (Ret.)
Col. Carl Bernard, USA (Ret.)
Robert Boyke
Edward Brady
Robert Brewer
Nelson Brickham
Col. John Bringham, USA (Ret.)
Comdr. Frank C. Brown, USN
Col. Bui Hop, ARVN
Cao Van Luong
John Cassidy
Col. Walter B. Clark, USA (Ret.)
William E. Colby
Lt. Col. John L. Cook, USA (Ret.)
Col. Henry F. Dagenais, USA (Ret.)
Col. Dang Van Minh, ARVN
Lt. Col. Dao Quan Hien, ARVN
Orrin DeForest
Col. Douglas Dillard, USA (Ret.)
Col. Griffin Dodge, USA (Ret.)
Rudolph Enders
Daren Flitcroft
George French
Robert French
Donald Gregg
Col. William Grieves, USA (Ret.)
Donald Halsey
Jack Harrell
John Hart
Brig. Gen. James A. Herbert, USA (Ret.)
Brig. Gen. Stuart A. Herrington, USA
Col. Horace L. Hunter, USA (Ret.)
Col. Huynh Van Trinh, PAVN
Lt. Col. Robert Inman, USA (Ret.)
Bruce Jones
Robert Komer
Lewis Lapham
Bruce Lawlor

Rear Adm. Irve C. LeMoyne, USN
Maj. Gen. Le Van Duong, PAVN
Le Van Thai
Command Sgt. Maj. Michael N. Martin, USA (Ret.)
Gary E. Masters
Gary Mattocks
Col. Chester B. McCoid, USA (Ret.)
Ralph McGehee
Henry McWade
Warren H. Milberg
Col. Lewis L. Millett, USA (Ret.)
Brig. Gen. Robert Montague, USA (Ret.)
Daniel Mudrinich
John Mullins
Nguyen An Tien
Nguyen Co Thach
Nguyen Ngoc Dien
Nguyen Thi Binh
Nguyen Trong Phuc
Gen. Nguyen Trong Vinh, PAVN
Col. Nguyen Van Cua, ARVN
Col. Nguyen Van Dai, ARVN
Evan J. Parker, Jr.
Lee Patten
Pham Huu Chinh (pseudonym)
Thomas Polgar
Lloyd Pomeroy
Felix I. Rodriguez
Peter Scott
Robert Simmons
Command Sgt. Maj. Michael Sinkovitz, USA (Ret.)
Frank Snepp
Thich Van Quan (pseudonym)
Lloyd Thyen
John S. Tilton
Tran Huu Dinh
Col. Tran Ngoc Chau, ARVN
Tran Van Dang
Brig. Gen. Tran Van Nhut, ARVN
Truong My Hoa
Col. Viet Lang, ARVN (pseudonym)
Lt. Gen. Vinh Loc, ARVN

Vo Van Dinh (pseudonym)
Robert Wall
James R. Ward
Quentin H. Watkins
Harvey Weiner
Richard Welcome
Gen. William C. Westmoreland, USA (Ret.)
Charles Whitehouse
John Wilbur
Rex Wilson
Stephen B. Young

Chapter 2   The Shadow Government and the Viet Cong

1. Central Intelligence Agency (hereafter cited as CIA), "The Vietnam Situation: An Analysis and Estimate," 23 May 1967, LBJ, Papers of the Capital Legal Foundation, Box 5, Folder CIA 238, chap. 3, 4.

2. CIA, Office of Research and Reports, "Viet Cong Manpower Recruitment," 21 November 1966, Widener, Film A413.6.1, Reel 3: 971-977, 1.

3. CIA, "Capabilities of the Vietnamese Communists for Fighting in South Vietnam," 13 November 1967, Special National Intelligence Estimate Number 14.3-67, LBJ, Papers of the Capital Legal Foundation, Box 6, Folder CIA 303-307, 22.

Chapter 3   The Shadow Government and the People

1. Shaplen, *Road From War*, 337.
2. *Rand Vietnam Interviews*, ser. V, no. 105, 18.
3. Quoted in Race, *War Comes to Long An*, 98.
4. *Rand Vietnam Interviews*, ser. V, no. 12, 22.
5. Quoted in Conley, *Communist Insurgent Infrastructure*, 349–50.
6. *Rand Vietnam Interviews*, ser. AG, no. 362, 2, 3.
7. Quoted in Herrington, *Silence Was Weapon*, 29.
8. Quoted in Henderson, *Why Vietcong Fought*, 65–66, 70.
9. *Rand Vietnam Interviews*, ser. DT, no. 143, 13, 14.
10. Ibid., ser. Z-ZH, no. 41, 6.
11. Quoted in Pike, *Viet Cong*, 122–23.
12. *Rand Vietnam Interviews*, ser. PIE, no. 42, 8–9.
13. Quoted in Conley, *Communist Insurgent Infrastructure*, 331.
14. Quoted in Trullinger, *Village at War*, 71.
15. *Rand Vietnam Interviews*, ser. PIE, no. 21, 8.
16. Quoted in Pike, *Viet Cong*, 229.
17. *Rand Vietnam Interviews*, ser. PIE, no. 20, 2.

18. Quoted in David Hunt, "Organizing for Revolution in South Vietnam: Study of a Mekong Delta Province," *Radical America* 8, nos. 1 and 2 (January–April 1974): 24.

19. Quoted in Chanoff and Toai, *Portrait of Enemy,* 155.

20. Quoted in Henderson, *Why Vietcong Fought,* 65.

21. Quoted in Race, *War Comes to Long An,* 161–62.

Chapter 4 The War against the Shadow Government: Before Phoenix

1. Race, *War Comes to Long An,* 226.

2. FitzGerald, *Fire in Lake,* 177.

3. Komer, *Bureaucracy at War,* 116.

4. Robert Komer, "Pacification: A Look Back and Ahead," *Army* (June 1970): 23.

5. Examples include Asprey, *War in Shadows;* Corson, *Betrayal;* and Krepinevich, *Army and Vietnam.*

6. For examples of these incidents, see Peterson, *Combined Action Platoons,* 38, 56–60, 68, 88; Hemingway, *Our War Was Different,* 56, 80, 158; and West, *The Village,* 114–27.

7. Montague, interview.

8. CIA, "Problems of Viet Cong Recruitment and Morale," 3 August 1967, Special National Intelligence Estimate Number 14.3-1-67, LBJ, NSF, National Intelligence Estimates, Box 5, Folder 14.3, North Vietnam, 3.

9. CIA, "Vietnam Situation" chap. 3, 7.

Chapter 5 The New Attack on the Shadow Government

1. Colby, interview.

2. Komer, interview.

3. Phillip B. Davidson, interview by Ted Gittinger, 30 March 1982, LBJ, Oral History Collection, interview 1, 28.

4. Statistics in House Committee on Government Operations, *U.S. Assistance Programs in Vietnam: Hearings before a Subcommittee of the Committee on Government Operations,* 92d Cong., 1st sess., 15, 16, 19, and 21 July and 2 August 1971, 181; and Chu Xuan Vien, *U.S. Adviser,* 7–8.

5. Thayer, *War without Fronts,* 36, 157; Cooper et al., *American Experience,* 3:265.

6. Wall, interview.

7. Brickham, interview.

8. Johnson, "Phoenix/Phung Hoang," 198–99.

9. Robert Komer to Gen. William Westmoreland, "Organization for Attack on VC Infrastructure," memo, 14 June 1967, CMH, 2.

10. Parker, interview.

11. Komer, interview.

12. For documentary evidence, see American Embassy, Saigon, to Secretary of State, Washington, "Phoenix Goes Underground," cable, 16 May 1973, CMH, 1–2. Americans who remained in Vietnam after 1972 confirmed that the attack on the VCI continued after the cease-fire.

Chapter 6   Targets

1. Le Van Thai, interview.
2. Mullins, interview.
3. American Embassy, Saigon to Secretary of State, Washington, "July Internal Security Assessment," airgram, 30 August 1971, CMH, 4.
4. Robert Komer, "The Phung Hoang Fiasco," draft, 30 July 1970, CMH, 2.
5. Scott, interview.

Chapter 7   Informants and Agents

1. Almy, interview.
2. *Rand Vietnam Interviews,* ser. Tet-VC, no. 2, 2.
3. Snepp, interview.
4. Polgar, interview.
5. Lapham, interview.
6. Gregg, interview.
7. Lawlor, interview.
8. Mudrinich, interview.
9. Flitcroft, interview.
10. McCoid, interview.
11. Vo Van Dinh, interview.
12. Wilson, interview.
13. Viet Lang, interview.
14. West, *Area Security,* 15–16.
15. Nguyen An Tien, interview.
16. Lawlor, interview.
17. Pham Huu Chinh, interview.
18. Mudrinich, interview.
19. Tran Van Nhut, interview.
20. Wilson, interview.
21. Allnutt, *Marine Combined Action Capabilities,* 41.
22. Cook, interview.
23. Thayer, *War without Fronts,* 50–51; Lewy, *America in Vietnam,* 272–73, 454.
24. Ward, interview.
25. Corson, *The Betrayal,* 119–20.

26. Bernard, interview.

27. Brown, interview.

28. Dao Quan Hien, interview.

29. Combined Document Exploitation Center (hereafter cited as CDEC), "Intensification of Political Activities," Doc. Log No. 06-1329-71, 10 March 1971, 1, in Pike Collection, unit 5, fiche 641.

30. MACCORDS-PHD, "Phung Hoang End-of-Year Report for 1970," 11 May 1971, CMH, 27.

31. Mattocks, interview.

32. Mudrinich, interview.

33. Milberg, interview.

34. See, for example, FitzGerald, *Fire in Lake,* 524. Neil Sheehan, "C.I.A. Says Enemy Spies Hold Vital Posts in Saigon," *The New York Times,* 19 October 1970, revealed the conclusions of the report to the public.

35. Enders, interview.

36. CDEC, "P.R.P. Assessment of Situation," Doc. Log No. 12-1198-68, August 1968, 3, in Pike Collection, unit 1, ser. 1, sec. 2, fiche 488.

37. Bureau of the Census, *Statistical Abstract of the United States: 1984* (Washington, D.C.: Bureau of the Census, 1983), 354.

38. *Rand Vietnam Interviews,* ser. AG, no. 573, 10.

39. Dillard, interview.

40. Masters, interview.

41. CDEC, "1970–1971 Winter-Spring Campaign," Doc. Log No. 01-1059-71, 4 October 1970, 1, in Pike Collection, unit 1, ser. 1, sec. 2, fiche 709.

42. Viet Lang, interview.

43. Mattocks, interview.

44. CDEC, "Governmental Activities," Doc. Log No. 03-2315-70, 10 February 1970, 9, in Pike Collection, unit 5, fiche 638.

45. John Paul Vann to Robert Komer, "Attack on the Infrastructure," memo, 5 March 1968, MHI, John P. Vann Papers, 2.

46. Masters, interview.

47. Dao Quan Hien, interview.

48. Simmons, interview.

49. Colby, interview; Parker, interview; Dillard, interview.

50. Gregg, interview.

51. Flitcroft, interview.

52. CDEC, "Some Features of Enemy Psywar, Chieu Hoi, and Espionage Activities and Friendly Countermeasures Last Year (1970)," Doc. Log No. 09-1261-71, April 1971, 8, in Pike Collection, unit 1, ser. 1, sec. 2, fiche 776.

53. MACCORDS-PHD, John Tilton to Maj. Gen. D. P. Bolton, "Phung Hoang Program," 4 August 1971, CMH, 1.

54. Lawlor, interview.

55. Viet Lang, interview.

56. "COSVN Resolution No. 9," July 1969, MHI, 60, 61.

Chapter 8 Prisoners: Interrogation, Torture, and Execution

1. Milberg, "Future Applicability of Phoenix," 36–37.

2. Pomeroy, interview.

3. Simmons, interview.

4. Quang Tri Province Report, May 1968, CMH, 2.

5. John G. Lybrand and L. Craig Johnstone, "The Phoenix Program in II Corps," 1 May 1968, CMH, 11–12, 15.

6. Almy, interview.

7. Mudrinich, interview.

8. Hunter, interview.

9. Lybrand and Johnstone, "Phoenix Program in II Corps," 11.

10. House Committee on Government Operations, *U.S. Assistance Programs*, 335.

11. Walsh, *SEAL!*, 141.

12. West, *The Village*, 56.

13. Welcome, interview.

14. Quoted in Maurer, *Strange Ground*, 355–56.

15. Ibid., 358–61.

16. B. G. Burkett, conversation with author.

17. Viet Lang, interview.

18. Holmes, *Acts of War*, 382.

19. Ward, interview.

20. Flitcroft, interview.

21. House Committee on Government Operations, *U.S. Assistance Programs*, 321, 357.

22. Senate Committee on Armed Services, *On Nomination of William E. Colby to be Director of Central Intelligence: Hearing before the Committee on Armed Services*, 93d Cong., 1st sess., 2, 20, and 25 July 1973, 108, 116–17.

23. U.S. Army Intelligence Command, "Rounder Post," dossier ZB 51 23 87, control symbol 1271 6004, 10 December 1971. Copy obtained by author from U.S. Army Intelligence and Security Command.

24. House Committee on Government Operations, *U.S. Assistance Programs*, 356.

25. Ibid.

26. No one seems to have noticed that during the 1971 hearings at which Osborn testified, another soldier refuted Osborn's claim that only enlisted men could become agent handlers. Michael Uhl, who spoke out against Phoenix, as Osborn did, said that he knew some officers who had taken a course in agent handling at Fort Holabird. See House Committee on Government Operations, *U.S. Assistance Programs*, 359.

27. The written records were mentioned in Senate Committee, *On Nomination of Colby*, 108.

28. Quoted in U.S. Army Intelligence Command, "Rounder Post," 265, 267.

29. Quoted in ibid., 315.

30. Quoted in Peter Kann, "The Hidden War: Elite 'Phoenix' Forces Hunt Vietcong Chiefs in an Isolated Village," *The Wall Street Journal*, 25 March 1969.

31. Tran Ngoc Chau, interview.

32. Scott, interview.

33. Lawlor, interview.

34. See, for instance, MACV, Maj. Gen. W. G. Dolvin, Directive No. 525-36, 18 May 1970, reprinted in House Committee on Government Operations, *U.S. Assistance Programs*, 238.

35. Lybrand and Johnstone, "Phoenix Program in II Corps," 11–12.

36. Dagenais, interview.

37. Patten, interview.

38. Quoted in Fawcett, *Hunters and Shooters*, 116.

39. Mullins, interview.

40. Lawlor, interview.

41. Wilson, interview.

42. Vo Van Dinh, interview.

43. Tran Van Nhut, interview.

44. Cassidy, interview.

45. Boyke, interview.

46. Thich Van Quan, interview.

47. Boyke, interview.

48. Simmons, interview.

49. CDEC, "Activities of Security and Armed Elements," Doc. Log No. 11-2394-70, ca. 1969, 8, in Pike Collection, unit 5, fiche 570.

50. Blaufarb, *Counterinsurgency Era*, 213.

51. In Colby and Forbath, *Honorable Men*, 230–31.

52. Viet Lang, interview.

Chapter 9   Ralliers, Documents, and Photographs

1. Chapters 20 and 21 discuss rallier statistics more fully.

2. Rodriguez, interview.

3. CDEC, "COSVN Directive 136 and Missions Assigned to Sub-Region 1," Report No. 6 028 0774 71, April 1970, 2, in Pike Collection, unit 1, ser. 1, sec. 2, fiche 649.

4. CIA, "COSVN Assessment of the Accelerated Pacification, Phung Hoang, and Chieu Hoi Programs," 13 July 1970, Suitland, Folder 101708, 5.

5. Donald Colin, "End of Tour Report," 19 August 1971, CMH, 12.

6. CDEC, "Some Features of Enemy Psywar," 8.

7. *Rand Vietnam Interviews*, ser. V, no. 66, 2.

8. CDEC, "Report on (Propaganda-Training Activities) during the 1st Quarter of 1971," Report No. 6 028 1197 71, 8 April 1971, 2, in Pike collection, unit 5, fiche 685.

9. Viet Lang, interview.

10. Le Van Thai, interview.

11. Wilson, interview.

Chapter 10   Misinformation

1. Vo Van Dinh, interview.

2. Jensen-Stevenson, *Spite House.*

3. McConnell, *Inside Hanoi's Secret Archives;* Keating, *Prisoners of Hope;* and Brown, interview.

4. Brady, interview.

5. Nguyen Van Dai, interview.

6. House Committee on Government Operations, *U.S. Assistance Programs,* 321.

7. Masayoshi Riusaki, Questionnaire, Command Historical Program, U.S. Advisory Group, IV CTZ, 13 March 1970, CMH, 3–4.

8. Scott, interview.

9. Dagenais, interview.

10. Tran Van Nhut, interview.

11. Tilton, interview.

12. Hunter, interview.

13. Le Van Thai, interview.

14. Harrell, interview.

15. Almy, interview.

16. Mullins, interview.

17. Gregg, interview.

18. Boyke, interview.

19. Gregg, interview.

20. Flitcroft, interview.

21. Lawlor, interview.

22. Quoted in Santoli, *Everything We Had,* 173.

23. Cassidy, interview.

24. Martin, interview.

25. Simmons, interview.

26. Dao Quan Hien, interview.

Chapter 11   The Challenge: Phoenix Centers

1. McWade, interview.

2. Lybrand and Johnstone, "Phoenix Program in II Corps," 5.

3. Hoang Ngoc Lung, *Strategy and Tactics,* 45.

4. Brady, interview.

5. Parker, interview.

6. MACCORDS, "Phung Hoang Reexamination (PHREEX) Study Briefing," 28 October 1971, CMH, 8.

7. MACCORDS-EVAL, Clarence Hannon, "Evaluation Report: Pacification in Quang Tri Province, I Corps Tactical Zone," 11 August 1968, Suitland, Box 33, Folder 101406, 2.

8. Binh Duong Province Report, July 1969, CMH, 3.

9. Lybrand and Johnstone, "Phoenix Program in II Corps," 4–5.

10. Phu Bon Province Report, August 1968, CMH, 6.

Chapter 12   Attempts to Make Phoenix and Phung Hoang Work

1. Flitcroft, interview.

2. Inman, interview.

3. Brady, interview.

4. Scott, interview.

5. McWade, interview.

6. Komer, "Phung Hoang Fiasco," 7.

7. Parker, interview.

8. Cook, interview.

9. MACCORDS-PHX, "Phung Hoang (Phoenix) Program 1969 End of Year Report," 28 February 1970, CMH, 8.

10. Phu Yen Province Report, September 1970, CMH, 4.

11. Bac Lieu Province Report, February 1969, CMH, 1.

12. Inman, interview.

13. Colin, "End of Tour Report," 7.

14. Scott, interview.

15. Lybrand and Johnstone, "Phoenix Program in II Corps," 13.

16. COMUSMACV to CinCPac, cable, 1 September 1970, CMH, 6.

17. MACCORDS-PHD, Alan O'Connor to John Tilton, "Phung Hoang Bloc Inspection of Binh Thuan Province," memo, 17 December 1971, CMH, 2.

18. See, for instance, William Colby, "Internal Security in South Vietnam—Phoenix," December 1970, CMH, Tab 57.

19. Binh Duong Province Report, May 1971, CMH, 2; Colby, "Internal Security in South Vietnam—Phoenix," Tab 57.

20. MACCORDS-PSG, "The Status of the Viet Cong Infrastructure Leadership: Long An and Phu Yen Provinces," 3 January 1970, Suitland, Box 53, Folder 101745, 1; Colby, "Internal Security in South Vietnam—Phoenix," Tab 57.

21. Brady, interview.

22. From MR 1 briefing, 7 August 1971, at the Phung Hoang Quarterly Conference, quoted in Dean to Jacobson, 31 August 1971, CMH, Appendix, 2.

23. Stephen Dukkony,"Completion of Tour Report," 2 February 1973, CMH, sec. 3, 4.

24. See MACCORDS-PHD, "Phung Hoang End-of-Year Report for 1970," 35–37.

Chapter 13   Other Intelligence and Operations Coordination

1. Ba Xuyen Province Report, August 1969, CMH, 3.

2. Le Van Thai, interview.

3. Viet Lang, interview.

4. Wilson, interview.

5. Harrell, interview.

6. Mullins, interview.

7. Wilbur, interview.

8. William Grieves to Frank Walton, "Analysis of NPFF—1969," 15 January 1970, CMH, 2–3.

9. Wilson, interview.

10. In Watson and Dockery, *Point Man*, 229.

11. Boyke, interview.

Chapter 14   The Nature of Operations

1. MACCORDS-EVAL, "Evaluation of NPFF in III CTZ," 3 December 1968, CMH, 18.

2. Viet Lang, interview.

3. Quoted in Lybrand and Johnstone, "Phoenix Program in II Corps," 8–9.

4. Thayer, *War without Fronts*, 211–12, presents statistics, derived from CORDS statistics, that separate neutralizations by "specific targeting" from those by "general targeting," but he does not define these terms. Apparently, Thayer did not regard "specific targeting" as gathering intelligence on a specific VCI and then mounting an operation against that particular person, which is how most American advisers, and I, define it. His figures for neutralization through specific targeting by military units are far too high for him to have used such a narrow definition.

5. Lionel Rosenblatt and Stephen Cummings, "Kontum Province Study," 17 March 1970, Suitland, Folder 101982, 50–51.

6. Mudrinich, interview.

7. Ngo Quang Truong, *Territorial Forces*, 136–37.

8. Lawlor, interview.

9. Clark, interview.

10. Scott, interview.

11. Quoted in Fawcett, *Hunters and Shooters*, 42.

12. Le Van Thai, interview.

13. LeMoyne, interview.

14. *Rand Vietnam Interviews,* ser. DT, no. 269, 6.

15. Harrell, interview.

Chapter 15   The Birds of Prey

1. Ngo Quang Truong, *Territorial Forces,* 89.

2. Ward, interview.

3. Rosenblatt and Cummings, "Kontum Province Study," 38.

4. Quang Tin Province Report, August 1968, CMH, 4.

5. Bruno Kosheleff and Stan Jorgensen, "The Situation in the Countryside, Quang Nam Province," 16 March 1970, Suitland, Folder 101986, 21.

6. Quoted in Trullinger, *Village at War,* 119.

7. Jerry Dunn, "Completion of Tour Report," 3 May 1970, CMH, 6.

8. Lt. Col. Cecil Simmons, "Completion of Tour Report," 8 July 1972, CMH, 5.

9. Clark, interview.

10. Lt. Col. James C. Cloud, "End of Tour Report," July 1970, CMH, 9.

11. MACCORDS-EVAL, Clarence Hannon, "Evaluation Report: Pacification Progress in Quang Nam Province, I Corps Tactical Zone," 27 July 1968, Suitland, Folder 101407, 1.

12. Mebane Stafford, "Completion of Tour Report," 20 December 1970, CMH, 7.

13. Komer, "Phung Hoang Fiasco," 6.

14. Dunn, "Completion of Tour Report," 7.

15. Scott, interview.

16. Dillard, interview.

17. Welcome, interview.

18. Boyke, interview.

19. Harrell, interview.

20. Viet Lang, interview.

21. Quoted in Hersh, *Price of Power,* 135. Brackets in original.

22. Lapham, interview.

23. Ward, interview.

24. Viet Lang, interview.

25. Wilbur, interview.

26. Enders, interview.

27. Herbert, interview.

28. Colby, interview.

29. Masters, interview.

30. Thayer, *War without Fronts,* 210.

31. MACCORDS-PHD, "Phung Hoang End-of-Year Report for 1970," Appendix 6.

32. JCSM, Gen. Earle Wheeler to Secretary of Defense, "U.S. Military Involvement in the PRU Program in the RVN," 8 December 1969, CMH, 1.

33. MACCORDS-PSCD-PRU, William Buckley to Deputy ACofS CORDS, "Provincial Reconnaissance Units (PRU)," 4 August 1971, CMH, 1.

34. Shackley, *Third Option*, 74. Shackley draws on the document cited in note 32.

35. Enders, interview.

36. Harrell, interview.

37. In DeForest and Chanoff, *Slow Burn*, 26.

38. Quoted in Orr Kelly, *Brave Men, Dark Waters*, 144.

39. Georgie Ann Geyer, "The CIA's Hired Killers," *True* (February 1970), reprinted in Senate Committee on Foreign Relations, *Vietnam: Policy and Prospects, 1970: Hearings before the Committee on Foreign Relations on Civil Operations and Rural Development Support Program*, 91st Cong., 2d sess., 17, 18, 19, and 20 February and 3, 4, 17, and 19 March 1970, 351.

40. Bui Tin, *Following Ho Chi Minh*, 52.

Chapter 16 The South Vietnamese

1. Lawlor, interview.

2. Kosheleff and Jorgensen, "Situation in Countryside," 36.

3. Tran Van Nhut, interview.

4. MACCORDS, "Phung Hoang Reexamination," 9.

5. MACDR-CR, Wilbur Wilson to William Colby, "Motivation of GVN Leadership in the Phung Hoang Program," memo, 24 June 1971, CMH, 2.

6. Komer, "Phung Hoang Fiasco," 5.

7. Dao Quan Hien, interview.

8. Herrington, *Silence Was Weapon*, 195.

9. Carl Bernard, "The War in Vietnam: Observations and Reflections of a Province Senior Adviser," October 1969, CMH, 3.

10. Viet Lang, interview.

11. See, for example, Stanley Resor to Melvin Laird, "Secretary of the Army Vietnam Trip Report, 20–28 August 1969," 6 October 1969, enclosure 1, James Siena, "The Phoenix Program," CMH.

12. Bernard, interview.

13. Komer, *Bureaucracy at War*, 30.

14. Colin, "End of Tour Report," 3–4.

15. CDEC, "Assessment of Situation in Mekong Delta—1968 to 1971," Doc. Log No. 02-1050-71, October 1970, 5, in Pike Collection, unit 1, ser. 1, sec. 1, fiche 83.

16. Neil Sheehan, *Bright Shining Lie*, 742.

17. Almy, interview.

18. Herbert, interview.

19. Komer, interview.

20. Pomeroy, interview.

21. Goodman, *Politics in War*, 212, 226–31.

22. Ibid., 212.

23. MACCORDS, Pacification Studies Group, "Pacification Attitude Analysis System," October 1970, Suitland, Box 78, Folder 102074, 13.

24. *Rand Vietnam Interviews*, ser. PIE, no. 48, 6.

25. Komer, "Phung Hoang Fiasco," 3.

26. ACofS CORDS to Chief of Staff, "NPFF/PRU Interim Report," 18 August 1969, CMH, 15. The GVN later claimed that Phoenix and Phung Hoang had killed 41,000 members of the VC shadow government between August 1968 and mid-1971. See Hersh, *Price of Power*, 81. CORDS statistics, which are presented in chapter 20 of this book, list only about 19,000 killed for this time period. In all probability, however, the 41,000 figure did not come from the official Vietnamese Phung Hoang reports but was instead a number concocted by the GVN to support its boasts.

27. Scott, interview.

28. Cooper et al., *American Experience*, 2:90.

29. Ninh Thuan Province Report, March 1971, CMH, 3.

30. Herbert, interview.

31. Mattocks, interview.

32. Wilbur, interview.

33. Harrell, interview.

Chapter 17   The Americans

1. Simmons, interview.

2. Bernard, interview.

3. Scott, interview.

4. Polgar, interview.

5. Harrell, interview.

6. Lawlor, interview.

7. Pomeroy, interview.

8. Herbert, interview.

9. Nguyen Duy Hinh, "The Pacification Adviser," in *The U.S. Adviser*, ed. Chu Xuan Vien (Washington, D.C.: U.S. Army Center of Military History, 1980), 156.

10. Parker, interview.

11. Bringham, interview.

12. Clark, interview.

13. Hoang Ngoc Lung, "The Intelligence Adviser," in *The U.S. Adviser*, ed. Chu Xuan Vien (Washington, D.C.: U.S. Army Center of Military History, 1980), 90.

14. Gregg, interview.

15. Komer, interview.

16. Collins, *Development and Training*, 129.

17. Hunt, *Pacification*, 276.

18. Komer, interview.
19. Hunter, interview.
20. Parker, interview.

Chapter 18   Neutralization of Non-Communist Civilians

1. Samuel Popkin, "Pacification: Politics and the Village," *Asian Survey* 10, no. 8 (August 1970): 667.

2. Young, *Vietnam Wars*, 213.

3. Clark, interview.

4. Harrell, interview.

5. Arrest statistics are from MACCORDS, "Phoenix Comments on International Security Affairs, Internal Security Study," 16 July 1969, cited in Johnson, "Phoenix/Phung Hoang," 417, and from Congressional Research Service, Library of Congress, *Summary, Safety Programs—Vietnam*, 14 April 1972, 7, cited in Fred Branfman, "South Vietnam's Police and Prison System: The U.S. Connection," in Frazier, *Uncloaking the CIA* (New York: Free Press, 1978), 115. I could not locate the originals of either of these documents, despite many hours of investigative work at numerous libraries and archives and, in the latter case, appeals to members of Congress. Statistics on the number of VCI killed are in Thayer, *War without Fronts*, 212.

6. James Sterba, "The Controversial Operation Phoenix: How It Roots Out Vietcong Suspects," *The New York Times*, 18 February 1970.

7. MACCORDS-PHX, John Mason, "Legal Processing and Significant Actions," 23 October 1969, CMH, 2.

8. "Vietnamization of the Phung Hoang (Phoenix) Program," discussion paper, 18 September 1972, CMH, 1. No author or originating organization is listed on the document, but CMH historian Dale Andradé informed me that the Office of the Secretary of Defense probably produced it.

9. MACCORDS, "Phoenix Comments on International Security Affairs, Internal Security Study," cited in Johnson, "Phoenix/Phung Hoang," 417.

10. Congressional Research Service, *Summary, Public Safety Programs*, 7, cited in Branfman, "South Vietnam's Police and Prison System," 115.

11. Colby, "Internal Security in South Vietnam—Phoenix," Tab 34.

12. Thayer, *War without Fronts*, 213.

13. Ibid.

14. MACCORDS-PSG, "Binh Dinh Province—The Challenge—1971," 12 June 1971, MHI, Annex F, 2.

15. Thayer, *War without Fronts*, 213.

16. Kien Giang Province Report, October 1971, CMH, 3.

17. MACCORDS-PH, John Tilton to DEPCORDS/MACV, "Current Status of the Phung Hoang Program," 9 August 1972, CMH, 1.

18. See Hunt, *Pacification*, 242–44.

19. House Committee on Government Operations, *U.S. Assistance Programs*, 236.

20. Cited in Lewy, *America in Vietnam*, 285.

21. Cited in Greenspan, *Modern Law of Land Warfare*, 158. A belligerent may also imprison high-level civilian political officials of enemy states as prisoners of war, 100.

22. Lewy, *America in Vietnam*, 286.

23. House Committee on Foreign Affairs, *Political Prisoners in South Vietnam and the Philippines: Hearings before the Subcommittee on Asian and Pacific Affairs*, 93d Cong., 2d sess., 1 May and 5 June 1974, 113–20.

24. Le Van Thai, interview.

25. Herrington, *Silence Was Weapon*, 196.

26. Lawlor, interview.

27. Welcome, interview.

28. West, *The Village*, 36.

29. Mullins, interview.

30. Simmons, interview.

31. Quoted in Judith Coburn and Geoffrey Cowan, "Training for Terror: A Deliberate Policy?" *The Village Voice*, 11 December 1969, 5.

32. Ibid., 6.

33. Erwin Knoll, "The Mysterious Project Phoenix," *The Progressive*, February 1970, 20–21.

34. Anthony Herbert, with James Wooten, *Soldier* (New York: Holt, Rinehart and Winston, 1973), 105.

35. Barry Lando, "The Herbert Affair," *The Atlantic Monthly*, May 1973, 78.

36. "The Herbert Case and the Record," *Army*, February 1972, 6–11.

37. Quoted in Maclear, *Ten Thousand Day War*, 264.

38. Quoted in Santoli, *Everything We Had*, 208–9, 213, 216–17.

39. B. G. Burkett, conversation.

40. Lawlor, interview.

41. Larry E. Cable, conversation with author.

42. Wall, interview; Enders, interview.

43. Burkett, conversation.

44. Joel M. Hutchins, *Swimmers among the Trees: SEAL Operations in the Vietnam War* (Novato, Calif.: Presidio Press, 1996), 210.

45. Michael Haas, review of *Swimmers among the Trees: SEAL Operations in the Vietnam War*, by Joel M. Hutchins, *Behind the Lines*, September/October 1996, 55–56.

46. Bailey, interview; Burkett, conversation.

47. Valentine, *Phoenix Program*, 343–45.

48. Ibid., 344.

49. Valentine cites Goldstein et al., *My Lai Massacre*, 145. This book contains the full text of the Peers Report.

50. See Goldstein et al., *My Lai Massacre,* 144–45. The policemen involved might not have even worked for the Special Police. The Peers Report and other available sources describe them as employees of the National Police but do not indicate whether they belonged to the Special Police branch of the National Police.

Valentine, *Phoenix Program,* 179–80, offers a similarly spurious account of the Hue massacre of 1968, which puts the blame on Phoenix instead of the VC. Again, he manipulates a source that actually supports the consensus view, namely that the Communists indeed killed several thousand people at Hue; see Karnow, *Vietnam: A History,* 530–31.

51. See, for example, FitzGerald, *Fire in Lake,* 516; Maclear, *Ten Thousand Day War,* 261.

52. MACJOIR-PHOENIX, Evan Parker, Jr., to Robert Komer, "Analyzing Size of VC Infrastructure," 22 June 1968, LBJ, Papers of the Capital Legal Foundation, Box 5, Folder CIA 229-232, 1–2; Thayer, *Systems Analysis View,* 10:65.

53. Parker, interview.
54. Harrell, interview.
55. Brady, interview.
56. Ward, interview.
57. Herrington, *Silence Was Weapon,* 196.
58. Simmons, interview.
59. Mullins, interview.

Chapter 19   Assassinations

1. Hersh, *Price of Power,* 135.
2. Szulc, *Illusion of Peace,* 46, 47.
3. Michael Drosnin, "Phoenix: The CIA's Biggest Assassination Program," *New Times,* 22 August 1975, 16.
4. Valentine, *Phoenix Program,* 13.
5. Quoted in ibid., 12.
6. Ibid., 340.
7. Burkett, conversation; Dale Andradé, conversation with author; Brown, interview.
8. Elton Manzione, letter to author, postmarked 10 February 1992.
9. Herrington, *Silence Was Weapon,* 13.
10. Wilbur, interview.
11. LeMoyne, interview.
12. Viet Lang, interview.
13. Dillard, interview.
14. Hunter, interview.
15. MACCORDS-PHD, Tilton to Bolton, "Phung Hoang Program," 1.
16. Greenspan, *Modern Law of Land Warfare,* 330–31, 467.

17. For these statistics, see Thayer, *War without Fronts*, 212.

18. Almy, interview.

19. Pomeroy, interview.

Chapter 20   Neutralization Statistics

1. Scott, interview.

2. Martin, interview.

3. Mudrinich, interview.

4. Enders, interview.

5. MACCORDS-PS, ACofS CORDS to CofS, "Phoenix and the NPFF," 29 April 1969, CMH, 2.

6. Khanh Hoa Province Report, October 1968, CMH, 3.

7. MACCORDS-PHD, "Phung Hoang End-of-Year Report for 1970," 16–17.

8. Lewy, *America in Vietnam*, 91–92.

9. Herbert, interview.

10. Thayer, *War without Fronts*, 209.

11. Ibid., 208, 209.

12. Harrell, interview.

Chapter 21   Actual Viet Cong Cadre Losses

1. *Rand Vietnam Interviews*, ser. Tet-VC, no. 9, 9.

2. Tran Van Tra, *Concluding 30-Years War*, 35.

3. Harrell, interview.

4. "COSVN Resolution 14," 30 October 1969, reprinted in Porter, *Vietnam: Definitive Documentation*, 2:549.

5. For examples, see CIA, "Summary of Viet Cong Activities in South Vietnam During July 1967," 30 August 1967, LBJ, NSF, Country File—Vietnam, Box 252-258, Folder CIA Intell Info Cables 7/27/67–8/31/67, 3 of 3), 12–13; MACV, "The Viet Cong Infrastructure: Modus Operandi of Selected Political Cadres," July 1968, CMH, 17–18; and MACCORDS-PHX, "Phung Hoang (Phoenix) Program 1969 End of Year Report," D-5, D-6.

6. Truong Nhu Tang, *Vietcong Memoir*, 201.

7. Quoted in Karnow, *Vietnam: A History*, 602.

8. Le Van Duong, interview.

9. Hersh, *Price of Power*, 80–81.

10. Quoted in Nayan Chanda, "The Phoenix Programme and the Ashes of War," *Far Eastern Economic Review*, 2 May 1985, 40.

11. For example, see Bergerud, *Dynamics of Defeat*, 314.

12. Enders, interview.

13. Lawlor, interview.

14. CDEC, "Assessment of Situation in SVN by (NVA) Senior General Vo Nguyen Giap and Various Officials of COSVN and SVNLA," Doc. Log No. 06-2469-70, 5 July 1970, Suitland, Folder 102058, 39–40. The National Archives declassified this document in September 1992 at my request.

15. CDEC, "Intensification of Political Activities," 1.

16. CDEC, "Communiqué on FWMAF/RVNAF Pacification Plan for 1971," Doc. Log No. 07-1338-71, 25 February 1971, 6, in Pike Collection, unit 1, ser. 1, sec. 2, fiche 761.

17. "Phoenix Plan Condemned as Terror Campaign," Liberation Radio Broadcast, 24 October 1969, translated and released on 27 October 1969, 1, cited in Andradé, *Ashes to Ashes,* 267.

18. CDEC, "PRP Central Committee Assessment of Situation in Binh Dinh Province, January–June, 1969," Doc. Log No. 09-5326-69, July 1969, 2–11, in Pike Collection, unit 1, ser. 1, sec. 2, fiche 522.

19. Almy, interview.

20. Nguyen Thi Binh, interview.

21. Tran Van Tra, "Tet: The 1968 General Offensive and General Uprising," in Jayne Werner and Luu Doan Huynh, eds., *The Vietnam War: Vietnamese and American Perspectives* (Armonk, N.Y.: M. E. Sharpe, 1993), 57.

22. DeForest and Chanoff, *Slow Burn;* Enders, interview; Rodriguez, interview; Viet Lang, interview.

23. "COSVN Directive No. 01/CT71," January–February 1971, reprinted in Porter, *Vietnam: Definitive Documentation,* 2:551.

24. CIA, "COSVN Assessment," 5, 6.

25. VNIT 482—#2, interview with Binh Dinh Phoenix Coordinator, 8 August 1969, CMH, Vietnam Interview Tape Files, 31, cited in Boylan, "Red Queen's Race," 353–54. Brackets in original.

26. Karnow, *Vietnam: A History,* 534.

27. MACCORDS-PHD, "Phung Hoang End-of-Year Report for 1970," 44.

Chapter 22 Additional Setbacks for the Shadow Government

1. Trullinger, *Village at War,* 142.

2. MACCORDS-PHX, John Mason to DEPCORDS/MACV, "Viet Cong Infrastructure (VCI) Command and Control Difficulties," n.d., CMH, 2.

3. CIA, "Effects of Pacification on Viet Cong in Tay Ninh Province," 28 July 1970, Suitland, Folder 101152, 2–3.

4. CDEC, "Resolution Adopted by the Phung Hiep District Party Committee," Doc. Log No. 08-1137-72, n.d., 12, in Pike Collection, unit 1, ser. 1, sec. 2, fiche 946.

5. Thayer, *War without Fronts,* 144, 149, 215.

6. Clark, interview.

7. Kosheleff and Jorgensen, "Situation in Countryside," 65.

8. Shaplen, *Road from War,* 337.

9. Herring, *America's Longest War*, 161.

10. *Rand Vietnam Interviews*, ser. AG, no. 545, 30.

11. Cao Van Luong, interview.

12. *Rand Vietnam Interviews*, ser. V, no. 48, 7.

13. Wiesner, *Victims and Survivors*, 225.

14. Kosheleff and Jorgensen, "Situation in Countryside," 44.

15. Quoted in Bergerud, *Dynamics of Defeat*, 305.

16. Race, *War Comes to Long An*, 271.

17. Kosheleff and Jorgensen, "Situation in Countryside," 11–12.

18. Senate Committee on Foreign Relations, *Vietnam: Policy and Prospects*, 103.

19. CDEC, "Anti-Pacification Activities," Report No. 6 028 1401 70, 20 May 1970, 3, in Pike Collection, unit 1, ser. 1, sec. 2, fiche 673.

20. Herrington, *Silence Was Weapon*, 34.

21. Truong Nhu Tang, *Vietcong Memoir*, 212.

22. CDEC, "Assessment & Strategy," Doc. Log No. 06-1790-70, 6 November 1969, 23, 25, in Pike Collection, unit 1, ser. 1, sec. 2, fiche 584.

23. CDEC, "Assessment of Situation in SVN," 20.

24. Shaplen, *Road from War*, 337; Tran Dinh Tho, *Pacification*, 149.

25. Binh Dinh Province Report, May 1971, CMH, 1.

26. Hoang Van Thai, *How South Vietnam Was Liberated*, 18, 98.

27. "COSVN Resolution 12," 7, 8, in Pike Collection, unit 1, ser. 1, sec. 2, fiche 1050.

28. "COSVN Directive 08/CT74," August 1974, reprinted in Porter, *Vietnam: Definitive Documentation*, 2:655.

29. Le Gro, *Vietnam from Cease-Fire to Capitulation*, 179.

30. Cited in Neil Sheehan, *Bright Shining Lie*, 724.

31. *Rand Vietnam Interviews*, ser. DT, no. 135, 22–23.

32. Snepp, interview.

33. Colin, "End of Tour Report," 12.

34. COMUSMACV to AIG 7051, cable, 18 January 1971, CMH, 1.

35. CDEC, "Report on the Situation and Achievements in Jul 69," Doc. Log No. 11-2038-70, 7, in Pike Collection, unit 1, ser. 1, sec. 2, fiche 567.

Chapter 23   The Shadow Government in Decline

1. "COSVN Resolution No. 9," 6.

2. "COSVN Directive 08/CT74," August 1974, reprinted in Porter, *Vietnam: Definitive Documentation*, 2:655.

3. In DeForest and Chanoff, *Slow Burn*, 186.

4. Quoted in Bergerud, *Dynamics of Defeat*, 218.

5. CDEC, "Activities of Security and Armed Elements," 30.

6. Ibid., 30–32.

7. CDEC, "Resolution Adopted by the Phung Hiep District Party Committee," 11, 13.

8. Mullins, interview.

9. CDEC, "Assessment of Situation in SVN," 1, 22, 27.

10. Thayer, *War without Fronts*, 157; Collins, *Development and Training*, 151. The ARVN figure is for 1971–72.

11. Prados, *Hidden History of Vietnam War*, 219–20. Emphasis in original.

Chapter 24   Abuse of the Population

1. CORDS and the GVN implemented a survey program called the Pacification Attitude Analysis System. Surveyors asked the villagers their opinions about the attack on the VCI and a host of other Allied activities, but the surveys are not very helpful. The surveyors did not venture into hamlets dominated by the VC. More important, many villagers were likely to suspect trickery and thus to speak insincerely when questioned by the surveyors, about whose identity and political allegiance they were not certain. Candid remarks might have offended someone and spelled trouble for the speaker. In addition, these studies (unlike the Rand interviews) do not contain much information that suggests the reliability of the source.

2. Tran Van Nhut, interview.

3. Viet Lang, interview.

4. National Security Study Memorandum No. 1, inserted in *Congressional Record*, 92d Cong., 2d sess., 10 May 1972, 16819.

5. Bergerud, *Red Thunder, Tropic Lightning*, 227.

6. See Lewy, *America in Vietnam*, 160, 331.

7. MACCORDS-EVAL, Hannon, "Evaluation Report: Pacification Progress in Quang Nam Province," 5.

8. Simmons, interview.

9. Quoted in Bergerud, *Dynamics of Defeat*, 214.

10. Cited in Lewy, *America in Vietnam*, 230–31.

11. Walzer, *Just and Unjust Wars*, 195–96.

12. Lewy, *America in Vietnam*, 450–53.

13. Christian Appy mistakenly thought that he had found the error. Appy, *Working-Class War*, 203, claims that Lewy omitted 222,000 civilian deaths misidentified as military deaths from his calculations. Appy bases this conclusion on Lewy, *America in Vietnam*, 445, table A-2. Lewy, 453, does include this figure, however, in the calculations presented in table A-8. Yet, Lewy's original figure of 365,000 total civilian deaths, which excludes the 222,000, already includes many, if not most, of the misidentified civilian deaths, a fact that Lewy apparently does not recognize. Lewy's 365,000 figure includes 115,000 killed by Allied bombing in North Vietnam and by VC executioners, plus 250,000 estimated killed in other war-related inci-

dents. Lewy arrives at the 250,000 figure by multiplying the number of people admitted to South Vietnamese hospitals for war-related injuries by the killed- to-wounded ratio of South Vietnamese soldiers. If one assumes that the wounded civilians who went to the hospitals often suffered their wounds in the same areas as civilians who were killed and counted as enemy dead—a safe assumption—then the method of extrapolating from hospital figures includes all civilians killed in the South aside from those executed by the VC, regardless of how the Allies identified them. As a result, the number of Communist military deaths might be close to the 444,000 estimated by Lewy because many civilians were indeed misidentified as soldiers, but the number of civilian deaths should be close to 365,000, not 587,000.

14. Millett, interview.

15. FitzGerald, *Fire in Lake,* 517.

16. Quoted in *Pentagon Papers,* Senator Gravel Edition, 1:255.

17. CIA, "The Pacification Effort in Vietnam," Special National Intelligence Estimate Number 14-69, 16 January 1969, Widener, Film A413.6, Reel 7: 547-555, 5.

18. *Rand Vietnam Interviews,* ser. DT, no. 109, 26.

19. Quoted in Grant, *Facing the Phoenix,* 297.

20. See chapter 18, note 11.

21. Scott, interview.

22. Lewy, *America in Vietnam,* 448–49.

23. Trullinger, *Village at War,* 169.

24. Simmons, interview.

25. *Rand Vietnam Interviews,* ser. AG, no. 580, 8.

Chapter 25   Changing Attitudes

1. *Congressional Record,* 93d Cong., 2d sess., 10 December 1974, 38986.

2. James Gibson, "Operation Phoenix," in *War in the Shadows,* ed. Samuel Lipsman (Boston: Boston Publishing, 1988), 72.

3. Baritz, *Backfire,* 268.

4. Col. Harry G. Summers, Jr., USA (Ret.), informed me that Currey actually was a U.S. Army Reserve chaplain and never served in Vietnam.

5. Cincinnatus, *Self-Destruction,* 121.

6. Spector, *After Tet,* 293–94.

7. Kolko, *Anatomy of a War,* 394–99, 480.

8. *Rand Vietnam Interviews,* ser. DT, no. 135, 5.

9. Ibid., 138–39.

10. Quoted in Hunt, "Organizing for Revolution," 61.

11. VCD 1116, "Extracts from Captured Documents Pertaining [to] Population Control," item 8, n.d., 9, in Pike Collection, unit 5, fiche 625.

12. *Rand Vietnam Interviews,* ser. AG, no. 545, 12.

13. Ibid., ser. AG, no. 372, 28.

14. Ibid., ser. AG, no. 573, 3.

15. Ibid., ser. V, no. 22, 4.

16. Ibid., ser. V, no. 72, 29.

17. Trullinger, *Village at War,* 110.

18. CDEC, "Activities of Security and Armed Elements," 8.

19. Quoted in Popkin, "Pacification," 664.

20. *Rand Vietnam Interviews,* ser. Tet-VC, no. 15, 4.

21. Tay Ninh Province Report, February 1968, CMH, 1.

22. *Rand Vietnam Interviews,* ser. V, no. 28, 5.

23. CIA, "Summary of Viet Cong Activities," 3–4.

24. Herbert, interview.

25. Wiesner, *Victims and Survivors,* 229.

26. Quoted in Maurer, *Strange Ground,* 311.

27. CDEC, "Resolution Adopted by the Phung Hiep District Party Committee," 7, 13.

28. Herrington, *Silence Was Weapon,* 67.

29. U.S. Agency for International Development, "United States Economic Assistance to South Vietnam, 1954–1975," 31 December 1975, unpublished report, 1:56. Copy obtained by author from USAID.

30. Quoted in Santoli, *To Bear Any Burden,* 215.

31. Stanford Research Institute, "Land Reform," 4:82–92.

32. USAID, "United States Economic Assistance," 2:257.

33. Thayer, *War without Fronts,* 242.

34. Bush, Messegee, and Russell, *Impact of Land to Tiller Program,* 43.

35. See, for example, Callison, *Land-to-the-Tiller,* 215.

36. Quoted in ibid., 224.

37. Ibid.

38. Brady, interview.

39. For an example, see Tran Dinh Tho, *Pacification,* 156.

40. Clark, interview.

41. Colin, "End of Tour Report," 13.

42. Trullinger, *Village at War,* 184–85.

43. *Rand Vietnam Interviews,* ser. V, no. 77, 6.

44. Tran Van Nhut, interview.

45. The Americans conducted some large surveys of villagers, including the Pacification Attitude Analysis System surveys, to determine their attitudes. These surveys generally confirm my own conclusions, but I have not cited them to support my arguments. As before, I consider them inappropriate for use as hard evidence, for I believe that both the methods of collection and the questions that studies try to answer contain too many flaws. For a good description of the surveys, see Thayer, *War without Fronts,* 173–93.

46. Clark, interview.

47. CDEC, "Directive of TA 020," Doc. Log No. 07-1616-70, 28 February 1970, 1, 2, in Pike Collection, unit 1, ser. 1, sec. 2, fiche 640.

48. Vietnam Documents and Research Notes, "Communist Guidance on 'New Phase' of the 'Revolution' in South Vietnam," Doc. No. 117, April 1974, 8, in Pike Collection, unit 1, ser. 1, sec. 2, fiche 1035–36.

49. Ibid., 7.

Chapter 26   The Impact of the New Attitudes

1. Michael Walzer, review of *America in Vietnam,* by Guenter Lewy, *The New Republic,* 11 November 1978, 31, 33. Walzer implies that the first of the two statements reflects the opinion of Lewy; because it actually does not, however, in all likelihood it represents the opinion of Walzer himself.

2. Bush, Messegee, and Russell, *Impact of Land to Tiller Program,* 88.

3. Metzner, *More Than a Soldier's War,* 156, 165.

4. Callison, *Land-to-the-Tiller,* 277.

5. "COSVN Resolution No. 9," 46.

6. Race, *War Comes to Long An,* 270.

7. CIA, "The Vietnam Situation," Special National Intelligence Estimate, 6 June 1968, LBJ, NSF, National Intelligence Estimates, Box 7, Folder 53, South Vietnam, 8, 9.

8. See, for example, Boylan, "Red Queen's Race," 474–76.

9. Quoted in Trullinger, *Village at War,* 164.

10. Quoted in Callison, *Land-to-the-Tiller,* 276–77.

11. Dukkony, "Completion of Tour Report," sec. 2, 3.

12. Thayer, *War without Fronts,* 63.

13. Vinh Loc, interview.

14. Le Gro, *Vietnam from Cease-Fire to Capitulation,* 179.

15. Quoted in Thompson and Frizzell, *Lessons of Vietnam,* 229.

Chapter 28   Reflections

1. David Hunt, "The Antiwar Movement after the War," in Jayne Werner and Luu Doan Huynh, eds., *The Vietnam War: Vietnamese and American Perspectives* (Armonk, N.Y.: M. E. Sharpe, 1993), 269.

2. Jacqueline Desbarats and Karl Jackson, "Research among Vietnam Refugees Reveals a Blood Bath," *The Wall Street Journal,* 22 April 1985.

3. Nguyen Ngoc Dien, interview.

4. Quoted in *Daily Report of the U.S. Foreign Broadcast Information Service: East Asia,* 2 June 1993, 57, cited in Kolko, *Anatomy of a War,* 570.

5. Nguyen Trong Phuc, interview.

6. Truong Nhu Tang, *Vietcong Memoir,* 268.

7. Quoted in Chanoff and Toai, *Portrait of Enemy,* 206.

8. Tran Van Nhut, interview.

9. Tran Ngoc Chau, interview.

10. Dao Quan Hien, interview.

11. Vo Van Dinh, interview.

12. Le Van Thai, interview.

13. Kevin Cullen, "Most Veterans Polled Say War with Iraq Is Just," *The Boston Globe,* 9 December 1990.

14. Ibid.

15. *Heaven and Earth,* dir. Oliver Stone, Warner Bros., 1993.

16. See Hayslip, *Child of War, Woman of Peace,* 290–96.

17. Veterans Administration, *Myths and Realities,* 28, 32.

18. Mattocks, interview.

19. Herbert, interview.

20. Ward, interview.

21. See, for example, MacPherson, *Long Time Passing,* 239.

22. Veterans Administration, *Myths and Realities,* 62.

23. Wilson, interview.

24. Brady, interview.

25. Ibid.

26. Harrell, interview.

27. Enders, interview.

28. George French, interview.

29. Weiner, interview.

30. Montague, interview.

31. McGehee, *Deadly Deceits.*

32. McGehee. interview.

33. Snepp, interview.

34. Ibid.

35. Boyke, interview.

36. Welcome, interview.

37. Ibid.

38. Almy, interview.

39. Simmons, interview.

40. Scott, interview.

41. Ibid.

42. Clark, interview.

43. Ibid.

44. Lawlor, interview.

45. Ibid.

Selected Bibliography

Allnutt, Bruce. *Marine Combined Action Capabilities: The Vietnam Experience.* McLean, Va.: Human Sciences Research, 1969.

Andradé, Dale. *Ashes to Ashes: The Phoenix Program and the Vietnam War.* Lexington, Mass.: Lexington Books, 1990.

Andrews, William. *The Village War: Vietnamese Communist Revolutionary Activities in Ding Tuong Province 1960–1964.* Columbia: University of Missouri Press, 1973.

Appy, Christian. *Working-Class War: American Combat Soldiers and Vietnam.* Chapel Hill: University of North Carolina Press, 1993.

Asprey, Robert. *War in the Shadows: The Guerrilla in History.* New York: William Morrow, 1994.

Aurora Foundation. *Report on the Violations of Human Right in the Socialist Republic of Vietnam: April 1975–December 1988.* Atherton, Calif.: Aurora Foundation, 1989.

Baritz, Loren. *Backfire.* New York: William Morrow, 1985.

Bergerud, Eric. *The Dynamics of Defeat: The Vietnam War in Hau Nghia Province.* Boulder, Colo.: Westview Press, 1991.

Bergerud, Eric. *Red Thunder, Tropic Lightning: The World of a Combat Division in Vietnam.* Boulder, Colo.: Westview Press, 1993.

Berman, Paul. *Revolutionary Organization: Institution-Building within the People's Liberation Armed Forces.* Lexington, Mass.: Lexington Books, 1974.

Blaufarb, Douglas. *The Counterinsurgency Era: U.S. Doctrine and Performance, 1950 to the Present.* New York: Free Press, 1977.

Boylan, Kevin. "The Red Queen's Race: The 173rd Airborne Brigade and Pacification in Binh Dinh Province, 1969–1970." Ph.D. diss., Temple University, 1994.

Bradford, Alfred. *Some Even Volunteered: The First Wolfhounds Pacify Vietnam.* Westport, Conn.: Praeger, 1994.

Braestrup, Peter. *Big Story: How the American Press and Television Reported and Interpreted the Crisis of Tet 1968 in Vietnam and Washington.* 2 vols. Boulder, Colo.: Westview Press, 1977.

Brooks, Douglas. "The Phoenix Program: A Retrospective Assessment." Master's thesis, Baylor University, 1989.

Bui Tin. *Following Ho Chi Minh: Memoirs of a North Vietnamese Colonel.* Translated by Judy Stowe and Do Van. Honolulu: University of Hawaii Press, 1995.

Burr, Jewett. "Land to the Tiller: Land Redistribution in South Viet Nam, 1970–1973." Ph.D. diss., University of Oregon, 1976.

Bush, Henry, Gordon Messegee, and Roger Russell. *The Impact of the Land to the Tiller Program in the Mekong Delta.* Saigon: Control Data Corporation, 1972.

Buttinger, Joseph. *Vietnam: A Dragon Embattled.* 2 vols. New York: Frederick A. Praeger, 1967.

Callison, Charles Stuart. *Land-to-the-Tiller in the Mekong Delta: Economic, Social, and Political Effects of Land Reform in Four Villages of South Vietnam.* Lanham, Md.: University Press of America, 1983.

Cao Van Vien. *Leadership.* Washington, D.C.: Government Printing Office, 1981.

Carhart, Tom. *The Offering.* New York: William Morrow, 1987.

Chanoff, David, and Doan Van Toai. *Portrait of the Enemy.* New York: Random House, 1986.

Chu Xuan Vien, ed. *The U.S. Adviser.* Washington, D.C.: U.S. Army Center of Military History, 1980.

Cincinnatus [Cecil B. Currey pseud.]. *Self-Destruction: The Disintegration and Decay of the United States Army during the Vietnam Era.* New York: W. W. Norton, 1981.

Colby, William, and Peter Forbath. *Honorable Men: My Life in the CIA.* New York: Simon & Schuster, 1978.

Colby, William, with James McCargar. *Lost Victory: A Firsthand Account of America's Sixteen-Year Involvement in Vietnam.* Chicago: Contemporary Books, 1989.

Collins, James Lawton, Jr. *The Development and Training of the South Vietnamese Army, 1950–1972.* Washington, D.C.: Government Printing Office, 1975.

Conley, Michael. *The Communist Insurgent Infrastructure in South Vietnam: A Study of Organization and Strategy.* Washington, D.C.: Government Printing Office, 1967.

Cook, John. *The Advisor.* Philadelphia: Dorrance & Company, 1973.

Cooper, Chester, Judith Corson, Laurence Legere, David Lockwood, and Donald Weller. *The American Experience with Pacification in Vietnam.* 3 vols. Arlington, Va.: Institute for Defense Analyses, 1972.

Corn, David. *Blond Ghost: Ted Shackley and the CIA's Crusades.* New York: Simon & Schuster, 1994.

Corson, William. *The Betrayal.* New York: W. W. Norton, 1968.

Davidson, Phillip B. *Vietnam at War.* Novato, Calif.: Presidio Press, 1988.

DeForest, Orrin, and David Chanoff. *Slow Burn: The Rise and Bitter Fall of American Intelligence in Vietnam.* New York: Simon & Schuster, 1990.

de Silva, Peer. *Sub Rosa: The CIA and the Uses of Intelligence.* New York: Times Books, 1978.

Duiker, William. *The Communist Road to Power in Vietnam.* Boulder, Colo.: Westview Press, 1981.

Duiker, William. *Sacred War: Nationalism and Revolution in a Divided Vietnam.* New York: McGraw-Hill, 1995.

Duncanson, Dennis. *Government and Revolution in Vietnam.* New York: Oxford University Press, 1968.

Elliott, David, and C. Thomson. *A Look at the VC Cadres: Dinh Tuong Province, 1965–1966.* Santa Monica, Calif.: Rand Corporation, 1967.

Elliott, David, and W. Stewart. *Pacification and the Viet Cong System in Dinh Tuong: 1966–1967.* Santa Monica, Calif., Rand Corporation, 1969.

Fall, Bernard. *The Two Viet-Nams: A Political and Military Analysis.* New York: Frederick A. Praeger, 1963.

Fawcett, Bill, ed. *Hunters and Shooters: An Oral History of the U.S. Navy SEALs in Vietnam.* New York: William Morrow, 1995.

FitzGerald, Frances. *Fire in the Lake: The Vietnamese and the Americans in Vietnam.* Boston: Little, Brown, 1972.

Ford, Ronnie. *Tet 1968: Understanding the Surprise.* London: Frank Cass, 1995.

Frazier, Howard, ed. *Uncloaking the CIA.* New York: Free Press, 1978.

Freeman, James. *Hearts of Sorrow: Vietnamese-American Lives.* Stanford, Calif.: Stanford University Press, 1989.

Galula, David. *Counterinsurgency Warfare: Theory and Practice.* New York: Frederick A. Praeger, 1964.

Gettleman, Marvin, Jane Franklin, Marilyn Young, and H. Bruce Franklin, eds. *Vietnam and America: A Documented History.* New York: Grove Press, 1985.

Gibson, James. *The Perfect War: Technowar in Vietnam.* Boston: Atlantic Monthly Press, 1986.

Goldstein, Joseph, Burke Marshall, and Jack Schwartz, eds. *The My Lai Massacre and Its Cover-Up.* New York: Free Press, 1976.

Goodman, Allan. *Politics in War: The Bases of Political Community in South Vietnam.* Cambridge: Harvard University Press, 1973.

Grant, Zalin. *Facing the Phoenix.* New York: W. W. Norton, 1991

Greenspan, Morris. *The Modern Law of Land Warfare.* Berkeley: University of California Press, 1959.

Hackworth, David, and Julie Sherman. *About Face.* New York: Simon & Schuster, 1989.

Halberstam David. *The Best and the Brightest.* New York: Random House, 1972.

Hargrove, Thomas. *A Dragon Lives Forever: War and Rice in Vietnam's Mekong Delta 1969–1991, and Beyond.* New York: Ballantine Books, 1994.

Hayslip, Le Ly, with James Hayslip. *Child of War, Woman of Peace.* New York: Doubleday, 1993.

Hayslip, Le Ly, with Jay Wurts. *When Heaven and Earth Changed Places: A Vietnamese Woman's Journey from War to Peace.* New York: Doubleday, 1989.

Hemingway, Al. *Our War Was Different: Marine Combined Action Platoons in Vietnam.* Annapolis, Md.: Naval Institute Press, 1994.

Henderson, William. *Why the Vietcong Fought: A Study of Motivation and Control in a Modern Army in Combat.* Westport, Conn.: Greenwood Press, 1979.

Herring, George. *America's Longest War: The United States and Vietnam, 1950–1975.* 2d ed. New York: Alfred A. Knopf, 1986.

Herrington, Stuart. *Silence Was a Weapon: The Vietnam War in the Villages.* Novato, Calif. : Presidio Press, 1982.

Hersh, Seymour. *The Price of Power: Kissinger in the Nixon White House.* New York: Summit Books, 1983.

Hickey, Gerald. *Village in Vietnam.* New Haven: Yale University Press, 1964.

Hickey, Gerald. *Accommodation and Coalition in South Vietnam.* Santa Monica, Calif.: Rand Corporation, 1970.

Hoang Ngoc Lung. *Strategy and Tactics.* Washington, D.C.: Government Printing Office, 1980.

Hoang Ngoc Lung. *Intelligence.* Washington, D.C.: Government Printing Office, 1982.

Hoang Van Thai. *How South Vietnam Was Liberated.* Hanoi: Gioi Publishers, 1992.

Holmes, *Acts of War: The Behavior of Men in Battle.* New York: Free Press, 1986.

Hosmer, Stephen, Konrad Kellen, and Brian Jenkins. *The Fall of South Vietnam: Statements by Military and Civilian Leaders.* Santa Monica, Calif: Rand Corporation, 1978.

Hunt, Richard. *Pacification: The American Struggle for Vietnam's Hearts and Minds.* Boulder, Colo.: Westview Press, 1995.

Hunt, Richard, and Richard Shultz, Jr., eds. *Lessons from an Unconventional War: Reassessing U.S. Strategies for Future Conflicts.* New York: Pergamon Press, 1982.

Infantry Magazine, ed. *A Distant Challenge: The U.S. Infantryman in Vietnam, 1967–1972.* Nashville, Tenn.: Battery Press, 1983.

Isaacs, Arnold. *Without Honor: Defeat in Vietnam and Cambodia.* Baltimore: Johns Hopkins University Press, 1983.

Jensen-Stevenson, Monika. *Spite House: The Last Secret of the War in Vietnam.* New York: W. W. Norton, 1997.

Johnson, Ralph. "Phoenix/Phung Hoang: A Study of Wartime Intelligence Management." Ph.D. diss., The American University, 1985.

Karnow, Stanley. *Vietnam: A History.* New York: Viking, 1983.

Keating, Susan Katz. *Prisoners of Hope: Exploiting the POW/MIA Myth in America.* New York: Random House, 1994.

Kelly, Francis J. *U.S. Army Special Forces 1961–1971.* Washington, D.C.: Government Printing Office, 1973.

Kelly, Orr. *Brave Men, Dark Waters: The Untold Story of the Navy SEALs.* Novato, Calif.: Presidio Press, 1992.

Kolko, Gabriel. *Anatomy of a War: Vietnam, the United States, and the Modern Historical Experience.* New York: New Press, 1994.

Komer, Robert. *Bureaucracy at War: U.S. Performance in the Vietnam Conflict.* Boulder, Colo.: Westview Press, 1986.

Krepinevich, Andrew, Jr. *The Army and Vietnam.* Baltimore: Johns Hopkins University Press, 1986.

Lanning, Michael, and Dan Cragg. *Inside the VC and the NVA: The Real Story of North Vietnam's Armed Forces.* New York: Ballantine Books, 1992.

Le Gro, William E. *Vietnam from Cease-Fire to Capitulation.* Washington, D.C.: Government Printing Office, 1981.

Leites, Nathan. *The Viet Cong Style of Politics.* Santa Monica, Calif.: Rand Corporation, 1969.

Leites, Nathan, and Charles Wolf, Jr. *Rebellion and Authority: An Analytic Essay on Insurgent Conflicts.* Chicago: Markham Publishing, 1970.

Lewy, Guenter. *America in Vietnam.* New York: Oxford University Press, 1978.

Lipsman, Samuel, ed. *War in the Shadows.* Boston: Boston Publishing, 1988.

Maclear, Michael. *The Ten Thousand Day War, Vietnam: 1945–1975.* New York: St. Martin's Press, 1981.

MacPherson, Myra. *Long Time Passing: Vietnam and the Haunted Generation.* Garden City, N.Y.: Doubleday, 1984.

Maurer, Harry. *Strange Ground: An Oral History of Americans in Vietnam, 1945–1975.* New York: Henry Holt, 1989.

McAlister, John T., Jr., and Paul Mus. *The Vietnamese and Their Revolution.* New York: Harper & Row, 1970.

McChristian, Joseph. *The Role of Military Intelligence, 1965–1967.* Washington, D.C.: Government Printing Office, 1974.

McConnell, Malcolm. *Inside Hanoi's Secret Archives: Solving the MIA Mystery.* New York: Simon & Schuster, 1995.

McCuen, John. *The Art of Counter-Revolutionary War: A Psycho-Politico-Military Strategy of Counterinsurgency.* Harrisburg, Pa.: Stackpole Books, 1966.

McGehee, Ralph. *Deadly Deceits: My 25 Years in the CIA.* New York: Sheridan Square Publications, 1983.

Metzner, Edward. *More Than a Soldier's War: Pacification in Vietnam.* College Station: Texas A&M University Press, 1995.

Meyerson, Harvey. *Vinh Long.* Boston: Houghton Mifflin, 1970.

Milberg, Warren. "The Future Applicability of the Phoenix Program." Master's thesis, Air University, 1974.

Ngo Quang Truong. *Territorial Forces.* Washington, D.C.: Government Printing Office, 1981.

Nguyen Duy Hinh and Tran Dinh Tho, *The South Vietnamese Society.* Washington, D.C.: Government Printing Office, 1980.

Nguyen Ngoc Huy and Stephen B. Young. *Understanding Vietnam.* Bussum, The Netherlands: DPC Information Service, 1982.

Nighswonger, William. *Rural Pacification in Vietnam.* New York: Frederick A. Praeger, 1966.

Oberdorfer, Don. *Tet!* Garden City, N.Y.: Doubleday, 1971.

Palmer, Bruce, Jr. *The 25-Year War: America's Military Role in Vietnam.* Lexington: University Press of Kentucky, 1984.

The Pentagon Papers, The Senator Gravel Edition. Boston: Beacon Press, n.d.

Peterson, Michael. *The Combined Action Platoons: The U.S. Marines' Other War in Vietnam.* New York: Praeger, 1989.

Pike, Douglas. *Viet Cong: The Organization and Techniques of the National Liberation Front of South Vietnam.* Cambridge: MIT Press, 1966.

Pike, Douglas. *War, Peace, and the Viet Cong.* Cambridge: MIT Press, 1969.

Podhoretz, Norman. *Why We Were in Vietnam.* New York: Simon & Schuster, 1982.

Popkin, Samuel. *The Rational Peasant: The Politics of Rural Society in Vietnam.* Berkeley: University of California Press, 1979.

Porter, Gareth, ed. *Vietnam: The Definitive Documentation of Human Decisions.* Vol. 2. Stanfordville, N.Y.: Earl M. Coleman Enterprises, 1979.

Powers, Thomas. *The Man Who Kept the Secrets: Richard Helms and the CIA.* New York: Alfred A. Knopf, 1979.

Prados, John. *The Hidden History of the Vietnam War.* Chicago: Ivan R. Dee, 1995.

Race, Jeffrey. *War Comes to Long An: Revolutionary Conflict in a Vietnamese Province.* Berkeley: University of California Press, 1972.

Rambo, Terry, Jerry Tinker, and John LeNoir. *The Refugee Situation in Phu-Yen Province, Viet-Nam.* McLean, Va.: Human Sciences Research, 1967.

Rodriguez, Felix I., and John Weisman. *Shadow Warrior.* New York: Simon & Schuster, 1989.

Rositzke, Harry. *The CIA's Secret Operations: Espionage, Counterespionage, and Covert Action.* New York: Reader's Digest Press, 1977.

Sansom, Robert. *The Economics of Insurgency.* Cambridge: MIT Press, 1970.

Santoli, Al. *Everything We Had: An Oral History of the Vietnam War by Thirty-Three American Soldiers Who Fought It.* New York: Random House, 1981.

Santoli, Al. *To Bear Any Burden: The Vietnam War and Its Aftermath in the Words of Americans and Southeast Asians.* New York: E. P. Dutton, 1985.

Scoville, Thomas. *Reorganizing for Pacification Support.* Washington, D.C.: U.S. Army Center of Military History, 1982.

Shackley, Theodore. *The Third Option: An American View of Counterinsurgency Operations.* New York: Reader's Digest Press, 1981.

Shafer, D. Michael. *Deadly Paradigms: The Failure of U.S. Counterinsurgency Policy.* Princeton, N.J.: Princeton University Press, 1988.

Shaplen, Robert. *The Road From War: Vietnam 1965–1970.* New York: Harper & Row, 1970.

Sheehan, Neil. *A Bright Shining Lie: John Paul Vann and America in Vietnam.* New York: Random House, 1988.

Sheehan, Susan. *Ten Vietnamese.* New York: Alfred A. Knopf, 1967.

Smith, Eric McAllister. *Not by the Book: A Combat Intelligence Officer in Vietnam.* New York: Ballantine Books, 1993.

Smith, Gary, and Alan Maki. *Death in the Delta: Diary of a Navy SEAL.* New York: Ivy Books, 1995.

Snepp, Frank. *Decent Interval: An Insider's Account of Saigon's Indecent End Told by the CIA's Chief Strategy Analyst in Vietnam.* New York: Random House, 1977.

Spector, Ronald. *After Tet: The Bloodiest Year in Vietnam.* New York: Free Press, 1993.

Stanford Research Institute. *Land Reform in Vietnam.* 5 vols. Menlo Park, Calif.: Stanford Research Institute, 1968.

Stein, Jeff. *A Murder in Wartime: The Untold Spy Story That Changed the Course of the Vietnam War.* New York: St. Martin's Press, 1992.

Summers, Harry G., Jr. *On Strategy: A Critical Analysis of the Vietnam War.* Novato, Calif.: Presidio Press, 1982.

Summers, Harry G., Jr. *Historical Atlas of the Vietnam War.* Boston: Houghton Mifflin, 1995.

Szulc, Tad. *The Illusion of Peace: Foreign Policy in the Nixon Years.* New York: Viking Press, 1978.

Thayer, Thomas. *War without Fronts: The American Experience in Vietnam.* Boulder, Colo.: Westview Press, 1985.

Thayer, Thomas, ed. *A Systems Analysis View of the Vietnam War: 1965–1972.* 12 vols. Arlington, Va.: Defense Documentation Center, Defense Logistics Agency, 1975.

Thompson, Robert. *No Exit from Vietnam.* New York: David McKay, 1969.

Thompson, W. Scott, and Donaldson Frizzell, eds. *The Lessons of Vietnam.* New York: Crane, Russak & Co., 1977.

Todd, Olivier. *Cruel April: The Fall of Saigon.* Translated by Stephen Becker. New York: W. W. Norton, 1990.

Tran Dinh Tho. *Pacification.* Washington, D.C.: U.S. Army Center of Military History, 1980.

Tran Van Don. *Our Endless War: Inside Vietnam.* San Rafael, Calif.: Presidio Press, 1978.

Tran Van Tra. *Concluding the 30-Years War.* Washington, D.C.: Foreign Broadcast Information Service, 1983.

Trooboff, Peter, ed. *Law and Responsibility in Warfare: The Vietnam Experience.* Chapel Hill: University of North Carolina Press, 1975.

Trullinger, James. *Village at War: An Account of Conflict in Vietnam.* Stanford, Calif.: Stanford University Press, 1994.

Truong Nhu Tang, with David Chanoff and Doan Van Toai. *A Vietcong Memoir.* San Diego: Harcourt Brace Jovanovich, 1985.

Valentine, Douglas. *The Phoenix Program.* New York: William Morrow, 1990.

Veterans Administration. *Myths and Realities: A Study of Attitudes toward Vietnam Era Veterans.* Washington, D.C.: Government Printing Office, 1980.

Walsh, Michael. *SEAL!* New York: Pocket Books, 1994.

Walzer, Michael. *Just and Unjust Wars: A Moral Argument with Historical Illustrations*. New York: Basic Books, 1977.

Watson, James, and Kevin Dockery. *Point Man: Inside the Toughest and Most Deadly Unit in Vietnam by a Founding Member of the Elite Navy SEALs*. New York: William Morrow, 1993.

Werner, Jayne, and Luu Doan Huynh. *The Vietnam War: Vietnamese and American Perspectives*. Armonk, N.Y.: M. E. Sharpe, 1993.

West, Francis J., Jr. *Area Security*. Santa Monica, Calif.: Rand Corporation, 1969.

West, Francis J., Jr. *The Village*. New York: Harper & Row, 1972.

Westmoreland, William. *A Soldier Reports*. Garden City, N.Y.: Doubleday, 1976.

Wiesner, Louis. *Victims and Survivors: Displaced Persons and Other War Victims in Viet-Nam, 1954–1975*. New York: Greenwood Press, 1988.

Williams, William Appleman, Thomas McCormick, Lloyd Gardner, and Walter LaFeber, eds. *America in Vietnam: A Documentary History*. Garden City, N.Y.: Anchor Press, 1985.

Woodside, Alexander. *Community and Revolution in Modern Vietnam*. Boston: Houghton Mifflin, 1976.

Young, Marilyn. *The Vietnam Wars 1945–1990*. New York: HarperCollins, 1991.

Index

liers, 108–9; recruitment of, 271–
72; seizure of hamlets by, 13–14;
surveillance system of, 156–57
Viet Minh, 3
Viet Nam Quoc Dan Dang, 28
Vietnam veterans, 353; portrayal of,
353–54; psychological effects on,
357, 358–59; reflections of, 353–65
villagers, South Vietnamese (*see also*
district and province chiefs; hamlets, South Vietnamese): alienation
of, 281–82; civilian deaths of, compared to other wars, 290–91, 394–
95n. 13; and elections, 313–15;
forced relocation of, 259–60, 303–
4; identification of corpses, 183–
85; and importance of family, 19–
20, 29, 68–69; as informants and
Allied agents, 65–66; and isolation
from family, 30; and land ownership, 21–22, 310, 320; and Marx-
ism, 20–21; mistreatment of, by
GVN and Allied forces, 281–97;
misunderstood by Americans, 20;

and Nationalism, 10; providing
false information by, 114–15; relationship to and support of Allies,
301–2, 304, 308, 394n. 1; relationship to and support of GVN,
42–44, 300, 316–18; relationship
to and support of VCI/Viet Cong,
18, 22–32, 268–69, 272, 290,
298–318
Vo Van Dinh, 351–52

Waldie, Jerome, 90
Wall, Robert, 51, 217–18
Ward, Jim, 355–56
wealth, influence of, 29–30
Weiner, Harvey, 359
Welcome, Rick, 361–62
Westmoreland, William C., 7; and
CORDS, 49; pacification *vs.* con-
ventional warfare, 44–45
Wilson, Rex, 356–57
women: Communist, 15; sexual
abuse of, 91

About the Author

ark Moyar is a native of Shaker Heights, Ohio, and currently resides in Chicago, Illinois. He graduated *summa cum laude* in history from Harvard University. His diverse awards and accomplishments include the David Donald Prize, the Charles Warren Undergraduate Prize Fellowship, the Deutscher Akademischer Austauschdienst scholarship for study in Germany, and selection to the U.S. Physics Olympiad Team. *Phoenix and the Birds of Prey* is his first book.